THE COMPLETE ENCYCLOPEDIA OF TERRORIST ORGANISATIONS

D0863524

THE COMPLETE ENCYCLOPEDIA OF TERRORIST ORGANISATIONS

PAUL ASHLEY

CASEMATE
Philadelphia

Published in the United States of America in 2012 by
CASEMATE PUBLISHERS
908 Darby Road, Havertown, PA 19083

Copyright © Paul Ashley, 2011

ISBN 978-1-61200-118-0

Published by arrangement with Frontline Noir, an imprint of
Books Noir, Scotland.

Cataloging-in-publication data is available from the Library of
Congress.

Cover design by Jim Hutcheson

Printed and bound in the UK

For a complete list of Casemate titles please contact:

CASEMATE PUBLISHERS (US)
Telephone (610) 853-9131, Fax (610) 853-9146
E-mail: casemate@casematepublishing.com

Introduction and Acknowledgements

I was serving with Her Majesties Armed Forces in a particular part of the world and was requested to find out some information on a suspicious chap who had travelled into our area. He was Spanish and the individual who requested the information wanted to know which flight he came in on. By chance I had flown in the day before and had sat next to chap, who was reading a Spanish newspaper, so the flight time and seat were easy. All I needed to get was his name from the flight manifesto. As it turns out he was a suspected terrorist. Once I had completed the task I became intrigued about terrorist organisations, and I wondered that if one army can provide information, training and expertise why don't terrorist organisations do the same. "Do they?" I thought to myself.

So I started to collect the names of terrorist organisations. This was long before the World Wide Web was introduced and we had the access that we now have. I read newspapers, magazines and various books and started to write down their names, which country they were from, any other names they went under and if they were linked to another organisation. Very soon I had bits of paper all over the place. Then along came my first computer and I opened up an excel spreadsheet and started to write them all down. Over the years there were hundreds and hundreds of names.

At some point I attempted to find a Terrorist Dictionary to see if there was one available in bookshops in the United Kingdom and the United States but did not find one. So I started to write my own. Over a long period of time it grew and grew. I could not place the information in the boxes of the excel spreadsheet and so had to start placing it in a word document. Again this got bigger and bigger. The result is what you are now reading.

In today's society terrorism affects us in many ways. Even if we do not see it, it is there lurking in the background, and more than we would like to imagine.

Terrorism is on our television sets, either on the news, in a documentary or as part of a plot in some episode of a thriller. In the United Kingdom we have had more than our fair share of terrorism in the past. That has now been superseded by the fundamentalists that strike without warning and with catastrophic results and in most cases anonymously. Now the world has its own problems with terrorist groupings. The people who carry out these attacks believe they are working for a divine purpose, and therefore everyone else is of a sub state, and for that reason they have no pity when carrying out an attack with mass casualties and fatalities.

We have seen the 9/11 pictures on our television screens from the United States, the results of the Madrid train bombings, the London bombings of 7/7, the siege of the school children from Russia and the Bali Bombings, to name but a few. These are some of the larger atrocities that have been carried out and resulted in changes in our lives. But what of the smaller incidents that are carried out under the term terrorism?

There are many reasons those individuals carry out terrorist acts. It could be that they are trying to impose their own ideology on a government or a populace, but today, the main impetus is religion and fundamentalism.

There are a lot of these groups around the world and unfortunately they will stay with us for a great number of years to come. These groups carry out single acts of terrorism, or if well organised, conduct well co-ordinated acts of terrorism. In some attacks various groups have come together to carry out deeds of terrorism. But how do we know who is linked together? I have attempted to resolve some of these questions and where positive links are made the appendix at the back of the book will inform the reader of which groups to look at to see what ideology links them together.

There are many more groups that are not mentioned in the book. The list is still ongoing. I have spent many hours, days, weeks and months collating these organisations. The websites that much of the information has come from is listed in another appendix. The reader, if they wish to know additional information about a group, can use them to glean more on the groups that they are interested in.

Without those websites this book would never have been put together and I thank those who have put those details on the World Wide Web for everyone to read. They are too many to mention and that's why I have opted to place them in an appendix of their own. All I have done is put the groups in a book form to make it easier for anyone who wants a quick reference to a particular part of the world or group to find and read about them.

Some of the groups in the book are no longer in existence, some are now legal government organisations that govern a country or sit in opposition to a government. In some cases, such as Greece, there are many groups that have committed a terrorist act and then never been heard of again. However, there are a lot of groups that still carry a current threat and care must be taken when visiting these site locations.

I hope those of you who have this dictionary find it useful in whatever you do, whether it be as a professional or just out of interest as a lay reader. Even if it makes people more aware of what goes on in, and around our world, regarding terrorism, then it would make life easier for law agencies around the world to operate.

My last paragraph is dedicated to those who fight terrorism in their own capacity, whether they are in the background or are soldiers on the ground who face terrorists on a daily basis. I have also battled against various groups so I understand more than those who sit behind a desk criticising what soldiers do to make their lives safer. Look after them as they are looking after you.

Paul Ashley

Dedication

I would like to dedicate this book to my wife Valerie Ashley. She has been a great help and when I was getting tired of it, Valerie would inspire me to carry on. Without her encouragement I would have never completed this dictionary. She had faith in what I was doing and I am extremely grateful for her encouragement.

I would also like to thank Colin (Charlie) Brown and his brother Fraser for all their help in the past.

Contents

Terrorist Encyclopedia

Numerical

1st Mechanical Kansas Militia

Continent: North America
Country: United States of America
Background:
The 1st Mechanical Kansas Militia was a small militia group known almost solely for its connection to a foiled plot to attack a 4th of July celebration at Fort Hood, Texas.

Led by Bradley Glover, a somewhat unstable but charismatic conspiracy theorist, the group's ideology was similar to that of other militia and so-called "Patriot" organisations. To that end, the group was staunchly anti-government and driven by conspiracies and paranoia. However, by openly advocating war against the United States government and being convinced that Chinese Communist troops were being trained on American soil, the 1st Mechanical Kansas Militia under Glover's leadership was considered to be one of the more extremist groups in the militia movement.

The group, which claimed to have 1,000 members (this claim was extremely dubious), was represented at the 3rd Continental Congress in 1996, a gathering of various militia movements. However, Glover and several other attendees found the Congress to be moderate and soon splintered off to plan violent action against the U.S. government.

This splinter group (which was unnamed and had no other members from the 1st Mechanical) met several times in 1997 with attendees including Kevin and Terry Hobeck from Ohio, Ronald Griesacker from the Republic of Texas militia group, and Merlon "Butch" Lingenfelter, Jr, a former UFO cult member. Also in attendance at these meetings were two undercover FBI agents, tasked with monitoring the group.

During these meetings, Glover and the other attendees hatched a plan to attack a 4th of July celebration at Fort Hood. Thanks to the FBI infiltration and a year-long investigation by the Missouri State Highway Patrol, the operation was foiled. Glover was sentenced to five years in jail for his role in the plot.

It is not clear whether the 1st Mechanical Kansas Militia played any role in the Fort Hood plot beyond Glover's involvement. In fact, it is somewhat possible that the 1st Mechanical never even existed beyond Glover's imagination. At various times, Glover claimed to be a commander of various groups with names such as the "Southern Kansas Regional Militia" and the "7th Division Constitutional Militia." Along with the 1st Mechanical, these group names are most likely aliases for the same band, and have not been heard of since Glover's capture.

The 1st Mechanical Kansas Militia has not been directly responsible for any terrorist incidents, and only gained notoriety due to the actions of its leader. The group has not been heard from since 1997 and is likely defunct.

Also known as 7th Division Constitutional Militia, Kansas Militia, Southern Kansas Regional Militia

1 October Antifascist Resistance Group

Abbreviation: GRAPO
Continent: Europe
Country: Spain
Background:
Originally established as the military arm of the outlawed Communist Party of Spain - reconstructed (PCE-R), the primary goals of GRAPO were the eviction of US and NATO forces from Spain and the creation of a new Maoist regime. In pursuit of these goals, GRAPO had conducted an urban terrorist campaign since 1975 utilising kidnappings, bombings and shootings directed against US and NATO facilities. It is thought that over 800 people have been killed during the course of their operations.

Links to French Action Directe, Italy's Red Brigades and Germanys Red Army Faction. GRAPO's structure has been built on a cellular concept for maximum internal security. The membership was broken down into two categories, Legal Commando's and Liberated Commando's. The Legal Commandoes were called to perform terrorist activity. The Liberated Commando's were an estimated twelve to fifteen full-time members who lived underground but whose identities were well known by the Spanish Police. A major anti-terrorist swoop in 1985 rounded up most of these individuals but later some of them were released.

2nd June Movement

Continent: Europe
Country: Germany
Background:
The 2nd of June Movement was a left-wing German terrorist group that operated in the mid 1970s. They never became quite as well known, or presented the persistent threat of the Baader-Meinhof Gang/RAF, and the groups often argued over ideology, although they remained operationally

allied. The 2nd of June Movement favoured an anarchist path, compared to the Marxist nature of Baader-Meinhof/RAF.

The 2nd of June Movement's name was a reference to the 2nd June 1967, the date on which German police killed pacifist protestor Benno Ohnessorg. The group was formed from an earlier German terrorist group, the West Berlin Tupamaros, whose members came from a German socialist commune called "Kommune I". The 2nd of June Movement is inactive.

See the West Berlin Tupamaros

3rd Continental Congress

Continent: North America
Country: United States of America
Background:

The 3rd Continental Congress was a loose alliance of militia and patriot groups in the United States. More a term for a meeting, rather than an actual terrorist group, several members and participants of 3rd Continental Congresses had been indicted on charges relating to terrorism. Like most so-called "Patriot" organisations, the 3rd Continental Congress was staunchly opposed to the United States government, which it viewed as corrupt and oppressive. The name "3rd Continental Congress" is a reference to the legislative bodies of the 13 colonies which would eventually declare their independence from Great Britain.

The 3rd Continental Congress first met in October 1996 in Kansas City, Missouri. According to news estimates, delegates from as many as 11 states attended the conference, including members of the Republic of Texas, the Michigan Militia, and the 1st Mechanical KS Militia. In April 1997, the Congress met again with an estimated 200 members present. Among those attendees were two undercover FBI agents.

During the 1997 Congress, several extremist attendees split off from the main group and discussed the violent overthrow of the U.S. government. This unnamed group of individuals met several times in 1997 with attendees including Kevin and Terry Hobeck from Ohio, Bradley Glover and Michael Dorsett from the 1st Mechanical KS Militia, Ronald Griesacker from the Republic of Texas, and the two FBI agents who had attended the 1997 Congress. From this infiltration, the FBI was able to foil a July 4th attack on Fort Hood mainly planned by Glover and Dorsett, and was able to uncover a huge cache of weapons held by the Hobecks. All members of this splinter group were eventually rounded up on weapons charges and were sentenced to various jail terms.

After the April 1997 meeting and subsequent FBI operation against the splinter faction, the 3rd Continental Congress faded away. In 2003, a man named William Flatt who called himself a "major general" with the Indiana Militia Corps issued a call for a revival of the Congress. Despite numerous postings on many militia and patriot websites, Flatt's call received little interest and the 3rd Continental Congress has essentially remained inactive.

In 2004, the 3rd Continental Congress launched a new website. While the site addresses common militia themes and arguments, there is no indication of any future action by the group.

15 May Organisation

Continent: Middle East
Country: Iraq
Background:
The group was formed in 1979 from remnants of Wadi Haddad's Popular Front for the Liberation of Palestine-Special Operations Group (PFLP-SOG). It was led by Muhammad al-Umari, who was known throughout Palestinian circles as Abu Ibrahim or the bomb man. The group was never part of the PLO. It was reportedly disbanded in the mid-1980s when several key members joined Colonel Hawari's Special Operations Group of Fatah.

The organisation claimed responsibility for several bombings in the early-to-middle 1980s, including a hotel bombing in London (1980), El Al's Rome and Istanbul offices (1981), and Israeli Embassies in Athens and Vienna (1981). Anti-US attacks include an attempted bombing of a Pan Am airliner in Rio de Janeiro and a bombing on board a Pan Am flight from Tokyo to Honolulu in August 1982.

Its location and area of operation was in Baghdad until 1984. Before it disbanded and then operated in the Middle East, Europe, and East Asia. Abu Ibrahim was reportedly in Iraq. External aid was probably received logistic and financial support from Iraq until 1984.

21 June

Continent: Europe
Country: Greece
Background:
21 June is a small Greek terrorist organisation. Their only known attack was a Molotov-cocktail attack on a Eurobank branch in September 2003 in the Thessaloniki region. 21 June was formed to protest the continued detention of seven protestors that were arrested in Thessaloniki during demonstrations against the EU summit on the 21st June 2003. Of the seven remaining in custody, three were Greek, one Syrian, one British and

two Spanish. The fire department estimated the damage from the attack at 50,000 Euros. It is unknown if 21 June had links to any of the more prominent anarchist terrorist groups in Greece.

21 June has not claimed an attack since September 2003 and is likely inactive. However, numerous anarchist groups currently operate in Greece, and it is possible that members of 21 June remain active with other like-minded organisations.

23rd of September Communist League Mexico

Continent: Central America
Country: Mexico
Background:

The 23rd of September Communist League was a Mexican terrorist entity that operated between 1973 and 1982. The group's name (commonly referred to by its abbreviated Spanish name, La Liga or its Spanish acronym LC-23S), commemorates a guerrilla assault on a military garrison in Chihuahua, Mexico that was led by a former schoolteacher, Arturo Gámiz, on the 23rd September 1965. La Liga was formed in March 1973 in Guadalajara, Mexico as an urban guerrilla organisation. However, the organisation was short-lived and its leaders were soon captured or killed. A second iteration of La Liga soon arose and continued operations through the early 1980s.

The primary objective of La Liga was to overthrow the Mexican government, controlled at that time by the Institutional Revolutionary Party, or Partido Revolucionario Institucional (PRI). However, the group's intent was not simply the institutionalisation of a purely Communist government in Mexico; rather, the group was avowedly against the ruling party in Mexico and saw Communism as a viable alternative. Therefore, La Liga was not an ideologically rigid organisation and instead espoused a mixture of Communism and anarchism. The group led a violent guerrilla operation in Mexico's urban centres, conducting kidnappings, bombings, and firearm assaults against soldiers, police officers, government officials, and civilians.

La Liga attacks, in large part, were sustained throughout the 1970s and early 1980s by incorporating additional members while other terrorist groups disbanded or were destroyed. However, the group was never able to gain the support of the Mexican population. While La Liga was initially formed by members of the Mexican middle class, the group unsuccessfully attempted to reach out to the working-class and students in order to broaden its struggle against the Mexican government. Internal ideological disputes and power struggles as well as a successful counterterrorist campaign by Mexico's security forces eventually destroyed the 23rd of September Communist League in 1982. No future group activity is expected.

Also known as La Liga, Liga 23 de Septiembre (L-23S)

32 County Sovereignty Movement

Continent: Europe
Country: United Kingdom and Ireland
Background:
The 32 County Sovereignty Movement (often abbreviated to 32CSM or 32csm) is an Irish republican political organisation that supports the Real Irish Republican Army's (RIRA) paramilitary activities. The 32CSM's objectives are:

(a) The restoration of Irish national sovereignty.
(b) To seek to achieve unity among the Irish people on the issue of restoring national sovereignty and to promote the revolutionary ideals of republicanism and to this end involve itself in resisting all forms of colonialism and imperialism.
(c) To seek the immediate and unconditional release of all Irish republican prisoners throughout the world.

Many of the 32 County Sovereignty Movement's founding members had previously been members of Sinn Féin and they were also involved with a sub-group within Sinn Féin called the 32 County Sovereignty Committee. The 32CSM are suspected to be aligned with the Real IRA.

The organisation was founded on the 7th December 1997 at a meeting in Fingal in Dublin by republican activists who were opposed to the direction taken by Sinn Féin and other mainstream republican politicians in the peace process, which would lead to the Belfast Agreement (also known as the Good Friday Agreement) the following year. The same division in the republican movement led to the paramilitary group now known as the Real IRA breaking away from the Provisional Irish Republican Army at around the same time. The 32 County Sovereignty Movement is often considered to be the 'political wing' of the Real IRA, although members reject the term.

Most of its founders had been members of Sinn Féin; some had been expelled from the party and others felt they had not been properly able to air their concerns within Sinn Féin at the direction its leadership had taken. Bernadette Sands McKevitt, a sister of hunger striker Bobby Sands and wife of Michael McKevitt, was a prominent member of the group until a split in the organisation.

The name refers to the 32 counties of Ireland which were established when the whole island of Ireland was under British rule. Twenty-six of these original counties now form the Republic of Ireland and the other six remain part of the United Kingdom.

Before the referendums on the Good Friday Agreement, the 32CSM lodged a legal submission with the United Nations challenging British sovereignty in Ireland. In November 2005 the 32CSM launched a political initiative titled Irish Democracy, A Framework For Unity.

This group has been subject to protests by the families of those who died in the Omagh bombing which was perpetrated by the Real IRA.

This group is currently designated as a Foreign Terrorist Organisation (FTO) in the United States as the group is considered to be inseparable from the RIRA. At a briefing in 2001, the spokesman for US Department of State stated that "evidence provided by both the British and Irish governments and open source materials demonstrate clearly that the individuals who created the real IRA also established these two entities to serve as the public face of the real IRA. These alias organisations engage in propaganda and fundraising on behalf of and in collaboration with the real IRA". This made it illegal for Americans to provide material support to the RIRA, requires US financial institutions to block the group's assets and denies alleged RIRA members visas into the US.

313

Continent: Asia
Country: Pakistan
Background:
313 is a Pakistani terrorist group formed by members of a number of other groups that have been banned in Pakistan, principally the Lashkar-e-Jhangvi, Harkat-ul-Mujahideen, Jaish-e-Mohammed, Harkat-ul-Ansar and Harkat-ul-Jihad-i-Islami. It appears, however, that 313 does not share the focus on Kashmir of the groups whose members comprise it.

In an intelligence report provided to Pakistani president Pervez Musharraf, it was reported that 313 had targeted a number of top Pakistani political officials. 313 also had undertaken anti-Shi'ite terrorism. The anti-Shi'ite ideology of 313 was apparent from a shooting attack on a bus in Karachi, which was timed to occur after Sunni passengers had left the bus to attend Friday prayers at their mosque, with the victims being only the Shi'ites remaining onboard.

No attacks have been attributed to 313 since October 2003; however, there have been no definitive reports on the demise of the group. Sectarian violence remains a problem in many parts of Pakistan.

2008 Uyghur Unrest

Continent: Asia
Country: China
Background:

Ethnic tensions in the Western region of Xinjiang, China, have a long history and date back since the Qing Dynasty annexed the territory in the 1700s. The Uyghur's as the original Turkic Muslim population in the area has at various stages tried to obtain self-determination. The Chinese central government has curbed independence movements consistently. The authorities see groups like the Hizb ut-Tahrir al-Islami (Islamic Party of Liberation) as terrorists and attribute them most of unrest activities of the last years.

Rumours go that on the 18th March that a Uighur woman had detonated a bomb on a city bus in Urumqi, escaping before its explosion. While officials deny the incident the International Herald Tribune reports of residents confirming the bombing.

On the 23rd March Muslim Uyghur's have held anti-government protests in the far western region of Xinjiang, China. Chinese officials are blaming separatists inspired by the 2008 Tibetan unrest . Demonstrators took to the streets at the weekly bazaar in Hotan. The authorities maintain tight controls on information from the area and reports of deaths or their denial could not be independently verified.

Residents of townships and villages near Gulja, a city in north-western Xinjiang, said that about 25 Uyghur's were arrested on the 4th April on a tip that people in the area were making bombs

A

Abkhazia Rebels

Continent: Asia
Country: Georgia
Background:
Abkhazia is a region in Caucasus. It is a de facto independent republic, with no international recognition. It is located within the internationally recognised borders of Georgia. Abkhazia is located on the eastern coast of the Black Sea, bordering the Russian Federation to the north. Within Georgia, it borders the region of Samegrelo-Zemo Svaneti to the east. Abkhazia's independence is not recognised by any international organisation or country and it is recognised as an autonomous republic of Georgia with Sukhumi as its capital.

A secessionist movement of Abkhaz ethnic minority in the region led to the declaration of independence from Georgia in 1992 and the Georgian-Abkhaz armed conflict from 1992 to 1993 which resulted in the Georgian military defeat and the mass exodus and ethnic cleansing of Georgian population from Abkhazia. In spite of the 1994 ceasefire accord and the ongoing UN-monitored and Russian-dominated CIS peacekeeping operation, the sovereignty dispute has not yet been resolved and the region remains divided between the two rival authorities, with over 83 percent of its territory controlled by the Russian-backed Sukhumi-based separatist government and about 17 percent governed by the Government of the Autonomous Republic of Abkhazia, recognised by Georgia as the legal authority of Abkhazia, located in the Kodori Valley, part of Georgian-controlled Upper Abkhazia.

Abu al Abbas

Continent: Middle East
Country: Iraq
Background:
Abu al-Abbas is an Islamist group that many believed to be responsible for the August 2004 kidnapping of James Brandon, a British journalist in Basra, Iraq.

On the 13th August 2004, a group of about 20 gunmen stormed the hotel where Brandon was staying and abducted him. Just hours earlier, a previously unknown Shia group calling themselves Abu al-Abbas threatened to kill anyone cooperating with British troops in response to a U.S. led attack on the Shia holy city of Najaf.

Shortly after Brandon was kidnapped, the gunmen released a video in which Brandon appeared with a hooded man who threatened to kill the journalist in 24 hours unless fighting stopped in Najaf. After about 20 hours, the kidnappers freed Brandon, purportedly at the orders of Muqtada al-Sadr, leader of the Shia rebel organisation Mahdi Army. It is unclear what connection the Mahdi Army had with the kidnappers, but securing the journalist's release was somewhat of a "publicity coup" for the Mahdi Army, who had been engaged in heavy fighting with coalition forces.

Although the Abu al-Abbas group never directly claimed responsibility for the kidnapping, it is highly likely that they were responsible. Aside from demanding the end of hostilities in Najaf, the group gave no indication as to their ideology or further aims. The name Abu al-Abbas is probably a reference to Abu al-Abbas as-Saffah, first Caliph of the Islamic Abbasid dynasty, and a revered figure amongst Shia Muslims. From both their name and their goal of ending fighting in Najaf, the group can be positively identified as a Shia Islamic organisation.

Kidnappings of foreign workers and journalists were extremely common in post-war Iraq. Sometimes the motive is simply monetary, but oftentimes kidnappers have concrete demands, such as the removal of specific troops from Iraq or the freeing of prisoners from U.S. custody. Although kidnappings are common, it is highly unusual that the Mahdi Army or any insurgent group would involve themselves in the freeing of hostages. To that effect, the Brandon kidnapping can be considered unique. In any case, Abu al-Abbas has not issued any public statements or claimed responsibility for further terrorist incidents since the kidnapping, and it is possible that the perpetrators were renegade members of the Mahdi Army looking for publicity.

Abu Bakr al-Seddiq Battalions

Continent: Middle East
Country: Iraq
Background:
This group was responsible for the kidnapping in Iraq of ten US-Turkish hostages. The group demanded that the employer leave Iraq within three days otherwise it would start to kill hostages. The ten were taken hostage in September 2004 and were released in October 2004 after the company employing the men had left Iraq.

Abu Bakr al-Seddiq Fundamentalist Group

Continent: Middle East
Country: Iraq
Background:

The Abu Bakr al-Siddiq Brigades is an Iraqi insurgent group responsible for two kidnappings which targeted foreigners in the country. The group first emerged in September 2004 after claiming responsibility for the kidnapping and subsequent killing of a Turkish man and an Iraqi whom the group accused of cooperating with Israel.

In October the group attained notoriety when they kidnapped and held hostage a Polish woman in Iraq. Their demands included the removal of Polish troops from Iraq and the release of female prisoners from U.S. custody in Iraq. Poland has been a strong ally of the United States during the war and subsequent occupation of Iraq. It was later revealed that the hostage, Teresa Borcz, was a dual Iraqi-Polish citizen who had married an Iraqi and lived in Iraq for many years. A videotape was released to al-Jazeera showing Borcz pleading for Poland to meet the kidnapper's demands. Poland did not negotiate with the group; however, Borcz was eventually released unharmed on the 19th November 2004.

The Abu Bakr al-Siddiq Brigades have not claimed a terrorist attack since the October 2004 kidnapping; however, there have been no reports of arrests or detentions of any group members. It is likely that members of the group remain active in the Iraqi insurgency.

Also known as Salafist Brigades of Abu Bakr Al-Siddiq

Abu Deraa

Continent: Middle East
Country: Iraq
Background:

Abu Deraa ("Father of the Shield") (real name: Ismail al-Zerjawi Hafidh), is an Iraqi Shiite warlord whose men have been accused of terrorising and killing Sunnis. His aim has apparently been to avenge Shiite deaths at the hands of Sunni militants in Iraq, though he has stated that he is fighting for all Iraqis and only targets the 'occupiers'. Abu Deraa operates out of Sadr City, which is also the stronghold of Shiite cleric Muqtada al-Sadr's militia, the Mahdi Army. He has gained a reputation for his command of Shiite death squads and brutal attacks targeting Sunni Muslims and cases of mass kidnappings in broad daylight. Many Shiites see him as a brave warrior who has inflicted misery on Sunni insurgents but Sunnis see him as a sectarian warlord who targets Sunnis because of their background.

He was also accused of orchestrating the kidnapping and assassination of Saddam Hussein's lawyer Khamis al-Obeidi. Abu Deraa's son was reported to have pulled the trigger. He is thought to have been recently disavowed, at least tacitly, by Muqtada al-Sadr due to his unmitigated killing sprees. Abu Deraa previously owned a small fish market in Sadr City prior to joining the al-Mahdi Army. The warlord has two sons currently in U.S. custody and another son with an amputated limb due to a U.S. airstrike.

In a statement released on the 4th December 2006, the Islamic State of Iraq claimed responsibility for the killing of Abu Deraa on a road north of Baghdad. The claim came three days after a statement released by the Islamic Army in Iraq that also claimed responsibility for the killing of Abu Deraa. It has been claimed that he had taken part in a by-proxy interview with Sydney Morning Herald conducted by veteran Middle East correspondent Paul McGeough on the 20th December 2006. His first exclusive interview was with Reuters news agency published on the 16th November 2006. Although no one is sure that he is still alive.

Also known as Father of the Shield

Abu Hafs al-Masri Brigades

Continent: Europe
Country: Spain, United Kingdom
Background:
The Abu Hafs al-Masri Brigade may be the name of an active al-Qaeda cell in Europe or the organisation that oversees al-Qaeda's European operations. Of course, the Brigade may exist in name only as well.

Named for infamous al-Qaeda terrorist Mohamed Atef aka Abu Hafs, the Abu Hafs al-Masri Brigade is known only through statements published through the London Arabic language daily al Quds al Arabi. Through this publication, the group has claimed responsibility for several large terrorist strikes, including the July London bombings, the 2004 Madrid train bombings, and the massive blackouts that occurred in North America in the summer of 2003. The attacks for which they claim responsibility are generally attributed to al-Qaeda, or al-Qaeda-linked groups. Ayman al-Zawahiri, al-Qaeda's number 2, has claimed responsibility for the organisation on more than one occasion. The group appears to be recently formed (as Atef was only killed in late 2001), but it may reflect only a name-change in memory of Atef for a pre-existing off-shoot or operational division of al-Qaeda.

Doubts of the group's existence stem from the fact that several of their claims are clearly false. The 2003 blackouts, for example, were caused by technical errors. The Abu Hafs group, however, referred to the incident as one of its "operations" - "Operation Quick Lightning in the Land of the Tyrant of This Generation."

This claim certainly calls the group's credibility into question. However, there is no conclusive evidence to show that all of their claims are false. What is clear in their statements, though, is that the group subscribes to the ideology of al-Qaeda. Abu Hafs al-Masri has publicly reiterated arguments made by Ayman al-Zawahiri and Osama bin Laden, such as the contention that westerners are themselves responsible for Islamist attacks on civilians because of their democratic systems.

The Abu Hafs al-Masri Brigade is most likely either a subset of al-Qaeda or a copy-cat group that has joined its jihad against the west. Its size and membership are unclear, as is its access to the al-Qaeda leadership, resources, and network.

The Abu Hafs al-Masri Brigade has accepted the call for a holy war against western civilisation most associated with al-Qaeda. The brigade attacks (or claims to attack) western civilians for their complicity in atrocities committed by western governments against Muslims worldwide. In July 2005, the group published a statement on the web that may have been meant to signal more attacks to European cells.

In February 2006, a statement signed by the Abu Hafs al-Masri Brigades appeared online threatening "bloody war" on Denmark. This was in relation to the controversy over the Muhammad cartoons published by the Danish newspaper Jyllands-Posten.

Abu Mus'ab al Zarqawi Battalion

Continent: Middle East
Country: Lebanon, Saudi Arabia
Background:

The Abu Mus'ab al-Zarqawi Battalion is a small Islamic extremist group founded in Saudi Arabia by Abdul-Raouf Saleh. As their name implies, the group emulates Abu Mus'ab al-Zarqawi, the leader of the al-Qaeda Organisation in the Land of Two Rivers who was killed on the 7th June 2006, in a U.S.-led attack. Subsequent statements from Battalion members revealed that they were merely inspired by al-Zarqawi, and not affiliated with al-Qaeda.

The Battalion has been linked to only one incident, the 12th September 2006, bombing of the U.S. Embassy in Damascus, Syria. Battalion operatives, armed with automatic weapons and hand grenades, drove to the Embassy gate with the objective to break into the compound and kill as many people as possible. However, Syrian guards, stationed at a post outside the Embassy's gates, successfully prevented the attackers from gaining entry. Three Battalion members and one Syrian guard were killed in a resulting shootout. The driver of a second vehicle filled with explosives, which arrived at a different entry point, was shot and forced to abandon the vehicle before any detonation could occur.

This attack was never explicitly claimed by any group. Initial reports implicated Jund al-Sham, an al-Qaeda offshoot that has been active in Syria, in the attack. However, further investigations as well as interviews with suspects uncovered Saleh's involvement, in particular his funnelling of money from Saudi Arabia to family members in Lebanon to purchase weapons for the attack. The weapons were then smuggled from Lebanon into Syria, where Saleh eventually arrived to plan attack operations. According to statements, the group originally planned to release a video of the attack.

All investigations surrounding the Abu Mus'ab al-Zarqawi Battalion produced no evidence of possible ties to larger terrorist groups, like al-Qaeda. While Syrian authorities arrested several group members, it is unclear at this time the status of their cases, particularly what charges have been filed and the timeline for criminal court proceedings.

It is unlikely that the Abu Mus'ab al-Zarqawi Battalion remains a threat to the region. Of greater concern, however, is that this group is part of a disturbing trend where "inspired" extremists commit attacks in the name of well-known militants whom they may not be affiliated with. Such arguments have been made regarding the 2004 Madrid subway bombings, claimed by the Abu Hafs al-Masri Brigade. Groups such as these can be considered a legitimate threat since it is virtually impossible to monitor their formation and initial planning. While they may only be capable of committing a single attack, the number of fatalities and amount of damage, as past attacks have shown, can be considerable.

Abu Nayaf al Afghani

Continent: Europe
Country: Spain
Background:
Little is known about Abu Nayaf al-Afghani, an al-Qaeda affiliated terror group that operates in Spain. The group is associated with al-Qaeda and its European cells, though the extent of the group's operational component is unclear. In April 2004, Abu Nayaf al-Afghani faxed a statement to a Spanish newspaper that claimed responsibility for an unsuccessful train bombing against a high speed train en route from Madrid to Seville. Several days later, the same group left a video tape by a mosque in Madrid, claiming responsibility for the infamous March 11 Madrid train bombings, despite the fact that this bombing occurred almost one month prior to Abu Nayaf al-Afghani's claim. Needless to say, the length of time

between the Madrid bombings and Abu Nayaf al-Afghani's claim has cast doubt on its authenticity. The bombings on the 11th March 2004 killed 191 people and wounded over 600. Ten bombs were planted and detonated nearly simultaneously on a busy commuter rail line south of Madrid.

Other sources attribute the March 11th attacks to the group Abu Dujana Al-Afghani Ansar Al-Qaeda Europe, which appears be an alias for Abu Nayaf al-Afghani. A separate Al-Qaeda linked organisation, the Abu Hafs al-Masri Brigade, also declared responsibility for the Madrid attacks, and although it faces similar questions about the validity of its claims, it is generally regarded by authorities as having carried out the attacks. While Abu Dujana Al-Afghani Ansar Al-Qaeda Europe and Abu Nayaf al-Afghani are likely the same operational group with aliases, the Abu Hafs al-Masri Brigade is probably an operationally distinct group loosely aligned with Abu Nayaf al Afghani. All of these groups are thought to share al-Qaeda's ideological convictions, though the extent to which they coordinate their actions is not fully known.

Abu Nayaf al-Afghani's political goals are less mysterious. The group seeks mainly to end Spanish support for American led efforts in the war on terror, citing "…Spanish…aggressions against Muslims in sending new troops to Iraq and announcing its intention to send new units to Afghanistan." The group's moniker contains two such references, as "Nayaf" refers to the Iraqi holy city of the same name ("Najaf" in Romanised Arabic), while "Afghani" is undoubtedly an allusion to American operations in Afghanistan.

One month after the Madrid bombings, Spain elected Prime Minister Jose Luis Rodriguez Zapatero's socialist government to power. He fulfilled his campaign promise to withdraw Spanish troops from Iraq in June 2004, satisfying one of Abu Nayaf al-Afghani's chief objectives. However, Zapatero doubled (from 250 to 500) the number of Spanish soldiers in Afghanistan, though whether Spanish support for this operation is sufficient to warrant further attacks is questionable. The group has not issued any claims of responsibility since their unsuccessful April 2004 attack. However, because of its affiliation and sympathy with al-Qaeda, as long as some level of Spanish support for American led operations in Afghanistan remains, the possibility of further attacks cannot be ruled out.

Also known as Abu Dujana Al-Afghani (of the) Ansar Al-Qaeda Europe

Abu Nidal Organisation

Abbreviation: ANO
Continent: Middle East
Country: Iraq, Libya, Syria
Background:
The Abu Nidal Organisation was an infamous Palestinian terrorist group

who split from the Palestinian Liberation Organisation (PLO) when the latter proposed the creation of the Palestinian National Authority in 1974. Group leader Sabri al-Banna aka Abu Nidal believed that no goal other than the total liberation of the Palestinian people was acceptable and that the only method by which to accomplish that goal was armed struggle. Abu Nidal hated Israel ("It is a crime to allow the Zionists to leave our land alive"), the United States ("Were it not for American support, the Zionist ghost would have long vanished from the world arena") and Arab leaders who have engaged politically with Israel or the West. Abu Nidal sometimes referred to these leaders as "Zionists who are not Jews," and they were the target of many of the ANO's attacks.

Abu Nidal Organisation was not a religious group, and Sabri al-Banna was primarily motivated by anger over the displacement of his family from Palestinian land during the 1948 Israeli War of Independence. During the 1980s, Abu Nidal was considered by terrorism experts to be the most dangerous international terrorist group in the world. However, Abu Nidal's extreme paranoia and frequent purges of those deemed disloyal weakened the Abu Nidal Organisation.

At its peak, the ANO had 400 members, but the organisation has been losing strength since the 1980s, when many of its operatives were arrested in South America. It has not attacked a Western target since the late 1980s. In August of 2002, the Iraqi government claimed that Abu Nidal had committed suicide in Iraq. Many believe that Saddam Hussein ordered the assassination, while others doubt that Abu Nidal is really dead. The remaining leadership of the organisation has publicly stated that the ANO did not die with its founder and that a new leader will be named. In any case, it is highly unlikely that the group will reactivate.

Also known as Arab Revolutionary Brigades

Abu Sayyaf Group

Abbreviation: ASG
Continent: Asia
Country: Philippines
Background:

The Abu Sayyaf Group (ASG), or Abu Sayyaf, is a radical Islamic terrorist group active in the Southern Philippines and Malaysia. ASG was designated as a foreign terrorist organisation by the United States in 1997. Its stated goal is the creation of an independent Islamic state encompassing parts of Southern Thailand, the island of Borneo, the Sulu Archipelago, and Mindanao, areas where Moro Muslims, a minority ethnic group in the Philippines, make up the majority of the local population. The ASG is known to target Filipino and Western Christians in the Southern Philippines, though the group's influence is thought to have expanded to the regional level recently.

The ASG was founded in 1991 by radical Moro National Liberation Front (MNLF) members who objected to the MNLF's negotiations with the Philippine government. Due to the ASG's predisposition toward violent tactics, which include high-profile bombings, armed attacks, assassinations, and beheadings, it is seen to be more radical than its mother group. Abu Sayyaf, which literally means "father of the sword" in Arabic, sees itself as the rightful inheritor of the legacy of armed Moro resistance in the region and the torchbearer in the struggle for the establishment of an Islamic state in Southeast Asia. Ironically, the group rocketed into prominence in the mid-1990s after two large scale plots (one to destroy 12 U.S. commercial aircraft simultaneously in mid-flight and one to assassinate Pope John Paul II) were foiled. It was thought to have two to five hundred core members mostly recruited from educational institutions and up to 2000 supporters.

Abu Sayyaf is largely self-financed through extortion rackets and kidnapping-for-ransom schemes. Allegedly, the ASG also receives a small level of logistical and material support from other extremist groups active in the region. The ASG provides safe haven for terrorist leaders from other groups and has local infrastructure in place to funnel money to plan and support attacks. It is also known to have substantial links to Jemaah Islamiya (JI) and factions of the Moro Islamic Liberation Front (MILF) that have yet to surrender to Philippine authorities.

The extent of the ASG's cooperation with al-Qaeda is thought to have diminished following the post-9/11 crackdown on the latter. Still, ASG members have trained in al-Qaeda camps in Afghanistan and some continued to receive operational guidance from al-Qaeda-affiliated terrorists hiding in or passing through the Philippines. The most famous of these contacts is 1993 World Trade Centre mastermind Ramzi Yousef, who met Abu Sayyaf founder and leader Abdurajak Janjalani in Afghanistan and trained ASG terrorists in bomb-making techniques. Osama bin-Laden's brother-in-law, Muhammad Jamal Khalifa, is thought to have provided the ASG with the bulk of its startup funding by laundering money through his charity, the International Islamic Relief Organisation.

Abu Sayyaf committed itself to Osama bin Laden's war against the "Jews and Crusaders" in February 1998. Later that year, Janjalani was killed by Philippine security forces and replaced by his younger brother Khadaffy Janjalani. After the death of the elder Janjalani, the group underwent a period of transition as Khadaffy Janjalani consolidated his power within the organisation, battling other contenders such as Galib Andang (aka Commander Robot) and Abu Sabaya for influence. Some experts suggested that the ASG moved away from its ideological and religious roots, engaging itself more in criminal activities (murder, robbery, kidnapping) with no apparent political or religious motive. It is also possible that this increase in criminal activity was due to the need to bolster the group's depleted coffers following the post-9/11 recommitment by governments the world over to disrupt and destroy terrorist financial networks. The group has certainly become more decentralised since Janjalani's death, a testament to the younger Janjalani's lack of leadership skills and religious legitimacy. The appointment of religious scholar Yasser Igasan to the ASG's top post in June 2007 may reflect the group's attempt to address this problem, though Igasan reportedly lacks military training.

The current goals of the ASG is the initiation of peace negotiations between the Philippine government and the MNLF (and subsequently the MILF) has served to divide the greater Moro resistance movement into those who seek a political resolution and those who use violence to achieve their objectives. The ASG has been strengthened by the addition of rogue MNLF and MILF elements dissatisfied with their respective groups' political approaches. Despite the concurrent efforts of the Philippine government and US counterterrorism advisers, the Abu Sayyaf Group remains a very active threat in the region and one of the main obstacles to peace in the Southern Philippines.

Accolta Nazinuale Corsa

Continent: Europe
Country: Corsica, France
Background:
Resistenza Corsa is a clandestine group that serves as the armed wing of the Accolta Nazinuale Corsa. Little is known about Resistenza Corsa beyond the facts surrounding their attacks and the group's statements that they are anti-drug trafficking, anti-immigrant, and anti-crime. The group appears to have been formed not long after the 2002 French presidential elections. In that election, the right-wing, anti-immigrant Front Nationale won as high a percentage of the Corsican vote as it traditionally claims in mainland France. Corsican police have speculated that the group could be a branch of the National Front for the Liberation of Corsica (FLNC).

In July 2003, Resistenza Corsa claimed a series of attacks in Northern Corsica against a furniture store, a vacation camp, a snack bar, and the car of an alleged heroin trafficker. A Resistenza Corsa member who communicated anonymously with a local television station claimed the attacks were committed to advance the group's anti-drug trafficking, anti-illegal immigration platform. The group warned that they would continue their attacks, possibly with napalm, if the police "failed to show a real willingness to fight drug trafficking." Resistenza Corsa also claims responsibility for a series of racist attacks against North African residents of Corsica that began in 2002.

Also known as Resistenza Corsa

Action Committee of Winegrowers

Abbreviation: CAV
Continent: Europe
Country: France
Background:
Little is known about Comite d'Action Viticole (CAV), a group that claims to act on behalf of discontented winegrowers in the Midi region of France. Midi winegrowers blame the state for failing to deal with problems of over-production and foreign competition in wine. The CAV's first attack was the 1999 bombing of a gas pipe in the Herault region. Two other attacks took place in the area on the same night, but CAV only claimed responsibility for the aforementioned bombing. In addition, in February 2002, the group bombed a train signal box on the Beziers-Narbonne high-speed line in the south of France, disrupting train traffic for 48 hours. This attack immediately followed a January riot at which thousands of protesters set palm trees and trash cans on fire. CAV's current goals are unknown.

Also known as Winegrowers Action Committee

Action Directe

Abbreviation: AD
Continent: Europe
Country: France
Background:
Action Directe (Direct Action, in English) first appeared in May, 1979, when it claimed responsibility for an attack on a French business organisation. Direct Action was a Marxist-Leninist organisation, whose ideology was based in the French "gauchiste" tradition. Early in its career, Direct Action focused its attacks on the French state, consistent with its goal of a revolutionary communist movement in France, although targets also included Israeli interests. This ideology changed with the changing political environment, notably after the election of the socialist Prime Minister in 1980. After this, much of the justification of the group's ideology was lost and their position became more marginalised. After a brief truce with the French government, Direct Action began to carry out attacks again, some under the Group Bakunin Gdansk Paris Guatemala Salvador (GBGPGS)

alias, with a new focus on anti-Americanism, tied to the "Euro-terrorist" movement of the time.

Although the group was ostensibly composed of both "domestic" and "international" factions, the group committed only a very small number of attacks outside France. The most well known of these was the 1985 car bombing of the American Air Force base at Rhein-Main, Germany, which was conducted in conjunction with the German terrorist organisation Red Army Faction (RAF). It is suspected that the GBGPGS was an alias for this "international" faction.

One of Direct Action's most noteworthy attacks, and it's one of its last, was the assassination of the head of Renault Corporation, Georges Besse in November 1986. Its 4 principal leaders, Nathalie Menigon, Jean-Marc Rouillan, Joelle Aubron and Georges Cipriani, were arrested in relation to this assassination in February, 1987. With the arrest of explosives expert Max Frerot soon after, the group was effectively decimated

The group had recently been in the news due to pressure on the French government to improve the living conditions of the Direct Action prisoners, some of whom have serious medical conditions and have faced long sentences of isolation. Another member of Direct Action, Helene Castel, who was indicted in France for participation in the 1980 bombing of a French banking group, was extradited from Mexico in August 2004 and faces a life sentence in prison.

Action Group Extreame Beate

Continent: Europe
Country: Denmark
Background:
Action Group Extreme Beate claimed responsibility for an attack on the house and car of Danish Integration Minister Rikke Hvilshoj in June 2005. Early in the morning, the group set fire to Hvilshoj's car and house. Hvilshoj, her husband, and her two children escaped the house and avoided any harm. The group issued a press release decrying the "racist refugee policy" of the Danish government. Denmark has a very strict immigration policy which is the cause of Action Group Extreme Beate's anger. The man who issued this press release had been arrested by the Copenhagen police and it was suspected that he carried out the attack. There is very little reason to believe that Action Group Extreme Beate will remain active following the arrest of the primary suspect for the Hvilshoj incident. It is highly likely that Action Group Extreme Beate was a name adopted by a lone operative who ended up in police custody.

Aden-Abyan Islamic Army

Abbreviation: AAIA
Continent: Middle East
Country: Yemen
Background:

The Aden Abyan Islamic Army (AAIA) emerged publicly in mid-1998 when the group released a series of communiqués that expressed support for Osama Bin Laden and appealed for the overthrow of the Yemeni government and operations against US and other Western interests in Yemen. Members of the sect adhere to the salafi religious faction, which is a small Sunni Muslim sect closely related to the Wahhabism theology practiced widely in Saudi Arabia. AAIA is suspected of being an offshoot of the Yemeni Islamic Jihad, a group believed to be funded by bin Laden. The majority of its members are former Mujahideen with experience in Afghanistan. The current status of the AAIA is unknown. Despite several press statements attributed to the AAIA and released in 2002, Yemeni officials claim that the group is operationally defunct.

The Islamic Army praised the attacks on US embassies in Tanzania and Kenya in August 1998 as "an heroic operation carried out by heroes of the jihad." It also announced its support for Osama bin Laden following the Americans' reprisal raid on his camp in Afghanistan, called on the Yemeni people to kill Americans and destroy their property. On 8th November 1998, then leader al-Mehdar, called on all members of the Yemeni parliament and Consultative Council to resign and demanded that President Ali Abdullah Salih "surrender" and face trial in accordance with the Shari'ah. His hostility towards the Yemeni government seemed to stem partly from his position as a member of a minority sect, but also from his view that Shari'ah law is not applied properly in Yemen.

Also known as Aden Islamic Army, Army of Mohammed and the Jaish Adan Al Islami, Islamic Aden Army, Islamic Army of Aden (IAA), Islamic Army of Aden-Abyan (IAAA), Jaysh Adan, Muhammad's Army

Affiche Rouge

Continent: Europe
Country: France
Background:

Affiche Rouge ("Red Poster" in English) was a faction of the French terrorist group Action Directe. Specifically, this faction was part of the "national" branch of Action Directe, and was led by André Olivier. Olivier's faction was based in Paris. The name of this faction was derived from a famous

Nazi WWII propaganda poster which depicted members of the French Resistance as criminals and terrorists. Olivier and a number of his accomplices were arrested in Lyon and St. Etienne in March 1986, effectively ending the operation of his faction.

Also known as Red Poster and see Action Directe

Afrikaner Resistance Movement

Abbreviation: AWB
Continent: Africa
Country: South Africa
Background:

The Afrikaner Weerstandsbeweging or AWB, meaning Afrikaner Resistance Movement, is a political and paramilitary group in South Africa under the leadership of Eugène Terre'Blanche. They are committed to the restoration of an independent Afrikaner republic or "Boerestaat" within South Africa. In their heyday they received much publicity both in South Africa and abroad as an extremist white supremacist group.

The AWB was formed in 7 July 1973 in a garage in Heidelberg, Transvaal, a town southeast of Johannesburg. Eugène Terre'Blanche, a former police officer, became disillusioned by then-Prime Minister B.J. Vorster's "liberal views," as well as what he viewed as Communist influences in South African society. Terre'Blanche decided to form the AWB with six other like-minded individuals, and was elected leader of the organisation, a position he holds to this day.

Their objective was to establish an independent Boerestaat ("Boer State") for Afrikaner people, existing separately from South Africa, which was considered too left wing by Terre'blanche. The AWB was formed in an attempt to regain the ground lost after the Second Boer War: they intended to re-establish the Boer Republics of the past — the South African Republic (Zuid-Afrikaansche Republiek) and the Republic of the Orange Free State (Oranje Vrystaat) — which the European and American governments had recognised in the late 1800s. The AWB flag is comprised of three sevens in a white circle upon a red background, forming a triskelion, highly similar to the Nazi swastika.

Despite the strong resemblance to the Nazi swastika and the historic admiration for Nazism among the far right in South Africa, Terre'Blanche publicly claims to distance the AWB from this interpretation of the emblem. He claims instead that the sevens, 'the number of JAHWEH', 'stand to oppose the number 666, the number of the anti-Christ'. Red is considered to represent Jesus' blood, while black stands for bravery and courage. The inner white circle symbolises the "eternal struggle". The AWB also uses the "Vierkleur" or the original flag of the once independent Transvaal Republic.

During the 1970s and 1980s, the AWB grew from the original 7 to several thousand white South Africans. They opposed the reform of Apartheid laws during the 1980s, harassing liberal politicians and holding large (and often quite rowdy) political rallies. Terre'Blanche used his flamboyant oratorical skills and forceful personality to win converts. He railed against the lifting of many so-called "Petty apartheid" laws such as the law banning interracial sex and marriage, as well as the larger and more important steps, such as limited political rights to Indians and Coloureds. During the State of Emergency (1984 to 1986) there were many reports of AWB violence against unarmed non-whites. The AWB was especially in opposition to the then-banned African National Congress in which members of the South African Communist Party played an important role. The ruling National Party considered the AWB to be little more than a fringe group, so while not officially endorsed, they were able to operate relatively unhindered. However in 1986, white police officers took the unprecedented step of using tear gas against Terre'Blanche and the AWB when they disrupted a National Party rally.

An economic crisis in the mid-1980s saw many poorer white South African families fall on hard times. The AWB instituted a programme to help the very poorest Afrikaner families. It was initially called the AWB Voedingskema (feeding scheme) and then the Volkshulpskema (people's help scheme), the programme contributed to the popularity of the AWB in the Afrikaner community. The scheme delivered a meal every day to 14,000 poor Afrikaner children in Pretoria. In the final 3 months of 1986 alone 300 tons of food was donated. In the winter, bedding was donated as well. Sympathetic mine owners and farmers 'arranged' jobs for unemployed Afrikaners on the farms and mines. Certain farmers also donated vegetables on an almost weekly basis to the poorest. Afrikaans singer Bles Bridges held a concert on March 3rd, 1987 in Pretoria and gave the 10,000 Rand raised to the AWB's People's Help Scheme.

In 1992, the AWB was beset by scandal when Terre'Blanche was found to be having an affair with journalist Jani Allan, with transcripts of their sexual relationship appearing in the South African press.

During the negotiations that led to South Africa's first multiracial elections, the AWB threatened all-out war. During the Battle of Ventersdorp in August 1991, the AWB confronted police in front of the town hall where President F W de Klerk was speaking, and three AWB supporters and one passer-by were killed in the conflict. Later in the negotiations, the AWB stormed the Kempton Park World Trade Centre where the negotiations were taking place, breaking through the glass front of the building with an armoured car. The police guarding the centre failed to prevent the invasion. The invaders then took over the main conference hall, threatening delegates and painting slogans on the walls, but left again after a short period.

In 1994, before the advent of majority rule, the AWB gained international notoriety in its attempt to defend the dictatorial government of Lucas Mangope in the homeland of Bophuthatswana. The AWB, along with a contingent of about 90 Afrikanervolksfront militiamen entered the capital of Mmabatho on March 10th and March 11th. During their entry to the homeland they were all observed indiscriminately shooting civilians and tossing grenades from their vehicles. After the black soldiers and police with Bophuthatswana Defence Force (they and the AWB were out in force to support president Mangope) witnessed these killings, they disappeared from the streets in protest. They later turned on the AWB/Volksfront militiamen at the airport at Mafikeng. One AWB member was shot and killed when the convoy attempted to leave the airport and continue on to Mmabatho. When in Mmabatho, the AWB and the Afrikaner Volksfront found themselves under continuous siege from both the Bophuthatswana Defence Force and Mmabatho citizens. When attempting to retreat from Mmabatho on the 11th March three AWB members were killed by Defence Force members after they had been wounded. The three exchanged fire with Defence Force soldiers and policemen from their Mercedes on reaching an intersection. One of the wounded, Andre Woolfaardt, requested an ambulance for an injured member and Menyatso allegedly replied, "Why didn't you bring your own ambulance". The journalists themselves were nearly fired upon by Bophuthatswana soldiers (they were saved by a jammed rifle) and Wolfaardt was killed at close range with an automatic rifle by Ontlametse Bernstein Menyatsoe whose words "What are you doing in my country?" were broadcast around the world by a television news crew. This proved to be a public relations disaster for the AWB and showed the world in stark terms that decades of white supremacy had come to an end. Despite this disaster, Eugène Terre'Blanche proclaimed the failed campaign a victory due to the fact that over a hundred Bophutatswana soldiers were killed and only three AWB members were killed.

On the 17th June 1997 Terre'Blanche was sentenced to six years in prison for assaulting a petrol station worker, John Ndzima, and the attempted murder of a security guard and former employee, Paul Motshabi. Terre'Blanche was released in June 2004 after serving 3 years in Rooigrond Prison near Mafikeng.During his time in prison he became a born-again Christian and claims he has moderated many of his more racist views and preaches reconciliation as 'prescribed by God'. However, the AWB website still claims these court cases and other scandals involving him were fabricated by the 'Black Government and the left wing media'.

Although primarily an Afrikaner movement, with Afrikaans as their sole official language, the AWB also had English-speaking white members. As Terre'Blanche's driver and AWB member, Jan 'J.P' Meyer, once remarked, "We have a large membership, even in parts of the country that we don't see as our (the Boervolk) homeland".

Ahl-e-Hadees

Continent: Asia
Country: Kashmir
Background:

Jamiat-e-Ahl-e-Hadees is a prominent religious organisation of Kashmir valley. Ahl-e-Hadees, founded following the demolition of the Babri Masjid in Ayodhya in December 1992, is claimed by India to be working at the behest of Pakistan's Inter-Services Intelligence. Ahl-e-Hadees is an all-India outfit with recruits from Bihar and Uttar Pradesh, operating in tandem with the Lakhmir Singh Rode group of the International Sikh Youth Federation. Indian intelligence reports suggest that the phase of the activity of these organisations began with the Taif Summit of the OIC in January 1981. Overseas Islamic organisations and their funds spawned a series of organisations in India and invigorated others. Mohammad Ramzan, chief of the Jamiat-e-Ahl-e-Hadees, was injured in an attack by militants on the 29th January 1999, when he was coming out of a mosque here after offering Friday prayers. He died on the 15th February 1999.

Ahlus Sunnah Wal Jamaah

Abbreviation: ASWJ
Continent: Europe
Country: United Kingdom
Background:

Ahlus Sunnah wal Jamaah (English: Adherents to the Sunnah and the community or Followers of Ahlus Sunnah wal Jamaah; alternately transliterated: Ahl ul-Sunnah Wa al-Jamma; ASWJ) is an Islamist organisation operating in the United Kingdom, intended to be a successor to the banned Al-Muhajiroun organisation. Founded in November 2005 in north London, its head was "Simon" Sulayman Keeler. Also attending the organisation's launch were Anjem Choudary, the former head of al-Muhajiroun, Abu Yahya, Abu Izzadeen and Abu Uzair. The group claims up to 1000 members, many of them members of the now-banned groups Al Ghurabaa and the 'The Saved Sect'.

ASWJ operates mainly through an invitation-only Internet forum set up in 2006 by Mizanur Rahman called "Followers of Ahlus Sunnah Wal Jama'aah Muntada", of which Anjem Choudary is a prominent contributor, under the screen name "Abou Luqman". The forum currently has 700 members. A reporter visiting the site found calls for holy war, and recordings of Osama Bin Laden, Ayman al-Zawahiri, and, notably, Omar Bakri Mohammed, the founder of al-Muhajiroun.

In February 2006 ASWJ helped organise the Islamist demonstration outside Danish Embassy in London in 2006.

In November 2006 the BBC programmes File on 4 and Newsnight, in an investigation into the radicalisation of young British Muslims reported that Omar Bakri is regularly broadcasting hate messages against the UK government and non-Muslim people via the internet, using a range of pseudonyms. His voice was reportedly confirmed by speech analysis experts to be that of Bakri. The BBC penetrated the broadcasts using undercover investigators from the group Vigil.

In December 2006, ASWJ issued a call on one of its websites for Muslims to fight the Ethiopian attack against the Islamic Courts Union in Somalia in whatever way possible, "financially, physically and verbally".

See the Al Muhajiroun, Al Ghurabaa and the Saved Sect.

Ahwaz Liberation Organisation

Abbreviation: ALO
Continent: Europe
Country: Netherlands
Background:

The Ahwaz Liberation Organisation (ALO), based in Maastricht in the Netherlands, was formed out of the remnants of three Iraqi-backed groups - the Democratic Revolutionary Front for the Liberation of Arabistan (DRFLA), People's Front for Liberation of Arabistan (PFLA) and the Arab Front for the Liberation of Al-Ahwaz (AFLA). It is a secular pan-Arabist group seeking independence from Iran. The DRFLA was the most notorious, having been sponsored by Saddam Hussein.

It was founded after the newly-installed Islamic government fired on Arab demonstrators in Khorramshahr, killing many of them. The DRFLA was behind the May 1980 Iranian Embassy Siege in London, taking a number of hostages in an effort to draw attention to its demands for the self-determination of the Arab population of Khuzestan. The British Special Air Service (SAS) stormed the building and freed the hostages.

The ALO's constituent groups operated as a mercenary force on behalf of Saddam's regime during the Iran-Iraq War, carrying out assassinations and attacking oil facilities. Bomb attacks on oil and power facilities have continued since the end of the Iraq War, although the ALO has not formally claimed responsibility. The ALO's leader, the self-styled "President of Al-Ahwaz" Faleh Abdallah Al-Mansouri, was living in exile in the Netherlands since 1989, shortly after the end of the Iran-Iraq War, gaining Dutch nationality. He declared himself to be the "President" of Al-Ahwaz, which he claims extends beyond Khuzestan, including much of the coast of Iran. However, during a visit to Syria in May 2006, he was arrested in Syria in May 2006 along with Iranian Arabs who were registered as refugees by the UNHCR. Although the Iranian government did not name the men who were taken into custody, officials said that the men arrested in Syria were Salafists who they accused of involvement in bomb attacks. However, the ALO's website makes no indication that it is motivated by a religious cause, but rather has stayed within the ideology of secular Arab nationalism.

Aitarak

Continent: Asia
Country: Indonesia
Background:

Aitarak (Indonesian for 'thorn') was the name of one of the most feared pro-Indonesia militia groups in East Timor during the late 1990s. On the 17th April 1999, the group conducted 12 murders at the Manuel Carrascaláo House Massacre in Dili. That same month members took part in the Liquiçá Church Massacre. At its height, the group was led by Eurico Guterres.

In 1999, following the autonomy referendum, during which East Timor citizens voted to separate from Indonesia and become independent, Indonesian military forces began a slow withdrawal from East Timor. In the course of this, they practiced what is referred to as the Timor-Leste Scorched Earth campaign, burning and destroying everything in their path.

They were assisted greatly in this by East Timorese pro-Indonesian militias. The militia groups for each district of East Timor were even more ruthless than the Indonesian military in most cases. Often, they knew their victims, and in many well-documented cases they had known their victims their entire lives, usually coming from the same villages or neighbourhoods.

The Aitarak gained the most notoriety, because they were the main militia group in the capital city and Dili district as a whole. It was here where international press were most present, and therefore the international press reported most what happened in Dili itself, and with the Aitarak.

Cases such as the Liquiçá Church Massacre, and the Suai Church Massacre, as well as Catholic nuns that were killed in Lospalos were largely unknown for a time.

Due to the ruthless manner in which the Aitarak killed and raped, they became infamous. They acted in a manner that indicated they had no fear of the press, or international reaction or consequences. In hindsight, it is quite apparent that the militia groups felt Indonesia would again gain control of East Timor, and those who had been faithful to the Indonesian government would be put in positions of power.

The exact number of victims killed by the Aitarak is unknown. It can easily be said that the number is in the hundreds. The most powerful of all the militias, Aitarak commanders could easily influence militia groups in other parts of East Timor, and did so on several occasions.

Although Indonesian military personnel and the government itself denied having any control over the militias, Indonesian military forces were present during nearly all the major incidents of mass murder. In the Liquiçá Church Massacre, investigators were baffled as to why none of the victims fled the immediate scene of the attack, until it was finally discovered through lengthy interviews that the church compound had been surrounded by Indonesian soldiers. The Indonesian military present did not enter and partake in the slaughter, but they did prevent any of the victims from fleeing.

Eurico Guterres, the commander of the Aitarak, held absolute control over not only the Aitarak, but also the Besi Merah Putih, and other militias throughout East Timor. Afterward, when suspects were being arrested and placed on trial for the carnage reaped on the East Timorese citizens during 1999, it was common to shift the blame to someone else. Militia members (Guterres included) regularly claimed that they acted on "orders" from someone else, or that they were merely a pawn with no control over what happened. Eurico Guterres was given 10 years in jail by the ad hoc Indonesian human rights tribunal, but is a free man today (as of February 2006) pending his Supreme Court Appeal. It is also well-known that he is now involved with Indonesia's second largest political party, PDI-P.

Also tried in the human rights tribunal were over a dozen Indonesian military and police officers. All were acquitted. They are all still actively serving in the country's Armed Forces and have each received promotions in rank since their East Timor service and trials ended.

Albanian National Army

Abbreviation: ABA
Continent: Europe
Country: Kosovo
Background:

The Albanian National Army (abbreviated ANA; Albanian: Armata Kombëtare Shqiptare, AKSh), is an ethnic Albanian terrorist organisation closely associated with the Kosovo Liberation Army — operating in the Republic of Macedonia and Kosovo under international administration from 2001. The group opposes the Ohrid Framework Agreement which ended the 2001 Macedonia conflict between insurgents of the National Liberation Army and Macedonian security forces.

It was formed in 2001 in the Republic of Macedonia and in 2003; the UNMIK declared it a terrorist organisation.

The ANA appeared in Kosovo in 2007. A video was aired by Kosovar television stations depicting a band of medium-armed, masked individuals intercepting cars. In October, 2007 the unit declared it would seize the Serb exclave of North Kosovo by force if the Kosovo Protection Force does not occupy it by the 1st November 2007. The United States State Department included it on the list of terrorist organisations as a result.

In early November of 2007, insurgents of the "Political Advisory Body of the Kosovo Liberation Army" suffered a minor crackdown, dubbed Operation Mountain Storm by the Macedonian armed forces in northwestern Macedonia. According to Macedonian authorities; six members of the KLA were killed.

On the 13th November 2007 a video was aired to the public, an exclusive interview with a leader of the ANA patrolling in the covert areas of North Kosovo, recruiting 20 new men. The leader stated that ANA stands at 12,000 men altogether and has called the Kosovar population for a boycott of then-forthcoming elections.

See the Kosovo Liberation Army

Alejo Calatayu

Continent: Central America
Country: Bolivia
Background:

Alejo Calatayu was a small commando unit in Bolivia which detonated a bomb at the home of an American DEA agent in Bolivia in 1987. Alejo Calatayu was most likely a group operating under the supervision of a local narcotics cartel. Such groups consistently targeted government officials as cocaine became an increasingly important aspect of the Bolivian economy in the 1980s. Alejo Calatayu's attacks were in protest of the arrival of US troops in Bolivia and the group has not been responsible for any incidents since 1987. Alejo Calatayu is no longer active.

Algetian Wolves

Continent: Asia
Country: Georgia
Background:

The Algeti Wolves (Georgian: Algeti Mglebi) are an extremist organisation in Georgia. On the 9th April 1994 assailants attacked the Tbilisi residence of the Russian special envoy, and the headquarters of Russian troupes in the Transcaucasus, with no injuries resulting. The Algeti Wolves claimed responsibility for the attack.

Also known as Algeti Mglebi

Alpha 66

Continent: North America
Country: United States of America
Background:

Alpha 66 is a paramilitary group funded by the US government, formed by Cuban exiles in Puerto Rico opposed to the Cuban government led by Fidel Castro. The group trained during the 1960s and 1970s in the Everglades for an eventual armed invasion of Cuba. The Cuban government, among others, has long considered the group to be a terrorist organisation.

Though an invasion never materialised after the failed Bay of Pigs invasion, the group continued its violent efforts against the Cuban communist government. In 1976, Miami Police Lieutenant Thomas Lyons and Detective Raul J. Diaz testified that groups including Alpha 66 had international terrorist ties and had sold $100 "bonds" in Miami to help finance their causes. The group was linked to a spate of bombings and assassinations in Miami during the 1970s, directed at moderate community leaders intolerant of the terrorist methods of certain anti-Castro groups against assigned communist officials and supporters. A week before Lyons and Diaz's testimony, broadcaster Emilio Milian had both his legs blown off in a car bomb outside his workplace.

Alpha 66 continues to be an organised entity. The current leader of this paramilitary group is believed to be Ferdinand de Montejo, who currently resides in Hollywood, Florida.

Also known as Cuban Liberator Army

Alex Boncayao Brigade

Abbreviation: ABB
Continent: Asia
Country: Philippines
Background:

The Alex Boncayao Brigade (ABB) was initially created as a faction of a pre-existing terrorist organisation, the New People's Army. The New People's Army (NPA) was formed in 1969 as the armed wing of a Filipino communist organisation. Since its inception, the NPA remained committed to the idea that a worker-peasant alliance manifested through a jungle-based guerrilla movement was the most likely path to revolutionary victory. In the early 1980s, a faction of the NPA called the Manila-Rizal committee grew increasingly vocal in their opposition to this strategy. In the minds of the Manila-Rizal committee, the NPA should concentrate more on urban terrorism. In 1984 Felimon "Popoy" Lagman recast the Manila-Rizal committee as an urban terrorist hit squad. Lagman named this new group the Alex Boncayao Brigade, in memory of a committee member who was killed in the 1970s. Between 1984 and 1991, the Alex Boncayao Brigade operated as a faction of the larger NPA. Due to continuing tensions between the NPA and its faction, the two groups finally severed ties in 1991.

Since 1995, the Alex Boncayao Brigade has demonstrated decreased adherence to a strictly communist ideology. Several terrorist incidents in the late 1990s were apparently initiated as anti-globalisation protests. In December 2000 the Alex Boncayao Brigade signed a truce with the Filipino military. Likely due to the ABB's government negotiations and its conciliatory implications, the NPA has begun to directly target its former ally. The NPA and ABB continue to target each others' members

Alfaro Lives, Damn it!

Abbreviation: AVC
Continent: South America
Country: Ecuador
Background:

The AVC initiated armed activities in Aug 1983 in the same fashion similar to the M19. by stealing swords used by an Ecuadorean national hero, Eloy Alfaro, a revolutionary leader and President of Ecuador in the early twentieth century and was killed in 1912. The AVC claimed to be non-Marxist but some of its members were known to have links to Cuba and Nicaragua. Some of its ideas was to form an opposition Government especially amongst the poor and to force the withdrawal of US and other foreign interests from Ecuador. One member was arrested in 1984 carrying documents that confirmed these ties and plans to approach Libya. The AVC had sent personnel to Columbia for training and participation in military operations under the leadership of M19. Throughout 1986 and 1987 the AVC suffered serious setbacks from Government security forces and essentially leaderless the group has conducted little terrorist activity since mid 1986.

Also known as !Alfaro Vive, Carajo! See the Tupac Amaru Revolutionary Movement, (MRTA).

Ali Suleiyman

Continent: Africa
Country: Somalia
Background:
Armed men stopped the car of an employee of the U.S. branch of Action International Contre La Faim (AICF). The security guard was killed and the employee and her driver were kidnapped by the men who were members of the Ali Suleiyman sub clan of the Majertain. The local Somali Salvation Democratic Front (SSDF) militia were contacted who pursued the kidnappers and caught up with them the next afternoon. Gunfire ensued but the aid worker was rescued unharmed. The kidnapping was apparently carried out to press the AICF's demands for a greater share of the power in the New Bari administration (local government).

Albanian National Army

Abbreviation: ANA
Continent: Europe
Country: The Republic of Macedonia
Background:
The Albanian National Army (ANA), despite its name, is a small, loosely-organised terrorist group – not a national army. The group, which grew out of insurgent Albanian groups that battled Macedonian troops in 2001, is opposed to the peace agreement that increased the rights of ethnic Albanians in Macedonia and conferred amnesty to the rebels. Instead, ANA favours the unification of areas populated by Albanians in several neighbouring Balkan states into an independent entity. They have protested Macedonian courts for "conducting political trials against innocent Albanians." Macedonian authorities, however, say the group's motives are more criminal, and that their attack on the court in Struga was in retaliation for the imprisonment of a group member thought to be involved in human trafficking.

The ANA's attack on the court in Struga has provoked fears that rebel activity in the area may be increasing. International officials, however, stress the supposed criminal motives of the group, and do not expect the group to grow stronger. Many of the group's rebels surrendered their weapons to NATO as part of the 2001 peace settlement.

The U.S. government has declined to place the ANA on its list of designated foreign terrorist organisations, and shares the opinion that it is more of a criminal gang. They do view the group, however, as a "threat to peace and stability in the Western Balkans," and have frozen their assets in the United States and prohibited Americans from engaging in transactions with the group.

Altaf Group

See the Mohajir Qaumi Movement Haqiqi (MQM-H) Alliance of Eritrean National Force

Continent: Africa

Country: Eritrea

Background:

In March 1999 representatives of ten Eritrean opposition groups formed the Alliance of Eritrean National Force, under the leadership of Abdullah Idriss, to overthrow the government of President Isaiyas Aferworki. The support given to the group by Sudan is a tit-for-tat policy, since Khartoum has accused Eritrea of supporting Sudanese opposition forces. The new group includes some veterans of the fragmented Eritrean politics, including the Eritrean Liberation Front - Revolution Council (ELF-RC) of Abdellah Idris, who will lead the new alliance.

Members of the Alliance include:

Eritrean Democratic Resistance Movement (Gash-Setit) [in southwestern Eritrea]

Eritrean Initiative Group

Eritrean Islamic Salvation Movement

Eritrean Kunamas Democratic Movement

Eritrean Liberation Front

Eritrean Liberation Front National Congress

Eritrean Liberation Front - Revolution Council

Eritrean People's Congress

Eritrean Revolutionary Democratic Front

Popular Democratic Front for the Liberation of Eritrea,

Ato [Mr] Ali Muhammad Sayyid Berhatu.

Alliance pour la resistance democratique

Abbreviation: ARD
Continent: Africa
Country: Congo
Background:

Mayi-Mayi is the main militia groups active in the Kivus region of Congo (Zaire). It is opposed to "Tutsi domination" and the Rassemblement congolais pour la democratie (RCD), but is otherwise seemingly without any clear objective and frequently change allegiances. No homogeneity exists between the various Mayi-Mayi groups, and the names of various commanders such as Louetcha, Padiri and Dunia frequently come up. As of late 1999 these forces were being re-supplied all over North and South Kivu to attack the positions of the Rwandan army. The Alliance pour la resistance democratique (ARD), based in the Fizi region, is believed to be a Mayi-Mayi front.

Also known as Mayi-Mayi

Amal

Continent: Middle East
Country: Lebanon
Background:

Amal was formed in 1975 by the Iranian Imam Musa Sadr. Despite the founder's Iranian heritage, Amal was expressly formed to protect and increase the influence of Lebanon's Shi'ite Muslim population. In addition, the group was interested in establishing a theocratic Islamic state. The group's name, Amal, has a double meaning. While Amal means "hope" in Arabic, it also represents an acronym of "Afwaj al Muqawama al Lubnaniya," or in English, "Lebanese Resistance Detachments."

In 1974, Musa Sadr founded the "Movement of the Deprived" to advance the political interests of the Shi'ites in Lebanon. Upon the outbreak of Lebanon's civil war in 1975, Musa Sadr established Amal as the military wing of the Movement of the Deprived. Amal, a non-state actor, would eventually kill dozens through its terrorist attacks. Amal gained legitimacy with an increasing number of Lebanese Shi'ites following Israel's invasion of Lebanon in 1978 and the accompanying clashes between Israelis and Palestinians in southern Lebanon.

With the death of Musa Sadr in 1978, Amal's leadership passed to Nabih Berri. As opposed to the clergyman Musa Sadr, Nabih Berri was a secular politician. Consequently, Berri was more interested in the nationalist goals of the Lebanese Shi'ites rather than any objectives to create a theocratic

Islamic state. Despite Berri's secularism, Amal benefited from the 1978-1979 Iranian revolution. From 1979 to 1982, Amal received financial assistance from Iran. In 1982, Iran founded Hezbollah to counter the Israeli forces that had entered Lebanon to destroy PLO's Lebanese base. With Hezbollah's founding, Amal lost Iran's financial backing. Around 1985, Syria initiated financial assistance to Amal.

Amal's significance has decreased substantially since its founding. The death of Musa Sadr, the group's founder, damaged the group. In addition, ongoing rivalries with Hezbollah have weakened the group. As a result of Amal's weakness, many of the group's members abandoned Amal to join Hezbollah.

Also known as Lebanese Resistance Detachments, Movement of Hope

American Front

Abbreviation: AF
Continent: North America
Country: United States of America
Background:

American Front (AF) is a skinhead group that was founded by Bob Heick around 1990. According to some sources, the group was founded in Portland, Oregon, while other sources locate AF's roots in San Francisco, California. Within a few years, AF had spread across the northwest and beyond. AF members have been arrested in Napa, San Francisco, Sacramento, Pennsylvania, Florida, Maryland and Washington. Heick, a high school dropout, first encountered racist skinhead culture in Britain in 1984. At the time, the racist organisation National Front was winning a war with anti-racist skinheads for control of the British skinhead movement. When Heick returned to the United States, he launched his own skinhead organisation, American Front. Membership in American Front is by application only, and the application implies that if a member betrays the organisation, the punishment is "death by crucifixion [sic]." (www.cgiaonline.org). This is a common attitude among skinheads, who are most brutal toward those who try to leave the movement.

AF members have committed heinous crimes. In 1991, police offers searching a Beaverton, Oregon residence from which AF members had been evicted found a "hit list" of Portland police officers who were to be targeted. In California and Washington during July of 1993, there was a series of bombings targeting public meeting places for blacks, gays and Jews in California and Washington. American Front members Wayne Paul Wooten, Jeremiah Gordon Knesal and Mark Kowaalski were convicted of committing two of those attacks: the bombing of the Elite Tavern (a gay club) on July 22, and the bombing of an NAACP meeting hall on July 20. According to U.S. Attorney Mike Yamaguchi, Wooten, Knesal and Kowaalski were part of a larger conspiracy to incite race war. The bombings seem to have been timed to coincide with the sentencing of the police officers convicted in the Rodney King case, presumably to take advantage of heightened racial tension connected with the case.

American Front's new leader is James Porazzo. Porazzo moved AF to Harrison, Arkansas, and made it the most explicitly Third Positionist group in America. The idea behind "Third Position" philosophy is to unify the extreme right and extreme left in their fight against the global capitalist system. Third Positionists are both socialist and racist. Porazzo advocates "socialist revolution in a racialist context," explaining "We propose a workable, realistic alternative, and that is Separatism! White autonomy, Black autonomy, Brown autonomy and death to the current twisted system.... The only other obvious route would be an eventual winner-take-all race war: I don't think anyone with any sense would want that.... [L]et me make it clear that American Front would rather fight the REAL ENEMY -- the system. [The system we must fight is] the dictatorship of the dollar. [The forces of global capitalism are controlled by] the Zionists and the Race that spawned them...a filthy, evil people the world would be better without. [Charging interest] is a filthy Jewish practice." (Porazzo, qtd in "Neither Left Nor Right")

American Indian Movement

Abbreviation: AIM
Continent: North America
Country: United States of America
Background:
The American Indian Movement (AIM) is an Indian activist organisation in the United States. AIM burst onto the international scene with its seizure of the Bureau of Indian Affairs headquarters in Washington, D.C., in 1972 and the 1973 standoff at Wounded Knee, South Dakota, on the Pine Ridge Indian Reservation. AIM was cofounded in 1968 by Dennis Banks, George Mitchell, Herb Powless, Clyde Bellecourt, Eddie Benton Banai, and many others in the Native American community, almost 200 in total. Russell Means was another early leader.

In the decades since AIM's founding, the group has led protests advocating Indigenous American interests, inspired cultural renewal, monitored police activities and coordinated employment programs in cities and in rural reservation communities across the United States. AIM has often supported other indigenous interests outside the United States, as well.

AIM was founded in Minneapolis, Minnesota on the 28th July 1968. Prior to its creation, several of the founding members of the AIM were incarcerated in the Minnesota penal system. It was from here that the ideologies that would define the initial course of the AIM would emerge. Clyde Bellecourt would be introduced to Eddie Benton Banai while imprisoned and resulted in a reintroduction to his Indian lineage. An American Indian Quarterly article reads: "The founders and leaders of AIM appear to have undergone some kind of ideological conversion experience which enabled them to accept their Indianness". It was at this time that Clyde Bellecourt came to the understanding that "he wasn't the dirty Indian he's been told he was by white students at school, where he went through all that racism and hatred". Vernon Bellecourt also spent time in the penal system, and under the guidance of his brother, ultimately became an early leader to the cause of AIM. This new ideology would become paramount to the future course of AIM and its leadership.

Founders of AIM, according to Peter Matthiessen's book In the Spirit of Crazy Horse, include Dennis Banks; Clyde Bellecourt, who directs the Peace Maker Centre in Minneapolis and administers U.S. Department of Labour job-development services; Eddie Benton-Benai, author and school administrator for the Red School House in Minneapolis and at Lac Courte Oreilles, Wisconsin; and Russell Means, who has worked as an actor and remains politically active, running for Governor of New Mexico and for president of the Oglala Sioux nation in 2002. Another well-known AIM member is Leonard Peltier, who is currently serving a prison term for his conviction in the murder of two FBI agents at the Pine Ridge Indian Reservation in 1975.

AIM's original mission included protecting indigenous people from police abuse, using CB radios and police scanners to get to the scenes of alleged crimes involving indigenous people before or as police arrived, for the purpose of documenting or preventing police brutality.

The tactics AIM adopted were premised on the fact that Indian activists failed to achieve results at the time of its founding. AIM believed that advocates for Indian interests who had worked within the American political system had not been effective. The political system simply ignored Indian interests. The AIM leadership decided at its founding that a more aggressive approach had to be adopted in order for their voices to be heard. Up to this time, Indian advocacy had been passive and comprised of the typical lobbying effort with the Congress and the state legislatures.

AIM used the American press and media to present its own unvarnished message to the American public. It did so by ensuring that the members of the press would have an event they wanted to cover for their respective newspaper or television/radio station. If successful, news outlets would seek out AIM spokespersons for interviews and receive its message. Instead of relying on traditional lobbying efforts with the Congress or state legislature, AIM directly sought out the American public to ensure it would get AIM's message. AIM was always on the lookout for an event that would result in publicity. Thus, the seizure of the Mayflower replica on Thanksgiving Day in 1970 during ceremonies commemorating the 350th anniversary of the Pilgrim's landing at Plymouth Rock, the occupation of Mount Rushmore in 1971, the Trail of Broken Treaties march and takeover of the Bureau of Indian Affairs headquarters in Washington, D.C. in 1972, AIM's occupation of Wounded Knee on the Pine Ridge reservation in 1973, the Longest Walk in 1978, and other events during the 1970s were designed to achieve this effect. All of these events were undertaken to ensure AIM would be noticed in order to highlight its belief that the rights of Indian people had eroded.

In view of the nature of its more provocative advocacy for Indian rights and the experience of other minority groups during the civil rights era, AIM encountered a similar reaction from the government. The Federal Bureau of Investigation (FBI) used paid informants to report on AIM's activities and its members. Local authorities and the FBI were also not averse to using violence against AIM or its members.

In 1973, AIM activists barricaded themselves in the hamlet of Wounded Knee on the Pine Ridge Reservation in South Dakota. They were alleged to have taken eleven hostages, which led to a seventy-one-day standoff with federal agents. In the ensuing trials most accused AIM members were acquitted.

The 1973 stand-off centred around AIM's allegations of federal and tribal police brutality on the Pine Ridge Reservation and allegations of brutality by a tribal group affiliated with the tribe's government Guardians Of the Oglala Nation (GOONS).

On the 26th June 1975, a gun battle between AIM members and FBI agents resulted in the shooting deaths of Joseph Stuntz and two FBI agents, Jack Coler and Ronald Williams. Leonard Peltier was eventually convicted of the agents' deaths. Many AIM activists claim that the AIM members who shot at the FBI agents were engaged in self-defence, and thus the killing was not a murder. Indeed, two of Peltier's co-defendants in the murder case were acquitted on grounds of self-defence in a separate trial. Peltier's critics, on the other hand, point out that both of the agents were shot and killed at close range after being wounded, one of them with his hands up. This killing and the subsequent conviction of Peltier have been major bones of contention between activists and FBI agents.

US Court of Appeals Judge Gerald Heaney concluded that "Native Americans" were partially culpable for the 1975 fire fight in which Stuntz,

Coler and Williams died, but that the federal government had "overreacted" during and after the 1973 Wounded Knee stand-off. Heaney said that overreaction created a climate of terror that led to the fatal shoot-out.

As of 2007, the Sioux nations have yet to accept a settlement they were offered in compensation for the Black Hills. Since 1973, several AIM-affiliated groups have set up camp at the Black Hills to resist what they see as an arbitrary settlement.

AIM maintained that Wounded Knee residents had invited their assistance in 1973 to defend their homes against official and vigilante attacks, but that the FBI then surrounded them, effectively holding the AIM members hostage. Many Wounded Knee residents dispute this, and say that the AIM occupation led to the destruction of their community and homes. Several trials of AIM members resulted from the confrontation, which resulted in some court-room brawls with U.S. Marshals, but few AIM members were convicted for their roles in the standoff.

AIM has been the subject of much controversy, some of it centring around the 1977 trial of Leonard Peltier, the AIM member convicted of the 1975 Pine Ridge murders of two FBI agents. Some activists doubt that he was responsible for these killings, and Amnesty International, among dozens of others throughout the world, has called for his release. Other activists say the murders occurred in a war-like environment, and that Peltier's role in the killings should be reviewed in that context.

Another famous AIM member was Anna Mae Pictou-Aquash, for whose 1976 murder two other 1970s AIM affiliates, John Graham and Arlo Looking Cloud, were indicted in 2003. Looking Cloud was eventually convicted. Graham was extradited from Canada to the US in December 2007. His trial was scheduled for June, 2008. In the decades before the indictments, some activists alleged that the FBI played a part or covered up her murder. In his book, American Indian Mafia, Former FBI Agent Joseph H. Trimbach alleges that several of the original activists were themselves involved as co-conspirators.

As is true with many national liberation movements (PLO, African National Congress), ideological differences emerged within AIM over the years. In 1993, AIM split into two main factions, each claiming that it was the authentic inheritor of the AIM tradition, and that the other had betrayed the original principles of the movement. One group, based in Minneapolis, MN and associated with the Bellecourts, is known as the AIM-Grand Governing Council, while the other segment of the movement, led by, among others, Russell Means, was named AIM-International Confederation of Autonomous Chapters.

The split was formalised when the latter group issued its "Edgewood Declaration" in 1993, citing organisational grievances and authoritarian leadership by the Bellecourts. However, ideological differences seem to have simmered for a long time, with the Grand Governing Council (GGC) presenting a spiritual, albeit more mainstream, approach to activism. The GCC tends toward a more centralised, controlled political philosophy. The autonomous chapters argue that AIM has always been organised as a series of decentralised, autonomous chapters, with local leadership that is accountable to local constituencies. The autonomous chapters reject the assertions of central control by the Minneapolis group as contrary both to indigenous political traditions, and to the original philosophy of AIM. The autonomous chapters within AIM, while also spiritually guided by indigenous ceremonialism, tend more toward third world national liberation strategies and indigenous nationalism, as recently embodied in the movement of the Zapatista Army of National Liberation in Mexico, and in the election of Evo Morales in Bolivia.

Anarchist Faction for Subversion

Continent: Europe
Country: Greece
Background:
Anarchist Faction for Subversion is a Greek terrorist organisation that has sporadically attacked vehicles of foreign diplomats and Greek government officials since 1998. The group's activity peaked in 2000 when it torched two German Embassy cars, one Lebanese Embassy car, on Egyptian Embassy vehicle, and the personal vehicle of the Jordanian cultural attaché. The group also set fire to a van belonging to a private security systems company, Vandehund.

Anarchist Faction for Subversion has not taken many opportunities to voice its political agenda. One statement, released after the attack on the Vandehund car, demanded the release of Nikos Maziotis. Maziotis was a prominent anarchist who placed a bomb in the Ministry of Industry and Development on the 12th December 1997 in solidarity with villagers revolting against the establishment of a multinational corporation in their area. This act as well as the group's name indicate that it is committed to facilitating anarchy and disorder through random arson against government officials.

Anarchist Faction for Subversion has not been active since late 2000. However, the current level of activity is roughly equivalent to the group's activity between its first attack in 1998 and its spike in 2000. Based on the group's sporadic actions in the past, it is difficult to predict whether the group will continue to commit arson.

An Gof

Continent: Europe
Country: United Kingdom
Background:

An Gof is the name of a Cornish nationalist terrorist organisation. The organisation takes its name from Michael An Gof (Cornish name Myghal An Gof), a leader of the Cornish Rebellion of 1497.

The extent to which this organisation was exaggerated by media or police is unknown. In one attack, a politician's letterbox was blown up with a bomb. It is uncertain whether other attacks were carried out by the same organisation.

In December 1980, a group calling themselves An Gof 1980 exploded a bomb at the courthouse in St Austell. In January 1981, they claimed responsibility for a fire at a Penzance hairdressers (the business was mistaken for the Bristol and West Building Society). Later in the decade, An Gof claimed responsibility for a number of fires, including one at the Zodiac Bingo Hall in Redruth. They also claimed responsibility for an attempted explosion at Beacon Village Hall in Camborne and placing broken glass under the sand at Portreath Beach in 1984.

A group claiming to be An Gof stated on the 12th March 2007 that it wants to destroy all English flags in Cornwall. A statement made by a spokesman for the group was faxed to the Cornish Branch of the Celtic League by an unknown person who withheld his or her telephone number and reads as follows:

"Out of respect for many of the decent and honourable Cornish people present today, we have asked our membership to remain inactive. We are aware that reputations were placed on the line by moderate Cornish Nationals who have been subject of death threats from the far right as well as threats of action by the police. However, we wish to make this point very clear: any attempts from here on to fly the hated and oppressive Flag of St. George of England which we know as the blood banner in this our Country will result in direct action by our organisation. For those who question our motives, we refer them to the events of 1497 and 1549 and the years of English Imperialistic repression which has followed. We shall not show the tolerance of those standing Vigil today and our action will be to remove and burn the flags of the English which may cause peripheral damage. An Gof 1497."

In March 2007 a group claiming to be the resurrected "An Gof" Cornish Terrorist group committed several acts of vandalism. This was followed on the 13th June 2007 with a declaration by a previously unheard of group called the CNLA or Cornish National Liberation Army which declared the restaurants owned by Jamie Oliver and Rick Stein to be enemies of the people and examples of the English cultural and fiscal invasion of Cornwall which had caused a financial hardship and a feeling of alienation for the Cornish people within their own duchy.

Animal Liberation Front

Abbreviation: ALF
Continent: Europe, North America
Country: Canada, United Kingdom, United States of America
Background:

The original Animal Liberation Front (ALF) formed in England in 1976, splintering off from the Hunt Saboteurs Association (HSA) to form a more militant organisation. The FBI claims that the American branch of the ALF began its operations in the late 1970s, but the group became more high profile in 1982, and then made the FBI's domestic terrorism list in 1987 with a multi-million dollar arson at a veterinary lab in California. ALF carries out direct action against animal abuse in the form of rescuing animals and causing financial loss to animal exploiters, usually through the damage and destruction of property. Because ALF actions are against the law, activists work anonymously, either in small groups or individually, and they do not have any centralised organisation or co-ordination. The Animal Liberation Front consists of small autonomous groups of people all over the world who carry out direct action according to the ALF guidelines. Any group of people who are vegetarians or vegans and who carry out actions according to ALF guidelines have the right to regard themselves as part of the ALF, according to their website and other materials.

Similar to activities in the United Kingdom and Canada, the American ALF has attacked medical and scientific research laboratories, butcher shops, and retail furriers. The organisation has claimed credit for the theft of research animals and the destruction of research equipment and records, as well as acts of vandalism and arson. In August of 2003, ALF activists claimed responsibility for the release of 10,000 mink from a mink farm in Washington State. In North America and the United Kingdom, most militant members of the ALF are young and from middle-class backgrounds.

The ALF's short-term aim is to save as many animals as possible and directly disrupt the practice of animal abuse. Their long-term aim is to end all animal suffering by forcing animal abuse companies out of business. The organisation claims to be nonviolent and activists are encouraged to take precautions not to harm any animal (human or otherwise).

ALF goals according to their website are as follows: 1. To liberate animals from places of abuse, i.e. laboratories, factory farms, fur farms, etc., and place them in good homes where they may live out their natural lives, free from suffering. 2. To inflict economic damage to those who profit from the misery and exploitation of animals. 3. To reveal the horror and atrocities committed against animals behind locked doors, by performing non-violent direct actions and liberations. 4. To take all necessary precautions against harming any animal, human and non-human.

Ansar al-Islam

Continent: Middle East
Country: Iraq
Background:

(Supporters of Islam). This is an extremist Kurdish group purportedly linked to Al-Qaeda. It is an offshoot of Jund al-Islam (Soldiers of Islam, a.k.a. Islamic Brigade) and has been engaged in fighting with the PUK since September 2001. Led by Mullah Krekar (a.k.a. Najm al-Din Faraj Ahmad), the military commander of Ansar al-Islam who is under house arrest in Norway. Krekar is the former military commander for the Islamic Movement of Kurdistan; he trained in Afghanistan. Krekar has denied any links to Osama bin Laden but bin Laden sent his greeting to the group in an audiotaped message in October 2003.

The group has been linked to the 19th August bombing of UN headquarters in Baghdad. Reports began surfacing in September 2003 that the group had split. There were widespread reports that the leadership changed in late 2003 and is now headed by Abu Abdallah al-Shafi'i (a.k.a. Warba Holiri al-Kurdi) who reportedly said in September that the group would change its name -- but declined to announce the name, London's "Al-Hayat" reported on the 5th September 2003.

Reportedly linked to the Kurdistan Islamic Group (KIG), led by Mullah Ali Bapir. Al-Shafi'i criticised the KIG in September 2003 for aiding U.S. forces in their attempt to crack down on Ansar militiamen. Al-Shafi'i added that other mujahedin groups inside Iraq had agreed to join up with Ansar Al-Islam.

The group claimed responsibility for the 1st February 2004 simultaneous attacks on Patriotic Union of Kurdistan (PUK) and Kurdistan Democratic Party (KDP) offices in Irbil, and the 17th March 2004 bombing of the Mount Lebanon Hotel in Baghdad. The group also claims to have participated in the April 2004 clashes against coalition forces in Al-Fallujah. The U.S. State Department designated the group a foreign terrorist organisation in March.

In Iraq it was thought to be defunct, but was attacked by US forces in April 2003 during the major combat phase and suffered major casualties. Those who remained alive fled into Iran and the group pretty much disintegrated. The original leadership is no longer in place. Some of the fighters within the group have drifted back into Iraq in small units where they have joined forces with other foreign and domestic Mujahideen in some cases and have also created some new resistance cells. There are alternate claims that the group has reorganised but this had not been validated.

See the Al-Qaeda and is an off shoot of Jund al-Islam (Soldiers of Islam a.k.a. Islamic Brigade) and possibly linked to the Kurdistan Islamic Group (KIG).

Ansar-e Hezbollah

Continent: Middle East
Country: Iran
Background:

Ansar-e-Hezbollah (Ansar is Arabic and means patrons or helpers) is a militant ultraconservative Islamist group in Iran. Along with the Basij, they are said to "represent a key element of the Islamic Republic's hold on power, its use of violent repression" of dissident gatherings. Its ideology revolves around devotion to Grand Ayatollah Ruhollah Khomeini and his belief in Valiyat al-faqih and elimination of foreign non-Islamic influences.

Ansar-e Hizbullah, or Followers of the Party of God or more literally Helpers of Hizbullah in Persian, is said to be a semi-official, paramilitary group formed in 1995 and consisting of "religious zealots who consider themselves" to be "preservers of the Revolution."

It is thought to be financed and protected by many senior government clerics. It is often characterised as a vigilante group as they use force but are not part of government law enforcement, although it may not meet the strict definition of the word inasmuch as the group pledge loyalty to the Supreme Leader of Iran Ali Khamenei and was thought to be protected by him.

It has been described as an "offshoot" or "vigilante associate" of the Iranian Hezbollah, a loose-knit movement of groups formed at the time of the Iranian Revolution to assist the Ayatollah Khomeini and his forces in consolidating power.

The Ansar-e-Hezbollah is known for attacking protesters at anti-government demonstrations, in particular during the Iran student riots, July 1999 and is thought to have been behind public physical assaults on two reformist government ministers in September 1998.

Ansar-e-Hezbollah is thought to have been behind death threats and a "series of physical assaults" on philosopher and ex-hardliner Abdolkarim

Soroush "that left him bruised, battered and often in tattered clothes."

Members typically wear full beards, dress in black clothes, green bandannas and attack using bars, chains, and similar weapons, sometimes while riding motorcycles. They have been described as "walking with the swagger that comes with being above the law."

Ansar Saddam Al-Jihadi

Continent: Middle East
Country: Iraq
Background:
This group first appeared on the scene claiming attacks on the 24th October 2004 and is made up of Saddam Loyalists. They are said to be an underground formation of highly motivated Ba'ath party militants established by Saddam Hussein in late 1998.

Anti Authority Erotic Cells

Continent: Europe
Country: Greece
Background:
Anti-Authority Erotic Cells has claimed responsibility for one attack: the bombing of a Thessaloniki office of Pfizer, the manufacturer of Viagra, on Valentine's Day 2000. No other information about the group is known. The group did not explain their motives when they called a local television station to claim responsibility for the attack. It seems likely that the group intended to be seen as part of the larger anarchist and anti-globalisation movement in Greece, given the fact that they bombed the office of an international company and chose to include "anti-authority" in their name. The group also, however, clearly intends to send some kind of message about sexuality. The fact that they did not clarify that message when they publicly claimed responsibility for the attack suggests that they expected someone other than the police or the general public to understand what they were trying to say about Viagra, Valentine's Day, and eroticism. The Greek police are unwilling to speculate on this puzzling group's motives.

The Anti-Authority Erotic Cells has not claimed responsibility for any attacks since it's first and is presumed inactive. The group is somewhat unusual in that it attacks in Thessaloniki rather than Athens. Relatively few groups have claimed responsibility for attacks in Thessaloniki. These groups include the Movement Against State Arbitrariness, the Revolutionary People's Struggle (ELA), Rigas Ferreos, Revolutionary Struggle, and the

Anti-Mainstream Self-Determination Faction. Greek police consider it possible that since these groups have attacked in the same city, they may share some of the same members.

Anti Olympic Flame

Continent: Europe
Country: Greece
Background:

A group calling itself "Anti-Olympic Flame" claimed responsibility for two arson attacks in Thessaloniki, Greece in spring 2004. Their first attack targeted a private security van, and in their claim of responsibility the group wrote, "We are asking young people to welcome the terrorism of the Olympic Games with a relay race of destruction and arsons against symbols of the state, against the commercial society and every authority." Their second arson attack targeted the vehicle of Deputy Consul of Cyprus, Panagiotis Georgiades. In this claim the group wrote, "In Greece and Cyprus and Turkey the enemies are to be found in banks and ministries. Let us crush the patriotic garbage on both sides of the Aegean."

Although little to nothing is known about Anti-Olympic Flame, their own statements show a proclivity towards anarchism and anti-capitalism. Their name alone expresses a disdain for Greece's hosting of the 2004 Olympics, which the group likely viewed as a celebration of wealth and commercialism.

Anti-Olympic Flame is one of many Greek groups that carried out small arson attacks in 2004 in Thessaloniki. In nearly all these cases, the attacks were perpetrated by loosely affiliated disgruntled individuals, rather than highly organised terrorist organisations. There is no reason to believe that Anti-Olympic Flame is an exception, and it is unlikely that the group will carry out any further attacks.

Anti Terrorist Liberation Group

Abbreviation: GAL
Continent: Europe
Country: France, Spain
Background:

The Anti-Terrorist Liberation Groups (GAL) was a Spanish paramilitary organisation that targeted Basque separatists and was active from 1983 until 1987.

The group, formed at a time when the Basque separatist group Basque Fatherland and Freedom (ETA) was at its height of activity, focused on destabilising ETA's safe havens in France, although they also carried out actions in Spanish territory. ETA, at this time, focused its attacks on Spain while its leadership remained in France, where the government did not persecute them, and even awarded some of its members political refugee status. The GAL's early activities consisted of bombings and revenge killings, initially pledging to kill an ETA member in retaliation for each death caused by the separatists. The group's first action was the kidnapping and killing of Jose Antonio Lasa and Jose Antonio Zabala in October 1983, both suspected members of ETA. Their bodies were not found until 1995, buried in quicklime and showing clear signs of torture. The group's notoriety reached new heights with the high-profile kidnapping of Segundo Marey in December 1983. The GAL claimed Marey was an ETA activist, but later released him when it emerged that he was merely a furniture salesman. Throughout the 1980s, the GAL had been accused of 23 to 28 murders in both France and Spain, as well as a number of other kidnappings. This period of Spanish History is known as "The Dirty War" (La Guerra Sucia).

Throughout the group's history there have been accusations of Spanish government support for the GAL. The GAL were linked to the Spanish Police's Anti-Terrorist Unit, as well as the Civil Guard, causing some to regard the group as a "para-police" unit. The GAL also employed French "mercenaries" to carry out some of their actions, especially in French territory. Although the Spanish public feared ETA terrorism, the GAL's support was limited due to the fact that as many as one third of its victims had no connection to ETA.

Legal processes linking the GAL to the Spanish government continued amid great controversy throughout the 80's and 90's, with a judicial inquiry and Supreme Court trial in 1994 finally proving a financial link between the group and the Interior Ministry. Money destined for "Reserved Funds" had been channelled to fund the GAL activities. Former Spanish Interior Minister Jose Barrionuevo and State Secretary for Security Rafael Vera were sentenced to 10 years in prison for embezzlement and involvement with the Marey kidnapping. Twelve Interior Ministry functionaries of the socialist government and senior police officers were incarcerated as well. During the proceedings of the case, it was also proven that the Spanish main intelligence agency, CESID (now CNI), was directly involved in the creation of the GAL. These proceedings put a cloud over the career of then-Prime Minister Felipe Gonzalez, whose government was repeatedly associated with heavy-handed policies toward Basque separatists. Trials involving the GAL have also been underway in France. After the Popular Party (Partido Popular) won the Spanish elections in 1996, Jose Maria Aznar's government granted pardons to a number of high ranking Interior Ministry functionaries that were in jail for GAL-related crimes. The group has not claimed any actions since 1987 and is considered to be inactive.

April 19 Movement

Abbreviation: M-19
Continent: South America
Country: Columbia
Background:

The founding of the terrorist group, April 19 Movement (M-19) was precipitated by the outcome of a Colombian presidential election. Former Colombian dictator-come-populist Rojas Pinilla ran for the presidency in 1970 as a member of the political party, National Popular Alliance (ANAPO). Under the banner of populism, ANAPO enjoyed wide support among the urban poor. On the 19th May 1970, Rojas Pinilla lost the presidential election, coming in a close second.

While ANAPO officially rejected violence as a retaliatory answer to the loss, some members of the group broke ranks. Rather than accept the results of the closely contested election, these individuals, now calling themselves M-19, decide to embark on a violent terrorist campaign that continued for two decades and cost countless lives. M-19, taking its name from the date of Rojas Pinilla's presidential loss, professes support for the poor of Colombia. Unlike earlier groups, such as the FARC and ELN, M-19 was not founded in the shadow of the Cuban socialist revolution of 1959. Instead of professing firm support of communist ideology, M-19 followed a more generalised leftist ideology of support for the poor and reform within the Colombian government.

The M-19 essentially ceased to exist in 1990. M-19, under intense pressure from the Colombian government's security forces, as well as right-leaning paramilitary groups, agreed to a ceasefire and shortly after laid down its arms permanently to become the Colombian political party, Democratic Alliance M-19. Predictably, some members rejected the cease fire, formed new terrorist groups, and continue to wreak violence and death throughout Colombia.

Also known as Movimiento 19 de Abril

Arab Fedayeen Cell

Continent: Middle East
Country: Lebanon
Background:

The Arab Fedayeen Cells claimed responsibility for three bombing attacks in Lebanon in 1986, all directed at Western-owned banks, both British and American. The group is also suspected in the abduction of a British journalist and murder of three other Britons in April 1986, apparently in response to the UK's role in the American attacks on Libya.

Both Canada and the United Nations consider the Arab Fedayeen Cells to be an alias of the Abu Nidal Organisation (ANO). The ANO was active in the Middle East at this time, and has a history of adopting aliases to claim certain attacks, such as those carried out by the Revolutionary Union of Socialist Muslims in 1984 and 1985. Abu Nidal received support from Ghadaffi's regime in Libya, further support for evidence of a link between the ANO and the timing of the attacks by the Arab Fedayeen Cells following American air strikes against Libya. The United States, however, had not officially listed the Arab Fedayeen Cells as an alias of the ANO, which it retains on its list of Designated Foreign Terrorist Organisations.

The Arab Fedaseen Cells had not claimed responsibility for an act of terrorism since 1986. The Abu Nidal Organisation, however, was still considered a viable terrorist threat by most observers. It had not specifically targeted Western interests since the late 1980's, but remains active in the Middle East and has targeted Palestinian and Jordanian diplomats in Lebanon. Speculation remains as to whether the ANO can survive the death of Abu Nidal, who was reported to have committed suicide in Iraq in 2002.

Arewa People's Congress

Continent: Africa
Country: Nigeria
Background:
The Arewa People's Congress is a recent organisation formed to protect the northern Nigerian interests. Northerners have been complaining of being marginalised by the Obasanjo government. Disgruntled military officers, serving and retired are said to be providing the growing 'private armies' with sophisticated weapons, which seriously threaten the country's budding democracy.

Argentine Anti-Communist Alliance

Continent: South America
Country: Argentina
Background:
Commonly referred to as the Triple A, the Argentine Anti-Communist Alliance was a right-wing, semi-official terrorist group active during the

mid-1970s. The Peronist government, led by Isabel Peron, the wife of former dictator Juan Domingo Peron, secretly created the Triple A in 1974 to terrorise radical left-wing groups responsible for hundreds of assassinations of police and military officials. The Triple A collaborated with the military and was staffed from police rolls, though the government officially pledged to bring the mysterious assassins to justice. The group was famous for assassinations, bombings, and torture. From 1974-1976, the Triple A waged war on Argentina's political left under the leadership of Jose Lopez Rega, the Minister of Social Welfare and a long-time advisor to the Perons.

The war between leftist terrorists and the Triple A grew out of a split between supporters of Juan Domingo Peron. Peron had attracted rabid support from both the left and the right. Leftists saw him as a populist who would bring about socialist revolution, while the right-wing supported his economic and political nationalism. When Peron was restored to power after a seventeen-year absence in 1973, he publicly cast aside his far-left supporters to build a better relationship with the church and economic elites. The left-wing of the Peronist movement, referred to as the Montoneros, became outcasts and took up arms. The violence escalated until military leaders staged a coup on the 24th March 1976 to restore order.

The leaders of the coup dissolved the Triple A in mid-1976. The army then took over the group's "counter-terrorism" responsibilities. What followed was a massive campaign of state terror against suspected subversives that resulted in as many as 30,000 deaths. This period, which lasted until 1983, is referred to as "the dirty war." The new military leaders used many of the same techniques, personnel, and even cars used by the Triple A. Thus, the Triple A is often described as the precursor to the state terror of the dirty war.

The Argentine Anti-Communist Alliance no longer exists as a terrorist group. It was dissolved in 1976 by the military junta which took control of the country on the 24th March of that year. The junta continued and expanded upon Triple A's terrorist activities against the radical left-wing and student groups until it collapsed in 1983.

Also known as Triple "A"

Arizona Patriots

Abbreviation: AP
Continent: North America
Country: United States of America
Background:
The Arizona Patriots were a loosely organised group of patriots that

subscribe to Posse Comitatus and Christian Identity ideology. The Patriots were white supremacist anti-Semites who sought to overthrow the American government. They began as paper terrorists, clogging the court system with bogus lawsuits. In the mid-1980s, however, the Patriots began planning more violent attacks on the government.

In 1984, the Arizona Patriots issued a document threatening to indict all Arizona public officials before a "patriot" grand jury unless they retired within 30 days. In 1986, the FBI ended a two-year undercover investigation of the group with the arrest of 10 members. The suspects were charged with plotting to bomb the Simon Wiesenthal Center, the LA office of the FBI, two offices of the Jewish Defence League, and a Utah IRS office. They were also planning to rob an armoured car in Nevada. Their plans for the robbery were extraordinarily complex, which is typical for the paramilitary radical right. The Patriots were going to use arrows with exploding tips, homemade mortars, and sleeping gas to attack the van, and they planned to detonate a bomb at the Hoover Dam just before the robbery in order to distract police. These crimes were inspired by The Turner Diaries, the same racist novel on which both Timothy McVeigh and The Order modelled their heinous crimes. The Arizona Patriots were essentially destroyed by the imprisonment of six of its members for involvement in the 1986 conspiracy, but there is some indication that the group may be resurfacing.

Armed Forces of National Resistance

Abbreviation: FARN
Continent: Central America
Country: El Salvador
Background:
In 1975, the Armed Forces of National Resistance emerged from an existing terrorist organisation, the Revolutionary Army of the People (ERP). The Armed Forces of National Resistance's leadership group consisted primarily of middle-class citizens with backgrounds in the Christian Democratic Party's youth movement. The group's ideology was principally expressed in actions against foreign corporations, investors, and governments. The Armed Forces of National Resistance expressly criticised the "imperialism" exported by Japan, Germany, North America, and Great Britain. FARN accused corporations from these areas of exploiting underdeveloped peoples for their own gain. The group also accused the associated foreign governments of complicity in the imperialist actions of the corporations.

From 1975 to 1980, the Armed Forces of National Resistance mainly engaged in urban warfare and the kidnapping of business executives. FARN gained publicity and supporters as a result of a series of high-publicity kidnappings. In 1980, FARN and four other rebel organisations joined the Farabundo Marti National Liberation Front (FMLN), an umbrella terrorist group with assistance from Cuba.

The Armed Forces of National Resistance existed as one part of an umbrella group from 1980 to 1991. On the 31st December 1991, the Farabundo Marti National Liberation Front signed a peace agreement with the El Salvadorian government. The Farabundo Marti National Liberation Front is no longer active as a terrorist organisation. Today, FMLN is a legal political party in El Salvador.

Also known as National Resistance, Resistencia Nacional (RN)

Armed Islamic Group

Abbreviation: GIA
Continent: Africa
Country: Algeria
Background:

The Armed Islamic Group (GIA) is an Islamic extremist group which aims to overthrow the secular Algerian regime and replace it with an Islamic state. The group began its violent activity in 1992 after Algiers declared the victory of the Islamic Salvation Front (FIS) "the largest Islamic opposition party" void, following the first round of legislative elections in December 1991. FIS was outlawed and many of its leaders arrested, and the group split into a moderate wing and a number of armed extremist factions, one of which was GIA.

GIA engaged in frequent attacks against civilians (especially journalists, intellectuals and secular schools) and government workers, sometimes wiping out entire villages in its area of operation. From 1993 to 1998, about 70,000 civilians were killed in surprise raids throughout the country. Also in 1993, GIA announced a campaign against foreigners living in Algeria, and subsequently killed more than 100 expatriates, predominantly Europeans. The group uses assassinations and bombings, including car bombs, and it is known to favour kidnapping victims and slitting their throats.

In an event that foreshadowed September 11th, the GIA hijacked an Air France Flight from Algiers to Paris on Christmas Eve in 1994 with 227 passengers and crew. Although the hijackers released some women, children, and elderly passengers before takeoff, an informant and some of the released hostages told the French that the hijackers actually wanted to fly the jet into the Eiffel Tower and explode it over Paris. All four hijackers were killed when French security forces stormed the aircraft.

Although the GIA has not targeted Americans in Algeria, some Algerian terrorists who have tried to attack the United States may be linked to the

GIA, according to the Council on Foreign Relations. In December 1999, Ahmed Ressam was arrested at the U.S.-Canadian border with a carload of explosives. Ressam is an Algerian who was living in Canada and he was convicted of plotting a millennium-eve attack on Los Angeles International Airport. Ressam also led authorities to alleged co-conspirators in Canada and the United States.

On the 29th September 2005, Algeria adopted by general referendum the "Peace and Reconciliation Charter" proposed by President Abdelaziz Bouteflika. The referendum came into effect in February 2006 and offers a pardon to militants on the run who surrender by August 2006 as long as they are not responsible for massacres, rapes or bombings of public places. Several members of GIA have already been released as a result of the charter. The most recent significant attacks undertaken by the GIA were conducted in August 2001. Some sources have alleged the organisation has become inactive due to the arrests and imprisonment of many of its members. Members of the GIA who wish to continue to conduct terrorist activities are believed to have joined the GIA's splinter group, the Salafist Group for Call and Combat (GSPC).

The GIA was formed when the military cancelled elections in 1992 after a fundamentalist party the Islamic Salvation Front (FIS) won the first round. This Algerian group was banned under the British anti-terrorist law and had its assets frozen on the 24th September 2001 by the US Government. The group has been eclipsed by the Salafi Group for Call and Combat.

Armed Islamic Group of Al-Qaida, Fallujah Branch

Continent: Middle East
Country: Iraq
Background:

This Muslim Group with many foreign fighters appeared on the scene in July 2003 and may have been led by Afghan war veteran Abu Lyad. They claimed responsibility for "all" the armed resistance against the US forces in Iraq in a four minute videotape aired on the Dubai-based Al-Arabiya satellite television station on the 13th Jul 2003. The group denies any affiliation with Saddam Hussein and was the first Iraqi group purporting links to Osama bin Laden's group Al-Qaeda. In their taped address, they encouraged the United States to "leave Iraq's territories and to live up to their promise." The taped address warned of more attacks that would aim to "break Americas back." The speaker on the tape purportedly resembled Abu Lyad who the US claims is a member of al-Qaeda, but there was no concrete evidence to this claim. European Governments often refer to Iyad as a Muslim Mujahideen. Iyad, who lost a leg in the Afghan war with the

Russians, has also fought in the Chechen jihad and was last positively identified in the Pankisi Gorge in Georgia in spring 2002.

Armed Revolutionary Nuclei

Abbreviation: NAR
Continent: Europe
Country: Italy
Background:

The Nuclei Armati Rivoluzionari (NAR, Armed Revolutionary Nuclei) was an Italian neofascist terrorist organisation active from 1977 to November 1981. It committed 33 murders in four years, and had projected to assassinate Francesco Cossiga, Gianfranco Fini and Adolfo Urso. An off-shoot of Terza Posizione, the group maintained close links with the Banda della Magliana criminal Roman organisation. The Banda della Magliana provided it logistical support (lodging, false papers, weapons and bombs, etc.) In November 1981, it was discovered that the NAR hid weapons in the Health Minister's basements. The first trial against them sentenced 53 persons on the 2nd May 1985, on charges of terrorist activities.

The NAR were directed by Valerio Fioravanti, his little brother Cristiano Fioravanti, Dario Pedretti, Francesca Mambro and Alessandro Alibrandi. Other important members included: Luigi Ciavardini, Gilberto Cavallini, Stefano Soderini, Franco Anselmi, Giorgio Vale, Massimo Carminati, Claudio Bracci, Stefano Bracci, Mario Corsi detto "Marione", Stefano Tiraboschi, Lino Lai, Paolo Pizzonia, Patrizio Trochei, Walter Sordi, Marco Mario Massimi, Pasquale Belsito, Fiorenzo Trincanato, Andrea Vian. In 1980, NAR member Giorgio Vale became the leader of Terza Posizione, which was used as a front for the NAR.

NAR members Giusva Fioravanti and Francesca Mambro have been sentenced as responsible for the 1980 bombing of the Bologna main train station which killed 85 people. It is however noteworthy that Fioravanti and Mambro, despite acknowledging their participation to a significant number of killings, always denied their implication in the bombing. Therefore, in spite of a definitive tribunal sentence, their involvement is still matter of debate. Stefano Delle Chiaie is also thought to have been the ARN architect of the Bologna massacre.

According to Magliana pentito Maurizio Abbatino, NAR member Massimo Carminati was the only one who could freely access to the weapon cache discovered by Italian justice in November 1981. Massimo Carminati not only held close links with the Banda della Magliana, but also with SISMI secret agents, in particular General Pietro Musumeci and colonel Giuseppe Belmonte, a member of Propaganda Due masonic lodge.

NAR members Gilberto Cavallini and Luigi Ciavardini (sentenced in 2007 to a 30 years prison term for the 1980 Bologna bombings) also assassinated on 23rd June 1980 the magistrate Mario Amato, charged of investigations on the radical right, as well as Francesco Evangelista on the 28th May 1980.

Armenian Secret Army for the Liberation of Armenia

Abbreviation: ASALA
Continent: Eurasia
Country: Armenia, Lebanon
Background:

The Armenian Secret Army for the Liberation of Armenia (ASALA) was the most well-known, well-organised, and prolific of the Armenian terrorist groups of the 1970's and 1980's. Founded in 1975 by Hagop Hagopian and Hagop Tarakciyan, ASALA operated mainly out of bases in Beirut. ASALA's primary objective was to increase awareness of the Armenian genocide and further the cause of Armenian independence. In 1915, Turkey (then the centre of the Ottoman Empire) attempted to eliminate systematically the sizable Armenian minority living within its borders; estimates of the final death toll range anywhere between a few hundred thousand to upwards of two million people. The anger of the Armenian people, both in Armenia and abroad, only grew with time. Turkey added fuel to the fire by refusing to acknowledge the scope of the killings or apologise publicly for them. Some Armenians hoped that, as the Holocaust had generated international support for the founding of Israel, increasing awareness of the Armenian genocide (brought on by terrorist acts) might help them gain an independent homeland. In addition to its nationalist mission, ASALA also promoted Marxism-Leninism and allied with other international terrorist groups with similar leanings, including the Irish Republican Army, Italian Red Brigades, and Kurdistan Workers Party.

Between 1975 and 1985, the ASALA claimed responsibility for more than fifty attacks, a number that goes up by ten or so if the actions of ASALA splinter groups are included. Most ASALA and ASALA-affiliated acts of terrorism were aimed at Turkish diplomats or Turkish interests in the Middle East and Europe. After a bombing at Paris' Orly Airport in 1983, the group began to split into competing factions and eventually disappeared altogether. No major act of international terrorism was committed by ASALA between 1985 and 1997, but in the latter year, the Turkish

Embassy in Brussels was bombed and a man called authorities claiming that the ASALA was responsible. However, experts doubt the veracity of this claim, and no further ASALA activity is expected. With the collapse of the Soviet Union, Armenia has become an independent, sovereign state, thereby fulfilling the major objective of most of the terrorists. Former terrorists now find themselves in the government or the military (or perhaps fighting the Azerbaijanis in the contested province of Nagorno-Kabakh), rather than conducting a campaign of international violence from the shadows.

Army for the Liberation of Rwanda

Abbreviation: ALIR
Continent: Africa
Country: Democratic Republic of the Congo
Background:

The Army for the Liberation of Rwanda (ALIR) was formed following the 1994 genocide in Rwanda. The events leading up to the terrorist organisation's formation began several decades earlier. The historical conflict in Rwanda has involved the two primary ethnic groups in the country, the Hutu and Tutsi. The Hutu are Rwanda's majority ethnic group with 84% of the population while the Tutsi comprise approximately 15 percent. In 1959, the Hutus overthrew the ruling king of Rwanda, an ethnic Tutsi. Following the takeover, thousands of Tutsis were killed while approximately 150,000 fled to neighbouring countries. The children of the Tutsi exiles eventually formed an insurgent group, the Rwandan Patriotic Front. In 1990 the Rwandan patriotic Front sparked a civil war. The Hutu regime would eventually commence a genocidal campaign in April 1994. Approximately 800,000 Tutsis and moderate Hutus were killed in the genocide. The Hutu regime's Armed Forces of Rwanda (FAR) and the government's civilian militia force, the Interahawme, executed the 1994 genocide. Despite the murderous campaign, the Tutsi forces eventually usurped the Hutu regime in July 1994.

Following the defeat of Hutu regime, those who had carried out the genocide feared retribution from the new government. Former members of the Armed Forces of Rwanda (FAR) and Interahawme fled Rwanda for the Democratic Republic of Congo (formerly Zaire). In the Democratic Republic of Congo (DRC), the former soldiers and militia members formed a terrorist group, called the Army for the Liberation of Rwanda (ALIR). ALIR's goals were to overthrow the new Tutsi-operated government and re-install a Hutu-dominated government. Some observers also believed that ALIR aimed to re-initiate the genocide of Tutsis.

In August 1998, Rwanda and Uganda backed a rebellion against the government of the Democratic Republic of Congo (DRC). Subsequently, DRC provided training, arms, and supplies to ALIR in exchange for ALIR's assistance in countering the rebellion. ALIR had now secured financial backing to counter the Rwandan government, one of ALIR's principal objectives. However, ALIR also targeted innocent civilians, including the murder of eight foreign tourists in 1999. In 2001 ALIR was superseded by another organisation, Democratic Front for the Liberation of Rwanda (FDLR). FDLR has forged alliances with other Rwandan insurgent groups, including some non-Hutu organisations. In 2002, Rwandan forces withdrew from eastern Congo and the DRC government ceased its financial support of ALIR/FDLR.

Army of God

Continent: North America
Country: United States of America
Background:

The Army of God is an underground network of terrorists who believe that the use of violence is an appropriate tool for fighting against abortion. An excerpt from the Army of God Manual says that the Army of God "is a real Army, and God is the General and Commander-in-Chief. The soldiers, however, do not usually communicate with one another. Very few have ever met each other. And when they do, each is usually unaware of the other's soldier status. That is why the Feds will never stop this Army. Never, and we have not yet even begun to fight." Pastor Michael Bray is the Chaplain of the Army of God. He hosts the annual "White Rose Banquet" honouring those imprisoned for anti-abortion violence. He also wrote the book "A Time to Kill," which provides a biblical justification for the use of violence against abortion providers. Bray has served time in jail for bombing abortion clinics. Bray's daughter is named after a murderer of an abortion doctor.

The Army of God manual is a "how to" for abortion clinic violence. It details methods for blockading entrances, attacking with butyric acid, arson, bomb making, and other illegal activities. The manual contains anti-abortion language as well as anti-government and anti-gay/lesbian language. The manual begins with a declaration of war on the abortion industry and continues, "Our Most Dread Sovereign Lord God requires that whosoever sheds man's blood, by man shall his blood be shed. Not out of hatred of you, but out of love for the persons you exterminate, we are forced to take arms against you. Our life for yours - a simple equation.... You shall not be tortured at our hands. Vengeance belongs to God only. However, execution is rarely gentle."

Several Army of God members have been involved in highly publicised incidents of terrorism. Eric Robert Rudolph was charged with the Atlanta Olympic bombing, as well as the bombings of an abortion clinic and a gay bar in Atlanta. Secondary bombs, designed to detonate after emergency service personnel arrived at the scene, were planted at both the abortion clinic and the gay bar. Another Army of God member, James Kopp, was convicted in the fatal shooting of clinic doctor Dr. Barnett Slepian in 1998. Kopp is believed to be connected with a half dozen other similar shootings that took place between 1994 and 1997. Clayton Waagner, the man who has claimed responsibility for sending over 550 anthrax threat letters to clinics in 2001, signed many of his threat letters with the name Army of God. He also posted threats to kill 42 individuals working at abortion clinics on the Army of God website. Past reports had noted the Army's increased anti-gay rhetoric and worry that this may be a precursor to attacks on gays and lesbians.

Army of Islam (Gaza Strip)

Continent: Middle East
Country: Gaza
Background:
Army of Islam (Arabic: Jaysh al-Islām), also known as Tawhid and Jihad Brigades, is the name used by the Dughmush-sometimes rendered "doghmush"- Hamula (clan) for their militant and takfiri activities. It is located at the Tzabra neighbourhood in the centre of the Gaza Strip bordered by Israel and Egypt.

Notorious for their kidnapping of BBC reporter Alan Johnston and capture of Israeli soldier Gilad Shalit, Army of Islam, which appears to draw inspiration from, or is linked to al-Qaeda, have also conducted at least one bombing of a Palestinian civilian target (an empty school) and a number of other kidnappings. The group has been previously closely related to Hamas, but has been since shunned by both Hamas and Fatah. The group has also been known as the organisation of al-Qaeda in Palestine.

They are also linked to the British-based Palestinian-Jordanian extremist Sheikh, Abu Qatada who they demanded be released in exchange for the BBC journalist Alan Johnston who they had kidnapped in Gaza

The group was reported to be an offshoot of the powerful Doghmush clan, which is renowned for extortion, smuggling, arms dealing and the ruthless dispatch of rivals, and has been dubbed "the Sopranos of Gaza City". In June 2006 an Israeli Defence Forces soldier Gilad Shalit was abducted from across the border in Israel. It was reported in the media that the attack was credited by several militant groups, one of which included the then previously unknown group calling itself the "Army of Islam".

In 2007 the group had kidnapped the BBC correspondent Alan Johnston. On the 25th June 2007 a video was released by Army of Islam showing Johnston with an explosive belt around his waist, with demands for the release of Muslim prisoners in British custody. The group, which also kidnapped ten members of Hamas, had claimed that they would have killed him if there had been an attempt to rescue him by force. On the 4th July 2007, after Gaza authorities arrested several members of Army of Islam including its spokesman, as well as threats of execution, Alan Johnston was handed over to Hamas officials and released after 114 days in captivity.

Army of the Corsican People

Continent: Europe
Country: Corsica, France
Background:
The Army of the Corsican people is a Corsican separatist organisation. The group is responsible for a series of small bombings beginning in late 2004. One of the bombings targeted Bordeaux's city hall as the city's mayor, Alain Juppe, was in court on corruption charges. The Army of the Corsican People's attack on Bordeaux marked a significant departure from past Corsican separatist violence by targeting mainland France. Previously, most attacks by Corsican separatists had been restricted to the island of Corsica. The group's intention is to minimise casualties while maximising the visibility of the Corsican separatist movement. The Army of the Corsican People claims to strive for an end to violence in Corsica and describes its attacks as warnings to France's ruling party, the Union for a Popular Movement (UMP).

While the Army of the Corsican People is a relatively new group, it is safe to say that it will continue low-level attacks in the immediate future. Corsican separatist violence is likely to become an increasingly problematic issue for the French government as the Army of the Corsican People strives to increase pressure on the UMP to relinquish control of Corsica.

Aryan Nations

Abbreviation: AN
Continent: North America
Country: United States of America
Background:
Aryan Nations (AN) is an umbrella group for factions of the Klan and

other right-wing extremists. Aryan Nations founder Richard Butler dubbed Aryan Nation's headquarters in Hayden Lake, Idaho, the "international headquarters of the White race," and the white supremacist community seems to agree. The RAND Institute describes Aryan Nations as the "first truly nationwide terrorist network."

Aryan Nations advocates Christian Identity, white supremacy, and neo-Nazism. Its goal is to form "a national racial state. We shall have it at whatever price is necessary. Just as our forefathers purchased their freedom in blood so must we. We will have to kill the bastards."

Until Aryan Nations lost its Hayden Lake property in 2000, the compound was the site of regular white supremacist festivals known as the World Congress of Aryan Nations. The festivals trained attendees in urban terrorism and guerrilla warfare and gave prominent white supremacists a chance to network. The group ran an "Aryan Nations Academy" in the early 1980s to teach young people the principles of white nationalism. The group has been reaching out to prisoners with a message of white supremacy since 1979.

During the 1990s, Aryan Nations suffered from internal struggles, and several key leaders departed. In September of 2000, a jury awarded Victoria and Jason Keenan $6.3 million in damages because the two had been chased and shot at by Aryan Nations guards outside the Idaho compound. Butler and Aryan Nations were bankrupted, and the Idaho compound was seized. The group has currently splintered into three factions: one headed by Butler (since deceased), one located in Pennsylvania and led by August Kreis and Charles Juba, and a group calling itself The Church of the Sons of YHVH/Legion of Saints (Church of the Sons of Yahweh), led by Ray Redfeairn (since deceased) and Morris Gulett.

See the Church of Jesus Christ Christian.

Aryan Republican Army

Abbreviation: ARA
Continent: North America
Country: United States of America
Background:
The Aryan Republican Army (ARA) was a militant group of Aryan Nations members and Christian Identity followers who committed 22 bank robberies in the Midwest during 1994 and 1995. They were one of many cells of violent racists that adopted the "leaderless resistance" structure advocated by KKK leader Louis Beam. They were, by some accounts, the most paramilitary and radical neo-Nazi group in the U.S. during their two-year robbing spree.

The ARA was named after the Irish Republican Army, and claims to have adopted its tactics and goals from the Irish Republican Army (IRA). It is clear, however, that the ARA was a far more extreme group than its Irish role model. The ARA's goals were nothing less than the overthrow of the U.S. government, the extermination of Jews, and the establishment of an Aryan state in North America. Members were required to read *The Turner Diaries*, a white supremacist fantasy novel that served as the inspiration for both Timothy McVeigh and The Order. Their main base of operations was Elohim City, an Oklahoma haven for militant racists. Timothy McVeigh called Elohim City two weeks before the bombing, and the possibility of a connection between McVeigh and the ARA is the subject of volumes of speculation by militia-watchers and conspiracy theorists.

The ARA's primary activities were robbing banks and stockpiling weapons and ammunition. During a typical bank robbery, an ARA member would enter with a pipe bomb and a pistol and threaten to kill both employees and customers of the bank. ARA members seem to have had a sick sense of Humour. They often committed robberies in costume, dressed as Santa Claus, the Easter Bunny, ATF or FBI agents, and Middle Eastern men. Part of the proceeds from the robberies were used to fund "White Terror Productions," a racist record label that recorded a CD dedicated to Sam and Vicki Weaver (who were killed at Ruby Ridge) and Richard Wayne Snell (a racist militant who was executed on the day of the Oklahoma City bombing for his role in an earlier plot to bomb the Alfred P. Murrah building.

The FBI was not actually aware of the existence of the ARA until one of its members was apprehended, since the group had not claimed responsibility for any of its robberies. When Richard Lee Guthrie was arrested in January of 1996 as a suspect in one of the 22 robberies that the ARA had committed, he told police about the ARA and gave them the location of four of his accomplices. Police then arrested Pete Langaan, Mark Thomas, Scott Stedeford, and Kevin McCarthy. Mike Brescia was arrested a year later. Guthrie hanged himself in his cell soon after fingering his associates. The other five members of ARA were all sent to prison for their crimes.

No further crimes have been connected with members of the Aryan Republican Army, and, as far as authorities know, the group ceased to exist when its six known members were arrested. According to Mike Reynolds of the Southern Poverty Law Centre, however, it is likely that associates of the group remain at large. "These people had a support system. They had safe-houses and very good false documents. They were clearly preparing for something beyond bank robberies."

Also known as Aryan Resistance Army

Asbat al-Ansar

Continent: Middle East
Country: Lebanon
Background:

Asbat al-Ansar (League of the Followers or Partisans' League) is a Sunni extremist group in Lebanon, chiefly made up of Palestinian refugees. Based in the Ayn al-Hilwah refugee camp in southern Lebanon, Asbat al-Ansar is thought to have links with al-Qaeda and other related Sunni extremist groups.

Palestinian refugee camps in Lebanon and Syria are havens for terrorist groups. While Hamas, Hezbollah, and al-Fatah generally dominate, smaller, more extreme groups, such as Asbat al-Ansar, operate on the fringes and draw membership from individuals alienated by the larger organisations. Asbat al-Ansar bases its ideology on Salafism, a branch of Islam whose adherents believe in a pure interpretation of the Koran and Islamic law. The group is virulently opposed to Israel, the West, and other religious sects in Lebanon such as the Shia, Christians, and Druze. In total, the group hopes to set up a Sunni Islamic state in Lebanon.

The group was formed in the late 1980s or early 1990s by Sheik Hisham Shreidi, a Palestinian refugee and preacher. Shreidi was killed in 1991 by al-Fatah rivals, and shortly after his death, the Asbat al-Ansar split in to three factions, Asbat al-Nour, Jama'at al-Nur and Jund as-Sham (Army of the Levant). Asbat al-Nour was allegedly founded by Hisham's eldest son Abdullah in a dispute over leadership with Ahmad Abd al-Karim al-Saadi (a.k.a. Abu Mohjen). Abu Mohjen was Sheik Hisham Shreidi's top lieutenant and widely accepted successor. Abdullah and his younger brother Mohammed, who also led the splinter group, were killed by al-Fatah gunmen in 2003 and 2004 respectively, and it is suspected that Asbat al-Nour has now rejoined Asbat al-Ansar. The other faction, Jund as-Sham, would later be incorporated into Abu Musab al-Zarqawi's Tawhid and Jihad network, and some reports have this faction at odds with the other two sectors of Asbat al-Ansar. However, Abu Mohjen was reportedly named a top deputy by al-Zarqawi in Iraq, and any disputes between the three factions of Asbat al-Ansar are believed to be minor. Abu Mohjen has been sentenced to death in absentia several times by the Lebanese government and is believed to be operating in Iraq or Lebanon.

In its early stages, Asbat al-Ansar was responsible for attacks on soft targets such as clubs, liquor stores, and movie theaters. The group was also thought to be responsible for attacks on rival militant and religious leaders, including Sunnis who the group deemed to be too moderate. In the late 1990s, apparently buoyed by funding from al-Qaeda, the group began attacking hard targets of greater significance. Asbat al-Ansar is thought to be responsible for killing four Lebanese judges in 1999, a rocket attack on the Russian Embassy in Lebanon in January 2000 (apparently to express solidarity with Chechen Rebels), several thwarted attempts to assassinate the American Ambassador, as well as a foiled plot to attack the Italian Embassy, the Ukrainian Consulate General, and Lebanese Government offices in 2004. The group also reportedly organised a coup attempt in 2000 which was carried out by its allies Tafkir wa Hijra, another Sunni extremist group in the region. The failed attempt left dozens of people dead, including Lebanese soldiers and civilians. Over the past few years, Asbat al-Ansar has been tied to a number of bombings at fast food restaurants in Lebanon, and has also been embroiled in an ongoing battle with al-Fatah over control of 'Ayn al-Hilwah which has cost many lives.

Despite denials from the group, Asbat al-Ansar almost certainly has ties to al-Qaeda and its related entities. Although Asbat al-Ansar is still dedicated to its goal of a Sunni Islamic state in Lebanon, many fear that the group has embraced the pan-Islamic ideals of Osama bin Laden, and is planning to extend its operations beyond Lebanon into Syria, Israel and Iraq. Although Asbat al-Ansar is relatively small, the group can be considered very dangerous and very active.

Also known as the Osbat al-Ansar, the League of Ansar (Supporters), the Partisans League Jama'at al-Noor (an off shoot group of Asbat al-Ansar), Band of Partisans, League of the Followers, Partisans' League, Usbat al-Ansar.

Aum Shinrikyo

Continent: Far East
Country: Japan
Background:

Aum Shinrikyo (Supreme Truth) is a Japanese cult founded in 1984. The group's original name was Aum Shinsen no Kai (Group of Gods/Supreme Beings), but it was changed to Aum Shinrikyo in 1989. Its leader, Shoko Asahara, was a charismatic and partially blind guru whose world-view evolved from an advocacy of esoteric mysticism to apocalyptic nihilism, which encouraged his followers to confront the Japanese establishment. His teachings involved a unique amalgam of Buddhism, Hinduism, Christianity, and New Age thought, with some elements also taken from Nostradamus' prophecies and even science fiction. Asahara claimed to have many supernatural powers and believed that he had attained enlightenment.

The cult started as a small group composed of Asahara and fifteen of his followers, and they focused on esoteric yoga. Within very little time however, Aum's numbers swelled, thanks to the charismatic leader's frequent lecture tours and travels abroad. Aum Shinrikyo actively recruited among professionals and students from Japan's top universities. The cult also enlisted over 300 scientists with degrees in biochemistry, medicine, genetic engineering and biology. At its peak, Aum had 10,000 members in Japan, with 35,000 in Russia. Aum also had offices in the U.S., Germany and Taiwan.

Aum Shinrikyo amassed a considerable amount of wealth over the years. Japanese police concluded the group owned over $1 billion in assets, the majority of which was obtained through membership fees, the sale of its literature, donations, tests, advanced courses and numerous businesses the organisation ran. From here Aum moved onto the chemical, import-export, software developing and mining sectors, to name a few.

Initially, Asahara preached meditation, introspection and non violence. In the late 1980s, he decided that Aum should run for office in the 1990 Japanese parliamentary elections. Despite Aum's campaigning, none of its members were elected. Because of this, Asahara was enraged and accused the Japanese government of rigging the elections. It was around this time that he started justifying murder on spiritual grounds. These ideas coalesced into a proper doctrine called 'poa' deeply influenced by Tantra Vajiriyana.

Asahara became increasingly paranoid and started to tell his followers about an approaching nuclear apocalypse, a war between Japan and the U.S. The cult began to assemble its own militia and reorganised its leadership structure as a shadow government. This cabinet had ministries in charge of different areas such as Science and Technology, Intelligence, and Construction. Asahara reserved for himself the title of Supreme Leader. The group was now fully poised to commit violent terrorist attacks in order to hasten the coming Apocalypse.

In June 1993, the cult attempted to release anthrax spores from its mid-rise Tokyo office building/laboratory. The attack failed as the group unknowingly using a non-lethal vaccine strain of Anthrax, and was thus ineffective.

In June 1994, Aum conducted a sarin gas attack in Matsumoto city, killing seven people and injuring 144 others. The targets were three judges sitting on a panel hearing a lawsuit over a real-estate dispute in which Aum Shinrikyo was the defendant. None of the judges died in the attack. Unfortunately, the authorities did not identify the terrorist nature of the action until after Aum's most infamous deed; the Tokyo subway attack.

In March 1995, Aum assaulted Tokyo's subway, in an attempt to stop a police investigation into Aum's activities. The cultists released sarin nerve gas, killing twelve people and injuring over 5,000 others. The attack was conducted at peak Monday morning rush hour. After the attack, Japanese police discovered that Aum Shinrikyo had accumulated hundreds of tons of chemicals in order to make enough sarin gas to kill millions of people. The production was conducted at the Satyan 7 facility in the Kamikuishiki complex, outside of Tokyo, near Mt. Fuji. The complex was designed to produce thousands of kilograms a year.

In the months following the subway attack the Japanese Metropolitan Police arrested Asahara and the main leaders of the sect Asahara was put on trial where he pleaded not guilty to all charges, claiming that his followers acted without his knowledge. Nevertheless, he was sentenced to death, although Asahara's attorneys appealed. Other Aum leaders received death sentences while some received life sentences. Many members have sought appeals, but Japanese courts have rejected most.

Oddly enough, and despite the scale of Aum's activities, the Japanese government did not outlaw Aum Shinrikyo. In 1997, a legal panel decided that its depleted membership and the public abandonment of its ambitions meant that Aum was not dangerous anymore. Enough suspicion remained however, to pass a special law that enabled Japanese authorities to monitor Aum activities for the following three years. This has been extended at the end of each period 3 year, with the last extension occurring in January 2006.

After Asahara's imprisonment and subsequent trial, Fumihiro Joyu, former Aum spokesman, became the new head of the organisation. It was under his leadership that Aum changed its name to Aleph in 2000. Aleph has now about 1,500 members. Since 2000, Aleph has moved to distance itself from Aum's goals and doctrine. It redefined Asahara as "founder" rather than "Supreme Leader" and forbid the use of poa. It has apologised for its past acts of terrorism and paid reparation to the victims of the Tokyo underground sarin attack.

However, Aleph's new direction has not been embraced by all of Aum's followers. Fissions between group members had begun to appear, with one faction led by Joyu and another by Tatsuko Muraoka and Asahara's biological children. Muraoka's faction reportedly followed Asahara's original teachings and continues to support the group's incarcerated former leader. It has been widely reported that the tensions have continued and it seems that a permanent split is imminent.

The group has not been directly involved in any terrorist violence since 1995. However, In 2000 Aleph members were discovered gathering sensitive information on nuclear power plants. The cult hacked into classified computer networks to obtain information about nuclear facilities in Russia, Ukraine, China, South Korea, Taiwan, and Japan. Also, in 2000, Russian Aum followers were allegedly planning on conducting a series of attacks against Japanese child care facilities, to try to gain Asahara's release. The

Japanese Aleph Headquarters has denied any connection with this plan.

Currently, Aleph is once again seeking contributions, selling publications to members, organising seminars, conducting training and selling computers. Authorities report approximately 1,650 people in Japan and 300 in Russia still believe in Asahara's teachings. The cult holds 50 seminars a month for current and potential members. Aleph has offices all over Japan, including Tokyo, and, reportedly maintains approximately 100 safe houses throughout the country. It has been reported that at least 700 members are monk-like devotees and that mind control techniques are still part of Aleph's activities.

Other names Aum Shinrikyo (means the "teaching the supreame truth" on the "Powers of destruction and creation in the universe.") Aleph ("To start anew") new name of the group as of 2000 Aum Divine Wizard Association (Name of the organisation prior to Aum Shinrikyo) Aum Supreme.

Azores Liberation Front

Continent: Europe
Country: Portugal
Background:

The Azores Liberation Front, more commonly known as FLA (Portuguese: Frente de Libertação dos Açores) was a right-wing terrorist paramilitary organisation with independentist goals that appeared in the Azores, right after the Carnation Revolution, that made violent attacks in 1975.

The organisation, which appeared in 1974, became very popular during the PREC (the first months after the revolution). As the Communists accumulated more power, fear of Portugal becoming a pro-Soviet puppet state started to grow and was inactivated by the right-wing. Besides, the PREC (with its nationalisation policies) became very unpopular among Azorean farmers and industrialists, mostly from São Miguel island who organised themselves to resist the "red danger".

Even though the organisation gained some support for some time, it was virtually dead by the end of the 70's. Autonomy was granted to the Azores and Madeira (where a similar organisation existed, the Frente de Libertação do Arquipélago da Madeira) by the Constitution of 1976, cooling the explosive situation, and the communist threat was slowly eroding.

Al or al

Al-Abud

Continent: Middle East
Country: Iraq
Background:

The al-Abud Network is a former insurgent group who was operating within Iraq during the Iraq War. First reported in the "Comprehensive Report of the Special Advisor to the DCI on Iraq's WMD", the group is alleged to have attempted to acquire chemical weapons for use in fighting against Coalition Forces. The al-Abud network was primarily comprised of members of Jaysh Muhammad (JM), an anti-Coalition group motivated by both political and religious elements. The politically motivated faction of JM has strong ties to the Sufi region, which once was highly favoured by Saddam during his rule. The Sufi region was home to many former Iraqi security forces, intelligence officers as well as police officers. It is believed through their former standing, political affiliations and business relationships; the group is able to acquire chemical precursors and weapons such as mortars through a "pre-OIF supply infrastructure." It is believe by the Iraq Survey Group that Jaysh Muhammad and Fallujah based insurgents were able to acquire chemical munitions, however those munitions were not yet located.

The al-Abud Network recruited, in late 2003, an Iraqi chemist in attempts to develop Tabun, and Mustard agents. The group was able to acquire Malathion pesticide and nitrogen mustard precursors, however it is believed they were unable to acquire further precursors for the final stages. From interrogation of key suspects in the 2004 raids against the network, the Iraq Survey Group (ISG) was able to ascertain the final goal of the group was to use the chemical agents within a mortar round, possibly for firing or detonation as an improvised chemical device. In December 2003, the recruited chemist failed to produce tabun; they did however create a poisonous compound due to the mixing of Malathion with other precursors of Tabun. In total nine mortar rounds were "weaponised" with the created compound. The mortars themselves are stated to have been an ineffective means of dispersal, due to the likelihood of the poison being consumed in the explosion. Following the failure to create Tabun, the insurgent group focused on attempting to create Nitrogen Mustard in February of 2004.

The al-Abud network recruited another chemist, one with more experience, who owned a small chemical lab in Baghdad. This chemist was unable however to produce the Nitrogen Mustard or binary mustard as the group had wanted. In mid 2004 this chemist was arrested and the contents of his lab seized. During the arrest it was noted the chemist had managed to produce small quantities of Ricin, in the form of ricin cakes, a substance that can easily be turned into poisonous toxic ricin. This chemist also created napalm and sodium fluoride acetate for the Jaysh Muhammad insurgents. It is currently believed the al-Abud network has been neutralised, however the leaders of the group as well as financiers remain at large and, the chemical munitions created remain unaccounted for.

Al Ahwaz Arab Peoples Democratic Front

Abbreviation: APDF
Continent: Middle East
Country: Iran
Background:

The al-Ahwaz Arab People's Democratic Front (APDF) is a London-based separatist group dedicated to the independence of Iran's Khuzestan region. Khuzestan, an oil-rich province in south-western Iran, is home too much of Iran's ethnic Arab minority. The ultimate goal of the group is to establish an independent, Marxist Arab state for the people of Khuzestan.

The APDF currently operates out of London after having been banned from Iran and is considered one of the most active al-Ahwazi groups. Largely a political organisation, the group lobbies for international acknowledgement of discrimination against Arabs in Khuzestan and seems to have a direct hand in the separatist agitation which occurs in the province. The APDF has been linked to several terrorist attacks, but while the group has lauded those who committed them, it has denied direct responsibility.

Most notably, the APDF was linked to a 12th June 2005 series of explosions that rocked Iran, killing at least 10 and injuring more than 85. Seven explosions went off in Ahwaz, the capital of Khuzestan, and Tehran on June 12, a week before the presidential election was held in Iran. Iranian media said it received three claims of responsibility for the attack, including one from the APDF. The group issued a statement denying responsibility and accusing the government of implicating them as an excuse to further crack down on separatist activity.

The APDF also played a role in the Khuzestan riots of April 2005. The riots occurred when a classified letter signed by former vice president Hojjatoleslam Hohammad Ali Abtahi was widely distributed. The letter called for Persian Iranians to settle in Ahwaz and the surrounding areas in an attempt to forcibly relocate the local Arab population. Upon hearing of this letter, thousands of Ahwazi Arabs took to the streets, clashing with police and targeting government property. The group encouraged these ri-ots, calling on Arabs in the region to rise up against the government and defend themselves. In an interview on Al Jazeera, an APDF spokesperson, Mahmud Ahmad al-Ahwazi aka Abu Bashir, accused the Iranian police of opening fire on a peaceful protest organised by the APDF amidst the riots. The statement provoked further outrage and, as a reaction, the Iranian gov-ernment temporarily shut down Al Jazeera's operation in the country.

The Iranian government has accused the APDF of being a means through which Western countries foment discontent within Iran and try to topple the Mahmoud Ahmadinejad administration. The Iranian government de-nies ethnic discrimination or conflict in the country. The APDF claims it receives no funding from any foreign nation and is opposed to "imperial" Western influence in the Middle East.

Despite proclaiming its independence from Western states, one of the primary purposes of the group at this point seems to be courting the atten-tion of foreign governments and international NGOs. Leaders of the group seem to have formed relationships with officials in at least a few Western countries including Britain, France, and Canada. They also continue to investigate and report on what they consider to be grave human rights violations in Khuzestan. It is extremely likely that the group also continues to have a hand in separatist violence in the region. It is unclear, however, whether members of the group directly participate in the violence or merely support it indirectly.

Also known as Al-Ahwaz Arab Popular Democratic Front, Arab People's Democratic Front, Democratic Popular Front for the Arab People of Ahwaz

al-Aqsa Martyrs' Brigade

Continent: Middle East
Country: Palestine
Background:
Al-Aqsa Martyrs Brigade is an active terrorist organisation committed to the creation of a Palestinian nation-state. The brigade is comprised of an unknown number of small militias, or cells. While never officially recog-nised by al-Fatah or its former leader Yasir Arafat, al-Aqsa Martyrs Brigade was predominantly comprised of terrorists who also belong to al-Fatah. There had been reports that Arafat approved payments to al-Aqsa Martyrs Brigade. In 2000, the brigades began to operate separately from al-Fatah and had been a significant factor in the current intifada.

Al-Aqsa Martyrs Brigade is a secular, nationalist terrorist group. While the organisation does not seek to create an Islamic state, it does use Islamic themes in its campaign. An example would be its self-appointed name, which refers to the al-Aqsa Mosque in Jerusalem. The group's specific objectives are to drive the Israelis from the West Bank, Gaza Strip, and Jerusalem. These areas would then become a Palestinian nation-state. At the outset, al-Aqsa Martyrs Brigade expressly targeted Israeli settlers and security forces in the West Bank and Gaza Strip. However, the group soon expanded its targets to include citizens in Israeli cities and Palestinians suspected of collaboration with Israel.

The goals of Al-Aqsa Martyrs Brigade were primary tactics of suicide bombings and firearms attacks. While the group's primary objective is to forcibly remove Israelis from the West Bank, Gaza Strip, and Jerusalem, the group also targets civilians and soldiers in Israel.

Al Bara Bin Malek Brigade

Continent: Middle East
Country: Iraq, Jordon
Background:
Al-Bara bin Malek Brigades is a specialised cell of suicide bombers within Abu Musab al-Zarqawi's al-Qaeda Organisation in the Land of the Two Rivers. The Brigades have launched numerous suicide operations against U.S. and Iraqi government targets and were reportedly responsible for the devastating November 2005 hotel bombings in Jordan that killed almost 60 people.

The formation of the group was announced in June 2005 in a posting on a Jihadist website by a man identifying himself as Abu Doujana al-Ansari, the leader of the Al-Bara bin Malek Brigades. The statement read: "We gladly inform our sheik Osama bin Laden and Abu Musab al-Zarqawi of the formation of al-Bara bin Malek Brigade." However, the group first emerged a month earlier when it claimed responsibility for the kidnapping of six Jordanians who were working in Iraq. The group released a video showing the abductees, and warned Jordanian companies not to cooperate with the United States. The fate of the hostages is as yet unknown.

Although al-Zarqawi most likely did not have a personal hand in forming the Brigades, the group can be considered a fully-incorporated outfit within al-Qaeda Organisation in the Land of the Two Rivers. In general, any suicide mission claimed by al-Zarqawi could be said to have been carried out by the Brigades. The group's name comes from a famous Muslim hero al-Bara bin Malek, who, according to legend, sacrificed himself in battle by being flung over a castle's ramparts to engage the enemy. Many Islamist terrorist groups use this story as a justification for suicide terrorism. Although the Brigades are no doubt a vicious Jihadist group like other cells within the al-Zarqawi network, their full-fledged embrace of suicide tactics suggests that the group is superlative in their extremism.

In November 2005, al-Bara bin Malek Brigades, operating under Abu Musab al-Zarqawi's terrorist network, were responsible for triple hotel bombings in Amman, Jordan. In a claim of responsibility a spokesman for al-Qaeda Organisation in the Land of the Two Rivers said of the attacks: "At this time of alienation, a group of heroes from al-Bara Bin Malek Brigade who love martyrdom and yearn for heaven… (selected the targets) and the time of execution was set as accurately as God willed." The Jordan bombing was unique in that it marked the movement of the Iraqi terrorist insurgency beyond the borders of Iraq. It remains to be seen whether groups such as al-Bara bin Malek Brigades will continue this trend, and perpetrate further attacks abroad. In any case, the group can be considered extremely active in Iraq, with the strong possibility that they will carry out suicide missions in other countries as well.

Also known as al-Bara bin Malek Martyrs' Brigades

Al Fatah

Continent: Middle East
Country: Israel, West Bank/Gaza
Background:
Headed by Yasser Arafat, Fatah Joined the PLO in 1968 and won the leadership role in 1969. Its commanders were expelled from Jordan following violent confrontations with Jordanian Forces during the period 1970-1971, beginning with Black September in 1970. The Israeli invasion of Lebanon in 1982 led to the group's dispersal to seven Middle Eastern countries, including Tunisia, Yemen, Algeria, Iraq and others. The group maintains several military and intelligence wings that have carried out terrorist attacks, including Force 17, the Hawari Special Operations Group, Tanzim and Al Aqsa Marytrs Brigade. In the 1960's and the 1970's, Fatah offered training to a wide range of European, Middle Eastern, Asian and African terrorist and insurgent groups. The organisation carried out numerous acts of international terrorism in Western Europe and the Middle East in the 1970's. It was linked to terrorist attacks against Israel and foreign civilians in Israel and the occupied territories. At the time it was thought to have a strength of between 6,000 to 8,000. It had close, longstanding political and financial ties with Saudi Arabia, Kuwait and other Persian Gulf States. These relations were disrupted by the Gulf crises in 1990-1991. Also has had links with Jordan. Received weapons, explosives and training from the former Soviet Regimes of Eastern European States. China and North Korea have reportedly provided some weapons in the past.

See the Palestine Liberation Organisation, Black September Organisation Force 17, Tanzim and Al Asqa Marytrs Brigade

al Gama'al-Islamiyya

Abbreviation: GAI
Continent: Middle East
Country: Afghanistan/Egypt
Background:

Egypt's largest militant group, active since the late 1970s, is also one of its most highly decentralised. The GAI began as an alliance of loosely organised cells whose leaders were in contact with one another. The majority of the cells developed after Egyptian President Anwar Sadat released many members of the nonviolent Muslim Brotherhood (MB) who had been imprisoned during Nasser's reign. Members who rejected the MB's nonviolent stance fragmented off into a variety of violent Islamist groups. The larger organisation's spiritual leader was Sheikh Umar Abd al-Rahman, but his influence had been lessened since his lifelong incarceration in the United States in 1996 for his involvement in the 1993 World Trade Centre bombing. The Group conducted a number of attacks on Egyptian security forces, government officials in Egypt, Coptic Christians, and on other perceived Egyptian opponents of Islam. GAI also claimed responsibility for the June 1995 attempted assassination of Egyptian President Hosni Mubarak in Ethiopia.

The group's founders, who are serving prison sentences in Egypt, first called for a ceasefire in 1997 and again in 1999. The 1997 ceasefire led to a split in the organisation into two independent, sometimes warring factions. Mustafa Hamza's faction supports the ceasefire, but the other, led by Rifa'i Ahmad, is believed to be responsible for ordering his radical faction to massacre a group of tourists at Luxor within months of the 1997 call for ceasefire. Ahmad's faction was based in Afghanistan and had been identified as having close links with Egyptian Islamic Jihad (EIJ), which uses its website to condemn ceasefire initiatives advocated by moderate GAI leaders. The group's March 1999 ceasefire was somewhat more successful, but Sheikh Rahman rescinded his support for the cease-fire in June 2000.

Senior members of the radical faction signed Osama Bin Laden's fatwa in February 1998 calling for attacks against the United States, and since 2000, a number of GAI cells have targeted Coptic Christians in Egypt. Ahmad published a 2001 book in which he justified mass casualty terrorist attacks. He seems to have disappeared since then and his current whereabouts are unknown. The radical faction was targeted by US-led attacks on Afghanistan after 9/11 and what remained of the faction is believed to have dispersed into Pakistan and various outlying regions, but may have regrouped. In March 2002, members of the group's moderate leadership declared the use of violence misguided and renounced its future use, prompting denunciations by much of the leadership abroad.

For members still dedicated to violent jihad, the main goal is the overthrow of the regime of President Hosni Mubarak and the establishment of an Islamist state in Egypt. Since allying themselves with al-Qaeda however, the faction likely has broader objectives, including attacks on the US.

Al Islambouli Brigades of al Qaeda

Continent: Asia
Country: Pakistan
Background:
The al-Islambouli Brigades of al-Qaeda is an Islamic terrorist organisation named after Lieutenant Khalid al-Islambouli, the man who assassinated Egyptian President Anwar Sadat in 1981. Al-Islambouli is considered one of the most well-known Muslim shahids (martyrs) of modern times, and his younger brother, Muhammad Shawqi al-Islambouli, was reportedly the group's leader.

The al-Islambouli Brigades were a suspected offshoot of the International Justice Group, which itself is believed to be an offshoot of al-Gama'a al-Islamiyya (GAI). Allegedly, the Brigades has strong ties to al-Qaeda, primarily through Muhammad Islambouli's capacity as the head of one of Osama bin Laden's Maktab al-Khidmat (Bureau of Services) in Peshawar during the Afghan War and has a similar Sunni extremist, anti-American ideology.

In its history, the group has been associated with several suicide bombings with such diverse targets as the Egyptian Embassy in Islamabad, Pakistani Finance Minister Shaukat Aziz, two Russian airliners, and a Russian metro station. However, it is unclear whether or not the group was actually responsible for any of these attacks.

Three Egyptian terrorist organisations claimed the November 1995 Islamabad embassy bombing, including al-Jihad and al-Islambouli Brigades' founding groups, al-Gama'a al-Islamiyya (GAI) and the International Justice Group. Pakistani officials concluded that members of al-Jihad conducted the attack and have prosecuted accordingly. Although the Islambouli Brigades are the only group to have publicly claimed responsibility for the July 2004 assassination attempt on Finance Minister Aziz, Pakistani officials believe that extremist group Jaish-e-Mohammed was responsible. Chechen terrorist leader Shamil Basayev claimed responsibility for the August 2004 Russian airliner and metro stations attacks, and his fighters are the most likely culprits given their attack history and tactical capabilities, although group leader al-Islambouli is known to have had contact with Chechen terrorists in the past.

Al-Islambouli Brigades of al-Qaeda was most likely not responsible for all the attacks claimed by them. The diverse locations and typologies of targets selected, as well as conflicting claims of responsibility among other groups are indicative of the involvement of distinct organisations. Even though no attacks have been claimed since 2004, members are likely to be active within other organisations associated with GAI or al-Qaeda.

Also known as Islambouli Brigade of Martyrs, Platoon of Marytr Khaled Islambouli, al-Islambouli Brigades, al-Qaeda Organisation

Al-Jama'a al-Islamiyyah al-Muqatilah bi Libya

Continent: Africa
Country: Libya
Background:
The Libyan Islamic Fighting Group (LIFG) also known as *Al-Jama'a al-Islamiyyah al-Muqatilah bi-Libya* was the most powerful radical faction waging "Jihad" against former Libyan leader Colonel Moammar al-Qadhafi. Shortly after the 9-11 attacks, LIFG was banned worldwide (as an affiliate of al-Qaeda) by the UN 1267 Committee. On 7th February 2006 the UN embargoed five specific LIFG members and four corporations, all of whom had continued to operate in England until at least October 2005. LIGF was founded in the fall of 1995 by Libyans who had fought against Soviet forces in Afghanistan. It aims to establish an Islamic state in Libya and views the current regime as oppressive, corrupt and anti-Muslim, according to the Canadian Security Intelligence Service. LIFG claimed responsibility for a failed assassination attempt against Qadhafi in February 1996, and engaged Libyan security forces in armed clashes during the mid-to-late 1990s. They continue to target Libyan interests and may engage in sporadic clashes with Libyan security forces. They strongly deny any links with al-Qaeda and are keen to emphasise that LIFG has never carried out an attack outside Libya or against civilians. On the 10th October 2005, the United Kingdom's Home Office banned LIFG and fourteen other militant groups from operating in the UK. Under the United Kingdom's Terrorism Act 2000, being a member of a LIFG is punished by a 10-year prison term. The Financial Sanctions Unit of the Bank of England acting on behalf of HM Treasury issued the orders to freeze all their assets.

Al-Ma'unah (Spiritual Brotherhood)

Continent: Asia
Country: Malaysia
Background:

On its website (http://al-maunah.tripod.com [Offline as of July 11, 2000]), the group describes itself as a non-governmental organisation "involved in the teaching of martial arts, particularly the development of one's inner power and the practice of Islamic traditional medicine."

Al-Ma'unah currently had more than 1,000 members in Malaysia and overseas in Brunei, Singapore, Egypt and Saudi Arabia, it said.

The group said followers can make enemies hurl backward without touching them, are "invincible from" weapons, fire or sharp objects and can tie enemies without using rope.

The site says that proponents of the Al-Ma'unah adhere to the teachings of the Koran and a Muslim cleric named Amin Razali who, it claimed, received enlightenment after spending five years studying paranormal sciences in a hut in Indonesia.

Mr. Amin is called a master of "inner power" on the Al Ma'unah Web site, capable of making enemies "drop to their knees or fall down with the blink of an eye."

Images on their Website show group members practicing rituals that include being burned by fire, scalded by boiling oil and having tree trunks hurled on their chests.

"Jihad is our way! Islam will be victorious!" says the Web site, which also includes photos of believers putting their hands in cauldrons of hot oil, having logs rolled over their chests and coming into contact with a flaming torch.

Al Qaeda

Continent: World Wide
Country: World Wide
Background:

Al Qaeda, or 'The Base', was formed in 1988 by Osama bin Laden and his associate Mohammed Atef to bring together Arabs who fought in Afghanistan against the Soviet invasion. It serves as a focal point or umbrella group for a global network that includes terrorist cells in various – currently estimated at over 60 – countries. The Al Qaeda gradually emerged out of the Maktab al-Khidimat (MAK - the "Services Office") which had maintained and continues to maintain offices in various parts of the world, including Afghanistan, Pakistan (especially Peshawar) and the United States – specifically the Alkifah Refugee Centre in Brooklyn. It had evolved considerably to emerge as a primary umbrella group, which funds and carries out terrorist activity of Islamist terrorists worldwide. The Al Qaeda is reported to have a global reach, and the countries where it maintains a presence include Algeria, Egypt, Morocco, Turkey, Jordan, Tajikistan, Uzbekistan, Syria, Xinjiang in China, Pakistan, Bangladesh, Malaysia, Myanmar, Indonesia, Mindanao in the Philippines, Lebanon, Iraq, Saudi Arabia, Kuwait, Bahrain, Yemen, Libya, Tunisia, Bosnia, Kosovo, Chechnya, Dagestan, Jammu and Kashmri, Sudan, Somalia, Kenya, Tanzania, Azerbaijan, Eritrea, Uganda, Ethiopia, as also in parts of the West Bank and Gaza. The dispersed nature of Al Qaeda cadres around the globe has provided Osama bin Laden command over a global terror network with capabilities to carry out lethal terrorist attacks.

Al Qaeda has forged alliances with like-minded fundamentalist groups such as Egypt's Al Jihad, Iran's Hezbollah, Sudan's National Islamic Front, as also terrorist groups in Yemen, Saudi Arabia, and Somalia. Al Qaida also has ties to the "Islamic Group," led at one time by Sheik Omar Abdel Rahman, the Egyptian cleric serving a life sentence since his 1995 conviction for his role in the bombing of the World Trade Centre in New York in February 1993 in which six persons were killed and thousands injured as also for hatching a plot to bomb the United Nations, FBI offices, and other New York landmarks. Two of Sheik Rahman's sons are reported to have joined forces with bin Laden in the late 1990s. Since 1992 bin Laden and other Al Qaeda cadres have targeted US military forces in Saudi Arabia and Yemen, as also those stationed in the Horn of Africa, including Somalia.

A common factor in all these groups is the use of terror for the attainment of their goal of the overthrow of what they perceive to be 'heretic' regimes and the establishment of an Islamist regime in such countries. The Al Qaeda sees the United States as providing support to the various 'heretic' regimes of the world, including Saudi Arabia, Egypt, Israel and the United Nations. The Al Qaeda has opposed the involvement of the US forces in the 1991 and 2003 Gulf War's and in Somalia in 1992. It has also opposed the continuing presence of US troops in Saudi Arabia after the 1991 Gulf War.

The Al Qaeda hierarchy has Osama bin Laden as the 'Emir' (chief) followed by other senior Al Qaeda leaders and leaders of the constituent groups. Laden is the undisputed leader, referred to as 'emir-general' or 'prince' by his followers, who must take a sworn oath to him, violation of, which is punishable by death. Reportedly, his two aides are Egyptians: Ayman al-Zawahiri, a physician and leader of Al Jihad, the Egyptian terrorist group responsible for the Luxor tourist massacre in 1997; and Mohammed Atef his military commander. The core membership of Al

Qaeda consists of Afghan war veterans from various countries of the Islamist world. According to reports, the Al Qaeda is horizontally integrated informally with over 24 constituent groups. Following bin Laden is the *Shura Majlis* (a consultative council). Four committees concerning the aspects of military, religio-legal, finance and media report to the Shura Majlis. Selected cadres of these committees, especially from the military committee are reported to carry out the operational commands vis-à-vis terrorist attacks across the world.

The Al Qaeda is reported to rely to a great extent on differentiation of cadres as also secrecy in order to achieve maximum operational effectiveness in terrorist attacks. While the basic organisational structure has remained more or less the same, holistically the organisation is reported to have evolved considerably since its inception in 1988. Using hi-tech means, Osama bin Laden is reported to be constantly monitoring the activities of the various constituent groups. The Al Qaeda group is not a small, tightly knit group with a clear command structure. It is a loose coalition of terror groups operating across continents. Al-Qaeda's terrorist operations are not carried out by one group led by one person, but are rather conducted by various groups with support and guidance from Al-Qaeda. Members of one terror cell of Al Qaeda do not necessarily know members of others. Al Qaeda terror cells are reported to remain inactive for long periods of time engaging only in fundraising and propagation activities. A terror cell may be suddenly called into action to carry out lethal terrorist operations. Sympathisers are recruited primarily to perform logistical activities. Unlike conventional terrorist organisations, the operational groups and Al-Qaeda are linked, not through direct chains of command, but by their common experience in the Afghan war against Russia as also a shared belief in a pan-Islamist identity, cemented further through communication of experience and provision of funds.

From 1988 until in or about 1991, the Al Qaeda was headquartered in Afghanistan and Peshawar, Pakistan. In 1992, the Al Qaeda leadership as also its military command shifted its headquarters to Sudan. With increasing US pressure on Sudan, bin Laden reverted back to Afghanistan in 1996, by which time the Taliban regime were controlling a major portion of that country's territory. From his hideouts in Taliban-controlled Afghanistan, Osama bin Laden provided financial and other material support, religious fervour and 'inspiration' to thousands of Al Qaeda cadres and affiliates throughout the world.

The avowed goal of Al Qaeda is to "unite all Muslims and establish a government which follows the rule of the Caliphs." The underlying rationale is the overthrow of what it perceives as the corrupt and heretical regimes of the various Islamist states, and their replacement with regimes that are based on the rule of *Shari'ah* (Islamic law). Al Qaeda is vehemently anti-Western, with the United States of America perceived as an enemy of Islam. Al Qaeda seeks to overthrow nearly all Muslim governments, because bin Laden regards most of them as being corrupted by Western influences. Another rallying aspect for the Al Qaeda network is the 'liberation' of Islam's three holiest places -- Mecca and Medina in Saudi Arabia as also Jerusalem.

Over the years, the Al-Qaeda has evolved from being a regional threat to US troops in the Persian Gulf to a global threat to US as also other countries it perceives as being enemies of Islam. The foundational strength of the Al Qaeda network is the ideological and personal bond among the Arab cadres who were recruited by bin Laden for the fight against the Soviet occupation of Afghanistan. Al-Qaeda currently encompasses members and factions of several major Islamist terrorist organisations, including Egypt's Islamic Group and Al-Jihad, Algeria's Armed Islamic Group, Pakistan's Harkat-ul-Mujahideen, the Islamic Movement of Uzbekistan, and opposition groups in Saudi Arabia. It is also linked to the Abu Sayyaf Islamic terror outfit in the Philippines.

In December 1999, US and Jordanian law enforcement authorities ascertained and thwarted two alleged attempts, one in the United States and one in Jordan, to attack US citizens celebrating the new millennium. The US attempt was masterminded by a pro-bin Laden terror cell of Algerian Armed Islamic Group cadres coming from Canada. In June 2000, Jordan began trying its 28 alleged millennium plotters, but 15 of those charged are still at large. Also in June 2000, Lebanon placed 29 suspected bin Laden associates on trial for planning terrorist attacks in Jordan. Reports have indicated that Al Qaeda has also ventured into experimenting with chemical and biological warfare.

Other names al Qaida, the al Qadr, the Base, the Group for the Preservation of the Holy Sites, the International Islamic Front for Jihad against Jews and Crusaders, the Islamic Army for the Liberation of Holy Places, the Islamic Army for the Liberation of Holy Shrines, Qa'idat al-Jihad.

Areas of operation: Afghanistan; Albania; Algeria; Australia; Austria; Azerbaijan; Bahrain; Bangladesh; Belgium; Bosnia; Egypt; Eritrea; FRY (Kosovo); France; Germany; India; Iran; Ireland; Italy; Jordan; Kenya; Lebanon; Libya; Malaysia; Mauritania; Netherlands; Pakistan; Philippines; Qatar; Russia; Saudi Arabia; Somalia; South Africa; Sudan; Switzerland; Tajikistan; Tanzania; Tunisia; Turkey; Uganda; United Arab Emirates; United Kingdom; United States; Uzbekistan; Yemen

Al Qaeda Organisation in the Land of Two Rivers

Continent: Middle East
Country: Iraq
Background:

Tanzim Qa'idat al-Jihad Fi Bilad al-Rafidayn is the current name of the terrorist group Tawhid and Jihad, formerly led by Abu Musab Zarqawi. The U.S. State Department has understood this new name, which is translated as The Al-Qaeda Organisation in the Land of the Two Rivers, to imply that Zarqawi saw his group as the centre of Jihadist activities in Iraq. This change was made after Zarqawi formally pledged his alliance to al-Qaeda in a letter addressed to Osama bin Laden recovered by Coalition forces in August 2004. Despite the change in name, the letter makes it clear that the goals of Zarqawi's group – to overthrow the interim Iraqi government and establish an Islamic state in Iraq by forcing out the U.S.-led coalition – remain constant. Al-Qaeda in the Land of the Two Rivers is believed to be comprised of foreign terrorists, elements of the Kurdish Islamist group Ansar al-Islam, and indigenous Sunni Iraqis.

The group issued claims of responsibility daily in Iraq for attacks on American and Iraqi security forces, often claiming several attacks in one day. The al-Qaeda Organisation in the Land of the Two Rivers uses a variety of tactics that include RPG attacks against armoured vehicles, guerrilla style attacks by armed militants, suicide bombings, and the kidnapping and beheadings of foreigners. A video released in May 2004 gained notoriety for depicting Zarqawi brutally beheading Nicholas Berg, a civilian American contractor in Iraq. However, the group has increasingly eschewed such tactics since Zarqawi swore allegiance with al-Qaeda. Instead, al-Qaeda in the land of the Two Rivers, which is believed to derive most of its domestic support from Sunni Arabs, targets (in order of priority) Shiite Arabs, who are seen pro-American betrayers of the true faith, Coalition forces and their local support, including the fledgling Iraqi security forces, and Kurds, who are perceived to act as a "Trojan Horse" for Jewish economic infiltration into Iraq.

In addition to frequent smaller scale attacks in Iraq, the group claimed responsibility for the bombing of three hotels in Amman, Jordan that left 67 people dead and injured more than 150. A stern rebuke issued by al-Qaeda number two, Ayman al-Zawahiri, shortly after the attack seems to have stopped the selection of targets outside of Iraq.

Zarqawi's letter to bin Laden revealed many problems that the former believed al-Qaeda in the Land of the Two Rivers would face in the coming years. The Sunni insurgent leader pointed out that as American forces are drawn down or removed from the front lines and indigenous Iraqi forces take their place, attacks perpetrated against security forces will increasingly be seen as anti-Iraqi attacks, rather than anti-occupation ones. Zarqawi confessed that his fighters' freedom of movement has become increasingly restricted and that the "future has become frightening". The local Sunni Iraqi resistance is inexperienced and has been unwilling to sacrifice for the cause, whereas battle-tested foreign Mujahideen are too small in number to affect significant change. Zarqawi went on to complain that the Sunni Iraqi masses have "no firm principles" and that "their religion is mercurial".

Additionally, the letter illuminated a strategic plan for victory, despite these odds. Importantly, Zarqawi highlighted the importance of the information warfare campaign, stating that the "pen and the sword complement each other". He targeted the Shia as the main enemy, hoping to incite sectarian strife and thus provoke the Sunni "silent majority" into armed action in the ultimate battle for the future of Islam.

In a speech broadcast over the internet on the 23rd January 2005, Zarqawi denounced the upcoming Iraqi elections, calling candidates "demi-idols" and voters "infidels." Zarqawi's statement, declaring a "fierce war" against democracy, accused the Americans of rigging the election to favour Iraq's Shi'ite population. Increased Sunni Arab participation in Iraq's December 2005 parliamentary elections offered hope to some that support for wider insurgency may be abating. However, violence resumed following a lull in attacks during the election, including attacks by al-Qaeda in the land of the Two Rivers. In January 2006, the group was one of six insurgent organisations to unify under the Mujahideen Shura Council. As of now, all attacks perpetrated by al-Qaeda in Iraq are claimed in the name of the Council. Zarqawi was killed in a U.S. airstrike in June 2006, though the impact that this will have on the Iraqi insurgency had yet to be determined.

Also known as the Al-Tawhid, the Al-Tawhid wal-Jihad Jama'a Tawhid wal-Jihad (the Society of Tawhid and Jihad), the Qaedat al-Jihad fi balad ar-Rafidayn (the Base [Qaeda] of Jihad in the Land of the Two Rivers), the Al-Qaeda in the Land of Two Rivers, the Al-Qaeda in Mesopotamia, also see the Tawhid and Jihad, Monotheism and Holy Struggle, Organisation of Jihad's Base in the Country of the Two Rivers, al-Qaeda in Iraq, al-Zarqawi Network

Al-Qaeda in Iraq

Abbreviation: AQI
Continent: Middle East
Country: Iraq
Background:
Al-Qaeda in Iraq (AQI) is a term to describe the Sunni militia group which

is playing an active role in the Iraqi insurgency. The group was led by Abu Musab al-Zarqawi until his death in 2006; it is now believed to be led by Abu Hamza al-Muhajir (aka Abu Ayyub al-Masri).

The group is a direct successor of al-Zarqawi's previous organisation, Jama'at al-Tawhid wal-Jihad. Beginning with its official statement declaring allegiance to the Osama bin Laden's al-Qaeda terrorist network in October 2004, the group identifies itself as Tanzim Qaidat Al-Jihad fi Bilad al-Rafidayn (QJBR) ("Organisation of Jihad's Base in the Country of the Two Rivers").

In a July 2005 letter to al-Qaeda deputy leader Ayman al-Zawahiri, al-Zarqawi outlined a four-stage plan to expand the Iraq War, which included expelling U.S. forces from Iraq, establishing an Islamic authority (caliphate), spreading the conflict to Iraq's secular neighbours and engaging in battle with Israel. Consistent with their stated plan, the affiliated groups were linked to regional attacks outside Iraq, such as the Sharm al-Sheikh bombings in Egypt, and the Aqaba rocket attack.

In January 2006, AQI created an umbrella organisation called Mujahideen Shura Council (MSC) in an attempt to unify Sunni insurgents in Iraq. However, its efforts to recruit Iraqi Sunni nationalists and secular groups were undermined by its violent tactics against civilians and its extreme Islamic fundamentalist doctrine. Because of these impediments, the attempt was largely unsuccessful.

AQI used to claim its attacks under the MSC, until mid-October 2006 when Abu Ayyub al-Masri declared the self-styled Islamic State of Iraq (ISI), an another front which included the Shura Council factions. The AQI now claims its attacks under the ISI, and claims it's answering to the Emir and leader of the organisation, Abu Abdullah al-Rashid al-Baghdadi. According to a study compiled by US intelligence agencies, the ISI have plans to seize power and turn the country into a Sunni Islamic state.

AQI is among Iraq's most feared militant organisations and many experts regard it as the United States' most formidable enemy in Iraq. Others suggest that the threat posed by AQI is exaggerated, and some scholars claim that a "heavy focus on al-Qaeda obscures a much more complicated situation on the ground."

According to a 2006 U.S. government report, this group is most clearly associated with foreign terrorist cells operating in Iraq and has specifically targeted international forces and Iraqi citizens. AQI's operations are predominately Iraq-based, but the United States Department of State alleges that the group maintains an extensive logistical network throughout the Middle East, North Africa, Iran, South Asia, and Europe. Over a three-month period in 2005, al-Zarqawi's affiliates were reportedly responsible for more than 1,700 attacks on Coalition and Iraqi forces in the city of

Mosul alone. Many of these were suicide attacks and improvised explosive device (IED) attacks, typically using cars and other motor vehicles. (In March 2007 the U.S.-sponsored Radio Free Europe/Radio Liberty analyzed al-Qaeda in Iraq attacks for that month. Al-Qaeda in Iraq had taken credit for 43 out of 439 attacks on Iraqi security forces and Shiite militias, and 17 out of 357 attacks on U.S. troops.)

Estimates for AQI numbers range from 850 – about 3 to 5 percent of the Sunni insurgency – to several thousand. In 2006 the State Department's Bureau of Intelligence and Research estimated that AQI's membership was in a range of "more than 1,000," putting AQI's forces at less than 1 percent of the insurgency. In 2007 the State Department dropped its base-level estimate, because, as an official explained, "*the information is too disparate to come up with a consensus number*".

According to both the July 2007 National Intelligence Estimate and the Defence Intelligence Agency reports AQI accounted for 15 percent of attacks in Iraq. However, the Congressional Research Service noted in its September 2007 report that attacks from al-Qaeda are less than two percent of the violence in Iraq and criticised the administration's statistics, noting that its false reporting of insurgency attacks as AQI attacks has increased since the "surge" operations began.

In 2004, AQI kidnapped Shosei Koda, a Japanese citizen and murdered him on October 30th. In November, the al-Zarqawi's network was the main target of the American Operation Phantom Fury in Fallujah. On December 19th, the group bombed a Shiite funeral procession in Najaf and main bus station in nearby Karbala, killing at least 60 in the Shiite holy cities. The group also reportedly took responsibility for a September bombing directed at U.S. forces that killed 35 children and seven adults in Baghdad.

In 2005, AQI largely focused on executing high-profile and coordinated suicide attacks. The group claimed responsibility for numerous attacks which were primarily aimed at civilians, the Iraqi Government, and Iraqi Security Forces, among them for attacks against the voters during the Iraqi legislative election and the coordinated suicide attacks outside the Sheraton Ishtar and Palestine Hotel in Baghdad on October 24. On April 2nd, AQI fighters attacked the Abu Ghraib prison in a combined suicide and conventional attack. In July, al-Qaeda claimed responsibility for the kidnapping and execution of Ihab Al-Sherif, Egypt's envoy to Iraq. A July 2005 three-day series of suicide attacks, including Musayyib marketplace bombing, left at least 150 people dead and more than 260 wounded. Al-Zarqawi also claimed responsibility for the September 2005 massacre of mostly Shiite unemployed workers in Baghdad, which killed about 160 people and injured 570.

The attacks blamed on or claimed by al-Qaeda in Iraq kept increasing in 2006. In one of the incidents, two American soldiers (Thomas Lowell Tucker and Kristian Menchaca) were captured, tortured and beheaded by the ISI; in another, four Russian embassy officials were abducted and executed. Iraq's al-Qaeda and its umbrella groups were blamed for multiple attacks targeting Iraqi Shiites, some of which AQI claimed responsibility for. In 2006, several key members of the AQI were killed or captured by the American and allied forces, including al-Zarqawi killed on the 7th June 2006, his spiritual adviser Sheik Abd-Al-Rahman, and the alleged "number two" deputy leader Hamid Juma Faris Jouri al-Saeedi.

The high-profile attacks linked to the group continued through the early 2007, as the AQI-led Islamic State claimed responsibility for attacks such as the March 23 assassination attempt of Sunni Deputy Prime Minister of Iraq Salam al-Zaubai, the 12th April Iraqi Parliament bombing, and the May capture and subsequent execution of three American soldiers. On the 3rd May 2007, the ISI leader al-Baghdadi was declared to have been killed in Baghdad, but his death was later denied by the group (later, al-Baghdadi was declared by the U.S. to be non-existent). There were also conflicting reports regarding al-Masri.

More recently, al-Qaeda seems to have lost its foothold in Iraq and appears to be severely crippled. There are three main reasons for this: violent attacks and intimidation against civilians have severely damaged their image and caused the loss of support among the population. The Sunni militias that previously fought together with AQI, have begun to work together with the Iraqi government and the Coalition troops. This has severely isolated the group. The troop surge has supplied military planners with more manpower to go after Iraq's al-Qaeda leaders. In fact, dozens of high-level officials have been captured or killed since the "surge" began.

In May 2007 the U.S. forces announced the release of dozens of Iraqis who were tortured by AQI as a part of the group's intimidation campaign. The U.S. also claimed the group was at least of one of the forces behind the wave of the chlorine bombings in Iraq which affected hundreds of people through the series of crude chemical warfare attacks since the late 2006. According to a rival insurgent faction, the group is even demanding money in return for "protection", killing members of the families (especially wealthy ones) when not paid

The attacks against civilians were often targeted at the Iraqi Shia majority in an attempt to incite sectarian violence. Al-Zarqawi purportedly declared an all-out war on Shiites while claiming responsibility for a series of September 2005 mosque bombings which killed at least 74 people. The same month, a statement claiming to be by AQI rejected as "fake" a letter allegedly written by al-Zawahiri, in which he appears to question the insurgents' tactics in attacking Shiites in Iraq.

U.S. and Iraqi officials accused AQI of trying to slide Iraq into full-scale civil war between Iraq's majority Shiites and minority Sunni Arabs with an orchestrated campaign of a civilian massacres and a number of highly provocative attacks against the high-profile religious targets. With attacks like the first al-Askari Mosque bombing in Samarra, the deadly one-day series of bombings which killed at least 215 in the Baghdad's Shiite district of Sadr City, and the second al-Askari bombing, provoking the Shiite militias to unleash a wave of retaliatory attacks, resulting in a plague of death squad-style killings and spiralling further sectarian violence. This religious/ethnic violence between the Iraqis is sometimes called the "civil war in Iraq" by the observers.

As of mid-2007, the majority of the suicide bombings targeting civilians in Iraq are identified by the military and government sources as being the responsibility of al-Qaeda and its associated groups.

AQI claimed an attempted chemical bomb plot in Amman, Jordan in April 2004. On the 3rd December 2004, AQI attempted to blow up a Iraqi-Jordanian border crossing, but failed to do so (in 2006, a Jordanian court sentenced Zarqawi (*in absentia*) and two of his associates to death for their involvement in the plot).

AQI also increased its operations outside Iraq by claiming credit for three attacks in 2005: Suicide bomb attacks against hotels which killed 60 people in Amman, Jordan, on the 9th November 2005; Rocket attacks that narrowly missed the USS *Kearsarge* and the USS *Ashland* in Jordan and which also targeted Eilat in Israel; Firing of several *Katyusha* rockets into Israel from Lebanon in December.

In addition, an AQI operative was arrested in Turkey in August 2005 while planning an operation to target Israeli cruise ships. In Lebanon, the Palestinian militant group Fatah al-Islam (which was defeated in the 2007 Lebanon conflict) was linked to AQI and led by Zarqawi's former companion who fought in Iraq. The AQI was also implicated in the 2006 German train bombing plot.

The first reports of a split and even armed clashes between AQI and its allies, and the other insurgent Sunni groups date back to 2005. In the summer of 2006, local Sunni tribes and insurgent groups, including the prominent Islamist-nationalist group Islamic Army in Iraq (IAI), began to speak of their dissatisfaction with al-Qaeda and its tactics, and openly criticised the foreign fighters for their deliberate targeting of civilian targets.

In September 2006, thirty Anbar tribes formed their own local alliance called Anbar Salvation Council (ASC), directed specifically to counter al-Qaeda ("terrorist") forces in the province, openly siding with the government and the U.S. troops. Since then, AQI forces have retaliated against local Sunni tribesmen and other insurgent groups for negotiating a deal(s) with the U.S. forces and the Iraqi government to route out al-Qaeda-aligned militants. The extremist group supposedly played a vital role in the assassination of Harith Dhaher Khamis al-Dhari, a Sunni nationalist insurgent leader who headed the Anbar-based group 1920 Revolution Brigade. On the 17th March 2007, scores of people were killed when a truck bomb exploded near a Sunni mosque in Fallujah where the local Imam had criticised the al-Qaeda in Iraq.

On the 17th April 2007, the IAI spokesman accused AQI of killing at least 30 members of the Islamic Army and alleged that the leader of the Islamic State of Iraq, al-Baghdadi, had "broken the Islamic law". The same statement also alleged that AQI has also killed members of the Jaish al-Mujahideen and Ansar al-Sunna insurgent groups, and called on Osama bin Laden to personally intervene to rein-in the al-Qaeda in Iraq. On the same day, ISI released an audio tape in which a man claiming to be al-Baghdadi attempted to soothe the tensions with other major Sunni insurgent groups. On the 1st May 2007, the government stated that al-Masri was killed by the ASC fighters. Four days later, AQI released an audio tape in which a man claiming to be al-Masri warned Sunnis not to take part in the political process, and claimed that reports of internal fighting between his group and other Sunni militia groups were "lies and fabrications".

In June 2007, the growing hostility between the foreign-influenced religious extremists and other Sunni nationalists led to gun battles between the groups in Baghdad. Meanwhile, the U.S. military began arming moderate insurgent factions on the promise to fight al-Qaeda in Iraq and not the Americans. The Islamic Army, however, reached a ceasefire with AQI on the 6th June 2007, yet still refusing to sign on to the ISI. There were reports that the Hamas of Iraq insurgents were involved in assisting U.S. troops in their Diyala Governorate operations against AQI in August 2007.

In September 2007, AQI claimed responsibility for the assassination of three people including the Sunni sheikh Abdul-Sattar Abu Risha (leader of the Anbar Awakening), sparking a revenge vow among 1,500 mourners. On 25th September 2007, a suicide bomber blew himself up in a mosque in the Iraq city of Baqubah, killing 28 people, including the leaders of Hamas of Iraq and 1920 Revolution Brigade, in the attack blamed on AQI that took place during a meeting at the mosque between tribal, police and guerrilla leaders.

Al Qaeda Organisation in the Islamic Maghreb

Continent: Africa
Country: Algeria, Mali, Mauritania, Niger
Background:

The al-Qaeda Organisation in the Islamic Maghreb (formerly known as the Salafist Group for Call and Combat (GSPC)) is a violent extremist group based in Algeria. The organisation has operated since 1996 and is now the most significant terrorist movement in Algeria. As the Salafist Group for Call and Combat, the group broke away from the Armed Islamic Group (GIA), which was the primary terrorist entity during the 1992-2000 insurgencies in Algeria. GIA aims to create an Islamist state in Algeria. While the GSPC broke away from GIA in 1998, both groups maintain the objective of overthrowing the secular Algerian government and establishing an Islamist state in the country. The word 'salafi' means fundamentalist, and Salafists believe in a "pure" interpretation of the Koran. While not all Salafists are extremists, GSPC's objectives are rooted in this ideology.

As a result of the long, bloody conflict from 1992-2000, which cost over 100,000 lives, GIA's support was relatively weak in Algeria. Using this weakness to its advantage, GSPC pledged to avoid inflicting civilian casualties in Algeria. While the group has in fact killed civilians, the numbers are significantly less than the casualties of the GIA. Instead, GSPC concentrated on targeting Algerian government and security forces, especially those in rural areas. The group has also pledged to attack Western targets and has been linked to several foiled attacks against U.S. and European targets in Western Europe. The GSPC has usurped GIA as the primary terrorist force in the country, and because of its minimal attacks against civilians, GSPC benefits from a larger support network in the country. According to some reports, GSPC has also been able to take over many of GIA's contacts with other extremists, including al-Qaeda allies. GSPC has publicly pledged its allegiance to many of these terrorist entities, and also officially pledged its allegiance to al-Qaeda in 2003. In early September 2006, Ayman al-Zawahiri publicly approved the merge of al-Qaeda with GSPC. The latter officially announced its name change in February 2007 in a public announcement following six near-simultaneous attacks of police stations in towns east of Algiers.

The al-Qaeda Organisation in the Islamic Maghreb is based in Northern Africa, specifically Algeria. However, the group is believed to be establishing links with groups across Northern Africa, and it also has links to an external network of extremists in Western Europe. The group has signalled its intent to target symbols of Western countries both inside and outside of Algeria, and it has also established a network to send North African militants to Iraq for suicide operations and as foot soldiers. Some intelligence experts fear the group is moving towards a global objective, along the lines of al-Qaeda, and may soon adopt similar tactics to al-Qaeda. Other experts argue that the Organisation does not have the resources to launch large-scale attacks outside of Algeria. However, the al-Qaeda Organisation in the Islamic Maghreb still appears dedicated to its primary objective, the establishment of an Islamist state in Algeria.

Recent arrests of members of the Organisation have uncovered plans for chemical attacks. In April 2005, a GSPC member, Kamel Bourgass, was convicted for "conspiracy to cause public nuisance by use of poisons and/or explosives. Bourgass's recent conviction did not represent the disruption of a vast terrorist conspiracy originally portrayed by British authorities, and, amidst a lack of hard evidence, many feel that the ricin plot was an over-blown threat. Bourgass was connected with the London-based GSPC cell led by Abu Doha, a known associate of Osama bin Laden who has also been linked with the foiled plot to blow up Los Angeles International Airport.

Also known as Al-Qaeda Committee in the Islamic Maghreb, Salafist Group for Call and Combat (GSPC), Salafist Group for Preaching and Combat

Al Qaeda in the Arabian Peninsula

Continent: Middle East
Country: Saudi Arabia
Background:
Al-Qaeda in the Arabian Peninsula is the name of the organised group of terrorists associated with al-Qaeda that operate within the Kingdom of Saudi Arabia. Although Saudi Arabia is the home of al-Qaeda's founder Osama bin Laden, the organisation ceased to be based there after bin Laden moved to Sudan and then Afghanistan. The precise relationships between this group and the larger network of al-Qaeda terrorists operating within the Kingdom remain unclear, although it is believed that they operate independently from the al-Qaeda central command, which remains in Afghanistan. The group has been suspected by both U.S. and Saudi authorities as being behind the al-Qaeda linked beheading of American contractor Paul Johnson.

The group was formerly led by Abdulaziz al-Muqrin, aka Abu Hajar, who was killed in a shootout with Saudi security forces in summer 2004 during a raid connected to the Paul Johnson investigation.

Experts believe that the death of al-Muqrin is a significant step toward the defeat of al-Qaeda within Saudi Arabia. They warn, however, that even though many of the original "Afghani" Mujahideen within Saudi Arabia are no longer active terrorists, the organisation is continuing to gain support from lower-class, unemployed Saudis. The group also is rumoured to have gained the support of some members of the Saudi Arabian security forces.

In early April 2005, Saudi security forces entered into a large armed battle with al-Qaeda militants in the city of ar-Rass, a city known as a centre of Islamic fundamentalist activity. As of April 5th, official sources indicated that 10 militants had been killed in the battle and ensuing standoff. Saudi media reported that among the dead was group leader Saud bin-Hammoud al-Otaibi.

The group has had a slew of leaders over the past few years as many prominent key figures in the organisation have been killed or captured by Saudi security forces as part of a crackdown on terrorism.

Also known as the Qaedat al-Jihad in the Arabian Peninsula, Al-Qaeda in the Land of the Two Holy Places, the Qaedat al-Jihad in the Land of the Haramain (Two Holy Places), the Fallujah Squadron (Cell Name), the Al-Haramain Brigades (Cell Name), the Al-Quds Brigade (Cell Name).

al Qaeda Sleeper Cell

Continent: North America
Country: United States of America
Background:

Attacks on the West have been conducted through two different types of terrorist organisations: the sleeper cell and the hit squad. The term "sleeper cell" means different things to different people, and is used to reference a variety of threats. Sleeper cells are groups of terrorists who are already in place and ready to act, as opposed to hit squads which are infiltrated into the target country shortly before an attack. Sleeper cells are trained and ready to carry out attacks at a designated time and place. According to some, the teams assembled in Nairobi and Dar es Salaam were classic al-Qaeda sleeper cells. Sleeper cells are loosely organised, and blend into communities easier through legitimate employment. There is very little to differentiate the embassy bombers from the September 11th teams. But some regard one or both as sleeper cells, while others classify one or both as mission specific outside hit squads. The Achilles heel of the later is an inability to cross international borders without attracting attention. The threat from the former is that they are effectively invisible until it is too late.

Prior to September 11th, counter-terrorism czar Richard Clarke mentioned to National Security Advisor Rice at least twice that al Qaeda sleeper cells were likely in the United States. In January 2001, Clarke forwarded a strategy paper to Rice warning that al Qaeda had a presence in the United States. After September 11 the Department of Justice was concerned about the possibility of additional terrorist attacks. There was great concern that additional "terrorist sleeper-cells" might become active and perpetrate further attacks. The FBI immediately sought to shut down any "sleeper" cells of terrorists who might be preparing another wave of violence. Sleeper cells are lodged in the immigrant communities. These have included the

Brooklyn cells in the first World Trade Centre bombing and the plot to bomb New York City landmarks, the Lyon cell in the 1994-96 attacks on French trains and the Meliani cell broken up across Europe in 2000-2001. Sleeper cells could develop from Muslim charities, foundations, academic groups and non-government organisations. Alienated segments of Muslim immigrant communities constitute a possible source of sleeper cells.

Al-Quds Brigade

Continent: Middle East
Country: Israel, Lebanon, Syria, West bank/Gaza
Background:

The al-Quds (Jerusalem) Brigades are the armed wing of Palestinian Islamic Jihad (PIJ). The al-Quds Brigades were previously known as the Sayf al-Islam Brigades and then al-Qassam. Unlike some terrorist organisations such as Hamas and Hezbollah, the PIJ does not maintain both an armed organisation and a separate network for social and political services. Therefore, there is not a significant difference between the al-Quds Brigades and PIJ as a whole.

According to an al-Quds Brigades commander, the military wing of PIJ has regional staff commands. Every member of the staff command is responsible for a cell that operates within the command's region and is at the head of a pyramid in that cell. The staff commanders monitor and carry out operations based on political decisions made by the PIJ leadership. All coordination among the cells takes place through the staff command.

The al-Quds Brigades' umbrella organisation, PIJ, is a violent offshoot of the Muslim Brotherhood, a Sunni Islamist religious movement that originated in Egypt and seeks broad social, moral, and political reforms based upon Islam. The PIJ is one faction within a loosely organised, highly secretive group of Islamic Jihad movements that span the Middle East.

The PIJ was founded in the late 1970s by a group of radical Palestinian activists living in Egypt led by Fathi Shaqaqi and Sheikh Abd al-Aziz Awda. Shaqaqi and Awda believed that the Muslim Brotherhood movement had become too moderate and had abandoned the Palestinian cause. PIJ believes that the annihilation of Israel and liberation of all of Palestine are prerequisites for recreating a pan-Islamic empire. PIJ stresses that the Arab-Israeli conflict is not a national dispute over territory but rather a fundamentally religious conflict. The group rejects any political arrangements or diplomatic activity to solve the conflict. PIJ believes that jihadist violence will inspire Palestinians to action and lead to the eventual destruction of Israel.

PIJ remains a relatively small organisation with a limited base of support.

PIJ remains dedicated to the violent destruction of Israel, shows no interest in joining the political process within the Palestinian territories, and will likely continue its attempts to injure Israel through acts of terrorism by its military wing, the al-Quds Brigades.

The construction of security fences by Israel along both the West Bank and Gaza border has made it more difficult for the al-Quds Brigades to execute terrorist attacks in Israel properly. However, Israel's large scale military operation against Hezbollah in the summer of 2006 triggered an increase in al-Quds Brigades' attacks. On the 2nd August 2006, they claimed responsibility for a rocket attack that struck an Israeli power plant in Ashkelon in southern Israel. Then on August 14th the al-Quds Brigades, along with other Palestinian terrorist organisations, claimed joint responsibility for setting up an ambush near an Israeli patrol near the southern gate of the Sofa military post. As such, the al-Quds Brigades and the PIJ as a whole remain a legitimate security threat in both the Palestinian territories as well as Israel proper.

Also known as Al-Qassam, Jerusalem Battalions, Jerusalem Brigades, Sayf al-Islam Brigades, al-Quds Battalions

Al Sadr Brigades

Continent: Middle East
Country: Lebanon, Syria
Background:

The al-Sadr Brigades formed after the mysterious disappearance of Lebanese Shiite spiritual leader Iman Musa al-Sadr. Al-Sadr, along with two companions, vanished during a visit to Libya in August of 1978. The al-Sadr Brigades is likely comprised of a small number of al-Sadr's supporters who may also be members of the terrorist group Amal, though the organisation's size and structure are not known. Lebanese Shiites have long suspected Libyan strongman Muammar al-Qaddafi of ordering al-Sadr's abduction and murder, though Libya insists al-Sadr boarded a plane to Rome following his arrival in Libya. However, Italian authorities found no evidence that he visited Rome. Al-Sadr had gone to Libya in an attempt to smooth over relations with Qaddafi, allegedly stemming from a personal dispute between the two men. Though the grounds for the clash are the subject of much speculation, it is clear that Qaddafi underestimated the international implications of abducting al-Sadr. The feud may also have arisen from religious differences, as Qaddafi leads an overwhelmingly Sunni nation, while al-Sadr headed a Shiite militia.

The al-Sadr Brigades' expressed aim is to secure Iman Musa al-Sadr's freedom. Using its contacts with other Shiite groups, such as Amal and

Hezbollah, the al-Sadr Brigades has pressured Libya to disclose al-Sadr's whereabouts. The group has also threatened to assault Libyan diplomatic personnel in Lebanon and promised to attack the Libyan embassy in Beirut were it to reopen. In 1984, the al-Sadr Brigades orchestrated the kidnapping of a Libyan diplomat, demanding the removal of all Libyan diplomatic personnel from Lebanon. After Libya complied, the diplomat was released. A similar attack occurred in 1988, when the Brigades kidnapped an alleged Libyan intelligence agent. The al-Sadr Brigades has also publicly pressured Hezbollah to arrest Libyan nationals and called for the Iranian government to demand that Libya account for al-Sadr's disappearance.

Continued Lebanese anger about al-Sadr's unknown fate has precipitated two crises in Lebanese-Libyan relations in 2000 and 2003, causing Libya to cease diplomatic relations. In 2002, the al-Sadr Brigades confirmed its long suspected suspicions of Libyan involvement, when Iran confirmed Imam Musa al-Sadr's death at the hands of Libyan agents. Despite this admission, conflicting reports regarding al-Sadr's fate continue to emerge, and the precise details of his disappearance remain unknown.

The al-Sadr Brigades are closely affiliated with Amal, a Shiite paramilitary and terrorist group founded by Imam Musa al-Sadr. Amal is an Arabic acronym for "Afwaj al Muqawama al Lubnaniya", meaning "Lebanese Resistance Brigades" in English. The word "Amal" means "hope" in Arabic. Al-Sadr founded Amal in 1975 to press Shiite influence in Lebanon. After al-Sadr's kidnapping, Amal was beset by internal power struggles and lost members to Iranian-sponsored Hezbollah. Despite this, Amal remains an influential Shiite organisation, due in part to close ties with Hezbollah, a group with similar political goals.

Questions remain as to the al-Sadr brigade's current objectives. Since a public acknowledgement in 2002 of the Imam's death, the group has issued several conflicting statements calling for al-Sadr's release and urging Hezbollah to assist in seeking retribution against the Libyan government. In addition, the al-Sadr saga is a continuing source of tension in Lebanese-Libyan relations. In spite of recent attempts at reconciliation, Former Libyan dictator Muammar al-Qaddafi's regime refused to admit any role in the Imam's disappearance, ensuring the continued enmity of Lebanese Shiites. Thus, future attacks remain a possibility.

B

Babber Khalsa International

Abbreviation: BKI
Continent: Asia
Country: India
Background:

Even after the terrorist-secessionist movement for Khalistan was comprehensively defeated in 1993, there remained a handful of terrorist organisations chiefly supported by Pakistan and some non-resident Indian Sikh groups who continue to propagate the ideology of Khalistan. One of the most prominent among them is the Babbar Khalsa International (BKI). It was among the oldest and most organised Khalistan terrorist groups. The BKI traces its origin to the Babbar Akali Movement of 1920 and is believed to have assumed its present form after the Baisakhi 1978-clashes between the Akhand Kirtani Jatha and Nirankaris and more particularly when some followers of Bibi Amarjit Kaur brought out some leaflets styling themselves as Babbar Khalsa after the killing of Nirankari chief Gurbachan Singh, on the 24th April 1980. Subsequently, the organisation started targeting all those who sympathised with the Nirankaris.

Sukhdev Singh Babbar and Talwinder Singh Parmar were the founding members of this organisation. The first unit of the BKI was founded in Canada in 1981 under the leadership of late Talwinder Singh Parmar. The organisation was active in the USA Canada, the UK, Germany, France, Belgium, Norway, Switzerland and Pakistan. Talwinder Singh Parmar, a co-founder of the BKI, formed the Babbar Khalsa (Parmar) faction in 1992, when he split from the BKI after serious differences erupted between him and its leadership. The Parmar faction has a presence in the UK, Germany, Belgium and Switzerland. The BKI wants an independent Sikh state called Khalistan.

Available evidence at the time suggested that the Babbar Khalsa is part of a terrorist network sponsored by Germany-based terrorist groups as well as Pakistan's external intelligence agency—the Inter Services Intelligence (ISI)—to revive terrorism in the Indian Punjab. The media reported in August 2001 and said a joint committee was formed in Germany to coordinate the activities of major terrorist organisations abroad. Gurdial Singh Lalli of the International Sikh Youth Federation (ISYF), Resham Singh of Babbar Khalsa and Harmeet Singh of Kamagata Maru Dal of Khalistan were the prominent leaders of this committee. The ISI was reportedly keen on forging coordination between Khalistani terrorists, terrorists operating in Jammu and Kashmir and some fundamentalist groups. Interestingly, the Pakistan government appointed Lt. Gen. (Retd.) Javed Nasir, a former chief of the ISI, as the Chairman of Pakistan Gurudwara Prabandhak Committee (PGPC), the body that administers Sikh shrines in Pakistan. The PGPC was formed in 1999. According to intelligence reports, Sikh terrorists camping in Pakistan were working under the direct supervision of General Nasir. Media reports at the time in April 2002 said the ISI has entrusted the Lashkar-e-Toiba (LeT) with the task of reviving terrorism in Punjab. The LeT will impart arms training to groups like the BKI, the ISYF and the Khalistan Zindabad Force (KZF). Reports also stated that the LeT had opened at least eight camps in Pakistan to train the Khalistanis. They were alleged to be at Kot Lakhpat, Chakwal, Gujranwala, Mianwali, Peshawar, Attock, Shahidan Da Banga and Gulbarg in Lahore.

Available evidence at the time also suggested that the BKI had established a nexus with Dawood Ibrahim, the fugitive Indian underworld kingpin residing in Karachi. The terrorists were liaising with the Dawood Ibrahim gang in Mumbai through whom they disposed of stolen cars and trucks to amass money, which was then sent to Wadhwa Sigh for procuring arms and ammunition. Some reports indicated that efforts were made by the ISI to help the BKI establish bases in China, but these initiatives were reportedly thwarted by the Chinese, who were not enthused by the project.

Badermeinhoff Gang

Continent: Europe
Country: Germany
Background:
Founded in the late 1960s, the Baader-Meinhof Group was a violent leftist organisation responsible for several decades of urban terrorism in the Federal Republic of Germany. The group attacked symbols of capitalist authority, including American targets, public buildings in West Germany, and notable German industrialists, charging that West Germany's post-war government was as repressive as Hilter's Nazi regime. Members embraced a blend of anti-capitalist and anarchist beliefs, protesting the Vietnam War and the occupation of Palestine and supporting other prominent leftist causes at the time.

The group referred to themselves as the Rote Armee Fraktion, or Red Army Faction (RAF), after the Japanese Red Army (JRA). The media, wishing not to legitimise the organisation, used the name "Baader-Meinhoff Group" to refer to the RAF.

The Baader-Meinhof Group's founder, Andreas Baader, his girlfriend, Gudrun Ensslin, and two others were the sole members of the group at its inception, bombing a pair of Frankfurt department stores in 1968. The four were imprisoned but released on an appeal which was later overturned, forcing them to go into hiding. Baader was re-arrested in April 1970, though he was able to escape in May with the help of Ensslin and a sympathetic left-wing journalist, Ulrike Meinhof.

Following the escape, Baader, Ensslin, Meinhof, and others trained in terrorist camps in Jordan operated by the Popular Front for the Liberation of Palestine (PFLP). They returned to Germany, where Baader, Ensslin, and a loyal following were responsible for several bombings, which would be sensationalised in the leftist press by Meinhof. The trio was captured in the summer of 1972, leading to the ascension of the RAF's "second generation", zealots dedicated solely to securing the release of the group's former figureheads.

The rise of the second generation marked not only a change in motivation but a change in tactics as well. For the next five years, the RAF went on an assassination and kidnapping spree, successfully targeting prominent executives and public officials. In 1976, Meinhof appeared to have hung herself in her prison cell, prompting a series of rumours regarding her possible extrajudicial execution.

The second generation's campaign culminated in the Deutscher Herbst (German Autumn) of 1977, when the group hijacked a Lufthansa plane with the help of the PFLP as a desperate attempt to free their leaders. Several days after the GSG-9, Germany's elite counter-terrorism unit, successfully stormed the plane, Baader and Ensslin were found dead in their maximum security prison cells. Official sources reported that they had committed suicide when it became apparent that the RAF's plot to free them had failed, though their deaths remain shrouded in controversy.

After the 1977 hijacking, the RAF's popular appeal dwindled steadily, though sporadic assassinations and bombings continued through the 1980s and early 1990s. Finally, in 1998, the group formally disbanded after five years of virtual inactivity.

Also spelt the Baader-Meinhof Group. See the Red Army Faction (RAF).

Bagranyan Battalion

Continent: Asia
Country: Georgia
Background:
The Bagramyan Battalion was composed of ethnic Armenians, living in the "break-away" Abkhazia region of Georgia and dedicated to the cause

of Abkhaz independence. Abkhazia, which sits in the northwest corner of Georgia, along the Black Sea coast, enjoyed more than fifteen years of full autonomy before it was absorbed by the Georgian republic in 1936. The breakup of the USSR in 1989 ushered in a resurgence of Abkhazian nationalism, along with calls for renewed independence from the Georgian government in Tblisi. In the spats of armed confrontation that followed, some ethnic Armenian residents of Abkhazia formed a separate battalion, the Bagramyan Battalion, to help drive the Georgians out. Occasional attacks against targets in Georgia were carried out by the Bagramyan battalion, including a high-profile attack against the administrative building of the village power grid in Mziuri. However, much of the Battalion's activities, like those of other Abkhaz pro-independence forces, have been directed against ethnic Georgians living in Abkhazia. As a result of these ethnic cleansing tactics, hundreds of thousands of ethnic Georgians now live as refugees in Russia and Georgia.

The situation in Abkhazia is tenuous but has stabilised somewhat since Russian peacekeepers were introduced in the late nineties. The Bagramyan Battalion has not been accused of any activities meeting the definition of terrorism since the Mziuri attack in May 1998. No further terrorist attacks are likely.

Balik-Islam

Continent: Asia
Country: Philippines
Background:

'Balik Islam,' are converts or returnees to Islam. Their shared belief is that Filipinos were originally Muslims before Spanish colonisers imposed Catholicism, so they are returning to their faith. An estimated 200,000 Filipinos have converted to Islam since the 1970s, joining about 4 million Muslims from the southern Philippines who are ethnically different from the heavily Christianised areas. At first, their numbers were too small to attract much notice from the authorities. That is, until Philippine Security Forces began focusing on the role of Muslim converts in extremist violence.

What they found was a disturbing pattern: Islamic insurgents were using cells of militant converts as terrorist operatives to strike targets in Manila. Police say a detained Balik Islam militant had confessed to planting a bomb on a ferry that killed more than 100 people in February 2004. Other detainees are linked to a foiled truck bombing in Manila that targeted the US Embassy. Although not all converts can be classified as terrorists there are a striking number that do assist with terrorism. They blend in to a population better and are hard to trace after an incident has occurred. These individuals are going to cause the Philippine and American Governments a lot of problems in the future.

Also known as Reverters, the Balik Islam Group. Also see the Rajah Solaiman Movement (RSM)

Baluch Liberation Army

Abbreviation: BLA
Continent: Asia
Country: Pakistan
Background:

The Baluch Liberation Army (BLA) represents the violent side of the struggle of the Baluch people to gain rights that they claim have been denied to them by the Pakistani government. Sources of discontent in Baluchistan include a desire for increased benefits from the region's mineral resources, an end to discrimination in government recruiting practices, and a more meaningful role for local Baluch government institutions in the construction of the Gwadar port in the region. The Baluch people were also involved in a violent struggle with the Pakistani government and military over these issues in the 1970s.

The group's membership includes many who, although too young to have experienced the Baluchi resistance movement of the 1970s, have lived abroad in the Gulf region and have acquired expertise in arms, ammunition and explosives. The BLA is thought to operate with a loose structure, with small autonomous cells able to carry out acts on their own without directives from above.

The BLA remains a threat to law and order in Baluchistan province. Several factors complicate the situation and could potentially internationalise the conflict. First, Pakistani security forces in Baluchistan are simultaneously fighting both armed Baluchi separatists and remnants of al-Qaeda and the Taliban in this area. Second, Pakistan alleges involvement of the BLA in the bombing at the China-funded Gwadar port. Third, armed Marri Baluch tribesmen who had been in exile in Afghanistan have begun to return to Baluchistan. These tribesmen are suspected of collaborating with the BLA, with whom they openly sympathise, although they have denied any official connection.

The BLA had recently claimed responsibility for the bombing of a crowded market in Quetta, which killed 11 and injured 27. Four vehicles, including a military vehicle, were also destroyed. Pakistani government sources claim that the military vehicle was not the target, while the BLA claimed responsibility but expressed "deep grief over the civilian casualties caused by the blast." Despite BLA's "regret," the group remains an active terrorist threat.

Baluch Liberation Front

Abbreviation: BLF
Continent: Asia
Country: Iran, Pakistan
Background:

The Baluchistan Liberation Front (BLF) separatist group was founded by Jumma Khan Marri in 1964 in Damascus, and played an important role in the 1968-1980 insurgency in Pakistani Baluchistan and Iranian Baluchistan. The BLF had support from Arab nationalist's leaders. Mir Hazar Ramkhani, the father of Jumma Khan Marri, took over the group in the 1980s.

From 1968 to 1973, the BLF was supported by Iraq in an Iranian Baluch revolt; it reduced its support to a low level after Iranian Baluchi leaders made a deal with the Shah of Iran. Iraq kept its ties with Iranian Baluchi and Central Baluchi. In 1973, Iraq supported the Baluchistan Liberation Front in a Central Baluchistan insurgency. In the same year, Pakistani authorities discovered arms in the Iraqi embassy in Islamabad that were intended for the BLF's use in Baluchistan. Pakistani Prime Minister Zulfikar Ali Bhutto dismissed the provincial government of Baluchistan. The move offended the Baluch, who responded by ambushing Pakistani army convoys. Baluchistan entered the Civil war, in which Pakistan deployed more than 80,000 troops in the Baluchi region.

In 1974, the Pakistani army bombed Baluchistan, killing 15,000 civilians. BLF fighters who returned to defend their families and bury the dead were killed in subsequent bombings which killed 5,000 Baluchi fighters. The survivors went to Afghanistan, where Iraq and the Soviet Union helped the BLF to reorganise.

Basque Fatherland and Freedom

Abbreviation: ETA
Continent: Europe
Country: Spain
Background:

Basque Fatherland and Freedom is a nationalist organisation dedicated to a separate nation-state for the Basque people, an ethnic group inhabiting areas of northern Spain and south-western France. There are between 2 and 2.5 million Basques in the region, many of whom speak an indigenous, non-Indo-European language called Euskara. Basque Fatherland and Freedom is usually referred to by its Euskara acronym, ETA.

ETA is one of Europe's most notorious and long-running terror groups.

It was founded in 1958 from the remnants of EKIN, another radical Basque separatist group. Both EKIN and ETA were created because of discontent with the moderate nationalism of the main Basque party, the Basque National Party. Since its founding, ETA has been responsible for hundreds of attacks in Spain, France, and elsewhere. It has also maintained ties with other terrorist groups both inside the Basque region and beyond, including the Irish Republican Army and Venezuela's Red Flag.

The bulk of ETA's attacks have targeted businesses and Spanish government officials, especially members of the security services and the judiciary. Its most common tactics are bombing and assassination. Similar to the IRA, ETA sometimes issues warnings prior to attacks.

The group's most notorious success was the assassination of Admiral Luis Carrero Blanco in December 1973. At the time, Blanco was seen by many as the most likely successor to Spain's dictator, Franco. He was killed when an underground bomb exploded beneath his car. More than twenty years later, ETA nearly assassinated Jose Maria Aznar, an opposition politician who later became prime minister.

The status of the Basque homeland changed significantly with the end of the Franco regime and the return of democracy in 1979. While Franco had sought to suppress Basque nationalism and separatism, the new democratic government offered significant autonomy to the Basque Provinces. In a deal completed in 1980, the Basque region acquired its own parliament, as well as control over taxation. Furthermore, Euskara became more prominent in public culture and education. The new autonomy, however, did not deter the radical separatists that comprised ETA.

ETA's level of activity has ebbed and flowed over the years. The group has attempted several cease-fires, including a 14-month one that lasted until December 1999. While there have been a number of ETA attacks since 2000, the group has claimed fewer victims and is believed to be shrinking. Spanish officials believe that recent crackdowns have led to a serious weakening of the group and sense that its future as a terrorist organisation may be limited. There are more than one hundred suspected ETA members in Spanish prisons today.

In the past several years, ETA has conducted sporadic attacks, including strings of bombings in September 2004, December 2005, and early 2006. However, these bombings were generally preceded by warnings and did not result in any deaths.

In March 2006, ETA declared a permanent cease-fire and expressed a willingness to join the political process. The decision may have been linked to the infamous Madrid train bombings of the 11th March 2004, which killed nearly 200 people. The attack was originally blamed on ETA, though it was soon discovered to be the work of militant Islamists linked to al-Qaeda. Like the Irish Republican Army, ETA leaders may have felt that the mass casualty terrorism practiced by some radical Islamist groups discredited its violent tactics—though this is not known for certain. ETA is famous for its secretive leadership structure.

In June 2007, ETA declared its March 2006 cease-fire null-and-void, though many had seen ETA's December 2006 bombing of an airport parking garage as an indication that the truce would not hold. An ETA spokesperson accused the Spanish government of interfering in Basque local elections as well as continuing with the prosecution and conviction of ETA members during the cease-fire.

It must be noted that ETA did not officially renounce violence or initiate steps to decommission its weapons (as the IRA did in July 2005) as part of its cease-fire declaration. ETA cease-fires have deteriorated into violence before.

Also known as Basque Fatherland and Liberty, Basque Homeland and Freedom, ETA

Bavarian Liberation Army

Abbreviation: BLA
Continent: Europe
Country: Austria
Background:
The Bavarian Liberation Army (BLA) (German: Bajuwarische Befreiungsarmee (BBA)) is an Austrian right-wing militant organisation. Its goal is to create a single, Teutonic, ethnically homogenous state. The BLA claimed responsibility for several letter-bomb attacks in 1995, which killed one German (Munich) and two Hungarian women.

Franz Fuchs, a self-declared BLA operator, was found guilty on the 10th March 2001 of 29 different bombings. Fuchs' attacks, primarily letter bombs, targeted minorities and refugees, as well as Austrian and German advocates for those populations. Fuchs' worst attack killed four Roma in Oberwart in 1995.

Black Brigade

Continent: Middle East
Country: Lebanon
Background:
Active in the mid-1980s, the Black Brigade was a small anti-Libyan terrorist cell that was dedicated to finding Lebanese Shia Imam Moussa Sadr, the founder of the terrorist organisation Amal, who vanished after visiting

Libya in 1978. It was suspected that former Libyan dictator Muammar Qadhafi, with whom Sadr had personal and religious differences, had Sadr killed. Qadhafi insisted that after Sadr's trip, the imam boarded a plane to Rome, though Italian officials have found no evidence to support this claim.

Due to the Black Brigade's small size, very limited number of attacks, and interests parallel to those of Amal, it can be inferred that some, if not all, Black Brigade members were also members of Amal. In the five years immediately following the imam's disappearance, a total of seven planes either belonging to Libyan Airlines, flying to Libya, or flying out of Libya were hijacked by Amal. These represented ultimately unsuccessful attempts to forcefully coerce Qadhafi to cooperate in the search for Sadr. Several Black Brigade gunmen attempted to secure the release of two Amal terrorists imprisoned in Cyprus for one of these hijackings by hijacking a Cyprus Airways plane en route to Libya. Black Brigade members were also responsible for other anti-Libyan actions, such as the attempted bombing of the Libyan Embassy in Beirut in 1983.

In 2002, Iran announced that it believed Sadr was killed by Libyan agents, though opinions on the imam's fate vary widely. To this day, Colonel Qadhafi maintains that Sadr returned safely from Libya and that he knows nothing about the imam's current location. The Black Brigade disappeared in the mid-1980s, and its members most likely were absorbed by larger Shia terrorist groups such as Hezbollah. For these reasons, attacks claimed by the Black Brigade are very unlikely to reappear, though attacks in the name of the imam may continue.

Also known as Black Brigades of Lebanon (BBL), Christian Anti-Moslem Organisation (CAO, CAMO), Lebanese Black Brigades (LBB)

Black Liberation Army

Abbreviation: BLA
Continent: North America
Country: United States of America
Background:

The Black Liberation Army was a militant splinter group of the Black Panther Party. Breaking away from the Black Panthers in the late 1960s, the stated philosophy of the BLA was to "take up arms for the liberation and self-determination of black people in the United States."

In the 1970s the BLA was responsible for numerous domestic criminal acts, including bank and armoured car robberies. In one of their more famous exploits, members of the BLA freed fellow BLA member Joanne Chesimard from prison where she was serving a life sentence for the murder of a state trooper. Chesimard fled to Cuba, where she is still living, and the US government has offered a reward of $1 million dollars for her capture. Members of the BLA were also charged in various terrorist plots including a plan to firebomb department stores in New York. In 1981, four members of the BLA were convicted for various charges including murder and armed robbery in a failed heist of a Brinks armoured car, which left one guard and two police officers dead. On the 25th March 1984, a man claiming to be "Lieutenant Spartacus" of the "Black Liberation Army," hijacked a Piedmont airlines jet with 58 passengers on board. The plane flew to Cuba where "Lieutenant Spartacus" found asylum. By the mid 1980s, with many of their members in jail or in exile, the BLA ceased to exist.

Also known as Afro-American Liberation Army

Black September Organisation

Abbreviation: BSO
Continent: Middle East
Country: Jordon, Lebanon, West Bank/Gaza
Background:

The Black September Organisation (BSO) was formed in 1971 as a clandestine wing of al-Fatah. BSO was founded with the objective to avenge the expulsion of the Palestine Liberation Organisation (PLO) from Jordan in September of 1970. This time was referred to as "Black September," hence the name chosen by the Black September Organisation. While Black September was originally described as a splinter group of al-Fatah, direct linkages between the groups were revealed with the arrests of BSO agents. Al-Fatah formed Black September in order to circumvent an al-Fatah declaration that they would not interfere in the domestic policies of Arab nations. However, some al-Fatah members planned to assassinate King Hussein, ruler of Jordan from 1953 to 1999. Hence, Black September was partially formed in order to pursue this specific objective.

While Black September failed several times to assassinate King Hussein, the group is notorious for a number of brutal, high-profile terrorist incidents. Black September expanded their list of targets from the Jordanian government to include Israeli and U.S. citizens and facilities. The group also carried out attacks against general "Western" targets. Black September is infamous for its attack against Israeli athletes and coaches at the 1972 Munich Olympics. In retaliation for the attacks against Israel citizens and facilities, Israel launched a significant response to eliminate the terrorist organisation. Israeli security forces retaliated against BSO terrorists in

Western Europe and Lebanon. Following the Israeli response, al-Fatah dissolved Black September in December 1974.

Upon al-Fatah's decision to dissolve Black September, many of the BSO members joined the Popular Front for the Liberation of Palestine (PFLP) and other active terrorist organisations. Attacks in the name of Black September continued long after the official dissolution. Black September is linked to attacks that occurred as late as 1988. Some terrorism officials believe these attacks were actually carried out by terrorists affiliated with other groups. Regardless, Black September is now inactive.

See the Fatah, Abu Nidal Organisation, 15 May Organisation, Arab Revolutionary Brigades (ARB), Revolutionary Organisation of Socialist Muslims (ROSM).

Black Star

Continent: Europe
Country: Greece
Background:

During the period between May of 1999 and October of 2002, Black Star was one of the most active terrorist groups in Greece. They are anti-American, anti-establishment, and anti-capitalist. The group has declared itself to be dedicated to "resistance against the mass organisations of US imperialism and to their local collaborators." (Morou, 7th October 2002) They believe that "the only terrorists are the US imperialist forces, their European allies, and their local capitalist associates." (FBIS London Bureau, 22nd June 2000) Black Star often demands the release of an imprisoned leftist "hero" (such as Dimitris Koufondinas, Simeon Seisidis, and Mumia Abu-Jamal) when calling to claim responsibility for an attacks. The group's favorite targets are the cars of embassies and diplomats, but they have also attacked the offices and cars of international organisations and businesses. One of their earliest attacks was against the Greek-Israeli Friendship Association, which may indicate that Black Star is anti-Israel.

Black Star's campaign of terror can be divided into two periods. During 1999, they attacked at least three times, and on all three occasions they used gas-canister bombs and attacked a building. The second period began in June of 2000. Between June and September of that year, Black Star attacked at least eight times, and on all eight occasions their chosen technique was setting cars on fire. This change in the group's methods and the six month period of inactivity at the beginning of 2000 suggests that the group may have been going through some kind of internal struggle or change. The group was inactive again for more than two years after September of 2000, but re-emerged in October of 2002 to show solidarity with Dimitris

Koufondinas (a member of the group 17N who had recently been arrested) by attacking a car with US license plates.

Also known as Mavro Asteri (Greek)

Black Panthers

Continent: North America
Country: United States of America
Background:

The Black Panther Party was formed in October 1966 in Oakland, California. The organisation, formed by Huey Percy Newton and Bobby Seale, supported Black Nationalism in the United States and criticised the U.S. as a racist, capitalist state. The Black Panthers believed that the United States government and economic structure systematically oppressed black people. Thus, the Black Panthers' "Ten Points," which detailed the group's beliefs and objectives, demanded freedom for all imprisoned blacks, exemption of black people from military service, and full employment of the black population. The Ten Points also reflect the group's leanings towards communism.

While the Black Panthers always advocated self-defence (in fact, the group's original name was the Black Panther Party for Self-Defence), the group stepped up its aggressive tactics following the April 1968 assassination of Martin Luther King, Jr. The Black Panthers did not subscribe to King's belief in non-violent protest, and began to arm their group members and provide military training. The Black Panthers gained support from some Americans due to their confrontational approach, as well as their programs for lower-class people such as the Free Breakfast for Children program. Beyond the Black Panthers' militaristic speech, certain group members had criminal records and had even jumped bail. This situation led to a series of confrontations with police, wherein both police officers and Black Panthers were killed. The police confrontations and internal fractionalisation severely limited the Black Panthers' operational capabilities. In the late 1960s and early 1970s, the Black Panthers leadership fled the country or went into hiding within the U.S. There were a series of high-profile airline hijackings; Black Panthers forced planes to Cuba, Algeria and North Korea, where they requested political asylum.

The Black Panthers had approximately 2,000 members in 1970, spread out throughout the United States. However, due to efforts by law enforcement and internal Black Panther rivalries, the group's leadership had either been captured or killed, or was in hiding or had fled the United States entirely by the early 1970s. By 1972, the Black Panthers was no longer operational. Some former Black Panthers members then joined the terrorist organisation, Black Liberation Army. The New Black Panthers, formed in the 1990s, is not associated with the Black Panther Party of the 1960s-1970s.

Also known as Black Panther Party for Self-Defence

Black Widow

Continent: Asia
Country: Chechnya, Russia
Background:

The Black Widows are female suicide bombers, usually of Chechen origin, many of whom lost husbands in the Chechen wars against Russia. In the Russian media, the term has been applied to any female suicide bomber regardless of ethnicity, as fears have increased of ethnic Russians converting to Islam and joining terrorist groups. Although some see the Black Widows as more of an overall phenomenon rather than an organised group, some attacks have been claimed by an entity calling itself the "Black Widows Brigade."

The first known "Black Widow" was Khava Barayeva, who blew herself up at a Russian military base in Chechnya in June 2000. An alert was issued to Russian security services in early 2004 for a woman popularly referred to as "Black Fatima," who was thought to be one of the principal recruiters of suicide bombers inside Russia. Many Chechen widows have been convinced by separatists that they have become burdens and that the loss of their husband was a punishment for their sins, leaving suicide bombing as their last resort. Some claim that potential suicide bombers are drugged and coerced into action and that extensive brainwashing techniques have been used on these women.

Leaders of the Chechen resistance movement have been split on the issue of the Black Widows. Recently deceased political leader Aslan Maskhadov, who had been acting as Chechen President, had disavowed connections to the Black Widows, although this claim was denied by Russian security officials. Warlord Shamil Basayev, the man responsible for the 2002 Dubrovka Theatre siege and the Beslan school massacre, has supported their actions, and has claimed to have personally trained 50 Black Widows.

Violence in the Caucasus region and the threat of suicide bombings continue to plague the region. Reports indicate that hundreds have died in these female suicide attacks, including approximately 150 in the summer of 2003 alone. The Black Widows will undoubtedly continue to gain recruits as the reservoir of widowed Chechen women grows commensurate to the death of rebel Chechen fighters. Officials in Moscow widely regard them as an active threat to peace and security in the region.

Also known as Chyornyye Vdovy

Boricua Popular Army

Continent: North America
Country: Puerto Rico, United States of America
Background:

The Boricua Popular/People's Army (Ejército Popular Boricua in Spanish) is a clandestine organisation based on the island of Puerto Rico, with cells throughout the United States. They campaign for and support the independence of Puerto Rico from what they characterise as United States colonial rule. The United States Federal Bureau of Investigation (FBI) classifies the Boricua Popular Army as a terrorist organisation.

Also known as Los Macheteros ("the Machete Wielders") and 'Puerto Rican Popular Army', their active membership is consisted by Puerto Rican men and women and was calculated by professor Michael González Cruz on his book Nacionalismo Revolucionario Puertorriqueño to be composed by approximately 5,700 members with an unknown number of supporters, sympathisers, collaborators and informants, with cells (usually consisting of between six and ten members) in the United States and other countries. Although a report by The Economist locates the number of active members at 1,100 excluding supporters. The group has claimed responsibility for numerous bombings, attacks against the U.S. military and armed robberies since 1978, and was led primarily by former FBI Most Wanted Fugitive Filiberto Ojeda Ríos until his death in 2005.

Also known as Los Macheteros (Machete Wielders)

Breton Revolutionary Army

Abbreviation: ARB
Continent: Europe
Country: France
Background:

The Armee Revolutionnaire Bretonne (ARB), or Breton Liberation Army, was created in 1971 as the armed wing of the Front de Liberation Breton (FLB), aka Breton Liberation Front. FLB had been established in 1963 to try and achieve the liberation of Brittany from France. The pro-independence, anticapitalist group Emgann ("Combat"), created in 1982, is considered the official front for the ARB. The group began its terrorist activities with a bombing in Roc-Tredudon in 1974, and an attack on the Chateau of Versailles in June of 1978. The group is believed to have been responsible for more than 200 attacks over the next 30 years. Until 2000, however, the group had successfully avoided human casualties (with the exception of two of its own members who were killed trying to defuse bombs they were afraid might injure someone), although they inflicted a significant amount of damage to property. In April of 2000, a McDonald's waitress died when a bomb blew up in her face as she opened a serving hatch at the restaurant in Quevert.

The group's strategy seems to have changed in the late 1990s, when it developed links with the Basque separatist movement ETA and helped the group to steal eight tons of dynamite from a quarry in Brittany. In July of 1998, the group gave an exclusive interview to a Basque paper "Gara," in which it claimed responsibility for a recent wave of attacks. The ARB said it would no longer limit itself to just symbolic actions, that (the government in) Paris never budged unless it believed it was under attack, and that the group would therefore pursue that goal.

The bombing of the McDonald's in Quevert coincided with the discovery of an unexploded bomb at a post office in Rennes. Both bombs contained explosives from the eight-ton cache that was stolen by Breton and Basque nationalists in 1999. The McDonald's attack was the last of almost 20 over an 18-month period between late 1998 and April of 2000. Targets included administrative offices, police precincts and utility installations, as well as the home towns of then-Prime Minister Lionel Jospin and Interior Minister Jean-Pierre Chevenement. The attack on the McDonald's is significant in that it would mark a turn toward anti-American and antiglobalisation goals. Four men were arrested, including Gael Roblin, 31, the spokesman of the main Breton autonomy movement, Emgann ("Combat"), which the prosecutors claim provided "theoretical justification" for a campaign of bombings, and Christian Georgeault, 48, the suspected ARB ringleader and former Emgann general secretary. All of the suspects denied ARB membership and responsibility for the attack.

Bretons have been fighting for independence since the region first unified under the Crown of France in 1524. The region lost all administrative autonomy in 1789, and the Breton language, related to Welsh and Cornish, was banned. Today, however, Brittany has as much autonomy as other French regions, and most town halls fly Brittany's black and white flag alongside the French official flag. In 1999, the ARB reiterated its goals to a Basque newspaper, saying, "France is not a dictatorship, but nor is there complete democracy in Brittany. When the French Constitution recognises the existence of a Breton people, the integrity of our territory, the Breton language, the conditions for a real democratic debate will be reunited. An armed struggle seems to us the only efficient means to obtain these conditions."

Also known as the Breton Resistance Army, Emgann

Brigades of Martyr Ahmed Yassin

Continent: Middle East
Country: Iraq
Background:

The Brigades of Martyr Ahmed Yassin was a previously unknown group that claimed responsibility for the killing of four U.S. security contractors in Fallujah, Iraq.

In March 2004, masked men ambushed a convoy of security contractors from the firm Blackwater Security Consulting as they drove through the restive streets of Fallujah, a hotbed of Iraqi resistance. The assailants raked the convoy with gunfire and threw grenades in to the vehicles, killing four of the six passengers. After the attack, the bodies of some of the victims were dragged through the streets by a mob, mutilated, and hung from a bridge.

Shortly after the killings, the Brigades of Martyr Ahmed Yassin claimed responsibility for the attack. The group said it was in response to the killing of Sheik Ahmed Yassin several days earlier by the Israeli military. Yassin was the spiritual leader of HAMAS, a Palestinian group responsible for hundreds of terrorist attacks. In a statement of claim, the group remarked that the killings were "a gift from the people of Fallujah to the people of Palestine and the family of Sheikh Ahmed Yassin who was assassinated by the criminal Zionists." The group also called for an end to the U.S. occupation of Iraq, but did not elucidate a specific ideology beyond these statements.

While the ambush of the contractors was well-planned, it is unlikely that the Brigades of Martyr Ahmed Yassin had been established before this incident. The ambush was just one in a series of attacks by multiple perpetrators on U.S. military and affiliated targets in Fallujah. It is possible that the Brigades took the opportunity to claim this incident as a way of venting anger over Yassin's death, and the actual perpetrators of this attack may not have been responsible for the public statements of claim. While it can't be proven that the Brigades of Martyr Ahmed Yassin was not actually an established organisation, the group has not been responsible for further attacks, and has not released any other public statements. Whether or not the Brigades of Martyr Ahmed Yassin was the actual perpetrator of the ambush incident, the group has not been heard from since, and is unlikely to re-emerge in the future.

Cambodian Freedom Fighters

Abbreviation: CFF
Continent: Asia
Country: Cambodia, United States of America
Background:

The Cambodian Freedom Fighters (CFF) are a militant organisation based in Long Beach, California that are dedicated to the overthrow of Cambodia's government. The group cites corruption, mismanagement, and perpetuation of inequality as some of the faults of the current regime, led by Prime Minister Hun Sen. CFF's leader is a middle-aged Cambodian-American accountant named Chhun Yasith. From his home in California, Yasith directs a network-in-place that stretches across North-eastern Cambodia and over the Thai border. Its members include Cambodian-Americans based in Thailand and the US, as well as former soldiers from the Khmer Rouge and Royal Cambodian Armed Forces. The group reportedly has nineteen brigades of unknown size, each led by a commander. In 1998, a world conference of all these commanders was held in Thailand to elect a board of directors. While the prospect of a terrorist group led by an accountant provoked smirks initially, the increasing violence of CFF activities has convinced Hun Sen's administration that the group represents a serious security threat.

The group's "coming out" occurred in November 2000, when seventy CFF militiamen led a coordinated attack on government buildings in Phnom Penh, killing at least eight people and causing significant damage to the facilities. One year later, the group exploded grenades near six government buildings. Luckily there were no fatalities. Cambodian President Hun Sen issued a warrant for the arrest of Chhun Yasith after the 2000 attack, but he has been unable to persuade the United States, which does not have an extradition treaty with Cambodia, to give him up.

Since 2001, the CFF has been inactive. The events of the 11th September 2001, and the subsequent announcement of a US-led global war on terrorism, has made it difficult for the US to turn a blind eye to Chunn Yasith's activities. Although Yasith remains in the country, his ability to stay here has been made conditional on the cessation of his involvement with all terrorism. No further attacks are expected.

Also known as the Cholana Kangtoap Serei Cheat Kampouchea

Canadian Hungarian Freedom Fighters Association

Abbreviation: CHFFF
Continent: North America
Country: Canada
Background:

The Canadian Hungarian Freedom Fighters Federation (CHFFF) was a small group of Hungarian expatriates in Canada. The "group" received notoriety in 1971 when one of their members (or perhaps their only member) Geza Matrai, jumped on Soviet Premier Alexei Kosygin's back and screamed "Long live Hungary," as Kosygin walked with Canadian PM Pierre Trudeau on an official visit to the Canadian Parliament. Kosygin was unharmed, and Matrai was sentenced to three months in jail. Matrai later ran unsuccessfully for a regional parliament seat in Toronto, but the CHFFF has not been heard from since the Kosygin incident. The Canadian Hungarian Freedom Fighters Federation is inactive.

Canary Islands Independence Movement

Continent: Africa, Europe
Country: Algeria, Spain
Background:

The Canary Islands Independence Movement was an ethnic Berber group that most likely surfaced in Algeria during the 1950s. Their primary goal was to create an autonomous state for native Berbers living on the Canaries. At the time the Islands were a territory ruled by the kingdom of Spain, and had been since the 1400s. After World War II, ethnic groups like the Berbers were severely repressed by the Spanish-controlled Franco regime, causing militants to become organised and take up arms against the dictatorship.

The Movement's first known attack took place on 3rd January 1977, when the Las Palmas (capital city of Grand Canary island) offices of South African Airways (SAL) were bombed. No injuries resulted from the attack, but there was significant property damage. Members of the Canary Islands Independence Movement did not state their reason for attacking SAL, but their decision was possibly linked to the airline's alleged discriminatory practice of flying only to certain African countries in which white people were likely to visit.

A second attack claimed by the Canary Islands Independence Movement occurred on the 27th March 1977, when a bomb exploded in a florist's shop at the Las Palmas Airport. While there were no fatalities, eight people were seriously injured. Subsequent threats of a second bomb in the airport forced Las Palmas' law enforcement to cease all air traffic to and from the airport until an investigation could be completed. All inbound flights were then re-routed to the Los Rodeos Airport on the neighbouring island of Tenerife. The Los Rodeos airport quickly became congested, causing flight delays in excess of eight hours. A Pan Am and KLM airplane, both 747 jumbo jets, collided on the Los Rodeos runway while preparing for takeoff. Later investigations indicated that as the KLM aircraft was taking off, it collided with the Pan Am aircraft that was taxiing on the tarmac. The accident was attributed to highly saturated use of the Los Rodeos Airport and dense fog that caused limited visibility. The investigation concluded that had the Las Palmas Airport not been closed due to the terrorist attack, the two airplanes may not have been using the Tenerife airport. The collision, which resulted in the deaths of 583 people, remains one of the largest disasters in aviation history.

The Canary Islands Independence Movement has been inactive since the late 1970s. Shortly after the death of Francisco Franco, a democratic constitutional monarchy was implemented in Spain that led to the creation of an autonomous Canaries Archipelago in 1982. Since gaining autonomy most militant groups that were active in the 1970s most likely ceased planning attacks and instead linked up with various political groups on the islands.

Also known as Movement for the Independence and Autonomy of the Canaries Archipelago

Carapaica Revolutionary Movement

Continent: South America
Country: Venezuela
Background:
The Carapaica Revolutionary Movement is a terrorist organisation operating in Caracas, Venezuela. The group supports the current government of President Hugo Chavez. While this organisation is not a member of the Bolivarian Circles, it does support the constitutionality of Chavez's rule and contests any efforts to remove Chavez from power. The Carapaica Revolutionary Movement has gone as far as attacking the Caracas Metropolitan Police because of the police's participation in controlling pro-Chavez street demonstrations. The Carapaica Revolutionary Movement also criticises the political organisation, Bandera Roja, for its alleged support of the Chavez opposition forces.

The membership of the Carapaica Revolutionary Movement is highly speculative. In August 2002, Venezuela's Scientific and Criminal Investigations

Corps (CICPC) claimed that several Carapaica members possessed criminal records for homicide, rape, and armed robbery. CICPC also indicated that some Carapaica members were dissident members of another Caracas terrorist organisation, the Tupamaro Revolutionary Movement. In a separate development, a group of women staged a November 2002 press conference to announce themselves as the female guerrilla wing of the organisation.

These descriptions and examples of the group's membership notwithstanding, in September 2002 STRATFOR Strategic Forecasting cited intelligence reports that the Carapaica Revolutionary Movement is principally comprised of former Venezuelan army personnel. The intelligence report estimates the group membership at 40 people. Finally, the report cites a direct link to the Chavez government, stating that the Venezuelan Interior and Justice Ministry trained and equipped this terrorist group. For its part, representatives of the Venezuelan government deny any relationship with the group. Furthermore, an official of the Interior and Justice Ministry publicly warned the Carapaica Revolutionary Movement that continued criminal violence by the group would be punished.

The current activities of the Carapaica Revolutionary Movement are not fully known. The group was implicated in an incident in 2003, although that linkage was not proven and could be tenuous. President Hugo Chavez remains in power, and there have been no indications that the Carapaica Revolutionary Movement has diminished its support for the embattled leader.

Also known as Carapaica Revolutionary Group

Che Guevara Anti-Imperialist Command

Continent: South America
Country: Argentina
Background:

The Che Guevara Anti-Imperialist Command is a terrorist organisation that operates in Argentina. It is named after Ernesto Guevara de la Serna (commonly known as Che Guevara), the iconic socialist revolutionary leader. In its history, the Che Guevara Anti-Imperialist Command has been associated with five attacks, four conducted on the same day. The organisation claimed responsibility for its first attack on the 25th July 2005, when two homemade bombs exploded outside the Buenos Aires City Legislature, damaging the building. Leaflets signed by the Che Guevara Commando left at the scene demanded the release of political prisoners who were arrested on the 16th July 2004 for attacking the legislature. Protests against the legislature's move to change the city's civil code had turned violent and resulted in the incarceration of 17 individuals.

Two Citibank branches, a Blockbuster video store, and a Ford car dealership were targeted on the 6th October 2005 in the group's second attack. The targets were bombed with rudimentary homemade incendiary devices. Conducted in the early morning hours, the bombings took place one day after the White House confirmed US President George W. Bush's visit to Argentina for the Summit of the Americas held in November 2005. Leaflets found at the scene of three of the bombings (the Citibank branches and Blockbuster) with anti-Bush and "anti-imperialism" slogans were signed either Che Guevara Anti-Imperialist Command or Colonel Dorrego Anti-Imperialist Command. In this case, "Colonel Dorrego" probably refers to one of the administrative centres of Buenos Aires, named for a former governor. It is likely that the Che Guevara and Colonel Dorrego Anti-Imperialist Commands are the same organisation.

The attacks conducted by the Che Guevara Anti-Imperialist Command were only several of the many demonstrations, both violent and peaceful, aimed at protesting the Summit of the Americas meeting and President Bush. Popular demonstrations against globalisation and the proposed Free Trade Area of the Americas drew thousands of participants. Several demonstrations turned violent when radical groups threw Molotov cocktails at police forces.

Given the group's name, the information divulged in their claim of responsibility, and the targeting of exclusively U.S. assets, it appears that the organisation opposes the Bush Administration, its capitalist interests in Argentina, and potentially globalisation as well. Additionally, the group's use of Che Guevara's name indicates that it may have socialist leanings.

Prior to these attacks, the Che Guevara Anti-Imperialist Command was an unknown entity. In addition, there has been no further public mention of the group since the attacks. As such, it remains unclear whether or not the group still exists. There is a possibility that the group had been formed merely to conduct those specific attacks and express public frustration over President Bush's visit and the Summit of the Americas. Achieving those objectives, the group may have ceased to exist. However, it is possible that the group or individuals associated with the group will conduct further attacks to protest the Bush Administration, "imperialism", and capitalism in the future.

Also known as Che Guevara Commando, Colonel Dorrego Anti-Imperialist Command

Christian Identity

Continent: North America
Country: United States of America
Background:

There is no single founder of the movement (Some think it to be Wesley Swift born in the 1800's. Others claim it can be traced back to the 1600's.), which developed over a period of seventy years and is still changing. Three people who were significant to its evolution are Reverend John Wilson, Edward Hine, and Howard Rand. Wilson and Hine began the movement as British Israelism in 1840. It developed into the Identity Movement when Howard Rand founded the Anglo-Saxon Federation of America in 1930 with the help of Wesley Swift, who was a member of the KKK. Later, Swift founded his own church, called the Church of Jesus Christ Christian, which developed into the Aryan Nations.

This movement has its origins in the 1800's America where it grew in the shadow of this country's developing and successful conquering of the American continent combined with racial prejudices. Many of the whites believed that North America was ordained by God and blessed by Him to be supreme in the world. All other racial groups were considered inferior. Early contributing movements to C.I.M. were the Nativist movement and Anglo Israelism.

Nativism was a philosophy that those not born in America (excluding American Indians) and were not Protestant, were harmful to the American System. In particular, a strong anti-catholic disposition was advocated. Manifestations of this philosophy resulted in physical persecutions of many Catholics in New York.

Anglo Israelism (also known as British Israelism) is the belief that the British and, therefore, the Americans and Canadians, are the true descendants of the ancient Israelites — the 10 lost tribes. The present Jews in Israel are really a false group descended from Cain. Identity believers usually act out their faith through social, military, and political agendas.

An early proponent of this movement, Charles Carroll, wrote a book called The Negro a Beast. He considered Negroes to be subhuman. The KKK is usually associated with this group.

The Christian Identity religion asserts that whites, not Jews, are the true Israelites favoured by God in the Bible. In most of its forms, Identity theology depicts Jews as biologically descended from Satan, while non-whites are seen as soulless "mud people" created with the other Biblical "beasts of the field." Christian Identity has its roots in a 19th-century English fad called British Israelism, which asserted that European whites were descended from the ten "lost tribes" of Israel and were thus related to Jews, who were descended from the other two Hebrew tribes mentioned in the Bible. But British Israelism, which was initially friendly to Jews, was adopted and transformed in the 20th century into a rabidly anti-Semitic creed by a number of racist preachers in the United States.

For decades, identity has been one of the most important ideologies for the white supremacist movement. In its hardest line form, it asserts that Christ will not return to earth until the globe is swept clean of Jews and other "Satanic" fluencies. In recent years, deep doctrinal disputes, the lack of a central church structure, and a shift among white supremacists towards agnosticism and racist variations of neo-Paganism have weakened the Identity movement and reduced the number of its adherents. The total number of groups counted in 2001 was 31.

The Christian Identity Movement is comprised of many radical fundamentalist Christian churches, extreme right-wing political groups, and survival groups. It is a complex, highly varied, and loosely organised movement whose fundamental teachings are based on the ideology that Anglo-Saxons are the direct descendents of the Ten Lost Tribes of Israel and are thus the true chosen people of God. Current groups that practice Christian Identity are associated with preaching hate, racism and genocide and condoning violence towards minorities, especially Jews. However, the original movement evolved from the British Israelism movement of the mid-nineteenth century, which did not start as a hate group nor did its leaders preach violence. Christian Identity took shape in early twentieth-century America, when it was influenced by American Nativism, the Ku Klux Klan, and various strands of anti-Semitism. By the 1970s and 1980s, Christian Identity ideology merged with anti-tax and paramilitary movements and rhetoric, and its actions became more violent. In its current form, Christian Identity is the unifying theology for a number of diverse groups; it provides its members with a religious basis for racism and a religious doctrine that allows believers to fuse religion with hate, conspiracy theories, and apocalyptic fear of the future.

The activities of Aryan Nations and similar groups led to a study conducted by the FBI, announced on the 20th October 1999 as "Project Megiddo." This study was intended to alert US law enforcement to what is described as "the potential for extremist criminal activity in the United States by individuals or domestic groups who attach special significance to the year 2000." An accompanying FBI statement mentioned that, "The threat posed by extremists as a result of perceived events associated with the year 2000 is real. The volatile mix of apocalyptic religious and New World Order conspiracy theories may produce violent acts aimed at precipitating the end of the world as prophesied in the Bible." The data for the report was collected over nine months by the FBI's domestic terrorism unit and was not supposed to be made public. However, the Centre for the Study of New Religious Movements, CESNUR, a cult apologist organisation, obtained a copy and placed it on their web site, at http://www.cesnur.org/test/FBI_004.htm . The Christian Identity movement was discussed at length in the Project Megiddo report because of its apocalyptic beliefs.

A theological system centred on a racist/anti-Semitic and white supremacy. It seems to use religious arguments to justify political agendas.

The following beliefs are held in common by most Christian Identity groups:

(1) A very conservative interpretation of the Christian Bible, which is their main sacred text. This interpretation includes a hatred of homosexuality and homosexuals, and a strict rejection of followers of other religions.

(2) A view of the white race, which is sometimes referred to as the Adamic Race or True Israelites, as superior to all others. The view that other races are the satanic spawn of Cain leads to a hatred of African Americans, Native Americans, and any person from "non-Aryan" countries.

(3) The belief that other pre-Adamic and non-white people were already in existence when Adam was created and that Adam and Eve were white. This leads directly to the belief that Anglo-Saxon Protestants are the true descendants of God's chosen people of the Hebrew Scriptures.

(4) That the commandment which forbids adultery does not refer to extramarital affairs but to racial adultery and interracial marriages. The tenth commandment in their view already bans adultery.

(5) That they are the direct descendents of God's chosen people, the Jewish people having descended from Cain. This belief is associated with extreme anti-Semitism within their movement. These beliefs can be summed up in what is referred to as the "two-seedline" doctrine: "Christian Identity followers assert that Adam was preceded by other, lesser races, identified as 'The beasts of the field' (Gen.1:25). Eve was seduced by the snake (Satan) and gave birth to two seed lines: Cain, the direct descendent of Satan and Eve, and Abel, who was of good Aryan stock through Adam. Cain then became the progenitor of the Jews in his subsequent matings with the non-Adamic races. Christian Identity adherents believe the Jews are predisposed to carry on a conspiracy against the Christian identity does not have a national organisational structure; rather, it is a grouping of churches throughout the country that follow its basic ideology. Some of these churches are as small as a dozen people and some have memberships in the thousands. The Southern Poverty Law Centre currently lists 602 active hate groups, of which 32 are specifically identified as Christian Identity groups (http://www.splcenter.org/intelligenceproject/ip-index.html). Some of the better

known organisations that follow Christian Identity beliefs include: Aryan Nations, American Nazi Party, Church of Jesus Christ Christian, Confederate Hammerskins, National Association for the Advancement of White People, Kingdom Identity Ministries, Posse Comitatus, Christian Research, Scriptures for America, White Aryan Resistance (WAR), and White Separatists Banner. Although many Internet search engines will not link to racist web sites, the *Nationalist Observer* prides itself on having the world's largest white racist internet links page: http://www.cwporter.com/RACISTLINKS.html . Recruitment is through extreme right-wing churches, survival groups, and word of mouth. Associates are generally are Ku Klux Klan, Aryan Nation, Nazi Party, White Separatists groups, etc. They link the Old and New Testaments of the Bible; some think sections of the U.S. Constitution were divinely inspired.

Chukakuha

Continent: Asia
Country: Japan
Background:

Chukakuha emerged following a 1957 division within the Japanese Communist Party. The forerunner of the Chukakuha was originally a Japanese Trotskyite organisation. In 1963, that organisation split into two groups, "Chukakuha" and "Kakumaruha." Chukakuha remained true to its communist roots, professing Marxist-Leninist insurgency beliefs. The group was one of 23 factions that comprised the Japanese New Left movement. Chukakuha was the largest of these leftist groups, as well as the largest terrorist insurgent group in Japan. Of the current fifty Japanese "New-Left" groups, Chukakuha remains the largest group. The group professed its communist beliefs through terrorist actions against the Japanese government, U.S. military and domestic facilities, the United Nations, and the G-7 SummiCombined with its communist beliefs, Chukakuha supports the associated cause of "anti-imperialism." The group has criticised what is sees as imperialistic organisations and facilities, such as the U.S.-Japan Security Treaty and transportation projects paid for by the Japanese government. Chukakuha strongly opposes the dispatch of the Japanese Self Defence Force to Iraq. Typically, Chukakuha commits its activities legally. But the group will revert to violent terrorist actions, specifically bombings that target government facilities.

Not to be confused with the separate terrorist organisation "Revolutionary Army (Kakumeigun)," Chukakuha and Kakurokyo have their own unofficial detached forces also called Revolutionary Army (Kakumeigun).

The group has previously shown its terrorist members to number around 200 with the group's overall supporters total approximately 3,500. Chukakuha has displayed reduced operational strength over the last few years, and its current membership is not known.

Also known as the Nucleus Faction, the Middle Core Faction the Central Core Faction, the Kansai Revolutionary Army, League of Revolutionary Communists - National Committee.

Combat 18

Continent: Europe
Country: UK
Background:

Founded as a strong-arm squad for the Nazi British National Party (BNP), C18 has established - frequently accompanied by lurid press headlines - such a formidable international reputation for itself as a violent Nazi hardcore group that others want to follow its example. The founder of C18 was the Nazi soccer hooligan thug and petty criminal Charlie Sargent who was soon joined by others thirsting for violent action on the streets. A key early recruit was Will Browning who took over as C18's leader in 1997 during a murderous feud with Sargent over money gathered from the sales of hate music CDs and other merchandise by ISD Records, the Nazis hated music group. In the conflict, Browning accused Sargent of robbing the movement and funnelling funds into his own pocket. In the ensuing clashes, Sargent and Martin Cross knifed Chris Castle, an ally of Browning, to death.

Before the internal dispute, Combat 18 - which never had formal members - had about eighty activists and about a hundred followers drawn from the BNP, the National Front, football hooligans and the bonehead scene around Blood & Honour, which C18 controlled for a period.

It also made its mark by setting up "Redwatch" - its own version of anti-Antifa - designed to intimidate and terrorise political opponents, Jews, ethnic minorities and police officers. Several C18 activists were subsequently convicted for violent assaults on opponents. As well as attacks on other people, C18 was active in firebombing private homes and the offices of progressive organisations, including the Communist daily paper, the Morning Star.

When not doing that, C18 was busy organising a plot to send letter bombs to its enemies from Scandinavia. Danish Nazi Thomas Nakaba, the man chosen as bomber, was arrested and the planned campaign was stopped before it started. The notion of orchestrated violence, in line with

US Nazi Louis Beam's strategy of "leaderless resistance" had hit the rocks of C18's ineptitude. However, not long after, in 2000, London nail bomber David Copeland, a BNP member, admitted to police before his conviction for the murder of three people, that he was influenced by C18 and the ideas it borrowed from US Nazi's.

C18 had spawned another violent group, the so-called Racial Volunteer Force (RVF). The RVF is linked to C18 but has an independent identity. It was formed by Mark Atkinson and Oldham-based activist John Hill because of their growing frustration Browning's inactivity. Most of the C18 events and socials that occur in Britain today take place under the name of the RVF.

The British authorities were becoming increasingly worried about the RVF's activities which, they believe, is collecting weapons and secretly exchanging bomb designs. Hill was in South Africa during the early 1990s and boasts that he learned bomb-making skills while there. In the spring of 2003, police raided a number of homes of people belonging to the RVF and C18. Among them were Atkinson and Hill.

The police also raided Kenneth Quinn, the leader of the Nazi November 9th Society. Based in Bedford, he was the name behind the RVF website and could yet face charges of distributing racist material on the Internet.

C18/RVF supporters were involved in the safe housing of Loyalist Volunteer Force (LVF) and dissident Ulster Defence Association (UDA) members in Bolton in North-west England.

In another development, the White Nationalist Party (WNP) was formed in Yorkshire as a right wing alternative to the BNP and the NF. Many WNP activists have been involved in the NF but the group is essentially the political wing of C18.

Combat 18 the numbers signify the initials of Adolf Hitler and represents Neo Nazis.

Combat 786

Continent: Europe
Country: United Kingdom
Background:
Combat 786 is an Islamic violent gang operating in the Northern English areas of Bradford and Oldham. It conducts assaults on white youths, justifying these actions as a response to attacks on Muslims by neo-Nazis and skinheads, and its name is a response to that of Combat 18, the gang it sees as its main enemy. 786 is the numerical value of the Arabic phrase at the beginning of the Qur'an, Bismillah al-Rahman al-Rahim, meaning "In the name of God, the most gracious, the most merciful".

Combat Organisation of the Polish Socialist Party

Abbreviation: OBPPS
Continent: Europe
Country: Poland
Background:

The Combat Organisation of the Polish Socialist Party (Polish: Organizacja Bojowa Polskiej Partii Socjalistycznej, abbreviated OBPPS), also translated as Fighting Organisation of the Polish Socialist Party; also known as bojówki (paramilitary units); Organizacja Spiskowo-Bojowa PPS (PPS Underground-Combat Organisation); Koła Bojowe Samoobrony Robotniczej (Workers' Self-Defence Combat Circles) and Koła Techniczno-Bojowe (Combat-Technical Circles), was an illegal Polish paramilitary organisation founded in 1904 by Józef Piłsudski.

Its operations reached their zenith about 1904-8, when it numbered over 2,000 members, including over 700 paramilitary personnel, and carried out over 2,500 operations. Afterwards it declined and was dissolved in 1911. Its goal was to create an armed resistance movement against the Imperial Russian authorities in partitioned Poland.

Committee for Liquidation of Computers

Abbreviation: CLODO
Continent: Europe
Country: France
Background:

The Committee for Liquidation of Computers (CLODO) was an anarchist organisation made up of self-identified "data processors" that targeted French computer companies in the 1980's. CLODO first surfaced in 1980, claiming responsibility for a series of minor attacks on computer companies in the Toulouse area, and releasing a statement to the French press that read, "We are workers in the field of data processing and consequently well placed to know the current and future dangers of data processing and telecommunications. The computer is the favourite tool of the dominant. It is used to exploit, to put on file, to control, and to repress." At the time, French police were convinced that CLODO was simply an outgrowth of Action Directe, a Marxist-Leninist group committed to the establishment of a communist government in France.

CLODO committed their most major terrorist attack in 1983 when they firebombed the Sperry-Univac Company in Toulouse. The message left by the group indicated that the attack was made in protest to the U.S. invasion in Grenada. Although no proof has ever been established that CLODO was affiliated with Action Directe, it seems likely that they had some linkages, but that CLODO was focused more on an anarchist worldview, as opposed to a Marxist-Leninist philosophy. The Committee for Liquidation of Computers has not been active since 1983.

Communist Combatant Cells

Abbreviation: CCC
Continent: Europe
Country: Belgium
Background:
The Communist Combatant Cells (CCC) was a Belgian terrorist organisation loosely committed to a communist ideology. The group was active for less than two years in the mid-1980s, primarily engaged in bombings within Belgium's borders. While the group was based in Belgium, their goals and targets were predominately international. CCC attacked perceived enemies of communism, specifically the North Atlantic Treaty Organisation (NATO), U.S. and international business firms, and the Belgian Employers Association.

The Communist Combatant Cells primarily targeted property rather than human representatives of capitalism, NATO, and the like. Nevertheless, CCC bombings led to several injuries and two deaths. In December 1985, police arrested CCC founder and leader Pierre Carette. His murder conviction on the 14th January 1986 essentially eliminated the Communist Combatant Cells. The Communist Combatant Cells has not been active since 1985.

Also known as Collectif des Prisonniers des Cellules Communistes Combattantes

Communist Liberation Faction

Continent: Europe
Country: Greece
Background:
The Communist Liberation Faction claimed credit for several small terrorist incidents in Marousi, Greece in February 2005. On the 1st February the group claimed to have set fire to a Kiss FM radio station van as well as to the Khalandri Tax Office. In a claim of responsibility the group stated that the attacks were a response to the "oppressive" Greek government and intended to establish "an atmosphere of terrorism-hysteria." No one was injured in the attacks.

Several weeks later the group claimed responsibility for another attack on a "Social Security Institution." In this claim, the group stated that the attack was in solidarity with "a former comrade," Mitsos Aivatzidhis, who apparently was struggling with a drug addiction and may have been in jail because of it (the claim was unclear).

Communist Liberation Faction is one of many small Greek arsonist groups known as "Gas Guys." These groups use arson to voice their discontent with Greek government policy and often espouse vague leftist or anarchist ideologies.

Although the group's attack in solidarity with a drug-addict friend is a bit odd, it can be assumed that Communist Liberation Faction is a typical Greek arsonist group. Such groups tend to perform a few small attacks and then fade away, and are likely little more than monikers adopted by discontented individuals. Communist Liberation Faction will likely not be responsible for future violence.

Communist Party of India - Maoist

Abbreviation: CPI-Maoist
Continent: Asia
Country: India
Background:
The Maoist Communist Centre of India (MCC) and the Communist Party of India (Marxist-Leninist) People's War (also known as the People's War Group or PWG) merged to form a new entity, the Communist Party of India-Maoist (CPI-Maoist) on the 21st September 2004, somewhere in the projected 'liberated zone'. Officially, the merger was announced on the 14th October 2004, by the PWG Andhra Pradesh 'state secretary', Ramakrishna, at a news conference in Hyderabad, on the eve of peace talks between the PWG and the State Government.

The merger is the consequences of initiatives that date back five years, when the PWG approached the MCC with a proposal of merger. In fact, since its inception on the 22nd April 1980, the PWG had been trying to bring all the Left Wing extremist groups (also called Naxalite) in India (numbering around 40) under its umbrella with the objective of overthrowing 'the bureaucrat comprador bourgeois and big landlords classes who control state power in collusion with imperialism' and 'to establish in its place the New Democratic State under the leadership of the proletariat' with the ultimate aim of establishing socialism and communism. The MCC had been its first target and talks had been on since the early 1980's. However, the discussions failed to progress initially as a result of turf wars and differences at the leadership level. Despite ideological commonalities and shared objectives, the pathways to the merger have been full of obstacles, with territorial and leadership clashes giving rise to an inter-necine conflict that lasted through much of the 1990s, as the two groups struggled for supremacy in different parts of then undivided Bihar, result-ing in the death of hundreds of cadres and sympathisers. However, con-tinuous interaction resulted in declining hostility between the two groups over time, and gradually increased operational cooperation and consolida-tion. The creation of Jharkhand State in November 2000 and anti-Maoist operations launched by the administration pushed the MCC and PWG into closer cooperation, and a truce was announced between them three years ago. Significantly, the PWG had earlier merged with the CPI-ML (Party Unity) of Bihar on the 11th August 1998.

The organisations shared their belief in the 'annihilation of class enemies' and in extreme violence as a means to secure organisational goals. However, significant ideological divisions did exist in the past, with the PWG ad-hering to a Marxist-Leninist 'line', while the MCC embraced Maoism. These differences have now been ironed out, with Maoism prevailing, in the words of PWG Andhra Pradesh State 'Secretary', as "the higher stage of the M-L (Marxist-Leninist) philosophy. Marxism-Leninism-Maoism will be the ideological basis guiding its (CPI-Maoist's) thinking in all spheres of its activities." The new entity has reaffirmed its commitment to the classical Maoist strategy of 'protracted armed struggle' which defines its objectives not in terms of the seizure of lands, crops, or other immediate goals, but the seizure of power. Within this perspective, participation in elections and engagement with the prevailing 'bourgeois democracy' are rejected, and all efforts and attention is firmly focused on 'revolutionary activities' to under-mine the state and seize power.

See the Naxalites (Maoists - India), the Peoples War Group (PWG),

Communist Party of Nepal-Maoist

Abbreviation: CPN-M
Continent: Asia
Country: India, Nepal
Background:
The Communist Party of Nepal-Maoist (CPN-M) is one of the largest and most potent Communist insurgent groups in the world. In little over a decade, the CPN-M has been responsible for hundreds of attacks on gov-ernment and civilian targets.

Although Nepal had been an absolute monarchy for many years, mass demonstrations in 1990 forced then-King Birendra to institute a consti-tutional monarchy and revoke an earlier ban on political parties. In short order a new constitution was drawn up and parliamentary elections were scheduled. Among over 20 parties on the ballot, the United People's Front (UPF), an umbrella party of the left, ran in the 1991 general elections. However, the UPF's Maoist wing (the CPN-M) performed extremely poorly, and was excluded from the next election in 1994.

With no outlet in electoral politics, the Maoists turned to insurgency to reach their goal of overthrowing Nepal's parliamentary democracy and transforming Nepalese society. Such a "transformation" would likely include a purge of the nation's elite class, a state takeover of private industry, and the collectivisation of agriculture.

The CPN-M's strategy and tactics are based on traditional Maoist guerrilla war principles. As part of its struggle against the current regime, the Maoists have targeted Nepalese parliamentarians, the Prime Minister, government ministries, and a number of educational institutions. International targets have occasionally been hit as well, largely in an effort to isolate the government. Two US embassy guards were assassinated by the Maoists in 2002, allegedly for anti-Maoist spying activities. Further attacks against diplomatic targets have been threatened in CPN-M press releases. Foreign commercial targets are also fair game for the Maoists, as they demonstrated in three attacks on Coca-Cola facilities and one attack on a Pepsi-Cola truck.

Despite a massive effort from the Royal Nepalese Army (at the behest of current King Gyanendra) to crackdown on the CPN-M, the group enjoys widespread support and is believed to control an estimated 70% of the Nepalese countryside. The CPN-M had an estimated strength of 10,000-20,000 armed cadres with an arsenal that has increased in both size and sophistication in recent years. In addition to receiving funds and support from expatriate Nepalese living in India, the group funds its operations through extortion, "taxation", and bank robberies. The group maintains bases in India as well as Nepal and enjoys support from many Indian insurgent groups, most notably the United Liberation Front of Assam and the Communist Party of India-Maoist.

In February 2005, ostensibly due to his inability to crush the rebels, King Gyanendra issued a state of emergency and dismissed parliament. Although this move was done purportedly to defeat the CPI-M, Gyanendra's powergrab seems to have only strengthened the rebel's position. Widespread opposition to the King's move amongst the Nepalese people has lent credence to the rebel movement and has served to improve ties between the CPI-M and other legitimate political parties. In April 2006, facing massive protests, King Gyanendra gave up absolute power and announced that parliament would re-assemble.

Presently, the re-birth of parliament seems to have had a positive effect on the CPI-M. While the group is enjoying a period of strength and has shown to be generally resolute in terms of its ideology, the group has taken steps to embrace the political process in order to achieve their goal of a Communist state in Nepal. In late-April the group announced a unilateral three month ceasefire. Scarcely a week later, the interim Nepalese parliament reciprocated by announcing an indefinite ceasefire of its own.

In November 2006, CPI-M and the Nepalese political establishment reached a peace deal which would see the rebels disarming under UN supervision and joining the Nepalese parliament as the second largest party. The peace agreement has been hailed as "historic" and a "landmark" for ending violence in Nepal.

Although this agreement is an extremely positive step, many in Nepal are sceptical. Until the CPI-M has shown that it has given up violence permanently, a radical departure to say the least, the group may continue to commit large-scale violence against both government forces and civilians in the near future.

Concerned Christians

Continent: North America
Country: United States of America
Background:
Monte Kim Miller formed the Concerned Christians in Colorado, during the 1980s. Created as an element of the Christian counter cult movement to combat New Age religious movements and anti-Christian sentiment, it has since become an apocalyptic Christian cult as the group adopted the less mainstream views of the millennium held by Miller. They disappeared from their homes and jobs in October 1998 and had been the subject of a search.

On the 3rd January 1999 they gained notoriety for being arrested and deported from Israel. The deportation was part of an Israeli effort to protect the Al-Aqsa mosque from extremist Christian groups, codenamed "Operation Walk on Water". The Concerned Christians were one of several independent groups who believed it must be destroyed to facilitate the return of Jesus Christ. The group is said to currently reside in Greece and its potential threat level has since been disputed.

Continuity Irish Republican Army

Abbreviation: CIRA
Continent: Europe
Country: United Kingdom and Ireland
Background:

The Continuity Irish Republican Army (Continuity IRA or CIRA) is a small group of hard-core dissident Irish republicans based in Northern Ireland and the Republic of Ireland. The CIRA remains true to the original principles of its founding group, the Irish Republican Army: it engages in terrorist activity in the hopes of evicting British military personnel from Northern Ireland and uniting all geographic areas of Ireland under Irish rule, severing all ties to the United Kingdom. The CIRA remains a determined hold-out as other republican groups are disarming and committing fully to peaceful politics. It has completely rejected the full disarmament of the IRA announced in the summer of 2005. The CIRA is the armed wing of Republican Sinn Fein (RSF), a supposedly political organisation which was itself designated a terrorist organisation by the U.S. State Department in July 2004.

The RSF and CIRA emerged in response to the moderation of the Irish Republican Army and Sinn Fein, its political wing, during the 1980s and 1990s. The break centred on the IRA's decision to accept seats won in Parliamentary elections in the Republic of Ireland, ending a decades-old policy of abstentionism. A group of dissidents, who thought the move a tacit acceptance of the legitimacy of the partition of Ireland between north and south, broke off and formed Republican Sinn Fein. The Continuity Irish Republican Army was then created as RSF's armed wing. Although Republican Sinn Fein created the Continuity IRA in 1986, the group did not become an active terrorist organisation until the mid 1990s.

The CIRA has been implicated in a number of attacks in the past decade. The group is best known for conducting small bombings, most of them non-lethal, such as tossed explosives and car bombs. In addition to bombings, CIRA attacks have included robberies, kidnappings, hijackings, and assassinations. The CIRA has also been linked to extortion and other economic crimes in Belfast.

The CIRA remains committed to armed struggle to free Northern Ireland from British rule. It is the only Irish republican group that has not declared a cease-fire since the 1998 Good Friday Accords. The group has publicly disavowed the disarmament undertaken by the IRA in 2005, viewing it as treason. In February 2006, the CIRA and RSF caused a stir in Dublin when they led a counter-demonstration against a Unionist march that sparked rioting. Also in February, the Independent Monitoring Commission, established in 2004 to monitor paramilitary organisations in Northern Ireland, reported that a CIRA breakaway faction, calling itself Oglaigh na hEireann (Volunteers of Ireland), had emerged although little is known about the splinter group.

Though the CIRA is small (most estimates place its size between 20 and 50, while UK justice officials put the number at "less than 200"), it is committed to armed struggle and should be considered dangerous. The group is a particular threat to peace in Northern Ireland as the other republican groups strive to maintain a peace accord and prove that they have disarmed.

Contras

Continent: Central America
Country: Nicaragua
Background:

The Contras is not a terrorist organisation in the usual sense. Following the 1979 Sandinista revolution, rebel groups formed to counter the new Nicaraguan regime. These groups were primarily distinct and separate organisations with a common goal of overthrowing the Sandinista government. The separate groups were collectively referred to as "counterrevolutionaries" or contras for short. In a noteworthy twist of circumstances, a former terrorist organisation, the Sandinistas, had reached the highest level of power in Nicaragua and were now forced to confront a new group of anti-state terrorists. Only this time, the terrorists aimed to overthrow the revolutionary Sandinistas.

Shortly after the Sandinista takeover, Argentine military advisors began to train the contras. Unfortunately for the contras, the Argentine military junta was in turmoil and unable to continue its support. By 1982 the United States of America had taken over the sponsorship of the contras. In 1985, the U.S. mandated that several of the contra groups consolidate under a unified structure. The contras formed the Unified Nicaraguan Opposition, which comprised of four of the five biggest contra organisations.

The contras continued to assail the Sandinista regime throughout the 1980s. During the conflict, both the rebel contras and the ruling Sandinistas perpetrated numerous human rights abuse. Because both the contras and Sandinistas were recipients of foreign aid, the conflict mushroomed to a degree greater than most internal terrorist insurgencies. In a certain sense, the contras were successful in their goal. Combined with internal and external pressure to negotiate a truce with the contras, the Sandinistas were eventually obligated to open up democratic elections. The 1990 Nicaraguan presidential election ended the Sandinista rule of Nicaragua.

Following the 1990 general election, the majority of contras demobilised and settled into civilian life. Some contras claimed that the Nicaraguan government did not properly distribute aid intended for the former rebels. Some small groups of re-formed contras have demonstrated limited activity since 1990.

Also known as Counter Revolutionaries

Cornish National Liberation Army

Abbreviation: CNLA
Continent: Europe
Country: United Kingdom
Background:

The Cornish National Liberation Army, abbreviated to CNLA, is a militant Cornish nationalist organisation that has threatened to carry out acts of vandalism and arson against commercial targets that it considers to be 'English'.

The CNLA claims to represent a merger of the An Gof (originally founded in 1980 and reformed in 2007) and the Cornish Liberation Army. It claims to receive funding from organisations based in other Celtic nations and Irish groups in the United States, and that some of its members have received training from the Free Wales Army, the Scottish National Liberation Army, and the Irish National Liberation Army, as well as the Provisional Irish Republican Army.

In June 2007, the CNLA issued threats against celebrity chefs Rick Stein and Jamie Oliver, who own restaurants in the area, as well as to customers of these restaurants. A 36-year-old man was later arrested for making the threats.

It has been described by the Cornish political party, Mebyon Kernow as a 'pseudo-terrorist group'. Dick Cole, spokesman for Mebyon Kernow, released a statement to various London papers in an effort to balance the positions adopted by mainstream Cornish political groups.

The group also opposes the flying of the English flag in Cornwall, and has threatened to destroy all English flags in the county.

There is little evidence as to the size of the CNLA other than an August 2007 interview in Cornish World Magazine in which they claim thirty members.

As of the 9th October 2007 the CNLA changed its name to the Cornish Republican Army or CRA, in response to copycat groups and supporters claiming to be CNLA. The announcement contained dismissals and admissions of various publicised CNLA attacks. It also confirmed that the activities threatened against Jamie Oliver and Rick Stein had been ceased.

In November 2007 Per Svenssonn, a writer for the internet periodical Ciudadanos Europeos, successfully gained an email interview with a member of the CRA through the Cornwall24 website forum. As well as confirming the name change, the interview outlined (among other topics) the structure of the organisation, confirmed official CRA attacks and suggested future plans.

When questioned on forthcoming events the CRA spokesperson answered:

"2008 promises to be an interesting year for the English occupying forces and their establishment. Beyond that, no comment."

Also known as Cornish Republican Army (CRA)

Corsican Army

Continent: Europe
Country: Corsica, France
Background:

Armata Corsa is the main rival of the Front de Liberation Nationale de la Corse (FLNC), the largest and oldest terrorist organisation in Corsica. Suspected leaders Francois Santoni and Jean-Michel Rossi left the group in 1998 out of discontent with the radicalisation of the party. Armata Corsa claims it is more purely "nationalist" than other Corsican groups known to have links to organised crime on the island. The group first claimed responsibility for five coordinated bomb attacks across the island, all directed at Departmental Amenities Directorate (DDE) buildings. Buildings in Ajaccio, Sartene, Porto-Vecchio, Corte and Calvi were damaged and another device was found two days later, unexploded at a DDE facility in Bastia. In claiming responsibility for the attacks, the group said that "the DDE participates directly in ruthless property speculation against Corsicans." Two months later, the group claimed responsibility for an explosion at an Italian-owned hotel in Bonifacio which destroyed the main part of the building. This attack was in keeping with the modus operandi of other nationalist groups which often target foreign-owned businesses on the island.

The primary goals of Armata Corsa include an independent Corsica, the transfer of imprisoned Corsican terrorists from Continental France to a prison in Corsica, and the eradication of organised crime (and nationalist group relationships with organised crime) in Corsica.

Also known as Armata Corsa

Covenant Sword and Arm of the Lord

Abbreviation: CSA
Continent: North America
Country: United States of America
Background:

The Covenant, Sword and Arm of the Lord (CSA) were a Christian Identity survivalist group founded by James Ellison. Ellison, a former minister, ran a Christian retreat on his property, located near the Missouri-Arkansas border. In 1978 Ellison had a vision of the race war that he believed would soon engulf America, and he transformed his retreat into a white supremacist paramilitary training camp dedicated to the principles of Christian Identity. According to Ellison, the CSA would be an "Ark for God's people" during the coming race war. By God's people, Ellison meant white Christians. Jews, he told his followers, were not really God's chosen people, but rather a demonic and inferior race.

CSA recruited at gun shows, where they invited people to sign up for CSA's "Endtime Overcomer Survival Training School." Students who attended CSA training were trained in weapons usage, urban warfare, wilderness survival, and "Christian martial arts." CSA also made money at gun shows by selling homemade machine guns, silencers, and explosives. The organisation's other source of cash was theft. Ellison encouraged his disciples to steal, citing the Israelites plundering of the Philistine's tents after David killed Goliath as Biblical justification.

Beginning in 1983, the CSA embarked on a crime spree that included the firebombing of an Indiana synagogue, an arson attack on a Missouri church, and the attempted bombing of a Chicago gas pipeline. On the 19th April 1985, 300 federal officers surrounded the CSA compound and demanded that the 100 or so heavily armed residents surrender. After a tense four days of negotiations, the CSA peacefully surrendered. Inside the compound, authorities found homemade landmines, U.S. Army anti-tank rockets, and a large supply of cyanide that the CSA was apparently planning to use to poison the water supply of an unspecified city. Eight of the captured leaders and members, including Ellison, were convicted and imprisoned, effectively destroying the group.

Croation Freedom Fighters

Abbreviation: CFF
Continent: North America
Country: United States of America
Background:
The Croatian Freedom Fighters (CFF) were dedicated to gaining Croatian freedom from Yugoslavia and the eventual destruction of the Yugoslavian state. Mostly through bombings, the group terrorised Yugoslavian business and financial interests in the United States, as well as American citizens of Yugoslavian descent. Members of the group were also implicated in the bombing of the Statue of Liberty in 1980, although many other groups also claimed this attack, notably the Puerto Rican terrorist group Armed Forces of National Liberation (FALN).

CFF's most famous attack came in 1976, when they hijacked a TWA Airliner en route from La Guardia to Chicago, demanding the release of

Croatian prisoners and the distribution of Croatian-independence propaganda in both France and the United States. The terrorists, led by Zvonko Busic, eventually surrendered to French authorities and were tried and convicted in the United States.

In 1987, Zvonko Busic escaped from his prison cell in Otisville, NY, but was quickly apprehended 2 days later after being caught sleeping behind a building in Otisville, NY, 40 miles away. The Croatian Freedom Fighters have not been heard from since then.

D

Dagastan Liberation Army

Continent: Asia
Country: Russia
Background:

The Dagestan Liberation Army was an Islamic extremist group that emerged in 1999 for the purpose of creating independence for the Republic of Dagestan. Dagestan shares similarities with the Republic of Chechnya (which has endured a history of violent extremism), such as having a predominantly Muslim population as well as being situated in Russia's northern Caucasus region. The Chechen rebels, who commit terrorist attacks in the name of an independent Islamic state of Chechnya, often include neighbouring Muslim regions like Dagestan in their desired Islamic country. In fact, in August 1991, Chechen-led rebels declared that Dagestan was an Islamic state. In staging attacks, Chechen rebels have bombed targets within Dagestan.

The Dagestan Liberation Army led a brutal bombing campaign in September 1999 that killed hundreds of innocent civilians. The group's targets were apartment buildings in Moscow, where residents were killed indiscriminately by TNT and cyclonite bombs. According to the terrorist group, the bombings were in retaliation for military action within the regions of Chechnya and Dagestan by the Russian air force. The Dagestan Liberation Army believes that any Russian activities within Dagestan or Chechnya are illegitimate as these regions deserve independence from Russia.

Investigations into the 1999 bombings continued up to 2004, when Russian security forces killed three terrorists who reportedly participated in the attacks. Other members have been apprehended and found guilty for terrorist acts. It is probable that the Dagestan Liberation Army is no longer operational as a major threat in the region. Active members most likely migrated to join larger groups that are based in the Caucasus region, fighting for independence.

Dagastani Shari'ah Jamaat

Continent: Asia
Country: Chechnya
Background:

Formed in 2002 under the name Dzhennet ("Paradise"), Dagestani Shari'ah Jamaat is a terrorist group active in the Dagestan region of Russia, northeast of Chechnya. The group's objectives are similar to those of most groups in the region, which include the expulsion of Russian influence from the region, the destruction of all "opponents of Sharia" including moderate Muslims, and the creation of an independent Dagestan under Islamic law. Dagestani Shari'ah Jamaat mainly targets political leaders and Russian security forces.

The Caucasus region has been plagued with a rising number of insurgent groups, largely due to having poorer economic conditions than other regions in Russia as well as high concentrations of minority ethnic and religious groups such as Muslims, Dagestanis, Ossetians, and Chechens. Russian officials fear that disparate groups may join together to form a united front with more substantial capabilities. Evidence of this concern lies in the fact that Dagestani Shari'ah Jamaat has strong connections with Riyad us-Saliheyn, the group led by late Chechen rebel leader Shamil Basayev.

Initially, Dzhennet's membership consisted of leader and founder Rasul Makasharipov and a handful of local militants that had combat experience in Chechnya. In June 2003, due to a concerted effort to recruit from local mosques and a timely merger with an unknown group, Makasharipov's group grew substantially larger, eventually organising into local brigades theoretically under his command. After a series of high-profile attacks in 2005, the group changed its name to its current form.

In addition to committing terrorist attacks, Dagestani Shari'ah Jamaat is active on the propaganda front, often claiming attacks on behalf of other extremist groups, publicising atrocities committed by Russian special forces in Chechnya, and publicly criticising Russian policies and commenting on political events, the most recent being the execution of Russian diplomats in Iraq and the Israel-Lebanon War of 2006.

In June 2005, Makasharipov killed himself after his safe house was surrounded by Russian security forces. It is thought that he was succeeded by Shamil Yusuf Kulinsky. The group made major headlines in August 2006 when it claimed responsibility for killing Bitar Bitarov, the Head Prosecutor of Buinaksk, Dagestan and Adilgerei Magomedtagirov, the Dagestani Interior Minister, in a pair of car bombs. Ironically, after Makasharipov's death in 2005, Minister Magomedtagirov had declared that "the entire group (Dagestani Shari'ah Jamaat)…is over and done with".

Despite renewed Russian efforts to combat the insurgency, Islamic extremism continues to be a problem in the Caucasus region. Dagestani Shari'ah Jamaat, as one of the more potent groups in the region, figures to remain a major security threat until more of an effort is made to address the social and economic issues at the root of the Dagestani terrorism problem.

Also known as Dzhennet (Paradise), Islamic Jamaat of Dagestan

Darul Islam

Abbreviation: DI
Continent: Asia
Country: Indonesia
Background:

Darul Islam was an Islamic group in Indonesia that was considered to be more closely related to extremists than to Jemaah Islamiyah. It was started in 1942 by a group of Muslim militias, coordinated by a charismatic radical Muslim politician, Kartosuwiryo. The group recognised only Shari'a as a valid source of law.

During the Indonesian National Revolution, Kartosuwiryo founded his own band of freedom fighters in West Java, called Hizbullah and Sabilillah. As a protest toward the Renville Agreement signed by Indonesian leaders in 1948, which ceded West Java to the Dutch, Kartosuwiryo proclaimed "Darul Islam" (meaning Islamic State) in West Java. Darul Islam did not disband itself after the transfer of sovereignty in 1949, resulting in a clash with the government of the Indonesian Republic. Rebellious movements in provinces such as Aceh and South Sulawesi joined the Darul Islam Movement in the 1950s. The movement was an alternative government to the Republic until 1962, when the leaders were captured or killed.

However, despite the group being dismantled, underground networks may have persisted. In the 1970s and 1980s, there were occurrences of 'Islamic' terrorism attributed to a group known as Komando Jihad. The leaders arrested from this group were found to be Darul Islam veterans.

Dashmesh Regiment

Continent: Asia
Country: India
Background:

The Dashmesh Regiment not to be confused with Khalistan Armed Force aka Dashmesh Regiment (Seetal Singh Matewal) was a separatist group responsible for several terrorist bombings of civilian targets in India during the 1980s and 1990s. The founding members were close friends and trusted lieutenant of Sant Jarnail Singh Bhindranwale, Amrik Singh and General Shabeg Singh.

In April, 1984 Sikh militants lobbed hand grenades into a religious house near their holy city of Amritsar, killing four and injuring 31. In many

Punjab towns terrorists on motorcycles shot up cars, banks and people in the streets. Two Hindu political leaders, both national figures, were gunned down. At week's end 23 had been killed and 80 injured. Responsibility for the new wave of killings was claimed by the Dashmesh Regiment, a previously unrecognised group of Sikh terrorists that counts moderate Sikhs as well as Hindus and the government among its sworn enemies.

On the 1st July 1985: A bomb hidden in luggage bound for India exploded in the international terminal of Rome's airport, injuring fifteen baggage handlers. The luggage arrived either from Beirut or from Athens. The suitcase was to be loaded on an Italian Alitalia flight to New Delhi. Responsibility for the attack was claimed by the Dashmesh Regiment

De Fes

Continent: Europe, Africa
Country: France, Morocco
Background:

The name "de Fes" refers to a cell of Islamic terrorists that operated out of the Moroccan city of Fez in the mid-1990s. Members of the Fez cell were responsible for an August 1994 shooting attack on the Atlas-Asni hotel in Marrakech, Morocco, that left two Spanish tourists dead.

In some ways, the name "de Fes" is somewhat of a misnomer. Although the members of the group launched their attacks from that city, in reality the group was based in France. All members were either Moroccan or Algerian immigrants to France, or had dual citizenship. The Fez cell was part of a larger terrorist network that included several members based in France and other cells in Moroccan cities.

While the Fez cell was solely responsible for the Atlas-Asni attack, other members of the larger network were involved in a shooting attack on a Jewish cemetery in Casablanca, and an aborted plan to attack tourist beaches. After the Atlas-Asni attack, a massive manhunt in both Morocco and France uncovered the network.

Although the Moroccan government accused Algerian militants from the Armed Islamic Group (GIA) of funding the Fez cell and those involved in the other attacks, there is no proof that GIA had any role.

The Fez cell was made up of three young French Muslims who had been recruited by network leaders from the immigrant slums outside of Paris. They were Stephane Ait Idir, Redouane Hammadi, and Tarik Falah. Idir and Hammadi were captured in Morocco with several other members of the network, and were sentenced to death for their role in the attacks. Falah fled to Germany where he was captured and extradited to France. In France, Falah was sentenced to five years in jail. The ringleader of the network, Abdelilah Ziyad, was sentenced to eight years in jail in France for his role in recruiting and organising the Atlas-Asni attack. Over 30 other members of the network were tried in France and Morocco respectively and were sentenced to terms ranging from a few years in jail to death.

The attacks carried out by the Fez cell and other members of the larger network were intended to destabilise the Moroccan regime and usher in an Islamic government. In reality, the group's actions led to a large crackdown on Islamic militants in both North Africa and France. The attacks also led to a clearer understanding of the threat that young, poverty-stricken French Muslims pose when encouraged and coerced by experienced Islamic militants. Although the Fez cell is inactive, other members of its network might be active in terrorist activities in Morocco, France, or elsewhere.

Death Squad of Mujahideen of Iraq

Continent: Middle East
Country: Iraq
Background:
The Death Squad of Mujahideen of Iraq is a terrorist organisation responsible for a lone kidnapping attack against a company providing logistical support to U.S. forces in the region.

On the 27th July 2004, armed members of the group abducted three Jordanian truck drivers and a businessman who worked for a company that transports supplies to U.S. troops. Members of the group demanded the hostages' company cease operations in Iraq in exchange for their release. After hearing the hostages were being held in a house on the outskirts of Fallujah, a local tribal leader, Sheik Haj Ibrahim Jassam, led an armed raid against the group on the 3rd August 2004, freeing the four men. Sheik Jassam stated that the group holding the hostages was comprised of 'outsiders' although this information has not been confirmed. Poorly protected drivers are easy targets for Iraqi terrorists who seize them in order to convince their companies to cease operations and hamper reconstruction efforts. Several companies in the Middle East have halted work in Iraq after employees were kidnapped.

Members of the Death Squad of Mujahideen of Iraq have not claimed responsibility for any terrorist attacks since 2004. However, given the continued presence of U.S. forces in Iraq and the companies that supply them, it is possible that the group remains active, despite not being responsible for recent violence. It is also somewhat likely that members of the group remain active within different insurgent organisations.

Also known as Mujahedeen of Iraq, the Group of Death

Democratic Forces for the Liberation of Rwanda

Abbreviation: FDLR
Continent: Africa
Country: Rwanda
Background:

The Democratic Forces for the Liberation of Rwanda was the primary anti-Rwanda rebel group during the latter part of the Second Congo War. It continues to operate, mostly within the eastern region of the Democratic Republic of the Congo. It is composed almost entirely of Hutu ethnics opposed to Tutsi rule and influence in the region. The group is often referred to as the FDLR after its original French name: the Forces Démocratiques de la Libération du Rwanda.

The FDLR was formed in 2000 after the Kinshasa-based Hutu command and the Kivu-based Army for the Liberation of Rwanda (ALiR) agreed to merge. It counts among its number the original members of the Interahamwe that carried out the 1994 Rwandan Genocide. It received extensive backing from, and cooperation from, the government of Congolese President Joseph Kabila, who used the FDLR as a proxy force against the foreign armies operating in the country, in particular the Rwandan Patriotic Army and Rwanda-backed Rally for Congolese Democracy. In July 2002, FDLR units still in Kinshasa-held territory moved into North and South Kivu. At this time it was thought to have between 15,000 and 20,000 members. Even after the official end of the Second Congo War in 2002, FDLR units continued to attack Tutsi forces both in eastern DRC and across the border into Rwanda, vastly increasing tensions in the region and raising the possibility of another Rwandan offensive into the DRC - what would be their third since 1996. In mid 2004, a number of attacks forced 25,000 Congolese to flee their homes.

Following several days of talks with Congolese government representatives, the FDLR announced on the 31st March 2005 that they were abandoning their armed struggle and returning to Rwanda as a political party. The talks were held in Rome, Italy and were mediated by Sant'Egidio. The Rwandan government stated that any returning genocidaires would face justice, most probably through the Gacaca court system. If all of the FDLR commanders, who are believed to control about 10,000 militants, do disarm and return, a key source of cross-border tensions would be removed.

On the 4th October 2005, the United Nations Security Council issued a statement demanding the FDLR to disarm and leave Democratic Republic of the Congo immediately. Under an agreement reached in August, the rebels had pledged to leave Congo by the 30th September.

Its leader, Ignace Murwanashyaka, was arrested in Mannheim, Germany, in April 2006, but released shortly thereafter.

In August 2007, the military announced that it was ending a seven-month offensive against the FDLR, prompting a sharp rebuke by the government of Rwanda. Prior to this, General Laurent Nkunda had split from the government, taking Banyamulenge (ethnic Tutsis in the DRC) soldiers from the former Rally for Congolese Democracy and assaulting FDLR positions, displacing a further 160,000 people.

In October 2007 the International Crisis Group said that the group's military forces had dropped from an estimated 15,000 in 2001 to 6-7,000 now, organised into four battalions and a reserve brigade in North Kivu and four battalions in South Kivu. It named the political and military headquarters as Kibua and Kalonge respectively, both in the jungle covered Walikale region of North Kivu. It also said that 'about the same number' of Rwandan citizens, family members of combatants, and unrelated refugees remained behind FDLR lines in separate communities.

Also known as Forces Democratiques de Liberation du Rwanda.

Democratic Karen Buddhist Army

Abbreviation: DKBA
Continent: Asia
Country: Burma (Myanmar), Thailand
Background:

The Democratic Karen Buddhist Army (DKBA) is the militant wing of the Democratic Karen Buddhist Organisation (DKBO). In 1994, the DKBO splintered off from the Karen National Union (KNU), the largest and oldest of Burma's insurgent groups. The Karen is an ethnic group in the north of Burma that has waged war against the ruling Burmese government for over 50 years. Heavily oppressed by the current military junta, many Karen live in refugee camps in Thailand.

The DKBO split off from the KNU for religious reasons. Most Karens are Buddhists, but the ruling hierarchy of the KNU was entirely Christian. When the DKBO split from the KNU, the ruling Burmese Junta, the State Peace and Development Council (SPDC), immediately took the opportunity to form an alliance with the DKBO. At present the DKBO, and their military wing, the DKBA, are fully funded by the SPDC. DKBA troops are essentially an SPDC militia, and have conducted brutal campaigns against both the KNU and innocent Karen villagers in Burma and Thailand. Although the DKBA is guilty of numerous atrocities, they cannot be defined as an independent terrorist group. Rather, the DKBA enjoy widespread support from the ruling junta, one example of the oppression and terror that the SPDC has exhibited throughout their rule.

Ostensibly, some DKBA members believe that after destroying the KNU, they will defeat the SPDC and establish an independent Karen state. Despite the massive losses that the SPDC/DKBA has inflicted on the KNU, there is virtually no chance that the DKBA would ever be able to fight the SPDC, their main suppliers for many years. Most DKBA members have joined the group mainly to avoid retribution from the ruling junta.

Also known as Democratic Karen Buddhist Association, Democratic Karen Buddhist Organisation, Progressive Buddhist Karen Nationals Organisation

Democratic Party of Iranian Kurdistan

Abbreviation: DPIK
Continent: Middle East
Country: Iran
Background:

The Kurdistan Democratic Party of Iran is a Kurdish opposition group in Iranian Kurdistan which seeks the attainment of Kurdish national rights within a democratic federal republic of Iran.

"Democratic Party of Iranian Kurdistan" (PDK-I) was founded in Mahabad, Iran, on the 16th August 1945. PDK-I replaced the Komeley Jiyanewey Kurd (Council of Kurdish Resurrection) which had been formed three years earlier. Just 159 days after its foundation on the 22nd January 1946, the Party, availing itself of expedient circumstances in a section of Iranian Kurdistan, established the " Republic of Kurdistan ", usually referred to by historians as the Republic of Mahabad , the reason being its choice of Mahabad as the capital.

The Republic of Mahabad lasted not more than 11 months. Following a pact signed by the Iranian central government and the ex-Soviet Union (which supported the PDK-I and the secession of the Kurdistan province from Iran), the Iranian army launched a vast offensive into the region, destroying the "Republic" on the 17th December 1946. The " Republic " having collapsed, a great number of PDKI leaders were imprisoned, of whom 20 people including Qazi Muhammad (Ghazi Mohammad or Qazî Mihemmed), head of the Party and president of the Republic, M. Hossein Seyfi-Ghazi, minister of Defence, and Abulghassem Sadri-Ghazi, a member of the Iranian Parliament from Mahabad, were hanged in the capital of the Republic, and the others in Saqez and Bukan.

In less than two years after the collapse of the Republic, PDKI started its political and organisational activities anew, striking roots in some parts of Iranian Kurdistan.

Following the collapse of Dr. Mossadegh's government in 1953, when democratic rights and freedoms of the peoples throughout Iran were suppressed, PDKI's activities came almost to a standstill. A great number of Party activists were either imprisoned or went underground, though they resumed their activities after a very short time.

Two widespread police raids against the Party in 1959 and 1964 dealt heavy blows to its organisation: some 300 Party activists were imprisoned, with an even greater number hiding away or fleeing Iran. Nevertheless, not having sunk into despair, the Party embarked on the task of reviving its organisation. Its activities picked up such a speed that in 1967-68, a large number of its members and high-ranking cadres started an armed insurrection, lasting 18 months, against the Shah's regime. But as this armed movement lacked a safe rear zone, the Shah's regime managed to crush it.

The Kurdish Iranians in Iranian Kurdistan and PDKI played an active part in the Iranian people's uprising against the Shah's dictatorship. A group of PDK-I leaders, who were living in exile either in neighbouring countries or in Europe, returned to Iran before the collapse of the monarchy, actively participating in the uprising of the Kurdish people and assuming the status of leadership in the movement.

The uprising of the Iranian people having succeeded, PDK-I declared its public activities in a meeting held in Mahabad, which was attended by representatives from all parts of Iranian Kurdistan. Despite the Party's sincere endeavours to settle its differences over the democratic rights and freedoms of the Kurdish people peacefully with the newly established regime in Tehran, the rulers in Tehran did not give into the PDK-I.

On the 13th July 1989, Dr. Abdul Rahman Ghassemlou, Secretary-general of PDK-I, and two of his collabourators, were assassinated in Vienna, Austria as they were negotiating with envoys of the Iranian regime, at the latter's invitation, for a peaceful solution to the Kurdish issue in Iran. Dr. Ghassemlou's successor, Dr. Sadeq Sharafkandi met with the same fate on the 17th September 1992 in Berlin where he had attended the Congress of the Socialist International.

Devrimci Sol (Revolutionary Left)

Abbreviation: DHKP/C
Continent: Asia
Country: Turkey
Background:
The DHKP/C (Revolutionary People's Liberation Party/Front) is a Marxist, anti-Western splinter group of the Turkish terrorist group Devrimci Sol (Dev Sol). Dev Sol originated as a splinter group of Devrimci Yol (Dev

Yol) which was itself a splinter group of the Turkish People's Liberation Party-Front (THKP/C). The THKP/C was an offshoot of the broader Revolutionary Youth movement (Dev Genc) within Turkey.

In the early 1990s, infighting within Dev Sol resulted in the emergence of two factions. Dursun Karatas, who founded Dev Sol by combining splintered factions of Turkish radical leftist groups in 1978, changed the group's name to DHKP/C in 1994. Bedri Yagan, also a founding member of Dev Sol, broke from the Karatas faction and created a new faction, THKP/C (not to be confused with the original THKP/C). Confusingly, the Yagan faction of DHKP/C is still often referred to as Dev Sol.

DHKP/C's ideology is similar to that of other radical Turkish leftists. The group believes that the Turkish government is a fascist regime, controlled by the domineering, imperialist forces of the West, especially the United States and NATO. The group seeks to destroy these Western influences through violence and Marxist revolution. In its early years, when it was still known as Dev Sol, the group focused largely on political assassinations. A crackdown by Turkish authorities in the early 1980s forced the group to restrict its activities, though in the late 1980s Dev Sol was able to increase its attacks against Turkish military targets.

Despite internal troubles, the DHKP/C has managed to retain the ideology and goals of the original Dev Sol movement. The group has continued to conduct violent attacks against Turkish government targets as well as against Western interests in Turkey. The group has also sought to bring attention to its imprisoned members by staging hunger protests. More recently, the group has been intensely outspoken against US military operations in Afghanistan and in Iraq. DHKP/C believes that these operations are proof of the imperialist intentions of the United States.

Also known as Dev Sol (Karatas Faction), Devrimci Sol (Karatas Faction), RPLP/F, Revolutionary Left, Revolutionary People's Liberation Party/Front

Dhofar Liberation Front

Abbreviation: DLF
Continent: Middle East
Country: Oman
Background:

In 1965, the Dhofar Liberation Front (DLF) was formed in the southernmost province of Oman, in opposition to the rule of Sultan bin Taimur. Dhofar had a population of only some 40.000 at the time (out of a total of 750.000 Omanis), and the revolutionary movement received considerable support from the locals aggrieved by their poor living conditions: the country was at the time still living in the 14th Century. Initially, frustrated DLF insurgents were supported by Saudi Arabia, Egypt, and Iraq, but with the time a strong Sino-Communist influence was to have established itself, and even those tribesmen willing to cease fighting were firmly discouraged from doing so. The DLF launched operations against the local Police and Army outposts on the 9th June 1965 and quickly gained control of all except the coastal areas in Dhofar. Even the RAF base at Salalah was threatened and had to be fortified. The Omani troops had considerable problems during operations in jagged mountain areas and the Provosts of the SOAF failed to provide adequate air support. The situation worsened in 1967, when the British vacated Aden, and the DLF established a number of bases inside what became South Yemen. The South Yemenis were soon providing plenty of support to the Dhofari rebels, which in the same year were organised into the "Popular Front for the Liberation of the occupied Arabian Gulf" (PFLOAG).

On the 7th August the insurgents launched their first significant operation, attacking the British base at Salalah – old capital of Dhofar, some 110km from the South Yemeni border – with mortars. Arab claims about the success of this operation were slightly more enthusiastic: according to radio Baghdad 49 British soldiers were killed and one "RAF Hunter shot down". Surely enough, by 1969 the PFLOAG advanced towards the coast and captured the city of Rakhyut. Due to rebel air defences proving increasingly dangerous, the SOAF was forced to move the centre of operations to Salalah, even if the HQs remained at Muscat, some 970km to the north. An increased number of British troops were now deployed in Oman as well, including one SAS squadron, the first operation of which was to chase away Iraqi volunteers that had infiltrated the Musandam peninsula.

The British knew that they would lose their position in Oman, if they would not be able to reverse the military situation: on the 23rd July 1970 a coup was staged and the Prince Qaboos ibn-Said brought to power. A new era for Oman was about to begin. The SAS began training the Omani troops. Simultaneously, a campaign for improving the standard of living and more social equity within the local society bought over many of the rebels. The final offensive against insurgents was launched by Omanis and Iranians in the Sarfait area, in October 1975.

Also known as Jabhat al-Tahrir al-Dhofar

Earth Liberation Front

Abbreviation: ELF
Continent: Europe, North America
Country: Canada, United Kingdom, United States of America
Background:

The Earth Liberation Front (ELF) is an international underground organisation consisting of autonomous groups of people who carry out direct action according to the ELF guidelines. It was founded in 1992 in Brighton, England by Earth First! members who refused to abandon criminal acts as a tactic when others wished to move Earth First! into the mainstream. The group jumped to North America in the mid-90's. Historically, the group has concentrated efforts on the timber industry and animal rights issues. More recent actions indicate that some ELF factions are also targeting suburban sprawl, with New York a hotspot for this type of activity. Within the past year, a number of under-construction condominiums and luxury homes have been set on fire by ELF operatives. Subsequent press releases describe an "an unbounded war on urban sprawl", adding that "we will not tolerate the destruction of our island" and "if you build it we will burn it." There is not a centralised organisation or membership to speak of in the ELF, so individuals or cells are driven only by their personal decisions to carry out actions.

According to the ELF website, which guides individual member's actions, "Any direct action to halt the destruction of the environment and adhering to the strict nonviolence guidelines, listed below, can be considered an ELF action. Economic sabotage and property destruction fall within these guidelines."

1) To inflict economic damage on those profiting from the destruction and exploitation of the natural environment; 2) To reveal and educate the public on the atrocities committed against the earth and all species that populate it; and 3) To take all necessary precautions against harming any animal, human and non-human.

The ELF advocates "monkeywrenching," a euphemism for acts of sabotage and property destruction against industries and other entities perceived to be damaging to the natural environment. "Monkeywrenching" includes tree spiking, arson, sabotage of logging or construction equipment, and other types of property destruction. Economic damage is often accomplished via acts of vandalism, ranging from breaking windows and gumming locks to setting fires and damaging equipment. Public education is typically achieved by means of anonymous press releases following acts of sabotage. Spray paint is also used to communicate messages and to claim responsibility at the site of sabotage.

Eastern Turkistan Islamic Movement

Abbreviation: ETIM
Continent: Asia
Country: China
Background:

The Eastern Turkistan Islamic Movement (ETIM) is an Islamist extremist group based in China's Xinjiang-Uygur Autonomous Region. ETIM is an ethnic Uygur separatist organisation that aims to create an Islamist state in the Xinjiang province.

The area commonly referred to as Turkistan is sometimes split into Western Turkistan and Eastern Turkistan. Western Turkistan was controlled by the Russian empire and then by the USSR, and so the area is also referred to as Russian Turkistan. The USSR treated this area as an autonomous region. Following the dissolution of the USSR, the region was split among five new republics, Kazakhstan, Kyrgyzstan, Tajikistan, Turkmenistan, and Uzbekistan. In contrast, Eastern Turkistan has long been a part of China and is sometimes referred to as Chinese Turkistan. Today, the region is officially referred to as the Xinjiang-Uygur Autonomous Region.

While the Eastern Turkistan Islamic Movement's name would suggest that the group is interested in creating an Islamic state exclusively in the Xinjiang province ("Eastern Turkistan"), some analysts have stated that the group aims to create a new state that would include portions of Turkey, Kazakhstan, Kyrgyzstan, Pakistan, Afghanistan, and Xinjiang. ETIM is not the only terrorist group committed to an Islamic state in the Turkistan area; the Islamic Movement of Uzbekistan (IMU) is another significant terrorist operation pushing for a theoretical Islamic Turkistan state.

Claims that ETIM has ties to al-Qaeda, Osama bin Laden, and the Taliban persist. Many reputable sources debate whether or not al-Qaeda has provided the group with training and financial assistance. The US Department of State, in its 2005 report on terrorism, states that ETIM is "linked to al-Qaida and the international jihadist movement" and that al-Qaeda has provided ETIM with "training and financial assistance". Another US government website reports that one ETIM leader was killed in a raid on al-Qaeda safe houses in Pakistan. The Chinese government has been known to exaggerate the connection between ETIM and al-Qaeda to enlist the support of the United States in endorsing China's social control tactics in Xinjiang. It is likely that members of ETIM have had contact with al-Qaeda elements, but no high-level contacts have been established. As far as the group's strength is concerned, ETIM has been described as a small terrorist operation and the group demonstrates limited allegiance among the ethnic Uyghur's of the Xinjiang province. Furthermore, China shows absolutely no signs of acquiescing to any of ETIM's terrorist demands. In fact, the Xinjiang province is important to China both for its strategic location and its abundant natural resources.

The Chinese government alleges that ETIM is comprised of eight major factions, which are committed to terrorist attacks in the name of an Eastern Turkistan Islamic state: Central Asian Uygur Hezbollah (Kazakhstan), East Turkistan Liberation Organisation (ETLO), Eastern Turkistan International Committee, Eastern Turkistan Islamic Movement (Afghanistan), Eastern Turkistan Islamic Resistance Movement (Turkey), Eastern Turkistan Youth League (Switzerland), Turkistan Party (Pakistan), and the United Committee of Uyghur's' Organisations (Central Asia). It is unclear whether or not most of these are actual terrorist groups, and if so whether or not these are actual factions of ETIM. ETLO is known to be a terrorist group that supports ETIM's cause and could possibly be an ally of ETIM's as well. ETIM has been implicated in terrorist plots against US interests in the Central Asia region, including a foiled plot to attack the US Embassy in Kyrgyzstan.

Also known as East Turkestan Islamic Party (ETIP)

Egyptian Islamic Jihad

Abbreviation: EIJ
Continent: Middle East
Country: Afghanistan, Egypt
Background:
This Egyptian Islamic extremist group merged with Bin Laden's al-Qaeda organisation in June 2001, but may retain some capability to conduct independent operations. The relationship between Jihad leader al-Zawahiri and bin Laden formally began in February 1998 when al-Jihad joined the International Front.

Following the group's founding in the late 1970s, Egyptian security authorities began a ruthless crackdown on al-Jihad in the 1980s, imprisoning, torturing and executing its members. The group then split into two factions, one led by al-Zawahiri, the other by Abbud al-Zumar, who is currently imprisoned. The latter faction has since disappeared as many of its members have been jailed. But al-Zawahiri's faction, also known as the

"Vanguards of Conquest" (Talaa'al al-Fateh), has thrived. In the mid-80s, al-Zawahiri moved the headquarters to Afghanistan and began recruiting Afghan Arabs. New cells of al-Jihad were trained in the mujaheddin camps of Afghanistan from which they set off on missions to Egypt. Al-Jihad militants were trained as suicide bombers (reputedly an al-Zawahiri specialty) and, for reasons of security and effectiveness; they formed into isolated cells working independent of one another.

Al-Jihad's primary goals today have merged with those of al-Qaeda, to include attacks on US and Israeli interests. Al-Jihad's original goals, which likely still have a place, include a violent overthrow of Egyptian President Hosni Mubarak, whom they see as corrupt, impious, and repressive, to be replaced by an Islamist state. Al-Jihad is unique among the Islamic movements, however, in that it views war against the Jews and Israel as an initial, essential step toward fulfilling the goals of Islam. According to the group, the only way to resolve the conflict with the Jews in Palestine is by direct violent confrontation. In 1990, one of the organisation's leaders, Sheikh Tamimi (author of a 1982 booklet called "The Obliteration of Israel: A Koranic Imperative"), expressed this principle in the following words: "The Jews have to return to the countries from which they came. We shall not accede to a Jewish state on our land, even if it is only one village."

The original Jihad was responsible for the assassination in 1981 of Egyptian President Anwar Sadat. It also claimed responsibility for the attempted assassinations of Interior Minister Hassan al-Alfi in August 1993 and Prime Minister Atef Sedky in November 1993. The group has not conducted an attack inside Egypt since 1993 and never targeted foreign tourists there.

Ejercito del Pueblo en Armas

Abbreviation: EPA
Continent: South America
Country: Venezuela
Background:
The Ejército del Pueblo en Armas, which means the Army of the People Under Arms in English, is a small Venezuelan paramilitary group that emerged in the central state of Lara in 2004, though it was founded earlier. The group has been associated with some minor violence in the region, including the deaths of four rural villagers in November 2004. EPA's first known terrorist attack occurred in May of that same year, when a fragmentation grenade exploded outside a Mormon temple in Valencia. No one was hurt, but the blast scattered leaflets bearing the EPA's name and

denouncing the church as a bastion of American imperialism and a vehicle for American intelligence activities.

The EPA is an ideological supporter of Venezuelan President Hugo Chavez. Chavez, president since 1998, has built his regime on a defiantly anti-capitalist and anti-American agenda. Though the EPA supports the president, they claim to receive no public funding. Its main mission, according to its statements, is to repel an impending American invasion of Venezuela.

Some observers have linked the EPA to the terrorist group Fuerzas Bolivarianas de Liberacion (FBL), the Bolivarian Liberation Forces. The FBL, founded in 1992, was responsible for several attacks on government officials in the mid-1990s, and now supports Chavez. The group has attacked both opposition politicians and foreign embassies in Venezuela in recent years. Both the FBL and the EPA have suspected links to Colombian anti-government rebels, particularly the FARC.

Chavez has publicly disowned the FBL, calling on members to turn in their arms and let the Venezuelan army deal with the American threat. The arrest of four EPA members in February 2005, including key spokesman Freddy Yepez, further indicates that the government does not publicly support these "Chavista" groups. Opposition politicians have publicly denounced the EPA and the FBL.

The EPA has been less active since the February 2005 arrests of Yepez and 3 other members. They have not been associated with any violence or terrorism since late 2004. The Chavez regime maintains its popularity with Venezuela's lower classes, and the country's bitter feud with the United States is still in full swing.

It is unclear what the future role of the EPA is in the Venezuela-U.S. confrontation. It is certainly possible that the group may carry out other attacks against American targets, particularly businesses, in Venezuela. At the same time, the February arrests may have crippled the group, or it may have been reabsorbed into the FBL. If the group continues to operate, it will remain criminalised and on the fringes of Venezuelan politics, but the anti-Americanism and anti-neo-liberalism that it stands for will continue to have momentum in the country.

Also known as Army of the People Under Arms in English

English Peoples Liberation Army

Continent: Europe
Country: United Kingdom
Background:
The English People's Liberation Army was a paramilitary English nationalist organisation.

The organisation may have originated as a split from the Maoist Working People's Party of England. The Army's ideology called for the independence of England from "Judeo-fascist" forces.

According to the Dictionary of Terrorism, it was "extremely weak" but had "undertaken isolated bomb attacks". In 1983, it claimed responsibility for a parcel bomb sent to the headquarters of the Campaign for Nuclear Disarmament.

Barberis et al claim that the organisation may have had links to the Oliver Cromwell Republican Party, founded in 1977. This minor organisation, led by Paul Pawlowski, later renamed the Republican Party of England, is best known for its leader's demonstration against the wedding of Charles and Diana in 1981.

Eritrean Islamic Jihad Movement

Abbreviation: EIJM
Continent: Africa
Country: Eritrea, Ethiopia, Sudan
Background:
The Eritrean Islamic Jihad Movement (EIJM) is an organisation that seeks to depose the current Eritrean government and install a new government based on the principles of Islamic law. Currently led by Shaikh Khalil Mohammed Amer, the EIJM was formed in 1980 and is the only opposition group that claims to represent the interests of Muslim Eritreans, who make up approximately half of Eritrea's population.

Though the EIJM is based in Khartoum, Sudan, it runs the majority of its operations in the western lowlands of Eritrea near the Sudanese border. During the 1998 border war between Ethiopia and Eritrea, Ethiopia formed an alliance with Sudan and the Eritrean political opposition to undermine the Eritrean government's ability to fight. The People's Front for Democracy and Justice (PFDJ), the ruling party in Eritrea, has alleged that these ties currently serve to facilitate weapons transfers and provide training sites and safe haven to EIJM rebels. It cites the rebels' use of weapons of Sudanese origin (such as Kalashnikov assault rifles and RPG-7 grenade launchers) as proof of foreign involvement in its internal affairs. The EIJM has also been known to recruit from Eritrean refugee camps in Sudan.

The EIJM is a product of many mergers and alliances, and today it includes the members of the former Munezemet Arrewad al Muslimin al Eritrea (Eritrean Pioneer Muslim Organisation), the former Jebhat Tahrir al Eritrea al Islamiya Wataniya (Eritrean National Islamic Liberation Front), the former Lejnet al Difae al Islami (Islamic Defence Committee), the former Harekat al Mustedafeen al Eritrea (Movement of Oppressed

Eritreans), and the former al Intifada Islamiya (Islamic Uprising). Due to the diversity that characterised its formation, the EIJM is made up of a motley crew of political dissidents from other political parties and liberation movements, religiously-moderate opponents of the ruling party, and radical Islamists as well. Of its support base, a very small minority approves of terror tactics, though all agree that Muslim interests are severely underrepresented in the government, which is controlled solely by the overwhelmingly-Christian PFDJ.

Since Eritrea defeated Ethiopia in Eritrea's war of independence in 1993, the PFDJ has ruled Eritrea under the authority of a one-party "transitional government." The EIJM, the Eritrean People's Liberation Front – Democratic Party (EPLF-DP), and the 13-member Alliance of Eritrean National Forces (AENF) represent Eritrea's main opposition groups.

The U.S. Department of State has listed the EIJM as an al-Qaeda affiliate, though it should be noted that due to the high degree of fragmentation within the EIJM, only the most radical factions of the group actually have a direct connection to al-Qaeda.

The EIJM claimed responsibility for several attacks in 2003, including the bombing of a hotel in Teseney, and the year culminated in a series of ambushes that claimed the lives of 46 Eritrean military personnel. Since then it has been relatively quiet, though no evidence suggests that the group is inactive.

Also known as Abu Sihel Movement, Eritrean Islamic Jihad (EIJ, Eritrean Islamic Reform Movement, Islamic Salvation Movement (Harakat al Khalas al Islami)

Eritrean Liberation Front

Abbreviation: ELF
Continent: Africa
Country: Eritrea, Ethiopia
Background:

The Eritrean Liberation Front (ELF) was formed by a group of Eritrean students and intellectuals in Cairo, Egypt in July 1960. The Eritrean Liberation Front's primary objective was straightforward, to secure Eritrean independence from Ethiopia. Between 1885 and 1952, Eritrea was governed by Italy and Great Britain, successively. In 1952, the United Nations federated Eritrea with neighbouring Ethiopia. While Eritrea gained some measures of autonomy, the resolution stopped short of creating an independent Eritrean republic.

The Eritrean Liberation Front (ELF) began offensive actions against the Ethiopian government in 1961. While the group initially displayed characteristics of a Muslim movement and later flirted with Marxism, the ELF was first and foremost a nationalist group working for Eritrean independence. The ELF was the primary nationalist movement from 1960 to 1970. However in 1970, an internal ELF dispute led to the creation of a splinter organisation, the Eritrean People's Liberation Front (EPLF). Following the split, the EPLF would usurp the ELF as the primary insurgent group.

In 1991 EPLF troops defeated Ethiopian troops in Eritrea. The EPLF then created a provisional government of Eritrea. In a 1993 Eritrean referendum, the Eritrean people voted for the creation of a fully independent Eritrea. The current president of Eritrea was once a member of the Eritrean Liberation Front. Eritrean president Isaias Afewerki joined the ELF in 1966. In 1970 he co-founded the Eritrean People's Liberation Forces.

Eritrean Peoples Liberation Front

Abbreviation: EPLF
Continent: Africa
Country: Eritrea, Ethiopia
Background:
Eritrean People's Liberation Front (EPLF), frequently misidentified as the Ethiopian People's Liberation Front, was a separatist group which fought for Eritrea's independence from Ethiopia from the 1970s until 1990, when Eritrea achieved sovereign status.

The EPLF was formed after a schism with the Eritrean Liberation Front (ELF) in the early 1970s. The predominantly Christian EPLF split from the largely Muslim ELF due to religious and political disagreements. Far more leftist than the ELF, the EPLF replaced the ELF as the primary rebel group in Ethiopia by the 1980s. The EPLF was generally considered to be a Marxist organisation, though leaders refused to identify themselves with Marxism throughout much of the war with Ethiopia. The EPLF long regarded the United States as an imperialist influence and enemy due to U.S. cooperation with Ethiopia.

Over several decades, the EPLF became regarded as one of the most well-organised guerrilla groups in Africa. The group recruited from within the Eritrean region and trained each soldier for nine months before sending them to fight. International civil rights organisations occasionally made claims that the EPLF was forcing Eritreans to enter the army, a charge the group vehemently denies. Through involuntary conscription or not, the EPLF, with the rival ELF, formed a rebel force of over 30,000 soldiers. The Ethiopian government designated 25,000 troops to fight the Eritrean rebels. International observers were impressed by the EPLF's emergence as a well-disciplined army and their ability to maintain strength without outside support. The EPLF was largely armed with abandoned or stolen weapons from the Ethiopian Army.

While fighting was consistent for more than 30 years, one incident in particular fuelled international outrage at the group. The EPLF attacked a convoy of 16 U.N. and seven Catholic Relief Services trucks carrying food on the 20th October 1987, burning all of the food. The EPLF claimed responsibility for the attack, saying they had found bombs and ammunition in the convoy. The U.S. and other international sources condemned the attack, insisting there were no weapons present and accusing the EPLF of using hunger as a weapon in its war with the Ethiopian government.

The EPLF was also accused at various points of carrying out random assassination campaigns against Eritreans they believed were cooperating with or helping the Ethiopian government. The EPLF said all those killed were tried in their absence and warned many times to stop their "crimes."

In 1990, the EPLF expelled the last of the Ethiopian troops from Eritrea, forming an interim government and holding a U.N.-supervised referendum on independence. The leader of the EPLF became the first president of Eritrea and the EPLF became the single ruling party. The group eventually renamed itself the People's Front for Democracy and Justice.

The Marxist People's Front for Democracy and Justice remains the only legal political party in Eritrea. The new Eritrean government has drafted a constitution but it has yet to be ratified. Parliamentary and presidential elections have been postponed indefinitely. As a terrorist group, the former Eritrean People's Liberation Front is inactive.

Also known as the Peoples Front for Democracy and Justice

Ethiopian People's Revolutionary Democratic Front

Abbreviation: EPRA
Continent: Africa
Country: Ethiopia, Sudan
Background:

The Ethiopian People's Revolutionary Army (EPRA) was the armed wing of the Ethiopian People's Revolutionary Party (EPRP). The EPRP was formed in 1972, initially as an anti-monarchy group, calling itself the "first political party in the country." Ethiopia's political scene changed fundamentally soon after this, with the overthrowing of Emperor Kaile Sellasie in 1974 and the rapid takeover of power by a military regime (the "Derg").

The EPRP, however, still remained on the outside of the Ethiopian political spectrum and was eventually banned by the Derg. The group was initially founded on leftist principles, although its current political and economic platforms have moderated and now advocate a democratic republic and a market economy.

The group's armed wing, the EPRA, was formed in 1976 and was primarily active in the Tigray and Gondar regions, where it fought both the Ethiopian military and other opposition groups, primarily the Tigray People's Liberation Front (TPLF). Actions against the EPRP/EPRA by the Ethiopian government were deemed the "Red Terror." The combined effects of this two-front war devastated the group nearly to the point of elimination, and it was forced to move its base of operations into Sudan by the mid-1980s. The EPRA effectively ceased to exist as a military entity at this time.

Although not part of the current government, the EPRP remains an active political organisation and operates under the Coalition of Ethiopian Democratic Forces (CODEF). The EPRA/EPRP's long-time rival, the TPLF, is now Ethiopia's dominant political organisation.

Fallujah Squadron

Continent: Middle East
Country: Iraq, Saudi Arabia
Background:

Little is known about this group but it made the headlines when it kidnapped Paul Johnson Jr a United States Citizen. Johnson, a 49-year-old worked for Lockheed Martin Corp. He was kidnapped in June 2004 in Riyadh and the group's demands for his release were that the Saudi government released al Qaeda prisoners and that all Westerners left the Arabian Peninsula.

In a statement they said: "As we promised, we the mujahedeen from the Falluja Squadron slaughtered the American hostage Paul Johnson after the deadline we gave to the Saudi tyrants," said a statement on the Web site that has been translated from the Arabic.

"So he got his fair share from this life and for him to taste a bit of what the Muslims have been suffering from Apache helicopter attacks. They were tortured by its missiles." Johnson worked on Apache attack helicopters in Saudi Arabia and had lived there for more than a decade.

Nothing else is known about this group and it could have been just the one incident that has brought it to light. With the current situation in Iraq (2008) it is possible that this group could emerge again or that it has been subsumed by other groups.

Farabundo Marti National Liberation Front

Abbreviation: FMLN
Continent: Central America
Country: El Salvador
Background:

The Farabundo Marti National Liberation Front (FMLN) was a Marxist-Leninist insurgency movement operationally active in El Salvador from 1980 to 1992. The goal of the FMLN was to overthrow the military dictatorship that had ruled El Salvador since 1930 and replace it with a Communist government. The group was named after Farabundo Marti, a Salvadoran Communist revolutionary that led an unsuccessful and brutally-repressed revolt in 1932, during the height of El Salvador's economic and social depression.

In 1980, the FMLN was formed as an umbrella group representing the common interests of the five main leftist organisations of El Salvador: the Central American Workers' Revolutionary Party (PRTC), the People's Revolutionary Army (ERP), the Farabundo Marti Popular Liberation Forces (FPL), the Armed Forces of National Resistance (FARN), and the Communist Party of the Armed Forces of Liberation (FAL). The FMLN served to pool the limited resources of these groups and coordinate the strategies and tactics of the Communist insurgency in El Salvador.

The FMLN was organised into a political wing responsible for propaganda and public diplomacy and a military wing responsible for armed operations. Initially, the FMLN developed a three-pronged strategy. First, they sought to secure their rural support base. Second, they conducted raids against government forces and economic infrastructure to de-legitimise the regime. Finally, they waged a propaganda war in urban areas with the aim of inciting a popular uprising against the government.

Politically-inspired by Communists the world over and financially-supported by the Communist regimes of Castro and the Nicaraguan Sandinistas, the FMLN conducted two relatively-conventional offensives in 1982 that were unsuccessful due to limited resources, an easily-disrupted supply chain exacerbated by communication difficulties, and internal disputes over command authority and strategy. After resolving some of these issues with a new influx of communications equipment and American-made weapons purchased on the black market and supplied by Nicaragua, the FMLN reached the height of its strength in 1983, numbering up to 12,000 members at one point. The FMLN embarked on what was to be its final conventional offensive in September 1983, escalating the scale and intensity of warfare in comparison to previous engagements. Still, the FMLN was not able to win decisively.

After the US provided military aid to the government of El Salvador, the FMLN was forced to shift strategies and wage fully-asymmetrical warfare. The whole movement trimmed its size, reorganised into smaller units more conducive to guerrilla warfare, and moved into urban areas, especially San Salvador. In the last half of the 1980s, the FMLN employed terrorist tactics such as kidnappings, arson, and bombings to destabilise the regime. Due to the substantial influence that American financial support had on strengthening El Salvador's counterinsurgency prowess, US assets in El Salvador also became targets during this time. Notably, four US Marine security guards were massacred at a roadside café in June 1985.

Thought it exhibited a great deal of organisational flexibility, the FMLN was dealt a death blow when the US decided to support the Salvadoran government. Still, politically-inspired violence, no longer in the form of direct engagement, continued until 1989. On the 31st December 1991, the FMLN reached a peace settlement with the Salvadoran government that allowed the FMLN to participate in political affairs. In exchange, the government cracked down on the notorious right-wing "death squads" that were responsible for a majority of the human rights violations that occurred during El Salvador's civil war. Today, the FMLN is one of the two main political parties in El Salvador and can no longer be considered a terrorist organisation.

Also known as Frente Farabundo Marti de Liberacion Nacional-Frente Democratico Revolucionario (FMLN-FDR)

Fatah

Continent: Middle East
Country: Palestine
Background:

The Movement for the National Liberation of Palestine (Fatah) was founded in the early 1960s by Yasser Arafat and friends of his in Algeria; Fatah was originally *opposed* to the founding of the PLO, which it viewed as a political opponent. Backed by Syria, Fatah began carrying out terrorist raids against Israeli targets in 1965, launched from Jordan, Lebanon and Egyptian-occupied Gaza (so as not to draw reprisals against Syria). Dozens of raids were carried out each year, exclusively against civilian targets.

Fatah's popularity among Palestinians grew until it took over control of the PLO in 1968. Since then it has been the PLO's most prominent faction, under the direct control of PLO Chairman Yasser Arafat. "Fatah" is a reverse acronym of the Arabic, *Harekat at-Tahrir al-Wataniyyeh al-Falastiniyyeh*. The word "Fatah" means "conquest by means of *jihad* (Islamic holy war)".

Note the grenade and crossed rifles, superimposed on the map of Israel in the emblem. This emphasises the dedication of Fatah, along with the other "liberation" groups, to the "armed struggle" against Israel, a euphemism for terrorism against civilians.

Headed by Yasser Arafat, Fatah joined the PLO in 1968 and won the leadership role in 1969. Its commanders were expelled from Jordan following violent confrontations with Jordanian forces during the period 1970-71, beginning with Black September in 1970. The Israeli invasion of Lebanon in 1982 led to the group's dispersal to several Middle Eastern countries, including Tunisia, Yemen, Algeria, Iraq, and others. It maintains several military and intelligence wings that have carried out terrorist attacks, including Force 17, the Hawari Special Operations Group, Tanzim and the Al Aqsa Marytrs Brigade.

In the 1960s and the 1970s, Fatah offered training to a wide range of

European, Middle Eastern, Asian, and African terrorist and insurgent groups. Carried out numerous acts of international terrorism in Western Europe and the Middle East during the 1970s. It has been linked to terrorist attacks against Israeli and foreign civilians in Israel and the occupied territories.

The organisation has had close, longstanding political and financial ties to Saudi Arabia, Kuwait, and other Persian Gulf states. These relations were disrupted by the Gulf crisis of 1990-91. Also has had links to Jordan. Received weapons, explosives, and training from the former USSR and the former Communist regimes of East European states. China and North Korea have reportedly provided some weapons.

See Force 17, Tanzim and Al Aqsa Martyrs Brigade

Fatah al-Intifada

Abbreviation: Continent: Middle East
Country: Palestine
Background:
Fatah al-Intifada (Arabic, Fatah Uprising) is a Palestinian militant faction founded by Col. Said al-Muragha, better known as 'Abu Musa'. The group is often referred to as the 'Abu Musa Faction'. Officially it refers to itself as the Palestinian National Liberation Movement - "Fatah" the identical name of the major Fatah movement. Fatah al-Intifada is not part of the PLO.

Originally part of Fatah, Fatah al-Intifada broke away from the organisation in 1983, during the PLO's participation in the Lebanese Civil War. The split was due to differences between Abu Musa and Yassir Arafat over a number of issues, including military decisions and corruption. Fatah al-Intifada was formed with Syrian support and quickly attracted a number of Palestinian guerrillas disillusioned with Arafat's role in Fatah and the Palestine Liberation Organisation (PLO). There was also a political dimension: the organisation took a more leftist view than the generally apolitical Fatah, and used socialist phraseology. Abu Musa is known to have advocated the view that the Lebanese Civil War was not a sectarian conflict, but a form of class war. Syria provided extensive backing as the Abu Musa forces attacked Arafat loyalists in Fatah, while several radical PLO organisations in the Rejectionist Front stayed on the sidelines. The fighting led to heavy losses on both sides, and helped Syria extend its influence into Palestinian-held areas of Lebanon. Fatah al-Intifada quickly fell under the dominance of the Syrian army, and came to be widely regarded as a Syrian puppet organisation.

In 2006, reports alleged that some 200 members of Fatah al-Intifada had broken away from the main organisation to form an extremist Islamist group by the name of Fatah al-Islam. This movement, which denied ties to Syria and was reportedly involved in conflict with the Syrian government, was based in the northern Lebanese refugee camp Nahr al-Bared, and professed sympathy for al-Qaida. According to newspaper reports, it was joined by Salafi activists from other countries, such as Pakistan, Jordan, Algeria and Bangladesh, but it remained on the fringe of Palestinian politics, viewed with suspicion by the larger, mainstream factions such as the PLO groups and Hamas. Fatah al-Islam took part in a series of violent shootouts with the Lebanese army in May 2007, with several tens of killed and extensive damage to and flight from the Nahr al-Bared camp.

During the 1980s, Fatah al-Intifada committed a number of attacks on Israel, including on Israeli civilians, but it has not been involved in violence against Israel since sometime before the Oslo Accords in 1993. The group is not believed to possess any capacity to attack targets in Israel or the Occupied Palestinian Territories.

Also known as Fatah Uprising, Abu Musa Faction, Palestinian National Liberation Movement. See Fatah al Islam

Fatah al Islam

Continent: Middle East
Country: Lebanon
Background:
Fatah al-Islam, (English: Conquest of Islam) is a radical Sunni Islamist group that first formed in November 2006. It has been described as a militant jihadist movement that draws inspiration from al-Qaeda. It became very well known in May 2007 and June 2007 after engaging in combat against the Lebanese Army in the Nahr al-Bared UNRWA Palestinian refugee camp. The United States Department of State classified the group as a terrorist organisation on the 9th August 2007.

Fatah al-Islam was led by a fugitive militant named Shaker al-Abssi, A Palestinian refugee who was born in Jericho in 1955, al-Abssi was once a pilot with the rank of colonel.

Al-Abssi's first militant activities can be traced to connections he established with a secular Palestinian militant group named Fatah al-Intifada in Libya, after it defected from the umbrella Fateh movement in 1983 . From Libya, al-Abssi reportedly moved to Damascus, where he made close ties with Fatah al-Intifada's number two in command, Abu Khaled al-Omla.

Syrian authorities arrested al-Abssi in 2000 and sentenced him to three years in prison on charges of smuggling weapons and ammunition between Jordan and Syria. The government later released him. He went to Iraq following the U.S.-led invasion in 2003 and fought alongside groups affiliated with Al-Qaeda. He is said to have become friends with a number of Al-Qaeda leaders there.

In 2004 Al-Absi was sentenced to death in absentia by a Jordanian military court for involvement in the assassination of U.S. diplomat Laurence Foley, after Syrian authorities refused to extradite him for trial. Abu Musab al-Zarqawi was also sentenced to death for the killing of Foley and was thought to have been an associate of Al-Abssi.

He briefly returned to Syria, where he again hooked up with al-Omla who helped him relocate to Lebanon, where he and a group of youth he met in Iraq set themselves up in the headquarters of Fatah Al-Intifada in the village of Helwa in the Western Beqaa in 2005. In May 2006, Al-Absi and this small group engaged in armed clashes with Lebanese soldiers that led to the killing of one young Syrian wanted by Damascus for fighting in Iraq.

Syrian intelligence services then summoned al-Omla to ask him about al-Abssi and his group. The investigation unmasked the close coordination between al-Omla and al-Abssi that had been kept from the pro-Damascus Secretary General of Fatah Al-Intifada, Abu Moussa, and by extension, from the Syrian authorities.

Al-Omla then reportedly ordered al-Abssi to leave the Western Beqaa, which is close to the borders with Syria, and head for refugee camps in northern Lebanon.

In November 2006 the Palestinian security committee in Al-Badawi refugee camp in Tripoli handed over two members of al-Abssi's group to Lebanese military intelligence. Al-Abssi was reportedly infuriated and decided to break with Fatah al-Intifada and establish his own group, Fatah al-Islam.

In November 2006 Fatah al-Islam set up a headquarters in the Palestinian refugee camp of Nahr al-Bared in northern Lebanon. The group seized three compounds in the camp that had belonged to the secular Palestinian militant group, Fatah al-Intifada. Al-Abssi then issued a declaration saying he was bringing religion back to the Palestinian cause.

In March 2007 Seymour Hersh, investigative reporter for New Yorker magazine, suggested that the Lebanese government was giving support to Fatah al-Islam, in order to defeat Hezbollah. Independently, Dr. Franklin Lamb, a researcher at the American University of Beirut, a Hezbollah expert and the author of "Hezbollah: A Brief Guide for Beginners", located at the time in Lebanon, makes similar allegations, in more detail. He claims that assistant to Secretary of State, David Welch negotiated with the Saudis and Saad Hariri of the American backed Siniora government to funnel aid to Fatah al-Islam, so that the Sunni group could eventually attack Shiite Hezbollah.

But Michael Young, a writer for Reason Magazine, casts doubts on

Seymour Hersh's claims. Additionally, Professor Barry Rubin, Director of the Global Research in International Affairs Centre, has alleged that Al-Abssi is in fact a Syrian operative engaged in destabilising the government of Lebanon.

Other indications that Fatah al-Islam, and specifically Fath Al-Islam leader Shaker Al-'Absi, may have Syrian support come from Samir Geagea, executive body chairman of the Lebanese Forces, who asked why if anyone is found out to be a Muslim Brotherhood activist, he receives a death sentence, and if he is very lucky, he gets hard labour. So how come Shaker Al-'Absi - who is no ordinary militant but a leader... and who committed a crime in Jordan and was sentenced to death there, and was arrested in Syria - has been released [from prison]?

The official spokesman for Fatah al-Islam is Abu Salim Taha. Fatah al-Islam supposedly has more than 150 armed fighters in the Nahr el-Bared camp. The group allegedly has about more than half a dozen Palestinian members. The bulk of its membership is said to made up of Syrians, Saudis, and other Arab Jihadists who had fought in Iraq, as well as approximately 50 Lebanese extremist Sunnis.

The Syrian ambassador said the leaders of the group were mostly Palestinians, Jordanians, or Saudis, and that perhaps a "couple of them" were Syrians.

The pro-Saudi Al Hayat newspaper reports that Fatah al-Islam has close ties to Syria, and that much of the leadership of Fatah al-Islam is made up of Syrian officers Fatah al-Islam casualties is mostly made of Saudis. There was also information that there are Chechen and Bangali fighters among this group. Fatah al-Islam's primary goals are to institute Islamic law in Palestinian refugee camps and to target Israel.

Also known as Conquest of Islam

Fatah Special Operations Group

Continent: Middle East
Country: Palestine
Background:
Part of Yasser Arafat's Fatah apparatus, the group is named after its leader commonly known as Colonel Hawari, who died in a car crash in May 1991 while travelling from Baghdad to Jordan. The group has ties historically to Iraq. Membership includes former members of the radical Palestinian 15 May organisation. The group carried out several attacks in 1985 and 1986, mainly in Europe and usually against Syrian targets. Also it has targeted Americans, most notably in the April 1986 bombing of TWA Flight 840 over Greece in which four Americans were killed. The future of group

remains uncertain following Hawari's death. The organisation has not recently engaged in terrorist activity. The group's areas of operations were in Middle Eastern countries and Europe and it was thought that the PLO was the main source of support.

Also known as Martyrs of Tel al-Za'tar, Amn Araissi or Hawari Group

Fedayan – Majority Faction

Continent: Middle East
Country: Iran
Background:
Among the armed leftist guerrilla groups operating in Iran in 1987, the Fedayan was the most active. The Fedayan was established when smaller groups operating in Tabriz, Mashhad, and Tehran merged in 1970. Its founders were university students and graduates who saw violence as the only means to oppose the Shah. As Iran's economic situation deteriorated in the mid-1970s, the Fedayan recruited workers from large manufacturing industries and the oil sector. Recruitment expanded to include such national and ethnic movements as those of Kurdish, Turkoman, Baluch, and Arab minorities. The Fedayan opposed both imperial and republican regimes but did participate fully in the Revolution, taking over various military barracks and police stations in Tehran, Tabriz, Hamadan, Abadan, and Shiraz in 1979. In early June 1980, the Fedayan split into two factions: the Fedayan "Minority" and the Fedayan "Majority." The "Minority" faction, which was actually the larger of the two, has consistently opposed the Republic and considered Khomeini "reactionary." It vehemently condemned the Tudeh's cooperation with Khomeini prior to 1983. It also rejected the armed activities of the Mojahedin and advocated instead the expansion of underground cells. The "Minority" faction refused to join the NCR because of Bani Sadr's past association with the Khomeini regime. Subsequently, the "Minority" faction, along with a number of smaller leftist groups, established a new organisation known as the Organisation of Revolutionary Workers of Iran.

Fedayeen Saddam

Continent: Middle East
Country: Iraq
Background:
Saddam's Fidayeen have received attention during the current crisis with Iraq (2003), as having played a prominent role in attacking American forces in the south of Iraq, as well as for apprehending captured Americans. Saddam referred to this "heroic" unit in his televised address on the 20th

February. It is important at this juncture to understand the nature of this Iraqi fighting unit.

Saddam's Fidayeen (also seen as Fedayin) can be roughly translated "as those who sacrifice themselves for Saddam." It is a paramilitary militia with the strength of about 30,000 to 40,000 men. It was established in 1995 by Saddam's oldest son Uday to maintain internal security in Iraq. By no means is it a professional fighting force, nor are its member recruited for suicide missions. The members are induced to join with higher salaries than regular Iraqi soldiers. Many members are youths in their early teens or young twenties. They are recruited solely on their loyalty to Saddam, (not Uday) and have had no prior combat experience. It has been erroneously referred to as an "elite" fighting force, when in reality it is known for its brute forces, rather than fighting prowess.

The Fidayeen fighters tend to come from Saddam's hometown of Tikrit or are recruited from his al-Bu Nasir tribe. They are usually paraded in the Iraqi press as masked men with white uniforms. The Fidayeen fighters are independent of the Iraqi Ministry of Defence and report directly to Uday. Nevertheless, the deputy commander of the unit is a General Midhahim Sa'ab Al-Tikriti, also from Saddam's hometown.

Prior to this conflict, the Fidayeen carried out patrols and anti-corruption campaigns against drug smuggling and prostitution. The Fidayeen operate above the law and have the jurisdiction to perform executions, sometimes in front of the victims' homes. It was notorious for conducting a campaign of beheading women during night time raids on the accusation that they were practicing prostitution. In reality, these women belonged to families hostile to the regime.

During a potential conflict in Baghdad, these forces along with the Special Republican Guard defended the city in earnest. Based on their past operations, they would have offered stiff resistance during the battle for Baghdad.

Fighting Jewish Organisation

Abbreviation: EYAL
Continent: Middle East
Country: Israel West Bank/Gaza
Background:
EYAL (a Hebrew acronym meaning Fighting Jewish Organisation) was a Jewish nationalist extremist group that operated in Israel and the West Bank. Although members traced their organisational model back to the Irgun and Stern Gang, two right-wing Jewish militias that committed terrorist attacks in British-mandated Palestine, EYAL can be seen as an

outgrowth of the Kach movement. Kach is a right-wing group founded by the late Rabbi Meir Kahane, an extremist who advocated the annexation of all disputed territories and the forced transfer of Arabs from those lands.

EYAL became active shortly after the 1993 Oslo Peace Accords; their main aim was to disrupt the ongoing peace process and to oppose steps taken by then Prime Minister Yitzhak Rabin to hand back the West Bank to the Palestinians. In September 1995, EYAL claimed initial responsibility for the shooting death of a Palestinian in the West Bank town of Halhoul, but later denied any involvement. Another small Jewish extremist group "Sword of David" also claimed responsibility for the attack, and other sources indicate that the shooting could have been a criminal affair.

In November 1995, Prime Minister Rabin was assassinated by a Jewish extremist named Yigal Amir. Although it is not conclusive that Amir was a member of EYAL, he certainly had ties to the organisation and its founder, Avishai Raviv. In a bizarre twist, it later emerged that Raviv was actually an agent for the Israeli Shin Bet, investigating right-wing groups. While some speculate Shin Bet actually founded EYAL to spy on other extremists, the Shin Bet denies this claim vehemently. In any case, EYAL dissipated shortly after Raviv was found to be a collaborator, and the remaining members most likely joined the Kach movement and its affiliate Kahane Chai. Since 1995, the group has been inactive and its members have most likely retired or joined other extremist groups such as Kach and Kahane Chai.

See Kach, Kahane Chai

First of October Antifascist Resistance Group

Abbreviation: GRAPO
Continent: Europe
Country: Spain
Background:

First of October Antifascist Resistance Group emerged during a transitional period precipitated by the death of Spain's dictator General Franco. The group was created as the armed wing of an illegal political organisation, the Communist Party of Spain-Reconstituted. First of October Antifascist Resistance Group, also known by its Spanish acronym GRAPO, was founded with the principal aim of overthrowing the Spanish government and replacing it with a Communist state. While its political wing, the Communist Party of Spain-Reconstituted, favours a Maoist ideology; GRAPO aims to create a Marxist state in Spain.

After General Franco's death in 1975, Spain adopted a parliamentary democracy. Three years later Spain transitioned to a parliamentary monarchy. Despite the government evolution, GRAPO has remained committed to the creation of a Marxist state. The group has engaged in terrorist activity to oppose Spain's membership in NATO. In addition to its attacks against the Spanish government, GRAPO is intensely anti-U.S. and has attacked U.S. targets. Specifically, GRAPO objects to U.S. military bases on Spanish territory.

Following the September 11 attack against the United States, GRAPO publicly supported the airplane attacks in New York and Washington, D.C. GRAPO has appeared increasingly weak over the past decade. In July 2003, GRAPO's long-time leader was sentenced to ten years in prison.

Free Aceh Movement

Abbreviation: GAM
Continent: Asia, Europe
Country: Indonesia, Malaysia, Sweden
Background:
The Free Aceh Movement (GAM) sought to establish an independent Islamic kingdom in the province of Aceh, located on the northern tip of the Indonesian island of Sumatra. It was formed in the mid-1970s and is-sued a formal declaration of independence in December 1976.

The GAM has had several principal grievances. Aceh was historically independent and never fully accepted Dutch colonial authority, yet was incorporated into the rest of Indonesia with its independence in 1943. The subsequent centralisation of power in Jakarta abolished much of Aceh's historical and political autonomy. Popular resentment increased after the Indonesian government pledged to allow for autonomy in religion and education for Aceh, yet never implemented this plan. Aceh's wealth of natural resources, mainly timber and natural gas, has also been exploited by the central government in Jakarta, which directly takes up to 90% of the revenue from Aceh's resources. Finally, the GAM opposed the brutal actions of the Indonesian military (TNI), which resulted in thousands of killings and mass exodus from the province. As well as continued military actions against the TNI, the GAM also targeted natural gas facilities of Exxon-Mobil.

In recent years, the GAM remained focused on the establishment of an independent Islamic kingdom in the province of Aceh. Although funding and equipment had been reportedly sent to the GAM from Iran and Libya, the group did not hold the anti-U.S. sentiment of the worldwide Islamist movement, and its leader, Hasan di Tiro, has even expressed support for the U.S. war on terror and claimed to actively seek American support. Talks with the Indonesian government began in 2000, mediated by the Henry Durant Centre in Switzerland, resulting in a number of cease-fires that did not hold. Jakarta stressed that special autonomy would be the goal of any negotiation, while the GAM held out hope for a referendum on independence – a critical rift responsible for the lack of real political progress.

Negotiations with Jakarta ultimately caused a split in the GAM, a situation widely unknown in the Western press. Hasan di Tiro, the group's founder living in exile in Sweden, led a faction that rejected any compromise with the Indonesian government, calling itself the Aceh Sumatra National Liberation Front (ANSLF). The rival faction, involved in the negotiations in Switzerland, was called the Free Aceh Movement Government Council (MP-GAM). Its leader, Teungku Don Zulfari, is based out of Malaysia. There was also internal complication in Jakarta regarding policy toward the GAM, in which the TNI, suspicious of talks, favoured using overwhelming military force to deal with the group. This stance led the TNI to place political pressure on the government for the imposition of martial law in Aceh.

U.S. policy toward the GAM has been influenced by the conflict in East Timor and the current war on terror. Eager to restore links with the Indonesian military after 1999, the U.S. pressured the GAM into accepting a political settlement based on autonomy within Indonesia, assuring Jakarta that it supported Indonesian territorial integrity. Realising the crucial role that Indonesia can play in the war on terror, Washington supported counter-terrorism training for the TNI while continuing to pressure the GAM. Although the U.S. never singled out the TNI for its human rights record in Aceh, it lobbied against the TNI's request for imposition of martial law.

As of summer 2005, the GAM continued its struggle. Attacks remained focused on Indonesian security personnel; however the group also targeted civilians both directly and indirectly. The GAM caused civilian casualties in its attacks on Indonesian police and military targets while also directly targeting civilian groups and infrastructure opposed to its activities. However, the tsunami disaster of 2004 would ultimately bring the GAM and the government back to the negotiating table.

In August 2005, the GAM and the Indonesian government signed a comprehensive peace accord. The deal called for the GAM to disarm, and for Aceh to be granted a form of local self-governance. Although this was not the full independence that GAM desired, all non-local TNI were to leave Aceh, and all GAM fighters would be granted amnesty. In December 2005, the GAM officially disarmed, and the TNI left Aceh as agreed. Although the group is officially inactive, peace deals have been broken before in Aceh, and only time will tell if the current agreement will hold up and end hostilities.

Free Papua Movement

Abbreviation: OPM
Continent: Asia
Country: Indonesia, Papua New Guinea
Background:

The Free Papua Movement (OPM) is a political organisation that seeks independence from Indonesia for the indigenous people of West Papua. Insurgent operations against the Indonesian government and security forces are run by the group's military wing, the Liberation Army of the Free Papua Movement (TPN). The OPM's fundamental goal is self-rule combined with a return to a traditional mode of life. Their public statements declare, "We are not terrorists! We do not want modern life! We refuse any kinds of development: religious groups, aid agencies, and governmental organisations just Leave Us Alone, Please!"

The former Dutch colony of West Papua, the western half of the island of New Guinea, came under temporary Indonesian control as part of an UN-managed "decolonization" of the Dutch East Indies in 1963. It became a permanent part of Indonesia in 1969, when roughly a thousand West Papuans were selected to vote in a referendum on inclusion with Indonesia under the Act of Free Choice. The legitimacy of this election has been questioned by a variety of groups over the past thirty years.

One of the major consequences of Indonesian citizenship for West Papua was inclusion in the government's transmigration program. Transmigration was intended to disperse the population from densely-populated islands to those more open for settlement. At one stroke, natural resources could be better exploited and individual citizens could greatly expand their economic opportunities. In the past 40 years, the transmigration program has brought many non-native Indonesians to West Papua. OPM decries this relocation as a serious threat to indigenous culture.

The OPM has been operating a limited rebel insurgency in the mountains of West Papua since the declaration of independence in 1961. The group conducts small-scale raids and attacks on government offices and military installations, including a weapons depot in 2003. Members of OPM often retreat into Papua New Guinea to hide, though the PNG government declares this to be illegal and recently burned buildings in a village where OPM members were hiding.

OPM continues to conduct military operations against Indonesian officials, property, and foreigners in the country in the hopes of securing independence for its people. While OPM does not have the complete support of the population behind it, it has been able to maintain persistent insurgent activity in West Papua.

Free Wales Army

Continent: Europe
Country: United Kingdom
Background:

The Free Wales Army was a paramilitary Welsh nationalist organisation, formed out of Lampeter, West Wales, by William Julian Cayo-Evans in 1963, as a replacement for the then supposedly moribund Mudiad Amddiffyn Cymru.

The organisation's objective was to establish an independent Welsh republic. The Byddin's White Eagle of Eryri symbol became a familiar sight, painted on walls and bridges throughout Wales. The Army's motto was "Fe godwn ni eto," Welsh for "We shall rise again." Its crest was Eryr Wen, a white eagle mounted on dark green shield, commonly seen in shorthand, with the flag of Wales on the top left hand corner.

The Byddin consisted of a number of commanding units leading a structure of ranks and volunteers. These commanding units were often isolated and worked within the tight precepts of army directives. Activities were largely limited to training in the Welsh countryside armed with surplus IRA equipment, and small–scale operations. Although the media treated this surreptitious movement with some ridicule, the authorities took them seriously enough to bring court action against the leading figures in 1969, resulting in lengthy prison sentences for them. The trial against the six leading members (including Julian Cayo Evans) was the longest lasting court case/trial seen in Wales to date.

The exact number of members who were active is unknown. The byddin consisted of a nationwide network consisting of 200 active members and many more sympathisers.

The smallest unit of the army was the Section, comprised of six volunteers. This was the basis of army organisation in any area. The Section volunteers lived in close proximity, and were available for service at short notice. At this level the Section Commander (highest ranking officer) worked closely with the Company Adjutant to oversee operations in their Cantref.

Four Sections formed one District Platoon. Four platoons formed one Area Company.

So as to avoid overlap of operations the commander in chief split Wales into five areas of operation each made up of their respective Cantrefi:

Gogledd Orllewin (North West Wales): Brown
Gogledd Ddwyrain (North East Wales): Red
Canolbarth (Central Wales): Green
De Orllewin (South West Wales): Black
De Ddwyrain (South East Wales): Blue
Also known by its Welsh name Byddin Rhyddid Cymru

Fullujah Mujahideen

Continent: Middle East
Country: Iraq
Background:

Fallujah Mujahideen is an active anti-coalition, Sunni extremist terrorist group with suspected ties to Abu Musab al-Zarqawi's al-Qaeda in the Land of Two Rivers. Operating exclusively in Fallujah, the group was responsible for many of the kidnappings of foreign nationals that took place between 2003 and 2004.

In contrast to the local resistance led by the similarly-named Fallujah Mujahideen Shura under Sheikh Abdallah al-Janabi, the Fallujah Mujahideen is made up of foreign fighters and is led by a Saudi, Abu Abdullah. Fallujah Mujahideen is organised like a small army, with five to six brigades consisting of five teams made up of roughly 100 men each. Compared to other indigenous insurgent groups, the Fallujah Mujahideen has better arms, equipment, and funding.

Despite the common goal of opposing the "U.S. occupation", the Iraqi resistance does not approve of the violent and "uncontrollable" nature of the foreign Fallujah Mujahideen, whose tactics and methods are seen by them as counterproductive. In fact, local spiritual leaders are often the ones responsible for negotiating the release of hostages taken by the Fallujah Mujahideen.

Though violence in Fallujah seems to have tapered as a result of a concentrated coalition effort to root out insurgents in the city, there is no indication that Fallujah Mujahideen had dismantled. Therefore, the group was considered to be active.

G

Gazteriak

Continent: Europe
Country: France
Background:

Gazteriak was a group of Basque separatists based in France. While the Basque region encompasses parts of Spain and France, Gazteriak was active primarily in the French Basque country. Gazteriak is a term from the Basque language of Euskara, which means Youth. Gazteriak was founded as a Basque nationalist youth movement but Gazteriak members have been connected to terrorist activities. The group focused their criticisms on the economic and social situation of Basque youth.

Gazteriak believes in a separate state for the Basque people. Their proposed Basque state would encompass parts of Spain and France. The largest Basque separatist organisation, the ETA, is based in Spain and has committed countless acts of violence since their inception. Gazteriak members have been linked to the ETA. Gazteriak was originally founded to support a Basque nationalist candidate in a local French election.

In the 1997, Gazteriak membership was estimated at 1,000 people. However, all of these members were not actively involved in terrorism. In 2000, the organisation essentially ceased to exist. In this year, Gazteriak and its Spanish counterpart, Jarrai, merged to create the organisation Haika. Shortly thereafter, Spanish authorities declared the newly formed Haika illegal.

Gods Army

Continent: Asia
Country: Burma (Myanmar), Thailand
Background:

God's Army was an ethnic Karen (also translated as Kayin) militant group in Burma that gained notoriety more for its bizarre leadership structure than its terrorist activity. The group was led by Johnny and Luther Htoo, twin brothers who were only nine years old when they formed the God's Army to fight against the ruling Burmese military junta.

The Karen people are an ethnic minority in Burma who have been fighting for an independent homeland for almost 50 years. Although violence has plagued Karen-majority areas for years, the Burmese army launched a massive operation in 1997, ostensibly aimed at wiping out Karen militants, but termed ethnic cleansing and genocide by many human-rights groups. The assault, dubbed "Operation Spirit King" was initiated in order to secure a gas pipeline. Thousands of Karen were killed, and at least 100,000 refugees flooded over the Burma-Thailand border. It was from this crackdown that the God's Army was born.

God's Army is a splinter group from the Karen National Union, the main Karen insurgent outfit in Burma. According to legend, the group was formed in 1997 after the Htoo brothers, angry at other Karen militants fleeing from the Burmese Army, successfully led a military operation in which they killed several Burmese soldiers despite being hugely outnumbered. Myths soon spread about the brothers, with many Karen believing that the boys had spiritual powers (the Karen religion is a blend of Christianity and animism) and were immune to bullets. By 1998, several hundred fighters had joined the God's Army to fight against the junta. The Htoo brothers reportedly were strict fundamentalist Christians and instituted a code of morality that prohibited drugs, alcohol, and meat products. After the media discovered the young leaders, the group became famous worldwide despite its limited impact on the Karen-Burmese conflict. As was the case with other Karen militant groups, the Burmese army launched a heavy crackdown on God's Army.

In January 2000, after the Burmese had inflicted heavy losses on the group, God's Army fighters (Johnny and Luther were not present) seized a hospital near the Thai-Burma border and held over 750 people hostage in an effort to secure medical assistance and communications for the group. After a day, Burmese security forces stormed the hospital and killed all of the hostage-takers. Many reports suggest that the God's Army cadres had surrendered before they were gunned down. The Burmese continued their crackdown, and in January 2001 the Htoo brothers fled to Thailand and surrendered to authorities. After their defection, the group essentially ceased to exist.

Despite several surprising victories over the course of their existence, God's Army never posed a serious threat to the ruling Burmese junta, and never came close to securing an independent homeland for their people. Despite this, the Htoo brothers shot the group to disproportionate fame due to their age. There is some disagreement as to whether the boys actually led God's Army, or were simply figureheads used by older militants to increase the group's numbers. Although some of the brother's followers might have re-joined the Karen National Union, God's Army is decidedly inactive. Luther remains in Thailand, while Johnny returned to Burma in

July 2006 where he surrendered to Burmese authorities. It is unknown why he decided to leave Thailand.

Also known as Gods Army of the Holy Mountain

Guatemalan National Revolutionary Unity

Abbreviation: URNG
Continent: Central America
Country: Guatemala
Background:

The Guatemalan National Revolutionary Unity (Spanish: Unidad Revolucionaria Nacional Guatemalteca, URNG-MAIZ or most commonly URNG) was a guerrilla movement that emerged in Guatemala in 1982. After a peace process brokered by the United Nations URNG laid down its arms in 1996 and became a legal political party in 1998.

The URNG was formed as guerrilla umbrella organisation on the 7th February by four revolutionary groups active in Guatemala: the Guerrilla Army of the Poor (EGP), the Revolutionary Organisation of Armed People (ORPA), the Rebel Armed Forces (FAR), and the National Directing Nucleus of PGT (PGT-NDN).

On the 23rd March 1982, retired General Efraín Ríos Montt came to power as the chairman of a military junta that began a violent "scorched-earth" counterinsurgency campaign in the indigenous highlands against the URNG and its supporters until he was toppled the following year.

By the time a civilian government returned to office in 1986, the URNG recognised that coming to power through armed struggle was out of the question, and they took initiatives to negotiate a political solution.

According to a report in NACLA's Report on the Americas (May/June 1997),

The government and army maintained that since they had "defeated" the URNG, they had no need to negotiate until the guerrillas had laid down their arms. The subsequent settlements ending the wars in Nicaragua and El Salvador stiffened the elites' resolve "never" to permit such an outcome in Guatemala.

But gradually, from 1986 to 1996, the army and government were drawn into a peace process moderated and verified by the United Nations and including other international actors as key players. Both sides made major concessions. Obligations were imposed on the government, including significant constitutional reforms, which were internationally binding and would be verified by the UN.

In 1987 URNG substituted PGT-NDN for the Guatemalan Party of Labour (PGT) in its leadership.

On the 29th December 1996, a peace agreement was signed by the government and the URNG in the presence of UN Secretary-General Boutros Boutros-Ghali, officially ending the 36-year Civil War. The Secretary-General of the URNG, Comandante Rolando Morán, and president Álvaro Arzú jointly received the UNESCO Peace Prize for their efforts to end the civil war and attaining the peace agreement.

In the last legislative election, held on the 9th November 2003, the party won 4.2% of the popular vote and 2 out of 158 seats in Congress. In the presidential election held the same day, its candidate Rodrigo Asturias won 2.6% of the popular vote. At the 2007 elections, the party won with 3.72 % 2 seats in the congressional elections. In the presidential election of the same day, its candidate Miguel Ángel Sandoval won 2.14 % of the popular vote.

See Revolutionary Organisation of Armed People (ORPA), Guerrilla Army of the Poor (EGP), Rebel Armed Forces (FAR), National Directing Nucleus of PGT (PGT-NDN)

Guerrilla Army of the Poor

Abbreviation: EGP
Continent: Central America
Country: Guatemala
Background:
The Guerrilla Army of the Poor (EGP - Ejército Guerrillero de los Pobres) was one of the four guerrilla organisations comprising the Guatemalan National Revolutionary Unity (URNG - Unidad Revolucionaria Nacional Guatemalteca) that negotiated and signed the Peace accords in Guatemala with the Government and the Army of Guatemala.

Initially, the guerrilla organisation went by the acronym NORC but soon became known as the EGP. On the 19th January 1972, the first guerrilla contingents entered the forests of the Ixcán, to the north of Quichė. As a communist organisation, it combined a vanguard party structure with paramilitary forces and a Marxist-Leninist ideology.

The EGP sought to organise and, to a certain extent, control elements of the Indigenous towns of Guatemala as an opposition to the dictatorial regimes of the late twentieth century.

Until the peace accords were signed on the 29th December 1996, the EGP was the guerrilla organisation with the greatest number of militants and territorial extension, although this level of influence was greatly diminished from earlier levels, particularly following the brutal 'pacification' of the countryside under General Efrain Rios Montt. At its peak, the EGP could rely upon a social base of approximately 250,000 people, divided in the following guerrilla fronts:

"Commander Ernesto Guevara", in the NW zone of the country and
    the Forest of the Ixcán.
"Ho Chi Minh" in the Ixil zone of Guatemala.
"Marco Antonio Yon Sosa" in the North Central region of the country.
"Augusto César Sandino" in the central zone of Guatemala.
"13 of November" in the Eastern zone.
"Luis Turcios Lima" in the South Coast.
"Otto René Castillo" in the capital of the country and suburban zones.

The Commander-in-Chief was Ricardo Ramirez de León, alias
Commander Rolando Morán, who became the first Secretary General of
URNG following the peace accords. The EGP were disbanded on the 15th
February 1997, two months after signing the accords, and were integrated
into the URNG, which today exists as a conventional political party.

Gush Emunim Underground

Continent: Middle East
Country: Israel
Background:
Gush Emunim Underground was a militant organisation formed by prom-
inent members of the Israeli political movement Gush Emunim that ex-
isted from 1979-1984.

In 1983, its members were involved in a retaliation attack after the murder of a yeshivah student in Hebron. In broad daylight, two men entered
the Islamic College of Hebron, spraying bullets and tossing a grenade.
They murdered three students and wounded thirty-three. The group was
best known, however, for masterminding a failed attempt at destroying the
Dome of the Rock in Jerusalem. Shin Bet agents arrested the members
during an attempted bus bombing in 1984 and during interrogation discovered the group's plot to blow up the pillars of the Dome of the Rock.
Three of the men were sentenced to life in prison for the Islamic College
attack. Controversially, their sentences were commuted three times, so they
left prison in less than seven years

Hamas

Continent: Middle East
Country: Palestine
Background:

Hamas is a violent outgrowth of the Muslim Brotherhood. The Muslim Brotherhood is a Sunni, Islamist, religious movement that originated in Egypt and seeks broad social, moral, and political reforms based upon Islam. From the late 1960s, Hamas' founder and spiritual leader, Sheikh Ahmed Yassin, was actively involved in non-violent Muslim Brotherhood activities in the Palestinian Territories, including preaching, education, and charity work. In 1973, Yassin established al-Mujamma' al-Islami (Islamic Centre), an umbrella organisation overseeing Muslim Brotherhood activities in the Gaza Strip. By the early 1980s, Yassin's ideology had begun to radicalise with Yassin more openly espousing violence against Israel.

After the outbreak of the first Palestinian intifada in December 1987, Hamas was established as the political arm for Muslim Brotherhood activities and Hamas members began actively promoting the uprising. In August 1988, Hamas released its official charter. Hamas is dedicated to creating an Islamic state in the territory of "Palestine" (all of Israel and Palestinian Territories). According to Hamas' charter, the land of Palestine has been endowed to Islam, and it is therefore the duty of all Muslims to liberate Palestine through violent jihad.

Hamas remains zealously dedicated to its violent, Islamist goals and seeks to destroy Israel and replace the Palestinian Authority with an Islamic state. While Hamas and the Palestinian Authority/PLO do cooperate occasionally, Hamas has generally presented itself as an Islamic counterweight to Arafat's secular government. Hamas has violently opposed any political compromises with Israel and has frequently used suicide bombings and rocket attacks against Israel to derail the peace process.

As part of its Islamist ideology, Hamas maintains an active network of social services within the Palestinian Territories. Hamas' substantial financial support has enabled it to provide social services, such as education, health care, and recreation services that the Palestinian Authority has been unable to provide. This social work has substantially increased popular support for Hamas, drawing political support away from the Palestinian Authority.

Hamas has been able to leverage its popular support into increased support for its terrorist activities.

In January 2006, Hamas ran candidates for Palestinian parliamentary elections. In shocking fashion, the group won a landslide victory, garnering 76 out of a possible 132 seats.

In its newfound position as a legitimate political party, Hamas has continued to maintain a hard line against Israel and remains an active militant group. In 2006, factional clashes with its main rival, al-Fatah, consumed the Gaza Strip and led to many deaths on both sides.

Also known as Harakat al-Muqawammah al-Islammiyya, Islamic Resistance Movement

Hamas Of Iraq

Continent: Middle East
Country: Iraq
Background:
Hamas Iraq is a Sunni militia group based in Iraq, which broke off from the 1920 Revolution Brigade on the 18th March 2007. The group has claimed to have released videos of its attack on US troops. The 1920 Revolution Brigade insists that Hamas Iraq was involved in assisting US troops in their recent Diyala operations against Al-Qaeda in Iraq. Iraqi Prime Minister Nuri al-Maliki has feared the US-armed 'concerned local citizens' are an armed Sunni opposition in the making, and has argued that such groups should be under the command of the Iraqi Army or police. On the 11th October 2007 the militia group joined a political council that embraced armed resistance against American "occupation".

Hezbollah

Continent: Middle East
Country: Lebanon
Background:
Hezbollah (Arabic for "Party of God") is an umbrella organisation of various radical Islamic Shi'ite groups and organisations which receives substantial financial and philosophical support from Iran.

The name Hezbollah comes from a Koranic verse promising triumph to those who join the Party of God. Hezbollah was founded in 1982 in Lebanon's Bekaa Valley by Shia clergyman educated in Iran, and it subsumed a number of Lebanese Islamic groups. Hezbollah's formation was a direct response to Israel's 1982 invasion of Lebanon designed to eliminate the Palestinian Liberation Organisation's base of operations. The group quickly became an effective fighting force thanks to training, weaponry, and funding from the Iranian Revolutionary Guard Corps operating in Lebanon. Hezbollah soon began running training camps in the Bekaa Valley and other parts of Lebanon that instructed members of Hezbollah and other terrorist organisations how to conduct assassinations, kidnappings, suicide bombings, and guerrilla warfare.

In the early 1980s, Hezbollah popularised suicide bombings as an effective terrorist tactic. In April 1983, Hezbollah allegedly blew up a van filled with explosives in front of the U.S. embassy in Beirut killing 58 Americans and Lebanese. Then in October 1983, Hezbollah is believed to be responsible for a truck bomb that detonated in the U.S. Marine barracks killing 241 American peacekeepers, and a simultaneous truck bombing at the French barracks that killed 58 French soldiers. These attacks contributed to the decision to withdraw U.S. forces from Lebanon the following year. Hezbollah also carried out a number of kidnappings of Westerners in Lebanon during the mid 1980s, in which they executed the hostages or traded them for money or weapons.

In addition to Lebanon, Hezbollah's security apparatus operates in Europe, North and South America, East Asia, and other parts of the Middle East, and it is believed to be responsible for a number of other high profile terrorist attacks. In 1985 Hezbollah members hijacked TWA flight 847 and held the 39 Americans on board hostage for weeks. In addition, the 1992 bombing of the Israeli Embassy in Argentina and the 1994 bombing of a Jewish cultural centre in Buenos Aires are attributed to Hezbollah. Furthermore, in June 1996, Hezbollah allegedly attacked the Khobar Towers housing complex in Dharan, Saudi Arabia, killing 19 U.S servicemen and wounding hundreds of others.

In May 2000, Israel elected to unilaterally withdraw from southern Lebanon because the costs of continued military occupation were deemed unacceptable. Hezbollah immediately declared victory and took advantage of their increased freedom of movement to establish themselves as a virtual state within a state in southern Lebanon. During these years, Hezbollah continued its transformation from a terrorist organisation capable of executing the periodic spectacular attack to a well-disciplined professional fighting force. Core Hezbollah operatives likely currently number around 1,000, with reservist strength ranging from 3,000 to 10,000 fighters. Hezbollah also received a massive influx of funding from its primary state sponsor, Iran, at a clip of approximately 100 million annually. Iran provided thousands of Katyusha rockets and other advanced military hardware to the group as well.

On the 12th July 2006, Hezbollah members crossed the Israeli border and kidnapped two Israeli soldiers and killed 8 others. In response, Israel began a massive bombing campaign and limited ground incursion designed to destroy Hezbollah infrastructure and eliminate Hezbollah fighters and weaponry. Throughout the 34 days of intense fighting, Hezbollah fired 100s of rockets into northern Israel on a daily basis. On the 11th August 2006; Israel, Hezbollah, and the Lebanese government agreed to a cease fire. While the fighting has slowed considerably since, debate continues about the rules of engagement for the United Nations' peacekeeping force in Lebanon and whether Hezbollah will be disarmed.

Hezbollah's stated objectives include the establishment of a Shiite theocracy in Lebanon, the destruction of Israel, and the elimination of Western influences from the Middle East. Over the last 20 plus years, Hezbollah has not only professionalised its military capabilities but also joined Lebanon's political process and enmeshed itself into the social fabric of Lebanese society.

After the end of Lebanon's 15 year civil war in the early 1990s, Hezbollah joined the country's nascent democratic multi-confessional political process and the group currently enjoys widespread support among Lebanon's Shia population. As of August 2006, Hezbollah is a minority partner in the Lebanese Cabinet, with two serving ministers and a third endorsed by the group, and it holds 14 seats in Parliament.

Hezbollah's political wing also runs a variety of social programs in southern Lebanon and south Beirut that provide schooling, medical care, and welfare to Lebanese Shia. In addition, the group possesses its own radio station and satellite television station, al-Manar. Al-Manar serves as the primary propaganda engine for Hezbollah and broadcasts anti-Israel and anti-America propaganda to the Islamic world in multiple languages.

Due to its involvement in Lebanese politics and vast network of social services, there is considerable debate among the international community concerning whether Hezbollah should be classified as a terrorist organisation. The U.S., Canada, Israel, and others classify Hezbollah strictly as a terrorist organisation, which limits the group's ability to raise funds and travel internationally. However, countries like Australia and the United Kingdom distinguish between Hezbollah's security and political wings, and other countries like Russia do not consider Hezbollah a terrorist organisation.

Also known as Islamic Jihad, Islamic Jihad for the Liberation of Palestine, Organisation of the Oppressed on Earth, Party of God, Revolutionary Justice Organisation, The Islamic Resistance

Hezbollah al Hejaz

Continent: Middle East
Country: Saudi Arabia
Background:

Hezbollah Al-Hejaz (English: Party of God in the Hijaz) is or was a militant organisation operating in Saudi Arabia, Lebanon, Kuwait, and Bahrain. It is outlawed in Saudi Arabia. Several of its members are wanted in the United States for their part in the 1996 Khobar Towers bombing. Charged with participating were Ahmed Al-Mughassil, Ali Al-Houri, Hani Al-Sayegh, Ibrahim Al-Yacoub, Abdelkarim Al-Nasser, Mustafa Al-Qassab, Abdallah Al-Jarash, Hussein Al-Mughis, and a Lebanese "John Doe." Five more are wanted on conspiracy indictments: Sa'ed Al-Bahar, Saleh Ramadan, Ali Al-Marhoun, Mustafa Al-Mu'alem, and Fadel Al-Alawe. The Saudi Hezbollah is considered as terrorist group in Saudi Arabia and in America.

Hizb-an-Nusra

Continent: Asia
Country: Uzbekistan
Background:
Hizb-an-Nusra (English: Party of Support) is an Islamist organisation which the Uzbek government considers to be terrorist in nature that has operated in Uzbekistan since 1999. Members of Hizb ut-Tahrir, an international terrorist organisation, created Hizb-an-Nusra in Tashkent out of dissatisfaction with Hizb ut-Tahrir's inability to overthrow the Government of Uzbekistan.

Akromiya, another Islamic Uzbek terrorist organisation, broke away from HT in 1996. Akromiya leader Akrom Yo'ldoshev's pamphlet Yimonga Yul (Way to Faith) criticizes HT's goal of creating an international caliphate for impracticality. Yudashev argues in favour of creating an Islamic state on a local level instead.

Hizb ut-Tahrir al-Islami

Continent: Asia
Country: Uzbekistan, Tajikistan, Kyrgyzstan, and Kazakhstan, as well as in China
Background:
Hizb ut-Tahrir al-Islami (Islamic Party of Liberation) a radical Islamic political movement that seeks 'implementation of pure Islamic doctrine' and the creation of an Islamic caliphate in Central Asia. The group's aim is to resume the Islamic way of life and to convey the Islamic da'wah to the world. The ultimate goal of this secretive sectarian group is to unite the entire ummah, or Islamic world community, into a single caliphate. The aim is to bring the Muslims back to living an Islamic way of life in 'Dar al-Islam' (the land where the rules of Islam are being implemented, as opposed to

the non-Islamic world) and in an Islamic society such that all life's affairs in society are administered according to the Shari'ah rules.

Its basic aim was struggle with infidels and the organisation of a universal caliphate embracing all Islamic countries. This objective means bringing the Muslims back to living an Islamic way of life in Dar al-Islam and in an Islamic society such that all of life's affairs in society are administered according to the Shari'ah rules, and the viewpoint in it is the halal and the haram under the shade of the Islamic State, which is the Khilafah State. That state is the one in which Muslims appoint a Khaleefah and give him the bay'ah to listen and obey on condition that he rules according to the Book of Allah and the Sunnah of the Messenger of Allah and on condition that he conveys Islam as a message to the world through da'wah and jihad.

The group - also known as the Islamic Party of Liberation - believes it can achieve its utopian Islamic state in three steps. The first involves educating Muslims about its philosophies and goals. In the second step, the Muslims would then spread these views among others in their countries, especially members of government, the military and other power centres. In the third and final step, Hizb ut-Tahrir believes its faithful will cause secular governments to crumble because loyalties will then lie solely with Islam - not nationalities, politics or ethnic identifications. At that point the group says a supreme Islamic leader; a Caliph like those of past centuries would rule all Muslims with both political and religious authority.

There is little information on the number of its members. It is active all over the world. Hizb ut-Tahrir now has its main base in Western Europe, but it has large followings in Uzbekistan, Tajikistan, Kyrgyzstan, and Kazakhstan, as well as in China's traditionally Muslim Xinjiang Province. Most of its members are believed to be ethnic Uzbeks. Its expansion into Central Asia coincided with the breakup of the Soviet Union in the early 1990s. By one estimate there are more than 10,000 followers in Central Asia. Hizb ut-Tahrir al-Islami has been active in Central Asia since the breakup of the Soviet Union.

The group has never been overtly involved in any violent actions, and Hizb ut-Tahrir has long claimed it wants to achieve its objectives through nonviolent means. It has so far not been involved in any known terrorist activities. One of the most secretive fundamentalist Islamic organisations, it remains a radical organisation. Hizb ut-Tahrir is not against violence as such. It is just against the use of violence now. But they still think jihad (holy war) is a positive concept.

In 1999, the group was blamed for a series of bomb attacks in the Uzbekistan capital, Tashkent. It is believed by some to clandestinely fund and provide logistical support to a wide range of terrorist operations in

Central Asia, and elsewhere, although attacks may be carried out in the names of local groups.

Also known as Islamic Party of Liberation

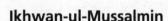

Ikhwan-ul-Mussalmin

Continent: Asia
Country: India
Background:
Indian security forces in Kashmir confront at least a dozen major insurgent groups of varying size and ideological orientation. The more prominent groups include the secular pro-independence Jammu and Kashmir Liberation Front (JKLF) and the radical Islamic and pro-Pakistani groups Hizb-ul-Mujahideen (HUM), Hizbollah, Harkat-ul-Ansar, and the pro-India Ikhwanul Muslimeen. In the summer of 1994 Pakistan's Inter Services Intelligence organised thirteen leading organisations into the United Jihad Council (Muttahida Jihad Council – MJC) under Commander Manzur Shah, the leader of Jamiat-ul-Mujahideen. Among the member organisations: Harakat-ul-Ansar, Hizb-ul-Mujahideen, Jamiat-ul-Mujahideen, Al-Jihad, Al-Barq, Ikhwan-ul-Mussalmin, Tariq-ul-Mujahideen.

The main Ikhwan facility is the Maktaba-i-Khidmat, originally established by the late Shaykh Abd Allah Azzam and now run by his successor Shaykh Muhammad Yussaf Abbas. It processes volunteers who are then dispatched to the numerous training camps run by Arab 'Afghan' militants inside Afghanistan.

Also known as Ikhwanul Muslimeen

Informal Anarchist Federation

Abbreviation: FAI
Continent: Europe
Country: Italy
Background:
The Informal Anarchist Federation (Federazione Anarchia Informale, FAI) has been described by Italian intelligence sources as a "horizontal" structure of various anarchist terrorist groups, united in their beliefs in revolutionary armed action. These groups oppose both the current European order and Marxism, which they see as solely a replacement of one form of oppressive authority with another. Groups comprising the FAI act both as separate organisations and also under the auspices of the FAI as a whole, and are known to format group campaigns.

The groups comprising the Informal Anarchist Federation are the "July 20th Brigade," the "Five C's," "International Solidarity," and the "Cooperative of Hand-Made Fire & Related Items." Each of these groups has also forged its own set of alliances outside of the FAI. Collaboration between these anarchist groups and more established Marxist groups, essentially in opposition to the principles of the FAI, have been a subject of debate in both anarchist circles and within the Italian security community. These claims have been bolstered recently with claims of solidarity between the FAI and the newest incarnations of the Red Brigades. The FAI and its constituent groups remain active and present a threat to public safety in Italy and across Europe.

See the July 20th Brigade, Five 'C's, International Solidarity, Cooperative of Hand Made-Made Fire and Related Items

Inner Macedonian Revolutionary Organisation

Abbreviation: IMRO
Continent: Europe
Country: Bulgaria
Background:

The Internal Macedonian Revolutionary Organisation (in Bulgarian: Vatreshna Makedonska Revoliucionna Organizacia, ____, in Macedonian: Vnatreshna Makedonska Revolucionerna Organizacija, ____), commonly known in English as IMRO, was the name of a revolutionary political organisation in the Macedonia and Thrace regions of the Ottoman Empire, as well as in Bulgaria, and after 1913 in the Macedonian regions of Greece and Serbia (later Yugoslavia). The organisation has changed its name on several occasions.

In the Republic of Macedonia and Bulgaria several right-wing parties carrying the prefix "VMRO" were established in the 1990s.

The organisation was founded in 1893 in Ottoman Thessaloniki by a "small band of anti-Ottoman Macedonian Slav revolutionaries, which later came to be dominated by Bulgarians." They considered Macedonia an indivisible territory and all of its inhabitants "Macedonians", no matter their religion or ethnicity". The organisation was a secret revolutionary society operating in the late 19th and early 20th centuries with the goal of making Macedonia an autonomous state, but which later became an agent serving Bulgarian interests in Balkan politics. It was led by Hristo Tatarchev, Dame Gruev, Petar Pop-Arsov, Andon Dimitrov, Hristo Batandzhiev and Ivan Hadzhinikolov. Its first name after Hristo Tatarchev's "Memoirs" was Macedonian Revolutionary Organisation (MRO). Ivan Hadzhinikolov in his memoirs underlined the five basic principles of the MRO's foundation.

The initial period of idealism for IMARO ended, however, with the Vinitsa Affair and the discovery by the Ottoman police of a secret depot of ammunition near the Bulgarian border in 1897. The wide-scale repressions against the activists of the Committee led to its transformation into a militant guerrilla organisation, which engaged into attacks against Ottoman officials and punitive actions against suspected traitors. The guerrilla groups of IMARO, known as "chetas" later (after 1903) also waged a war against the pro-Serbian and pro-Greek armed groups during the Greek Struggle for Macedonia.

Interahamwe

Continent: Africa
Country: Rwanda
Background:
The Interahamwe (meaning "those who stand together" or "those who work together" or "those who fight together") is a Hutu paramilitary organisation. The militia enjoyed the backing of the Hutu-led government leading up to, during, and after the Rwandan Genocide. A majority of the killings were perpetrated by the Interahamwe and ragtag portions of the militias that joined during the war.

Robert Kajuga, a Tutsi, was the President of the Interahamwe. The Second Vice President of Interahamwe was Georges Rutaganda. The Interahamwe was formed by groups of young Hutu males who carried out the Rwandan Genocide acts against the Tutsis in 1994. The Interahamwe formed the Genocidal Radio System which was used to broadcast where the Tutsis were fleeing.

For over a half a century, Hutus and Tutsis lived together in Rwanda. The Tutsis were the minority group who were largely herders, while the Hutus, the majority, worked the fields. After European influence came into the region, mainly Belgian, things changed significantly. The Belgians took the Tutsis side claiming they were the superior upper class. After years of being treated as peasants by the Belgians, the Hutus rebelled against the Tutsis and Belgians. The Interahamwe was formed to carry out the slaughtering of the Tutsis.

Following the invasion of the Rwandan capital Kigali by the Western backed Rwandese Patriotic Front (RPF), many Rwandan civilians and members of the Interahamwe fled to neighbouring countries, most notably to what at the time was Zaire, now Democratic Republic of Congo and Tanzania. It has been nearly impossible to bring the Interahamwe to justice because they did not wear uniforms or have a clearly organised group of followers. They were the neighbours, friends and co-workers of Tutsis.

Throughout the war, members of the Interahamwe moved into camps of refugees and the internally displaced. There, the victims were mixed in with the enemy and to this day it cannot be proven who killed who. With the Kagame regime still in power, members still take part in border raids from the refugee camps.

During the war, hundreds of thousands of Rwandan Hutu refugees fled to Zaire, along with many members of the Interahamwe, Presidential Guard, and the RGF, collectively becoming known as the Rassemblement Démocratique pour le Rwanda (roughly, Democratic Rally for Rwanda). Following the recruitment of significant numbers of Congolese Hutu the organisation took the name Armée de Libération du Rwanda (ALiR).

Iraqi Revenge Brigades

Continent: Middle East

Country: Iraq

Background:

Iraqi Revenge Brigades is a group that claimed responsibility for the January 2005 kidnapping of Minas Ibrahim al-Yusufi, leader of the Iraqi Democratic Christian Party. Al-Yusufi, a Swedish citizen born in Iraq, was taken from his car along the Baghdad-Mosul highway. Shortly after his abduction, a group calling themselves the Iraqi Revenge Brigades announced they were holding al-Yusufi and demanded a ransom of four million dollars (later lowered to $400,000) for his release. Over the course of a month, the Brigades released two videos showing al-Yusufi pleading for his life and imploring King Gustaf of Sweden, the International Federation of Christian Parties, the Iraqi Constituent National Assembly, and the Association of Muslim Scholars to help secure his release.

On the 18th March al-Yusufi was released by the Iraqi Revenge Brigades. Although official sources remarked that no ransom had been paid, this claim could not be verified. Most recently, the group was responsible for the January 2006 kidnapping of Jill Carroll, an American freelance journalist on assignment for the Christian Science Monitor. Carroll was freed in March 2006.

Kidnapping of foreigners is extremely common in post-war Iraq, although the motives behind such abductions vary greatly. Sometimes the perpetrators have concrete demands, such as the removal of specific troops from Iraq or the freeing of certain prisoners from U.S. custody. In other cases the perpetrators simply want to kill their hostage to invoke fear and to deter further foreign involvement. In the case of the al-Yusufi kidnapping, as it is with many other abductions, the motive seems to be purely monetary. At no time did al-Yusufi's kidnappers air any grievances or make any demands beyond compensation. To that end, although the Iraqi Revenge Brigades have not been responsible for further attacks or abductions, it is quite possible that the group is still active and looking to kidnap foreigners or wealthy Iraqis, simply for financial gain.

Also known as Al-Isawi Martyr Brigade, Brigades of Vengeance, Iraqi Vengeance Brigades

Iraultza

Continent: Europe
Country: Spain
Background:
Iraultza, meaning Revolution in the Basque language, was a small Basque militant armed group of the Trotskyist tendency that may be remembered for being the only one of its kind not to have killed anyone except two of its own members, who died preparing an explosive device in the early 1990s. Soon after the group, that had been active for about a decade with small attacks of explosives that never aimed to cause any personal victim, announced its dissolution.

Irish National Liberation Army

Abbreviation: INLA
Continent: Europe
Country: United Kingdom and Ireland
Background:
The Irish National Liberation Army (INLA) is a republican paramilitary organisation operating in Northern Ireland. Founded by Seamus Costello on the 8th December 1974, the INLA is the armed wing of the Irish Republican Socialist Party (IRSP) and a splinter group of the Official Irish Republican Army (Official IRA).

The Official IRA, with its Marxist-inspired ideology, emerged in 1969 following the split of the Irish Republican Army (IRA) into the Official and Provisional factions. In 1972, following a series of politically damaging attacks against civilians; the Official IRA declared a ceasefire and announced its intention to join the political process. Republican dissents, desiring a continuation of the armed struggle against the British presence in Northern Ireland, broke away from the organisation and formed the INLA in 1974.

As a paramilitary organisation in Northern Ireland, the INLA espouses a unique ideology of militant republicanism coupled with a Marxist-Leninist political and social approach. The organisation fights to unite all 32 counties of Ireland under an independent communist Irish state. Currently six counties in Northern Ireland remain part of the United Kingdom and 26 counties comprise the Republic of Ireland.

Members of the INLA have conducted attacks against British security forces, Northern Ireland's police forces, Protestants (civilians and paramilitaries), and rival republicans through the use of bombings, assassinations, and armed attacks. The group's most publicised attack occurred in May 1979 when it claimed responsible for the assassination of Airey Neave, a prominent member of the British Parliament and close political supporter of Margaret Thatcher. Airey Neave was killed by a car bomb shortly before the 1979 election that resulted in the selection of Margaret Thatcher as Prime Minister. In 1997, three imprisoned members of the INLA assassinated Billy "King Rat" Wright, the Loyalist Volunteer Force (LVF) leader also ensconced in Maze prison.

Shortly after its formation, the INLA was engaged in a bitter feud with its founding group, the Official IRA, which sought to destroy the faction. In the 1980s, the INLA was almost torn apart by factionalism, intra-republican rivalries, criminality, and arrests. One such rivalry involved an armed group composed of former INLA members, the Irish People's Liberation Organisation, that attempted to annihilate the INLA in 1987.

On the 22nd August 1998, the INLA declared a ceasefire although it remains opposed to the Good Friday Agreement. Its ceasefire was declared just days after the 1998 Omagh bombing in Northern Ireland. Although the attack was attributed to another republican terrorist group, the Real IRA, the INLA has been implicated as providing supplies for the bombing, including transportation vehicles.

While the INLA has not conduct any recent terrorist attacks, the group remains heavily involved in organised crime and narcotics trafficking and has not disarmed its membership. Several security sources have alleged that INLA members remain active through the use of cover names such as the Catholic Reaction Force (CRF) and People's Republican Army. Despite its ceasefire, the INLA continues to pose a threat to Northern Ireland and its fragile peace process.

Also known as Catholic Reaction Force (CRF), People's Liberation Army (PLA), People's Republican Army (PRA)

Irish Peoples Liberation Organisation

Abbreviation: IPLO
Continent: Europe
Country: United Kingdom and Ireland
Background:
The Irish People's Liberation Organisation was a small Irish republican

paramilitary organisation which was formed in 1986 by disaffected and expelled members of the Irish National Liberation Army whose factions coalesced in the aftermath of the supergrass trials. It developed a reputation for intra-republican violence and criminality, before being forcibly disbanded by the Provisional Irish Republican Army in 1992.

The IPLO emerged out of a split in the Irish National Liberation Army. After the 1981 Irish Hunger Strike, in which three of its members died, the INLA fell apart from within. The mid 1980s saw the virtual dissolution of the movement as a coherent paramilitary force. Factions associated with Belfast and Dublin respectively, fell into dispute with each other. When INLA man Harry Kirkpatrick turned supergrass, he implicated many of his former comrades in various terrorist activities and many of them were convicted on his testimony. After this, the death knell seemed close to sounding for the movement. It could be argued that by this time the INLA, and the associated political group the Irish Republican Socialist Party (IRSP) no longer existed as coherent national organisations. As a result, members both inside and out of prison broke away from the INLA and set up the IPLO. Some key players at the outset were Tom McAllister, Gerard Steenson, Jimmy Brown, Martin 'Rook' O'Prey and Harry Flynn. Ironically Steenson had attempted to have Flynn killed in 1981.

The IPLO's initial priority was to destroy the Irish Republican Socialist Movement from which it had split, and most of its early attacks reflected this, being more frequently against former comrades than on the security forces of the British state in Northern Ireland. The destructive psychological impact of the feud on the communities that the combatants came from was huge as it was viewed as a fratricidal conflict between fellow republicans.

The INLA shot and killed IPLO's leader Gerard Steenson in March 1986, and following revenge killings by the IPLO, the organisations agreed to go their separate ways.

The IPLO was increasingly becoming involved in the drugs trade, especially in ecstasy, and was becoming a haven for those who fell out of favour with the Provisional Irish Republican Army: the portents for its future were not good. A fallout over the proceeds of one transaction cost the life of Jimmy Brown, reputedly the only IPLO leader with any political aspirations or ability. A full-scale feud followed between two factions terming themselves, "Army Council" - led by Jimmy Brown and "Belfast Brigade" (Sammy Ward) which led to the 3000th killing of the Troubles Hugh McKibbon a 21 year old "Army Council" man. Brown had been the previous victim. This was one feud which made no pretence of being anything other than a lethal squabble over money and drugs. The organisation which had claimed it wanted to destroy the INLA because of the INLA's alleged criminality had become everything it claimed to have set out to oppose, and was turning inward destroying itself.

The INLA however regrouped and moved on under the leadership of Hugh Torney aka "Cueball". He was deposed as Chief of Staff (leader) in 1995 and there then followed another bloody feud between Torney's supporters and those who supported others including Gino Gallagher who was shot dead by a gunman hired by Torney's supporters. The INLA and IRSP are still in existence today without any obvious evidence of further splits to come.

Eventually, the Provisional IRA - by far the largest armed republican group in Ireland - decided enough was enough and mounted a major operation to wipe out the IPLO. On Saturday 31st October 1992 approximately one hundred IRA members systematically wiped the IPLO from the face of Belfast killing Belfast Brigade leader Sammy Ward, kneecapping several more and only sparing their lives on condition of their unconditional surrender and disbandment, which was forthcoming from both factions within days.

According to the Sutton database of deaths at the University of Ulster's CAIN project, the IPLO was responsible for 22 killings during the Troubles. Among its victims were twelve civilians, six INLA members, two loyalist paramilitary figures and two members of the British security forces.

Irish Republican Army

Abbreviation: IRA
Continent: Europe
Country: United Kingdom and Ireland
Background:

Founded over eighty years ago, the Irish Republican Army (IRA) is arguably the longest-operating terrorist organisation in Western Europe. Despite its longevity, the group remains committed to its founding goal, an Ireland fully independent of Great Britain. Ireland was ruled by Great Britain from the 18th century until 1921. Between 1919 and 1921, Irish separatists engaged in a violent guerrilla war on British forces within Ireland. By 1921, the Irish separatists, led by the political party Sinn Fein, had reached an agreement with the United Kingdom called the Anglo-Irish Treaty. With the signing of the treaty, the UK agreed to grant full independence to the southern 26 counties of Ireland while retaining sovereignty over the remaining six northern counties which would soon be known as Northern Ireland.

Following the signing of the Anglo-Irish Treaty, a civil war erupted in Ireland between pro-treaty and anti-treaty factions. While the acceptance of the treaty was ratified by referendum, there was a large minority that continued to find the creation of Northern Ireland an unacceptable compromise. In 1922, the IRA was founded by members of the anti-treaty faction who had participated in the guerrilla war against the British, lost the civil war and continued to refuse to recognise the legitimacy of the Republic of Ireland or Northern Ireland.

In 1969, the commencement of the almost thirty-year period collectively known as the "Troubles," the IRA split into two rival factions, the Official and Provisional IRA. The Official IRA, with its Marxist-oriented ideology, was opposed to an armed campaign against the British and would later declare an indefinite ceasefire in 1972. Although there have been recent accusations of criminal involvement, the Official IRA is not active in a military capacity. Hard-line members of the IRA, espousing the traditional republican ideology and opposed to the Official IRA's leftist leanings, formed the Provisional IRA in order to escalate the armed campaign against the British troop presence in Northern Ireland and protect Catholic civilians. After 1972 ceasefire declared by the Official IRA, the Provisional IRA became the de facto IRA, desiring the removal of British troops and the unification of Northern Ireland and the Republic of Ireland.

The IRA seeks to unite all 32 counties into one Irish state, independent of Great Britain. Due to their opposition to the 1921 Anglo-Irish Treaty, the IRA does not recognise the legitimacy of the governments of both Ireland and Northern Ireland although these views have been moderated in recent years. Bombings (particularly car bombs), assassinations, kidnappings, punishment beatings, extortion, smuggling and robberies have been conducted by the organisation in Northern Ireland, Ireland, and mainland Great Britain. Although its primary targets have been the British military and police in Northern Ireland, the IRA has also carried out operations against Protestants (paramilitaries and civilians) and British government officials, police and civilians in mainland Great Britain and Europe. Advanced warning for bombing attacks was occasionally given in order to minimise civilian causalities. After several instances of damaging police informant infiltrations, the IRA reorganised itself into small cells, called Active Service Units, under the leadership of the Army Council, to maintain operational security.

In August 1994, the IRA declared a cease-fire. While the cease-fire briefly broke down in 1996, negotiations resumed in the summer of 1997 following the election of Tony Blair as Prime Minister. The cease-fire culminated in the watershed moment of the Good Friday Agreement in 1998. In the Good Friday Accords, the IRA made a drastic shift in their policy and agreed to work towards a united Ireland only in peaceful terms. From the signing of the Accords on the 12th April 1998 through the end of the year, many held out the possibility that the IRA had finally given up its terrorist tactics. However, while the IRA had theoretically agreed that a peaceful solution was the only option; their actions demonstrated that violence was still a viable option. Members continue to engage in criminal activities such as smuggling and robbery.

Violent splinter groups, such as the Real IRA and Continuity IRA, were formed in opposition to the IRA's participation in a ceasefire and the peace process, heightening sectarian tensions. Despite temporary setbacks, negotiations continued, and in 2001, the IRA announced that it would begin to disarm. Furthermore, in July 2002 the IRA issued a public apology to the civilian victims of its attacks. Despite these promises, it was not until July 2005 that the IRA formally ordered an end to their armed campaign, pledging to use non-violent means to achieve their goals. In September of that year, an independent commission set up to oversee the disarmament process, the Independent Monitoring Commission, reported that the IRA had in fact scrapped their arsenal. This is seen as a major step by the group in upholding their pledge to abstain from violence.

Some believe that the efforts the IRA has taken in recent years demonstrate its real commitment to peace and an end to its terrorist activity. Although disarmament is a huge step forward, it remains to be seen if the IRA's non-violence pledge will be backed up with further action, and whether the organisation has permanently committed to leave terrorism behind. The continued presence of loyalist paramilitary organisations, violent Republican splinter groups, and sectarian tensions have the potential to drag the IRA back into terrorism.

Also known as Provisional Irish Republican Army (PIRA), Provos

Irrintzi

Continent: Europe
Country: France, Spain
Background:
Little is known about the Basque nationalist group, Irrintzi. Basque people inhabit territory in northern Spain and south-western France known as Euskal-Herria and their struggle to establish a separate nation-state has gained notoriety following the establishment of violent organisations such as Basque Fatherland and Freedom (ETA). Named after a whistling cry that was once utilised as a Basque war cry, the group claimed responsibility on the 12th October 2006 for five bombings in August in French Basque country.

On the 19th August a rudimentary homemade explosive device was left at the holiday home of French Defence Minister Michele Alliot-Marie. An anonymous caller warned police officials of the device which failed to detonate. Street violence associated with ETA supporters was rampant around this time following a statement by the ETA, published in the Basque newspaper Gara that the peace crisis was in crisis and warning against attacks on Basque citizens.

On the 12th October a communiqué issued by Irrintzi claimed responsibility for the device and four other unspecified attacks in French Basque country. It remains unclear how many of the remaining four explosives detonated. In the communiqué, group members demanded that the French government participate in peace negotiations with ETA, stated that Euskal-Herria is not for sale, and listed several common Basque demands such as recognition of the Basque people and a referendum for the Basque to decide their future.

No attacks have been claimed by Irrintzi since October 2006. It is possible that Irrintzi was merely a cover name for ETA members, observing a March 2006 ceasefire, or that ETA supporters claimed the attack during a period of supporter-led violence in August. Given the continued tensions among Basque nationals, Spain and France despite peace negotiations, future attacks remain possible whether conducted by Irrintzi or another Basque nationalist group.

Islamic Armed Group of al Qaeda, Fallujah Branch

Continent: Middle East
Country: Iraq
Background:
This Muslim group with many foreign fighters appeared on the scene in July, 2003 and may have been led by Afghan war veteran Abu Iyad. They claimed responsibility for "all" the armed resistance against US forces in Iraq in a four-minute videotape aired on the Dubai-based Al-Arabiya satellite television station on the 13th July 2003. The group denies any affiliation with Saddam Hussein and was the first Iraqi group purporting links to Osama Bin Laden's Al-Qaeda. In their taped address, they encouraged the United States to "leave Iraq's territories and to live up to their promises". The taped address warned of more attacks that would aim to "break America's back." The speaker on the tape purportedly resembled Abu Iyad, who the US claims is a member of Al-Qaeda, but there is no concrete evidence to this claim. European governments often refer to Iyad simply as a Muslim Mujahideen. Iyad, who lost a leg in the Afghan war with the Russians, has also fought in the Chechen jihad and was last positively identified in the Pankisi Gorge in Georgia in spring 2002. A report issued on the 20th April 2003 from the "Headquarters of the Arab Mujahideen in Iraq" was signed

by Abu Iyad, which may indicate that Iyad was one of the top commanders of the foreign Mujahideen in Iraq and if he has not previously had links to Al-Qaeda, he may have recently been recruited by the group.

Islamic Front for the Liberation of Palestine

Abbreviation: IFLP
Continent: Middle East
Country: Lebanon
Background:

The Islamic Front for the Liberation of Palestine (IFLP) was a faction of the Palestine Liberation Organisation (PLO) that was most active in the 1980s and early 1990s. While their name incorporates a faith subtext, their public statements did not stress religion as a motivating factor. Their goal, as with other groups within the PLO network, was to establish an independent Palestinian state. However, at times the IFLP adhered to a strict militant philosophy that was distinct from their allied groups. In 1990, the IFLP criticised the PLO for condemning Palestinian Fedayeen (commando) operations against Zionist settlers, stating that the PLO response was devoid of national and militant substance and would be seen as a blessing for American policy in the region. IFLP spokesmen called for the PLO to retract the statement.

The IFLP claimed their first attack in 1986 with the bombing of Israeli soldiers in Jerusalem. Killing one person and injuring sixty-five. Later that year, IFLP operatives in Beirut held three Americans hostage in an attempt to force the U.S. to support the emerging Intifada in the West Bank and Gaza. The next documented attack from the IFLP occurred on the 2nd May 1990, when a firebomb was thrown at the offices of the Jordanian-Soviet Friendship Society in Amman. The reasons for the attack, as stated by IFLP spokesmen, were to retaliate against the Soviets for plotting against the Palestinian cause, and to protest the emigration of Soviet Jews to the Palestinian region. No one was killed or injured in the attack.

The IFLP has been inactive since 1990. When the First Intifada ended in 1991, members of IFLP most likely joined larger groups with similar ideologies (such as the PLO, Al-Fatah, or Hamas) that had the resources to sustain influence in the Palestinian region.

See the Palestine Liberation Organisation (PLO)

Islamic Jihad Brigades

Continent: Middle East
Country: Iraq

Background:

The Islamic Jihad Brigades is a terrorist organisation currently operating in Iraq; the group first emerged following the US offensive in Iraq. In December 2004, the Islamic Jihad Brigades killed two American construction workers, Dale Stoffel and Joseph Wemple. The terrorist group claimed these two contractors were agents of the Central Intelligence Agency (CIA) and American military. In fact, the two men were employed by CLI USA, an American construction company. Following the attack, terrorist members of the group posted a video, which displayed personal identification papers belonging to the deceased men.

Approximately a month later, the Islamic Jihad Brigades kidnapped a Lebanese contractor working in Iraq. The terrorist group again taped a video, this time showing the kidnapped man, Gebrayel Abdi Azar, along with four masked terrorists. The group demanded that Azar's company leave Iraq within seven days or he would be killed. Azar's company, the al-Darjani Group, suspended operations and Mr. Azar was subsequently released.

The Islamic Jihad Brigades' targets are not limited to contractors working in Iraq; in September 2004, the terrorist group threatened to attack Iraq's universities if the schools continued to be taught in a coeducational manner. The group claimed that the men and women could not be taught in the same setting because of the immoral environment of the Iraqi universities. The Islamic Jihad Brigades are therefore not solely focused on expelling US forces, but clearly demonstrate strict Islamic underpinnings within their terrorist philosophy.

The Islamic Jihad Brigades show no indication that they have ceased their terrorist actions against either the United States or affiliated multinational businesses operating in Iraq.

Islamic Jihad Group Uzbekistan

Abbreviation: IJG
Continent: Asia
Country: Uzbekistan
Background:

The Islamic Jihad Group (IJG) is a violent terrorist organisation responsible for several high-profile bombings in Uzbekistan. Islamic Jihad Group is a splinter organisation from the Islamic Movement of Uzbekistan (IMU), another terror group operating in Central Asia.

The IJG was previously unknown until April 2004 when the group claimed responsibility for a series of suicide bombings around Tashkent and Bukhara, which killed 47 people. The attacks targeted local government offices, as well as a crowded market. Although IJG released a statement claiming responsibility for the bombings, officials doubted the existence of the unknown group, and blamed other extremist organisations.

On the 30th July 2004, IJG carried out simultaneous bombing attacks on the US Embassy, the Israeli Embassy, and the Uzbek Prosecutor General, killing at least two people and wounding several. The attacks were highly sophisticated, and they cemented IJG's status as a real terrorist threat in Central Asia. In their claim of responsibility, the IJG wrote:

"A group of young Muslims executed martyrdom operations that put fear in the apostate government and its infidel allies, the Americans and Jews. The mujahidin belonging to Islamic Jihad Group attacked both the American and Israeli embassies as well as the court building where the trials of a large number of the brothers from the Group had begun. These martyrdom operations that the group is executing will not stop, God willing. It is for the purpose of repelling the injustice of the apostate government and supporting the jihad of our Muslim brothers in Iraq, Palestine, Afghanistan, the Hijaz, and in other Muslim countries ruled by infidels and apostates."

Although IJG has not publicly elucidated their goals and philosophy, from their background and statements it is clear that they are deeply opposed to the current authoritarian-secular rule in Uzbekistan, and wish to set up an Islamic state in its place. Besides being closely linked with IMU, many officials speculate that IJG has close ties to al-Qaeda given the sophisticated nature of their attacks and targets.

On the 25th May 2005, the US State Department designated Islamic Jihad Group as a Specially Designated Global Terrorist Group. The United Nations shortly followed suit. Although IJG has not claimed responsibility for any attacks since 2004, it is highly likely that the group will continue attacks in the near future.

See the Islamic Movement of Uzbekistan (IMU)

Islamic Jihad for the Liberation of Palestine

Abbreviation: IJLP
Continent: Middle East
Country: Lebanon
Background:
Islamic Jihad for the Liberation of Palestine (IJLP) was a Lebanese radical Shia group that claimed credit for the 24th January 1987 abduction of three American and one Indian professors - Alann Steen, Jesse Turner, Robert Pohill, Mithal Eshwar Singh - from Beirut University College in West Beirut: They were eventually released.

IJLP is not to be confused with the similarly named Islamic Jihad

Movement in Palestine, which is made up of Palestinians active in attacking Israeli military and civilian targets in Israel/Palestine and based in Damascus.

Islamic Salvation Front

Abbreviation: FIS
Continent: Asia
Country: Algeria, Germany, United States of America
Background:

The Islamic Salvation Front (FIS) was initially created as a network of small, informal mosque groups. After Algerian constitutional reforms allowed the creation of political parties for the first time, the FIS filed for legal recognition and was certified as a political party in September 1989. The group won more than 50% of the votes during municipal elections in June 1990. In March 1991, a new electoral law proposed expanding the number of seats in Parliament from 295 to 542, clearly favouring regions in which the Front de Liberation Nationale (FLN), "the main Algerian political party," had strong support. In response, the FIS called for a general strike, which over several days, lead to escalating violence between militants and the security forces, and an eventual imposition of martial law. The threat of jihad against the army prompted them to arrest Abassi al Madani and his second-in-command, Ahmed Belhadj, on charges of conspiracy against the state. An additional 700 or so Islamists were soon taken into custody, joining some 2300 others already imprisoned.

When elections were held in December 1991, the FIS again surprised the secular parties by winning 44% of the Parliamentary seats (188 of 430 contested seats), while the FLN won only 15. Of the remaining 199 seats to be decided in the second round of elections (the second round decides those seats in which no candidate received a clear majority of the votes during the first round), the FIS was the leading party for 144 (i.e., although they did not receive more than 50% of the votes in that constituency, they still received more votes than their opponents in the first round). Fearing an Islamist takeover of the government, the Army cancelled the second round of elections scheduled for January 1992, removed the President from office, appointed a five-member High Council of State, made the FIS illegal and arrested many of its leaders.

Although FIS leadership initially remained ambiguous about the use of violence by its followers, imprisoned deputy leader Belhadj endorsed the armed struggle and indicated unity with an explicitly violent group, Abdelkader Chebouti's Mouvement Islamique Arme (MIA) in January of 1993. A breakdown in an attempted dialogue between the regime and the

FIS in late 1993 led a number of senior FIS leaders to defect to the more extreme Groupe Islamique Armee. To counter the influence of the GIA, the FIS officially created an armed wing in July of 1994, the Arme Islamiques du Salut (AIS), although this name had been used since 1993 to refer to the variety of armed groups loyal to the FIS. Although the FIS distanced itself from the GIA's civilian massacres, a January 1995 car bomb at the police headquarters in Algiers killed forty-two people and injured 286. In September of 1997, the FIS declared a ceasefire and in July of 1999, a new Algerian government formed an accord with the FIS and issued an amnesty for several thousand AIS guerrillas. FIS leaders Abassi Madani and Ali Belhadj were released from prison in 2003.

The AIS is no longer considered to be an active insurgent group. A unilateral ceasefire was declared in September 1997. A 16-point plan issued after the first round of voting in 1991 declared the group's intention to expand Sharia law to all areas of public and private life in Algeria, including in particular, women's dress and work. The group also declared its intent to reform government at all levels.

Also known as Armee Islamique du Salut (AIS), Army of Islamic Salvation, Front Islamique du Salut, Islamic Salvation Army

J

Ja'amat al Tawhid Wal Jihad

Abbreviation: JTJ
Continent: Middle East
Country: Iraq
Background:

Jama'at al-Tawhid wal-Jihad (Arabic: Group of Monotheism and the Holy Struggle) was a radical Salafi militant group in the Sunni Iraqi insurgency which was led by Jordanian national Abu Musab al-Zarqawi.

Foreign fighters were widely thought to play a key role in the decentralised network, although some analysts say it may have also had a considerable Iraqi membership. Following Zarqawi's 17th October 2004 pledge of allegiance to Osama bin Laden's al-Qaeda network, the group gradually became popularly known as al-Qaeda in Iraq (official name Tanzim Qaidat al-Jihad fi Bilad al-Rafidayn).

Jama'at al-Tawhid wal-Jihad was started by Abu Musab al-Zarqawi, other foreigners, and local, mostly Kurdish Islamist sympathisers. Zarqawi was a Jordanian who had travelled to Afghanistan to fight in the Soviet-Afghan War, but had arrived after the departure of the Soviet troops; instead he busied himself with reporting on the fighting of others. After a trip home, he eventually returned to Afghanistan, running an Islamic militant training camp near Herat in Afghanistan. Zarqawi started the network originally with a focus on overthrowing the Jordanian kingdom, which he considered to be un-Islamic in the fundamentalist sense. Eventually, Zarqawi developed a large number of contacts and affiliates in several countries. His network may have been involved in the late 1999 plot to bomb the Millennium celebrations in the U.S. and Jordan.

Following the U.S.-led invasion of Afghanistan, it is believed that Zarqawi moved westward into Iraq, where he may have received medical treatment in Baghdad for an injured leg. It is believed that he developed extensive ties in Iraq with Ansar al-Islam ("Partisans of Islam"), a Kurdish Islamist militant group that was based in the extreme northeast of the country. Ansar had alleged ties to Iraqi Intelligence; Saddam Hussein's motivation would have been to use Ansar as a surrogate force to repress the secular Kurds who wanted a "free Kurdistan" (In January 2003 Ansar's founder, Mullah Krekar, has staunchly denied any such contacts with Saddam's regime). Zarqawi's operatives have been responsible for the assassination of the U.S. diplomat Laurence Foley in Jordan in 2002.

Following the 2003 U.S-led invasion of Iraq, JTJ was developed as a militant network composed of foreign fighters and remnants of Ansar al-Islam to resist the coalition occupation forces and their Iraqi allies. In May 2004 JTJ joined forces with another Islamist organisation, the Salafiah al-Mujahidiah group of Abu-Dajanah al-Iraqi. Many of foreign fighters were not the group members, but once in Iraq they became dependent on Zarqawi's local contacts.

The stated goals of JTJ were to force a withdrawal of U.S-led forces from Iraq, topple the Iraqi interim government and assassinate collaborators with the "occupation," marginalise the Shiite Muslim population and defeat its militias, and to subsequently establish a pure Sunni Islamic state. Presumably, if and when those goals are achieved, the global Jihad would continue to establish a pan-Islamic state and remove Western influence from the Muslim world.

JTJ differed from other Iraqi insurgent groups considerably in its tactics. Rather than just using conventional weapons and guerrilla tactics, it has relied heavily on suicide bombings, mostly with vehicles, targeting a wide variety of groups but most especially Iraqi Security Forces and those facilitating the occupation. U.S and coalition forces, the United Nations (UN), foreign civilians, humanitarian organisations, Iraqi Shia and Kurdish political and religious figures, Iraqi police and security forces, and Iraqi interim officials have also been targeted. The group have assassinated several leading Iraqi politicians.

Zarqawi's militants have been known to use a wide variety of other tactics, however, including targeted assassinations and kidnappings, the planting of improvised explosive devices, mortar attacks, and beginning in a late June 2004 offensive urban guerrilla-style attacks using rocket-propelled grenades and small arms. TWJ was also known for the brutal beheadings of foreign and Iraqi hostages, which were then distributed on the Internet in video footage attributed to the group.

JTJ cites various texts from the Qur'an and the Sunnah (traditions) of Muhammad that they perceive to support their tactics. They refer to the tradition of the prophet Muhammad where he said to the people of Mecca when conquering them, "By the one in whose hand the soul of Muhammad is in, I came to you with slaughter" narrated in the books of Hadith (traditions). They also quote Muhammad saying, "Whoever slaughters a non-Muslim (at war with Islam, i.e. those perceived to be 'enemy occupiers') sincerely for the sake of Allah, Allah will make hellfire prohibited upon him." as well as many verses of the Qur'an calling Muslims to fight invading non-Muslims and even behead them, such where Allah says in the

Qur'an, "when you meet the non-Muslim (enemies in battle) strike their necks." The group's spiritual advisor was Abu Anas al-Shami.

This group's name, which is usually abbreviated as JTJ or most often shortened to Tawhid and Jihad, Tawhid wal-Jihad and sometimes Tawhid al-Jihad (or just Al Tawhid or Tawhid).

Also known as Group of Monotheism and the Holy Struggle

Janashakti

Continent: Asia
Country: India
Background:

The Communist Party of India (Marxist-Leninist) Janashakti is a left-wing extremist group operating in India's southern Andhra Pradesh state. Officially created in July 1992, Janashakti was formed from a merger of seven small left-wing organisations who had split off from the Communist Party of India (Marxist-Leninist). The reason for the split, as given by Janashakti, was that CPI (M-L) was not sufficiently revolutionary in their methods, and had acceded to the demands of larger ruling parties.

Janashakti is like many leftist organisations in India; their philosophy is an amalgam of many different strands of communist thought. Although the group's name implies Marxist-Leninist philosophy as being paramount, Janashakti also embraces Maoist doctrine and are often referred to as a "Maoist" group in the Indian press. The group's stated goals are revolution and implementation of a communist government in India.

Although the group originally employed legal methods and put out candidates for the Andhra Pradesh assembly, a series of schisms and with-drawals from the organisation led to a radicalisation within party ranks. By the late 1990s, Janashakti was solely a militant outfit, dedicated to violent struggle and the boycott of elections.

Since that time, Janashakti members have been responsible for numerous acts of violence in Andhra Pradesh, including assassination of political leaders, murder of police officers, bombings, and arson. In October 2004, the Andhra Pradesh government initiated peace talks with several Maoist groups, including Janashakti. The talks were ultimately a failure, and Janashakti resumed its attacks on the state.

Janashakti is still active in Andhra Pradesh, but the killing and imprisonment of many of its top leaders, have severely limited the group's operational capability to wage "revolution." In an extremely telling decision in August 2005, the Andhra Pradesh government re-banned several Maoist groups, but Janashakti was not among them. This is due to the perceived lack of threat from the group. In any case, Janashakti reportedly has 200-300 armed militants still under their command, and the possibility for further attacks in Andhra Pradesh remains high.

Also known as Communist Party of India (Marxist-Leninist), Janashakti

Janjaweed Militiamen

Continent: Africa
Country: Sudan
Background:

Much of the violence in Sudan, which has created over 1 million refugees, has been attributed to militias known as the Janjaweed.

The word, an Arabic colloquialism, means "a man with a gun on a horse." Janjaweed militiamen are primarily members of nomadic "Arab" tribes who've long been at odds with Darfur's settled "African" farmers, who are darker-skinned. Until 2003, the conflicts were mostly over Darfur's scarce water and land resources—desertification has been a serious problem, so grazing areas and wells are at a premium. In fact, the term "Janjaweed" has for years been synonymous with bandit, as these horse- or camel-borne fighters were known to swoop in on non-Arab farms to steal cattle.

The Janjaweed started to become much more aggressive in 2003, after two non-Arab groups, the Sudan Liberation Army and the Justice and Equality Movement, took up arms against the Sudanese government, alleging mistreatment by the Arab regime in Khartoum. In response to the uprising, the Janjaweed militias began pillaging towns and villages inhabited by members of the African tribes from which the rebel armies draw their strength—the Zaghawa, Masalit, and Fur tribes. (This conflict is entirely separate from the 22-year-old civil war that has pitted the Muslim government against Christian and animist rebels in the country's southern region. The Janjaweed, who inhabit western Sudan, have nothing to do with that war.)

Both victims and international observers allege that the Janjaweed are no longer the scrappy militias of yore, but rather well-equipped fighting forces that enjoy the overt assistance of the Sudanese government. In testimony before the Senate Foreign Relations Committee in June 2004, a field researcher with Human Rights Watch stated that the Sudanese army was openly recruiting horse-owning Arab men, promising them a gun and a monthly salary of $116 in exchange for joining a Janjaweed cohort. The International Crisis Group says that money that gets paid to the Janjaweed "comes directly from booty captured in raids on villages," giving them an additional incentive to act with extreme brutality.

There are numerous reports from international aid workers maintaining that Janjaweed raids are preceded by aerial bombardments by the Sudanese air force, that Janjaweed commanders are living in government garrison towns, and that Janjaweed militiamen wear combat fatigues identical to those of the regular army. Those who've interviewed refugees from Darfur also allege that Janjaweed commanders are using racism as a rallying point, encouraging their charges to rape the dark-skinned villagers they encounter during their raids. The Sudanese government has strongly denied offering any support to the Janjaweed.

Japanese Red Army

Abbreviation: JRA
Continent: Asia
Country: Japan, Lebanon
Background:

The Japanese Red Army (JRA) formed after breaking away from the Red Army Faction, a military arm of the Japanese Communist League. The JRA and its predecessor sprang from the vigorous student protest movements of the 1960s. The JRA sought to overthrow the Japanese monarchy and bring about an international communist revolution. They formed close ties with Palestinian revolutionary movements through the efforts of the JRA's leader, Fusako Shigenobu. The group became one of the most feared and infamous terrorist organisations in the world during the 1970s by hijacking several commercial airliners and holding the French embassy in The Hague hostage. The JRA's bloodiest attack was a 1972 assault on Tel Aviv's airport, in which three JRA members killed 24 people and wounded 80. In 1975, the JRA embarked on a successful campaign to free all of its imprisoned members by taking hostages and using them as bargaining chips.

At its peak, the JRA had between 30 or 40 members. In 1981, however, the JRA publicly stated that it was considering the rejection of violence as a political tool. In 1983, Shigenobu told the Japanese press that the group had "left the way of absolute terror." Despite this, the JRA continued to plan and execute attacks during the 1980s, although they were on a much smaller scale than the group's previous activities. In 1987, the Japanese government began a successful campaign to locate and arrest the JRA's leadership with the apprehension of Osamu Maruoka. Fusako Shigenobu was arrested in November of 2000, and while imprisoned, she announced, "I will disband the Japanese Red Army and launch new fights". Terrorism experts believe Shigenobu's declaration to be genuine, and the Department of State removed the JRA from the list of designated Foreign Terrorist Organisations in 2001.

Jarri

Continent: Europe
Country: Spain
Background:

Jarrai is an illegal socialist youth organisation, established in the Basque Country and Navarre. It was founded in 1979, the Supreme Court declared it as a terrorist organisation linked to ETA on the 19th January 2007. The qualification of "terrorist" was to continue the path undertaken years ago outlawing all organisations that make up the so-called abertzale left, to be declared by the justice department as part of the "environment of ETA". On the 4th February 2007 18 of the 19 members of Jarrai were arrested.

Jemaah Islamiya

Abbreviation: JI
Continent: Asia
Country: Indonesia, Malaysia, Philippines
Background:

Jemaah Islamiyah, which means "Islamic Community," was formed in Johor, Malaysia around 1993. While Jemaah Islamiyah did not exist as a violently brutal terrorist entity until 1993, the group's roots began to take shape years earlier. In 1973 two Muslim clerics, Abdullah Sungkar and Abu Bakar Bashir, formed a pesantren in Solo, Indonesia called Pondok Ngruki. At this time, the men were supporters of Darul Islam, a conservative Islamic movement. In addition, the two clerics had formulated the radical goal of creating an Islamic state in Indonesia.

In 1978, Sungkar and Bashir were arrested in Indonesia for subversive activities. Upon their release, the men left Indonesia for Malaysia and settled in the Indonesian-expatriate community in Johor. No longer living in Indonesia, the two men now expanded their radical goals beyond the original objective of an Islamic state in Indonesia. Sungkar and Bashir now supported the creation of an Islamic state across Southeast Asia to include Singapore, Indonesia, Malaysia, Brunei, southern Thailand, and southern Philippines.

Upon the eventual formation of Jemaah Islamiyah (JI) around 1993, the group actively advocated the use of violence to attain its goals. By the late 1990s, JI was recruiting and training extremists for the purpose of terrorist actions in Southeast Asia. Jemaah Islamiyah has shown the ability and willingness to inflict significant casualties on innocent civilians (including tourists) and those they believe to be allied with "Western interests." JI was linked to several bombings in 2000. The terrorist violence, often brutal and fatal, continues to this day. On the 12th October 2002, Jemaah Islamiyah inflicted the horrific Bali bombings, killing over 200 people.

In August 2003, JI leader Hambali (real name: Riduan bin Isomoddin) was captured. While the arrest surely damaged the group, JI remains an active and significant terrorist threat in Southeast Asia. The group is suspected of having a role in a triple-suicide bombing which struck Bali on the 1st October 2005, killing 20.

Jihad in Sweden

Continent: Europe
Country: Sweden
Background:

Jihad in Sweden is the name of a group which claimed responsibility for an aborted firebomb attack on an Iraqi polling station in Sweden in December 2005. In addition, the group allegedly had plans to bomb a Christian organisation's headquarters in response to a pastor's negative comments about the Prophet Mohammed. Although the group claimed to be acting as a faction of al-Qaeda, there is no proof to support this supposition.

In their lone attack, the members of Jihad in Sweden attempted to throw a Molotov cocktail through a window at an Iraqi polling station in Kista, Sweden. The station had been set up for expatriate-Iraqis living in Sweden to vote in the December 2005 Iraqi parliament elections. Three men carried out the attack and broke a window at the station before being scared off by guards. Investigators found numerous other incendiary devices on the perpetrators' escape route, but the attackers were not immediately apprehended.

In a claim of responsibility sent to a Swedish newspaper and postmarked a day before the attack, the previously unheard of al-Qaeda organisation for Jihad in Sweden claimed that the attack was merely a "precursor," and warned people against participating in the election or going near polling stations. The letter was signed by a person calling himself the "highest spokesman for al-Qaeda in Sweden." Despite this warning, no further attacks occurred.

Several weeks later, Swedish security forces arrested three suspects in connection to the attack. The men were Nima Nikain Ganjin, an Iranian-Swede, Albert Ramic, a Bosnian-Swede, and Andreas Fahlen, an ethnic Swede. The three men were put on trial and charged with "attempted terrorist offences" and conspiracy to commit terrorism. During the course of the trial it emerged that the three men were not al-Qaeda members but were inspired by the group and admired the concept of jihad. The men admitted that they had also planned to attack the Word of Life Church, a fundamentalist Christian organisation whose pastor had allegedly called the Prophet Mohammed a "paedophile." The attack was aborted because the men could not afford to travel to the church, belying the amateur nature of the group. Ultimately the three men were convicted on all counts and sentenced to varying terms in jail ranging from eight months to three years.

The arrest of the members of Jihad in Sweden effectively ended the group's existence. While it is quite clear that the group was not officially tied to al-Qaeda, Jihad in Sweden is an interesting example of how jihadist behaviour has slowly crept its way into Europe. Although Jihad in Sweden will not be responsible for further attacks, it is highly likely that similar al-Qaeda inspired groups will be active in Europe for a long time.

Also known as Al-Qaeda Organisation for Jihad in Sweden

Jundallah

Continent: Asia
Country: Iran
Background:

Jundullah (Army of God) is a Sunni terrorist organisation with links to al-Qaeda that is based in Balochistan. It is a part of the Baloch insurgency in Pakistan and in Iran's Sistan and Baluchistan Province. Being affiliated/mistaken with the Pakistani Jundallah, the Iranian Jundullah changed its name to: "Peoples Resistance Movement of Iran" (PRMI). Jundallah claims that it has 1,000 fighters and has killed Iranian soldiers. The group has been identified as a terrorist organisation by Iran and Pakistan.

Peoples Resistant Movement of Iran (PRMI), former Jundallah of Iran, is believed to have emerged on the scene in 2003 and it is known for attacks against high profile Iranian targets, especially government and security officials. Despite Iranian claims of PRMI's connection with the Pakistani Jundallah, no proof of such link has been found by independent sources. Iran also accuses the United States and other foreign elements of backing PRMI, possibly from Pakistani territory with Islamabad's support, despite Pakistan's history of cooperating with Iran to suppress Baloch nationalism, whereas PPMI adamantly denies any connections to al-Qaeda or the Taliban, as well as foreign governments such as the United States and Great Britain. In an interview with Dan Rather, Rigi describes the Iranian military as "cowardly" and in that video, he cut's a person's head off in front of the camera, in Al-Qaeda style.

The group's leader is known to be Abdolmalek Rigi (also known as Emir Abdul Malek Baloch). In a May telephone interview with Rooz, (Iranian online newspaper), Rigi defended PRMI's use of violence as a just means to defend Baloch and Sunni Muslim interests in Iran and to draw attention to the difficult economic situation and ethnic discrimination of the Baloch people, whom he describes as Iran's poorest. Significantly, Rigi declared himself an Iranian and Iran as his home. He also denied harbouring separatist aspirations. According to Rigi, PRMI's goal is to improve the life of Iranian Baloch and Sunnis and not to separate from Iran or even demand autonomy.

Jund al Sham
Justice Army of Defenceless People

Abbreviation: EJPI
Continent: Central America
Country: Mexico
Background:

The Justice Army of Defenceless People (EJPI) was a short-lived terrorist organisation that operated in Mexico during the late 1990s. Emerging in January 1997, the group was implicated in a handful of attacks, the last of which occurred on the 7th January 1998. Although group members justified their violent actions with various rationalisations, the prevailing complaint was the government's treatment of the indigenous people of Chiapas, Mexico. The group conducted one specific attack in response to a massacre of forty-five indigenous people living in Chiapas on the 22nd December 1997.

According to statements made by group members following several attacks, the group believed that government corruption and the economic policies of neo-liberalism have negatively impacted the economic well-being of "defenceless people." In addition, the EJPI accused the government of carrying out violent attacks against Mexican citizens.

Uniformed members armed with AK-47s operated in the Mexican state of Guerrero, which is also home to a larger terrorist organisation, the Popular Revolutionary Army (EPR). In 1998, Guerrero's Prosecutor General's Office has alleged that one EJPI attack was actually carried out by the EPR. Due to its limited number of attacks, it is possible that the EJPI was actually a cover name used by EPR members. The Justice Army of Defenceless People has not conducted any attacks since January 1998 and is presumed inactive.

Also known as Avenging Army of Defenceless People

Kabataang Makabayan

Abbreviation: KM

Kach

Continent: Middle East
Country: Israel, West Bank/Gaza
Background:

Kach is a Jewish nationalist extremist group in Israel founded by the late Rabbi Meir Kahane. In 1968, Rabbi Kahane founded the Jewish Defence League (JDL), a US organisation dedicated to protecting American Jews. The JDL became increasingly militant, espousing violence and vigilantism to curb anti-Semitism. In 1969, Kahane emigrated to Israel, and by 1971, he had established an international office of the JDL in Israel. The Kach movement (Hebrew for "Thus") emerged from this international JDL office.

Rooted in extremist Jewish ideology, Kach sought to restore the Biblical land of Israel by annexing all the disputed territories of Israel and forcibly removing all Arabs. Preaching the motto of "terror against terror," Kach openly espoused violence against Arabs and actively participated in anti-Arab activities in Israel. As part of its extremist ideology, the group also espoused violence against the Israeli government. In the mid 1970s, Kahane sought to transform Kach into an organised political party, running twice unsuccessfully for the Israeli Knesset. In 1984, Kahane was successfully elected to the Knesset. However, in 1988, Israeli law was amended to forbid racist groups from participating elections, effectively barring Kach from the political scene.

Despite the assassination of Rabbi Kahane in 1990, the Kach movement, and its closely affiliated splinter group, Kahane Chai, remained active in Israel. Kach has vehemently opposed the peace process, threatening and using violence against both Arabs and Israeli government officials. Following the signing of the Oslo peace accords between Israel and the PLO in 1994, a Kach supporter killed 29 people in a mosque in Hebron. As a result of this attack, Israel formally outlawed Kach and designated it as a terrorist organisation. Despite its being outlawed, Kach continues its anti-Arab activities within Israel. While the group has not officially claimed many attacks since being outlawed, Kach praises and supports any violence against Arabs.

In February 2005 Israeli Prime Minister Ariel Sharon accused Kach activists of threatening government officials who supported his plan of "disengagement" from Gaza. Sharon warned that the tension between those who supported and those who opposed his plan had the potential to lead to bloodshed. Although Kach did not officially carry out any attacks, shortly before the disengagement plan was to be executed, a Jewish IDF deserter named Eden Natan-Zada carried out a shooting attack on a bus full of Arabs in Shfaram, Israel. Natan-Zada was not a known member of Kach, but is said to have been inspired by the movement.

The United States designates Kach and its affiliate Kahane Chai as terrorist organisations, a designation which Kach rejects, and has challenged in U.S. courts. In October 2006, a U.S. federal court of appeals ruled that Kach was correctly designated and would remain on the FTO list for the foreseeable future.

Also known as Kakh. See Kahane Chai

Kahane Chai

Continent: Middle East
Country: Israel, West Bank/Gaza
Background:
Kahane Chai is an offshoot of Kach, the religious extremist group formed by Rabbi Meir Kahane. Following Kahane's assassination in 1990, his son Binyamin Kahane formed Kahane Chai (which means Kahane lives). Although Kahane Chai and Kach are designated separately, Kahane Chai is essentially an alias for Kach as the two groups have a shared core leadership and are referred to interchangeably in the media. The differences between Kach and Kahane Chai cantered around personal squabbles between Binyamin Kahane and the leaders of Kach, but such differences have disappeared since Binyamin Kahane was killed in 2000.

Kahane Chai, along with Kach, was banned from politics in Israel in 1994 following Dr. Baruch Goldstein's killing of 29 Muslims in the Cave of the Patriarchs. Goldstein was a member of Kach and statements in support of his actions by Kach and Kahane Chai led to their ban. Despite this ban, Kahane Chai is still very active in Israeli society and its leaders openly recruit new members and criticise government policy.

Kahane Chai is a violent group that aims to reinstate the ancient Biblical kingdom in Israel. It aims for expulsion of Arabs from Israeli territory and the creation of a Jewish theocracy. The group has been linked to a bombing attempt at the schoolyard of an Arab all-girls school and has been designated as a terrorist group by many foreign governments due to its constant intimidation of Arabs throughout Israel. The group has in recent years refrained from major terrorist activity as it is attempting to convince the Israeli government to lift the ban on Kahane Chai.

Kahane Chai increased its level of activity in protest of Ariel Sharon's plan to dismantle settlements in the Gaza Strip and West Bank. Viewing such a step as a violation of the principle that Jews deserve control of the holy land, the group issued many ominous warnings. The most serious threats levelled by Kahane Chai involved threats on the lives of politicians who supported the disengagement plan as well as an announcement of plans to derail train tracks in protest of the new policy. In any case, although opposition to disengagement was widespread, it was rarely violent, and Kahane Chai did not carry out any terrorist attacks.

Also known as Kach

Kata'ib al Khoul

Continent: Asia
Country: Russia
Background:
Kata'ib al-Khoul is a radical Islamic group operating in the Russian Republic of North Ossetia, which shares a southern border with Georgia and eastern border with the Russian Republics of Ingushetia and Chechnya. These three Russian Republics make up part of the North Caucasus region in southern Russia, which has experienced radical Islamic insurgent violence originating in Chechnya spill into both Ingushetia and North Ossetia. Kata'ib al-Khoul has similar goals to other Islamic nationalist insurgent groups in the region. The group seeks to end Russian control of North Ossetia and establish an independent Ossetian state. Many of Kata'ib al-Khoul's public statements appear on pro-Chechen websites, which leads to the possibility that the group has ties with Chechen insurgents.

In its short history, the group has conducted attacks by planting bombs and participating in small arms gunfire. Kata'ib al-Khoul first targeted gambling establishments in March 2006 because they considered the facilities immoral and corruptive influences on the Ossetian people. However, the group has also displayed its willingness to attack the Russian military along with Russian police in North Ossetia. It has even attempted to plant spies in the Russian government. In spite of these attacks, Russia has refused to acknowledge the existence of Kata'ib al-Khoul, stating that an Islamic insurgent group could not exist in a predominantly Orthodox Christian Republic. Some believe the group's members are from neighbouring Republics.

As recently as October 2006, Kata'ib al-Khoul re-affirmed its desire to attack Russian military planes. At the end of November, a statement from the group on a Chechen separatist website offered rewards for the assassination of several prominent Russian officials. A sum of $50,000 each was offered for the killing of two specific battalion commanders in the Russian military, and the same amount was offered to for the assassination of Chechen Premier Ramzan Kadyrov.

The statement elicits that, since Kata'ib al-Khoul is offering a bounty for other sympathisers to carry out operations, they may have abundant financial sources. Although it is difficult to approximate their funding situation, Kata'ib al-Khoul is likely to remain a moderate threat to the region in the foreseeable future.

Also known as Jamaat Kataib al-Khoul, Kataeb al-Ghoul, Kataib al-Khoul, Kataib al-Khoul Jamaat

Khmer Rouge

Continent: Asia
Country: Cambodia
Background:

The Khmer Communist Party was established in Cambodia, 1951. Originally sponsored by Vietnam, Khmer Communist Party was dedicated to the formation of a Cambodian socialist state. The party planned to follow the Maoist approach of initiating widespread revolution through initial insurgent activities in the countryside. By 1960, Khmer Communist Party was moving beyond merely expressing Maoist philosophies; the group was now actively engaging the Cambodian government in battle. Utilising terrorist tactics, the terrorist group would battle the Cambodian government from 1960 to 1975. During this time, Cambodia's long-time leader Norodom Sihanouk dubbed the guerrilla organisation the Khmer Rouge.

Sihanouk had a complicated relationship with the Khmer Rouge. While he sometimes allied himself with the group, at other times the insurgent group would challenge government forces. In 1970, Lon Nol overthrew Sihanouk's government, at which time Sihanouk found refuge in Beijing, China. Any confusion regarding Khmer Rouge's complicated relationship with the Cambodian government ended once Lon Nol took power. Khmer Rouge battled Lon Nol's government from 1970 to 1975. On the 17th April 1975, Khmer Rouge captured the capital city of Phnom Penh. Khmer Rouge governed Cambodia from 1975 to 1978. The terrorist organisation-turned-state government enacted an infamously brutal campaign against Cambodian citizens. Following the model of an agricultural-socialist state, Khmer Rouge emptied urban centres and forces the evacuees to work for agricultural communes. The Cambodian people were severely mistreated and overworked under Khmer Rouge's rule. In addition, the new government executed its educated citizens. During Khmer Rouge's three and a half year rule, an estimated 1.5 million people were killed though executions, starvation, and brutal working conditions.

In December 1978, Vietnamese forces invaded Cambodia and removed Khmer Rouge from power. However, Khmer Rouge was still a substantial threat and played a significant role in the civil war that continued for over a decade. In 1991, the Paris Peace Accords were signed, which guaranteed democratic elections and a ceasefire. Khmer Rouge broke the cease-fire at various periods between 1991 and 1998, reverting once again to its terrorist activities. Khmer Rouge's ability to engage in significant terrorist actions decreased throughout the 1990s. The remaining vestiges of Khmer Rouge surrendered on the 5th December 1998, ending the Khmer Rouge insurgency.

Knights of the Tempest

Continent: Middle East
Country: West Bank/Gaza
Background:
Knights of the Tempest is an armed splinter group formed from the Palestinian ruling party, al-Fatah. The group emerged in October 2005 when they claimed responsibility for the kidnapping and shooting of two Palestinian men in the Gaza Strip. The victims, who both survived, were accused of collaborating with Israel.

In their claim of responsibility, the Knights said they had acted because Palestinian security forces had previously ignored their calls to move against collaborators. The group also said the men had made a full confession, and that a Muslim cleric was consulted in order to mete out a proper punishment. The two captives were apparently shot in the legs, had their identity cards seized by the group, and were placed under house arrest.

From their public statements, it appears that the Knights of the Tempest are a more radical and religiously motivated splinter group from the generally secular al-Fatah movement.

This particular group seems particularly concerned with Palestinian collaborators, a common cause of anger amongst Palestinian militants. In the past, vigilante groups such as the Knights have captured and lynched dozens of alleged Palestinian collaborators, always without a trial. These collaborators are most often accused of providing information on militant leaders and planned terrorist attacks to Israeli security and intelligence forces.

The Knights of the Tempest have only claimed responsibility for one vigilante attack. However, after Israeli disengagement in August 2005, violence and unrest has wracked the Gaza Strip. As long as anarchy persists in this territory, it is likely that groups like the Knights and others will continue to take the law in to their own hands.

Also known as Knights of the Storm

Kosovo Liberation Army

Abbreviation: KLA
Continent: Europe
Country: Macedonia, the Republic of Serbia and Montenegro
Background:

The Kosovo Liberation Army (KLA) formed in Macedonia in 1992 with the goal of uniting the ethnic Albanian populations of Albania, Kosovo, and Macedonia into a "Greater Albania." Their name recognised that the province of Kosovo, officially part of the new nation of Serbia, was their most important and difficult target. The KLA was not based on a single rigid, hierarchical structure, but instead operated in dispersed cells. These cells did wear uniforms and maintain some form of chain of command, however. The group remained basically unknown until 1995, when it began carrying out small arms and sabotage attacks against Serbian Police outposts in Kosovo. The KLA also conducted vicious reprisal attacks against Kosovars accused of cooperating with the Serbians. The escalating violence forced the Serbian government to respond, but their response was, by almost any standard, far too aggressive; many innocent men, women, and children died as a result.

As the Serbian crackdown against the KLA grew increasingly brutal, the group's ranks swelled. An organisation that began 1998 with no more than 500 members was estimated to be 12,000 to 20,000 strong by the beginning of 1999. When the US-led coalition attacked Serbia in defence of the Kosovars in January 1999, the appearance of imminent victory drew even more ethnic Albanians to the KLA flag. The KLA militias played a critical role in the coalition victory, forcing Serbian forces out into the open where American and allied airpower could punish them. Since the end of the war in Kosovo, questions have surfaced about the worthiness of the KLA as a US ally. Accusations of ties to drug-running, foreign terrorism, and organised crime have surfaced, and the UN occupation force has had some difficulty convincing the KLA to lay down its weapons. The point may be moot however, as the de facto autonomy now enjoyed by the Albanians in post-war Kosovo has decreased the urgency of the KLA cause. No terrorist attacks have been claimed by the KLA since the beginning of the war, but isolated reprisals against the handful of Serbs remaining in Kosovo have continued.

The goal of establishing a Greater Albania has been dropped by all but the "hard core" of the KLA. The group has not engaged in a recognised act of terrorism since before the 1999 war, and no future attacks are likely unless the Serbian government attempts to reassert its authority over the province.

Kumpulan Mujahin Malaysia

Abbreviation: KMM
Continent: Asia
Country: Indonesia, Malaysia, Philippines
Background:
Kumpulan Mujahidin Malaysia (KMM) is an Islamic group based in Malaysia, specifically in the Malaysian states of Perak, Johor, Kedah, Selangor, Terengganu and Kelantan, as well as the federal territory of Wilayah Persukutuan. KMM is dedicated to overthrowing the current Malaysian government and then creating an Islamic state in its place. The group, however, does not limit its planned Islamic state to Malaysia, but also aims to include Indonesia and the southern Philippines, thus creating a pan-Southeast Asian Islamic state.

Many of KMM's members have trained in terrorist camps in Afghanistan, and certain members fought in the Soviet-Afghan war. KMM has forged ties with other extremist Islamic groups in the region, including Jemaah Islamiyah (JI) and Laskar Jihad. Jemaah Islamiyah's leaders had Abu Bakar Bashir and Riduan bin Isomoddin, aka Hambali, allegedly advise them and assist KMM leaders.

The Malaysian government, utilising the Internal Security Act (ISA), has detained dozens of KMM members. Also through the ISA, KMM's alleged leader is currently being held by the Malaysian government. KMM members have allegedly been involved in assassinations, bombings, robberies, and planning terrorist attacks on foreigners. Due to KMM's alliance with Indonesian terrorist groups, KMM members have also been involved in terrorist attacks against Christians in Indonesia.

See Jemaah Islamiyah, Laskar Jihad

Kurdistan Democratic Party

Abbreviation: KDP
Continent: Middle East
Country: Iraq
Background:
The Kurdish Democratic Party (KDP) is an organisation operating in

northern Iraq. Founded by Mustafa Barzani in 1946, the KDP constitutes Iraq's largest Kurdish advocacy group. The group seeks greater autonomy for Kurds within Iraq and the eventual creation of Kurdistan as an independent nation-state. As a people, Kurds are indigenous to a geo-cultural region commonly referred to as Kurdistan that is composed of territory from Iran, Iraq, Syria, and Turkey. Estimated at about 30 million people, the Kurds comprise one of the largest stateless ethnic groups in the world. Currently within Iraq, Kurds have established a de facto autonomous region, complete with an elected parliament, police force, schools, tax collectors, and an army.

Throughout its history, the KDP has targeted many organisations. Its main targets have been the Iraqi government under Saddam Hussein and Kurdish political rivals, the Patriotic Union of Kurdistan (PUK) and the Kurdistan Workers' Party (PKK). KDP rebels conducted full-scale armed attacks and helped to incite rebellions against Hussein's regime, most notably during the Iran-Iraq War, Operation Desert Storm, and Operation Iraqi Freedom. In order to assist in toppling Saddam Hussein, Iran provided quite a substantial portion of the KDP's funding. After Hussein's defeat in 1991, Iraqi Kurds and the KDP established a semi-autonomous Kurdish region in Iraq under the protection of Operation Provide Comfort's northern no-fly zone.

The KDP's rivalry with the PUK has been attributed to disputed sovereignty over some territories in northern Iraq and the deflection of Jalal Talabani to form the PUK in 1974. Both groups conducted frequent armed attacks against each others' forces, attempting to gain strategic territory. However, in 1998, the two groups signed a peace agreement and now share control of the Kurdistan Regional Government. After accusing the PKK of provoking Turkish air strikes, attacking food supply trucks, and preventing Iraqi Kurdish refugees from returning, the KDP (allegedly funded by Turkey) conducted attacks against the PKK. By expelling the PKK from Iraqi territory, the KDP ensured the PKK would not be able to launch attacks against Turkey from Iraqi territory, a major concern of Turkey's.

As a result of the KDP's alliance with PUK to form the Kurdistan Regional Government and the fall of Saddam Hussein's regime, KDP rebel forces are unlikely to conduct violent attacks in the future. Naturally the organisation will continue to fight for an independent Kurdistan, but the KDP has been trying to establish itself as a political organisation working for the peaceful attainment of Kurdistan.

Also known as Kurdish Vengeance Brigade, Kurdistan Freedom Falcons, Kurdistan Freedom Falcons Organisation

Kurdistan Workers Party

Abbreviation: PKK
Continent: Eurasia
Country: Turkey
Background:

The Kurdistan Workers' Party (PKK) is a leftist Kurdish nationalist organisation. The PKK was founded in 1974 by a group of Turkish students of ethnic Kurdish descent who were active in communist circles within Turkey. The group, led by Abdullah Ocalan, operated informally until 1978, when it formalised its agenda. Influenced heavily by Maoist doctrine, the PKK's goal was to incite a revolution that would free the Kurdish people and establish an independent Kurdish state. When it was founded, the group was violently opposed to the Turkish government, believing that a Kurdish state could only be established if the oppressive and colonialist Turkish government was defeated.

During the early 1980s, the group focused its attention on consolidating its resources and powerbase. In 1980, prior to the military coup in Turkey, the PKK fled Turkey and established training camps in the Bekaa valley, part of Syrian-controlled Lebanon. By 1984, the PKK had initiated its first armed attacks in the Anatolia regions of Turkey. The PKK targeted Turkish government facilities and personnel in Anatolia and frequently attacked Kurdish civilians who "collaborated" with the Turkish government. Some reports claim that the PKK killed over 30,000 civilians within Turkey during the mid-80s. In the late 1980s and early 1990s, in an effort to win increased support from the Kurdish peasantry, the PKK altered its leftist secular ideology to better accommodate and accept Islamic beliefs. The group also abandoned its previous strategy of attacking Kurdish civilians, focusing instead on government and tourist targets.

During the early 1990s, the PKK continued its strategy of actively attacking Turkish government and tourist assets in an effort to destroy the Turkish regime. The group has also targeted Turkish interests in Western Europe. In 1999, the PKK's leader, Abdullah Ocalan, was arrested in Kenya and extradited to Turkey where he faced the death penalty on terrorism charges. (Though convicted, Turkey abolished the death penalty in 2002, and his sentence was changed to life imprisonment.) The arrest of Ocalan seriously weakened the PKK. Following his arrest, Ocalan declared a unilateral cease-fire and announced his desire to establish a "peace initiative" with Turkey on Kurdish issues. The PKK affirmed Ocalan's wishes, purportedly disavowing its violent history.

In 2002, the PKK changed its name to the Kurdistan Freedom and Democracy Congress (KADEK), supposedly committing itself to non-violent activities. In 2003, KADEK announced a three-stage "road map" for peacefully resolving the issue of Kurdish autonomy. Despite the cease fire, the group continued its military training and planning and continued to threaten violence. In 2003, KADEK announced that it was dissolving itself and creating a new pan-Kurdish organisation called the Kurdistan People's Conference (KHK) that would seek Kurdish rights through negotiations with Turkey. Turkish officials have dismissed these moves as public relations tactics. It remains unclear what the outcome of this reorganisation will be. In late 2003, the KADEK sought to engineer another political face-lift, renaming the group Kongra-Gel (KGK) (Kurdistan People's Congress) and brandishing its "peaceful" intentions, while continuing to commit attacks and refuse disarmament.

The cease-fire with the Turkish government ended in the spring of 2004 and violence continued. In April 2005 the group officially decided to revert to its original name. In August 2005, the group announced a one-month ceasefire and said that they would hold indirect peace talks with the Turkish government.

Talks between the Kurdistan Workers' Party and the Turkish government, however, have failed to progress; violence linked to the PKK continues across Turkey, particularly in the southeast. The group claimed responsibility for three ambushes of Turkish forces in early March 2006, alleged to be retaliation for the deaths of seven PKK members in February. The group is also suspected in several small bombings in early 2006, including a bombing in Ankara on the 8th March that killed three people and injured eighteen.

Also known as KADEK, KHK, Kongra-Gel (KGK), Kongreya Azadi u Demokrasiya Kurdistan, Kurdistan Freedom and Democracy Congress, Kurdistan People's Conference, The People's Congress of Kurdistan

L

Lashkar e Omar

Abbreviation: LeO
Continent: Asia
Country: India
Background:

Lashkar-e-Omar (LeO) was a new terrorist group reportedly founded in January 2002 and is a conglomerate of Harkat-ul-Jihad-i-Islami (HuJI), Lashkar-e-Jhangvi (LeJ) and Jaish-e-Mohammed (JeM) cadres. It was formed after the arrests of several front-ranking Islamist leaders in Pakistan following President Pervez Musharraf's address to the nation on the 12th January 2002, in which he committed himself to dismantling the structures and networks of terrorism based in his country. The etymology of Lashkar-e-Omar is yet not clear. According to some reports at the time, it was named after Mullah Mohammed Omar, chief of the Taliban militia. Other reports indicated that the name is allegedly a direct homage to Syed Ahmed Omar Sheikh, a front-ranking JeM terrorist who was, on the 15th July 2002, sentenced to life by an Anti-Terrorism Court in Hyderabad, Sindh, for his role in the abduction-cum-murder of US journalist Daniel Pearl.

The LeO first came into prominence in November 2001 when it reportedly claimed responsibility for an attack on a church in Bahawalpur in Punjab. Police personnel and 17 Christians, including five children, were killed and nine others injured when six unidentified gunmen opened indiscriminate fire at a church in Model Town, Bahawalpur, on the 28th October 2001.

Their version of Islam is akin to that of the Taliban militia of Afghanistan. The LeO's ideological underpinning is a mixture of Islamist fundamentalism and totalitarian thinking.

Official sources at the time had indicated that what makes Lashkar-e-Omar a serious threat is the fact that most of its cadres are members of the same class and camp trained by Amjad Faruqui. Faruqui, a HuJI terrorist, is wanted for his involvement in the murder of Pearl. LeO also has suicide cadres in its ranks. The LeO was allegedly involved in the suicide bombing outside the Sheraton Hotel in Karachi on the 8th May. In that incident, 14 persons, including 12 French nationals, were killed. Security agencies suspect that there exist more LeO fidayeen (suicide) squads and that these would target foreign nationals, particularly Americans and Britons residing in Pakistan.

The LeO has close linkages with the Al Qaeda and several terrorist groups active in the Indian State of Jammu and Kashmir. Karachi based Al-Rashid Trust (ART) is reportedly funding the Lashkar-e-Omar. The ART is one of the 27 groups and organisations listed by US State Department on the 22nd September 2001 for involvement in financing and supporting a network of international Islamist terrorist groups.

Lashkar e Taiba

Abbreviation: LeT
Continent: Asia
Country: Pakistan, India, Kashmir
Background:

Lashkar-e-Tayyiba (LeT) is the armed wing of the Pakistan-based religious organisation, Markaz-ud-Dawa-wal-Irshad (MDI). MDI is an anti-US missionary organisation formed in 1989. The LeT is one of the three largest and best-trained groups fighting in Kashmir against India. In 1994, the LeT became one of the primary recipients of funds from Inter-Services Intelligence (ISI), Pakistan's external intelligence agency, after the Jamaat-e-Islami and the HM refused to accept new conditions attached to ISI money. The LeT agreed to support Kashmir's merger with Pakistan, to attack the Hindus in the Jammu Division, and to assist in training alienated Muslim youth in the rest of India. Along with the HuA and Al Badr, the LeT is thought to be responsible for a majority of the violence in the State.

In December 2001, the United States designated the group a foreign terrorist organisation. Pakistan subsequently banned LeT and froze its assets. LeT reorganised in an attempt to separate its military actions in Kashmir from its religious undertakings in Pakistan.

The LeT's agenda is outlined in a pamphlet titled "Why are we waging jihad." It includes the restoration of Islamic rule over all parts of India and propagates a narrow Islamic fundamentalism based on the Wahabi sect. The LeT challenges India's sovereignty over the State of Jammu and Kashmir. It seeks to bring about a union of all Muslim majority regions in countries that surround Pakistan. LeT is also a member of Osama bin Laden's International Islamic Front for Jihad against the US and Israel, as well as of the United Jihad Council.

Also known as Jama'at ud Da'awa

Laskar e Toiba

Abbreviation: LeT
Continent: Asia
Country: India
Background:

Formed in 1990 in the Kunar province of Afghanistan, the Lashkar-e-Toiba (also known as Jama'at-ud-Da'awa) is based in Muridke near Lahore in Pakistan. Its first presence in Jammu and Kashmir (J&K) was recorded in 1993 when 12 Pakistani and Afghan mercenaries infiltrated across the Line of Control (LoC) in tandem with the Islami Inquilabi Mahaz, a terrorist group then active in the Poonch district of J&K. The LeT is outlawed in India under the Unlawful Activities (Prevention) Act. It was included in the Terrorist Exclusion List by the US Government on 5th December 2001. The US administration designated the Lashkar-e-Toiba as a FTO (Foreign Terrorist Organisation) on the 26th December 2001. It is also a banned organisation in Britain since the 30th March 2001. The group was proscribed by the United Nations in May 2005. The military regime of General Pervez Musharraf banned the Lashkar-e-Toiba in Pakistan on the 12th January 2002.

The LeT's professed ideology goes beyond merely challenging India's sovereignty over the State of Jammu and Kashmir. The Lashkar's 'agenda', as outlined in a pamphlet titled "Why are we waging jihad," includes the restoration of Islamic rule over all parts of India. Further, the group seeks to bring about a union of all Muslim majority regions in countries that surround Pakistan. Towards that end, it is active in J&K, Chechnya and other parts of Central Asia.

It is closely linked to the Inter-Services Intelligence, the Taliban and al Qaeda. India's National Security Adviser M. K. Narayanan said on the 11th August 2006, that the Pakistan-based Lashkar-e-Toiba is part of the "al Qaeda compact" and is "as big as an omnipotent" as the international terror network. "The Lashkar today has emerged as a very major force. It has connectivity with west Asia, Europe....Actually there was a LeT module broken in Virginia and some people were arrested. It is as big as an omnipotent as al Qaeda in every sense of the term." Asked how significant the al Qaeda connection was in India, Narayanan said LeT was the "most visible manifestation" of the al Qaeda in India.

LeT has an extensive network that runs across Pakistan and India with branches in Saudi Arabia, United Kingdom, Bangladesh and South East Asia. The organisation collects donations from the Pakistani community in the Persian Gulf and United Kingdom, Islamic Non-Governmental Organisations, and Pakistani and Kashmiri businessmen. It receives considerable financial, material and other forms of assistance from the Pakistan government, routed primarily through the ISI. The ISI is the main source of LeT's funding. Saudi Arabia also provides funds.

The LeT maintains ties to various religious/military groups around the world, ranging from the Philippines to the Middle East and Chechnya primarily through the al Qaeda fraternal network. The LeT has also been part of the Bosnian campaign against the Serbs.

It has allegedly set up sleeper cells in the U.S. and Australia, trained terrorists from other countries and has entered new theatres of Jihad like Iraq. The group has links with many international Islamist terrorist groups like the Ikhwan-ul-Musalmeen of Egypt and other Arab groups. LeT has a unit in Germany and also receives help from the Al Muhajiraun, supporter of Sharia Group, (Abu Hamza Masari- of Mosque Finsbury Park, North London) and its annual convention is regularly attended by fraternal bodies in Saudi Arabia, Kuwait, Yemen, Bahrain, Oman, Kosovo, Bangladesh, Myanmar, USA, Palestine, Bosnia, Philippines, Jordan, Chechnya, etc. It also has links with the International Sikh Youth Federation (Lakhbir Singh Rode).

Laskar Jihad

Continent: Asia
Country: Indonesia
Background:

Laskar Jihad (Army of Jihad or Holy War Warriors) is a violent paramilitary organisation in Indonesia that emerged out of a sectarian conflict between Muslims and Christians in the Maluku (Molucca) Islands, which caused the deaths of thousands in the late 1990s and early 2000s. Laskar Jihad saw itself as a protector of the Muslim population of Maluku, and a harbinger of Jihad, dedicated to converting Christians and bringing Islamic law to Maluku and greater Indonesia. Although the group ascribed to Salafist Islam, Laskar Jihad can also be described as a nationalist group as they were interested in maintaining the territorial integrity of Indonesia, and not creating a pan-Islamist state.

The Maluku Islands conflict has roots that stretch back nearly 400 years. Unlike the rest of Indonesia which is 90% Muslim, Maluku has a slight Christian majority, and tensions between the two religions have always been high. The Christian community in Maluku was favoured by the Dutch colonialists who ruled Indonesia until 1945, and Christians even fought for the Dutch in the Indonesian war of independence. Even after the Dutch left, the Christian community in Maluku enjoyed a higher economic and social status than their Muslim neighbours. It was not until the 1980s that the Muslim population in Maluku began to close the gap, competing for jobs and resources once dominated by the Christian population. In early 1999, tensions boiled over, leading to wide-scale rioting and eventually open war between the two communities.

For a year the conflict raged, with the Indonesian government seemingly unable to stem the tide of violence. In response to a perceived Christian "onslaught" against the Muslims of Maluku, Laskar Jihad was established in January 2000 by Jafar Umar Thalib, an Indonesian of Arab descent who fought for the Mujahideen in Afghanistan against the Soviet Union. The group was made up entirely of volunteers, mostly from the Indonesian island of Java. At its peak the group's strength might have numbered over 10,000 fighters. After training in Java, Laskar Jihad members were sent to Maluku where their presence escalated the conflict rapidly. Laskar Jihad members destroyed villages, killed thousands of people, and forcibly converted many Christians to Islam, complete with ritual circumcision for both men and women. Although the group saw itself as a protector of Muslims, Laskar Jihad waged a "holy war" against innocent Christians in an effort that some have termed ethnic cleansing or genocide.

Laskar Jihad was believed to be aided by Islamist elements in the Indonesian military and also had admitted links with other Islamist terror groups such as the Taliban in Afghanistan, Abu Sayyaf in the Philippines and Kumpulan Mujahidin Malaysia (KMM). The group also had unproven but suspected links with al-Qaeda, as many allege that al-Qaeda members trained in Laskar Jihad camps in Java.

After quickly establishing itself as the most powerful military force in Maluku, Laskar Jihad sought to expand its influence into other ethnic conflicts in Sulawesi, Aceh, and West Papua. In Maluku, the group consolidated its power further and attempted to set up Sharia law on the islands. Despite Laskar Jihad's actions, the Indonesian government was reluctant to clamp down on the group, lest it appear anti-Islamic. Although the government did make several attempts to disarm and prohibit the group from operating, Laskar Jihad was essentially above the law.

In March 2002, the Indonesian government brokered a peace deal in Maluku, stemming the conflict which had killed thousands. Laskar Jihad's main battlefield was now essentially peaceful, but the group continued operations in other parts of Indonesia. On the 12th October 2002, Laskar Jihad announced they were disbanding. Some sources say the group was forced to disarm by the Indonesian government, while others say the group ended their military operations to focus on gaining political power. Just hours after their announcement, a powerful bombing perpetrated by Jemaah Islamiya, another Islamic terrorist group in Indonesia, killed over 200 people in Bali. Laskar Jihad leadership denied any role in the bombing, and said their announcement to disband had nothing to do with the attack. While most people accept this explanation, the timing of Laskar's announcement is an almost unbelievable coincidence.

As Laskar Jihad closed their offices and deactivated their website, many feared that the moves were nothing more then a ploy to avoid a government crackdown. Indeed, although Laskar Jihad activities have ceased in Maluku, various reports say the group has re-formed, and as recently as October 2005, was operating in the Indonesian province of West Papua as well as the Solomon Islands. At present, at this time it is impossible to say that the group is inactive, and it is quite possible that Laskar Jihad could re-emerge as a dangerous and violent force in Indonesia.

Also known as Army of Jihad or Holy War Warriors

Liberation Army Fifth Battalion

Continent: North America
Country: United States of America
Background:

The Liberation Army Fifth Battalion was the name of a group that claimed responsibility for the 1993 bombing attack on the World Trade Centre in New York City. A van loaded with over 500 pounds of explosives was parked in the underground parking structure of one of the towers. Upon detonation, the blast ruptured a hole in floors up to the third story and caused significant structural damage. The goal of the attack was to weaken the foundation of the tower, causing it to collapse on the second tower. Even though this did not occur, six people were killed and over one thousand were injured.

The attack was the first and only mention of the Liberation Army Fifth Battalion. A letter released to the New York Times newspaper days after the attack stated that the reasons for the bombing were to force the U.S. to stop support for Israel and end "interference" in Middle East affairs.

Investigations into the attack led to the arrests of ten suspected Islamist militants, including key planners of the attack: Mohammed Salameh, Mahmud Abouhalima, and Ramzi Ahmed Yousef. All three men were convicted between 1994 and 1998 and received the maximum sentence of 240 years in prison.

Information that emerged following the attack indicates that the Liberation Army Fifth Battalion was merely a name chosen by Ramzi Yousef and did not represent an authentic organisation. While it is uncertain whether the terrorists were actually members of larger organisations, it is clear that they had linkages to other groups. Yousef's uncle, Khalid Sheik Mohammed, a high-ranking al-Qaeda member who planned many attacks, including the September 11th, 2001 hijackings, reportedly help finance Yousef in the 1993 bombing. Al-Gama'a al Islamiyya (GAI) leader Sheik Omar Abdel Rahman was a convicted co-conspirator in the attack as well as a long-time associate of Egyptian Islamic Jihad (EIJ) and al-Qaeda.

Since the Liberation Army Fifth Battalion refers to those Islamic extremists involved in the 1993 World Trade Centre bombing, it seems unlikely that the name will be used in future attacks. Those involved who were not prosecuted or incarcerated have probably sought out roles in larger organisations like al-Qaeda, GAI, or EIJ.

Liberation Army of Chameria

Continent: Europe
Country: Greece, Albania
Background:
Liberation Army of Chameria (Albanian: Ushtria Çlirimtare e Çamërisë) is a reported paramilitary formation in the northern Greek region of Epirus. However, it has been disputed that the organisation is a Greek front. The organisation is reportedly linked to the Kosovo Liberation Army and the National Liberation Army, both ethnic Albanian paramilitary organisations in Serbia and the Republic of Macedonia respectively. As of 2001, the Greek police reported that the group consisted of approximately 30-40 Albanians. It reportedly does not have the support of the Albanian government.

Liberation Front of Brittany

Abbreviation: FLB
Continent: Europe
Country: Brittany
Background:
The Liberation Front of Brittany (French: Front de Libération de la Bretagne or FLB) is a militant group founded in 1963 to promote the "liberation of Brittany from France". Brittany is a province in northwest France, and was an independent Celtic duchy until it was claimed by the French in the sixteenth century.

The first known FLB attack occurred in June 1966 when a municipal tax office in St Brieux was bombed, and a note signed by the FLB claimed that they would continue to carry out a campaign of violence against these "occupying symbols of Brittany."

In the years following, the FLB carried out attacks against administrative structures, such as electrical installations, police barracks and statues - mainly by bombing them. The amount of attacks peaked in 1968.

However, the FLB ensured that no physical injuries or deaths would result from their attacks, which they wished to remain purely symbolic. They thus gained a reputation in the international community as the "smiling terrorists." There are even reports that the only two known FLB victims during this period were two FLB militants themselves, who were killed while trying to defuse a bomb they were afraid may hurt civilians.

Although created by young Bretons in the early 1960s, the FLB enjoyed popular support, evident in the 1969 arrest of numerous FLB suspects which revealed that members came from very diverse backgrounds: businessmen, housewives, students, farmers, and even clergy. Some of these suspects were put on trial, which only bolstered the Breton "liberation" movement as it was perceived to be further suppressive action by the government. This period was also marked with a rise in the number of students enrolling in Breton language courses, as being able to speak Breton was seen as legitimising one's position as a Breton militant.

Factions in the FLB emerged in the early 1970s which led to the creation of the militant Breton Revolutionary Army (Armée Révolutionnaire Bretonne, or ARB). This group acted separately from the FLB and proved to be the durable faction that is still existent today. It is important to note that there were several Breton liberation groups, and so the original FLB should not be confused with the others. This includes the Democratic Breton Union (still an existing political party that does not wish to be linked at all with the FLB and ARB - listed terrorist organisations) and the ARB, although this group did stem out from the FLB.

Liberation Front of Quebec

Abbreviation: FLQ
Continent: North America
Country: Canada
Background:

The Liberation Front of Quebec was formed in February 1963. This terrorist organisation, commonly referenced by its French acronym FLQ, based its ideological foundations on two defining goals. The first objective was to secure Quebec's separation from Canada. Throughout its history, FLQ remained committed to independence for the Quebec province. The Liberation Front's second goal was to improve the condition of Quebec's working class population. Within the first few years of its existence, the FLQ would harden its socialist rhetoric through principles of Marxism.

The majority of the FLQ's terrorist attacks occurred between 1963 and 1972. It was in October 1970 that the continuing terrorist actions of Quebec separatist groups came to a head. During this violent period, known as the "October Crisis," the Liberation Front of Quebec went on a violent rampage throughout Quebec. The violence prompted the Canadian government to authorise the War Measures Act on the 16th October 1970. The expanded powers granted by the law led to the capture of 500 suspected separatist terrorists.

The government crackdown combined with a public backlash against FLQ's terrorist actions, severely limited the group's operations post-1972. The group resurfaced in the late 1970s but has been dormant since then. In 1995 Raymond Villeneuve, one of FLQ's co-founders, created a new terrorist organisation, the Quebec National Liberation Movement. Villeneuve vowed to use intimidation and violence to expel English speakers from Quebec province, and thereby move a step closer to Quebec independence.

Also known as Quebec Liberation Front

Liberation Tigers of Tamil Eelam

Abbreviation: LTTE
Continent: Asia
Country: Sri Lanka
Background:

The Liberation Tigers of Tamil Eelam (LTTE), arguably the most lethal and well organised terrorist group in the world, began its armed campaign in Sri Lanka for a separate Tamil homeland in 1983. Under the Prevention of Terrorism Act, 2002 (POTA) in India, the LTTE is a proscribed organisation. On the 4th October 2003, the United States re-designated the LTTE as a Foreign Terrorist Organisation (FTO) pursuant to Section 219 of the US Immigration and Nationality Act. The LTTE has been proscribed, designated or banned as a terrorist group by a number of governments - India, Malaysia, USA, Canada, UK, Australia - countries where the LTTE has significant terrorist infrastructure for disseminating propaganda, raising funds, procuring and shipping supplies to support their terrorist campaign in Sri Lanka.

The LTTE was formed on the 5th May 1976, under the leadership of Velupillai Prabhakaran, and has emerged as perhaps the most lethal, well organised and disciplined terrorist force in the world. Headquartered in the Wanni region, Prabhakaran had established an extensive network of checkpoints and informants to keep track of any outsiders who enter the group's area of control.

Terrorism in Sri Lanka began in 1970 with the formation of a militant student body called the "Tamil Students Movement" to protest government plans to limit access of Tamil students to universities. Very soon this movement went underground and turned to overt terrorist activities. Violence escalated in Jaffna from 1972 onwards, beginning with the publication of a new constitution seen by the Tamil United Liberation Front (TULF) as anti-Tamil. The year 1972 saw the formation of two Tamil terrorist groups – the Tamil New Tigers (TNT) and Tamil Eelam Liberation Organisation (TELO), splinter groups of the original Tamil Students Movement. In July 1983, countrywide riots and clashes between Sinhalese and Tamils left thousands of Tamils dead and several hundred thousand as refugees. Large numbers of Government forces were deployed in the north and east provinces. This period marks the beginning of the LTTE guerrilla campaign against the Sri Lankan Government.

The LTTE aimed to create a separate homeland for the Tamils known as the Tamil Eelam (state) in the Northern and Eastern provinces of Sri Lanka. The Tigers controlled most of the northern and eastern areas of Sri Lanka but have also conducted operations throughout the island.

Apart from the military operations which the LTTE conduct in the North-eastern parts of the country against Government forces and the highly successful suicide killings operations in other parts of the country, a major aspect of the LTTE's operations is its publicity, fund-raising and military procurement strategies.

The LTTE ran a wide network of publicity and propaganda activities with offices and cells located in at least 54 countries. The largest and most important centres are located in leading western states with large Tamil expatriate communities, most notably the UK, France, Germany, Switzerland, Canada and Australia. In addition to these states, the LTTE are also known to be represented in countries as far-flung as Cambodia, Burma, South Africa and Botswana. Its publicity networks covering Europe, Australia and North America also include radio and TV satellites.

Apart from publicity, another important aspect of LTTE's strategy is fundraising. The majority of financial support comes from six main areas, all of which contain large Tamil Diasporas: Switzerland, Canada, Australia, the UK, the US, and the Scandinavian countries. The LTTE has established a wide network of offices and cells practically across the globe. They had secured a considerable degree of visibility in the United Kingdom – the headquarters of its "International Secretariat" – as well as in Canada, France, Germany, Holland, Switzerland, Italy, Sweden, Denmark, Norway, Australia and South Africa. These networks of offices and cells carry out propaganda, organise the procurement and movement of weapons and raise funds from the Tamil Diaspora.

There were also reports that the LTTE raised money through drug running, particularly heroin from Southeast and Southwest Asia. The LTTE is in a particularly advantageous position to traffic narcotics due to the highly efficient international network it has developed to smuggle munitions around the world. Many of these arms routes passed either directly through or very close to major drug producing and transit centres, including Burma, Thailand, Cambodia, southern China, Afghanistan and Pakistan.

Military and arms procurement played a vital part in the LTTE's battle against the Government sources. The LTTE arms network was headed by Tharmalingam Shanmugham, alias Kumaran Pathmanathan and colloquially known as "KP." At the heart of the KP's operations was a highly secretive shipping network. The ships frequently visited Japan, Indonesia, Singapore, South Africa, Burma, Turkey, France, Italy and Ukraine, scouting for arms. In addition to setting up a number of lucrative businesses, the LTTE established a state-of-the-art boatyard that manufactured a dozen different boats, including a mini-submarine for debussing divers.

Liberation of Achik Elite Force

Abbreviation: LAEF
Continent: Asia
Country: India
Background:

The Liberation of Achik Elite Force (LAEF) is a Garo militant group that was formed sometime in 2005. In an appeal in the first week of October 2006, the LAEF outlined the reasons of its existence: "LAEF stands to fight for a separate Achik state after studying the scenario of the State. It is learnt that the citizens of our land have been ill-treated and discriminated in every field – socially, politically and economically by the Khasis and Jaintias of Meghalaya making our people lag behind in the development process." It also appealed to the Achik (Garo) people "to co-operate and join hands to fight for a peaceful movement for an independent separate Achik State."

According to a 5th September 2007-report, the LAEF was trying to regroup in the Garo Hills with the help of some other militant groups, including the National Socialist Council of Nagaland-Isak-Muivah (NSCN-IM). Police sources stated some of its cadres had fled to Dimapur in Nagaland and were in constant touch with the NSCN-IM leaders. Shortly after his arrest from Jorabhat, the LAEF chief Peter Marak was interrogated and as per his statement, the NSCN-IM had provided the LAEF with as many as 15 AK-47s, 25 automatic M20 pistols and three highly powerful Universal Machine Guns besides over a hundred hand grenades, Assam Tribune reported on the 23rd August 2007. He also claimed that all the armaments were paid for by his organisation. A 22nd June 2007-report stated that the group had established a link with the National Socialist Council of Nagaland –Khaplang (NSCN-K).

Assam Tribune reported on the 23rd August 2007, that "the LAEF has since its inception in 2005 been rumoured to be patronised by members of a prominent political party from Meghalaya."

Libyan Islamic Fighting Group

Abbreviation: LIFG
Continent: Africa
Country: Libya
Background:
Libyan Islamic Fighting Group (LIFG), now allied to the National Transitional Council, was dedicated to two principle objectives. The founding goal of the terrorist group was to overthrow the formerLibyan government led by Muammar Qadhafi. LIFG was founded on thebelief that Qadhafi and his government were un-Islamic and should be overthrown. LIFG members had attempted, but failed, to assassinate Qadhafi. From the time it was founded until the late '90s, LIFG attacked Libyan security forces in armed altercations. The LIFG continued to target interest of the former Libyan government.

The Libyan Islamic Fighting Group also maintains a second objective beyond Libya's border, to contribute to the international jihadist campaign. This objective has become increasingly central to LIFG's activities and overall goals. LIFG has demonstrated significant (though denied) ties with al-Qaeda and others in the international jihadist movement. In fact, it is suspected that certain LIFG senior leaders maintain positions in al-Qaeda's senior command structure. LIFG is suspected as one of the terrorist entities to provide materials for the May 2003 suicide bombings in Casablanca.

While LIFG is essentially an indigenous Libyan Islamist terrorist group, the group is now demonstrating a proclivity for more global terrorist operations. LIFG is principally compromised of Libyans who fought in the Soviet-Afghan war. The Libyan veterans returned to their country with the aim of creating an Islamic state in Libya. In time, LIFG pledged its support to jihadist groups throughout the world. In addition to its links to al-Qaeda, the Libyan Islamic Fighting Group has ties to extremist groups in Egypt and Algeria. Abdelhakim Belhadj of the LIFG became the commander of the Tripoli Military Council after the rebels took over Tripoli during the fighting for the capital in 2011

Also known as Fighting Islamic Group, Libyan Fighting Group.

Lord's Resistance Army

Abbreviation: LRA
Continent: Africa
Country: Congo, Democratic Republic of the Sudan; Uganda
Background:

Based in Northern Uganda and Sudan, the Lord's Resistance Army seeks to destabilise and overthrow the government of Uganda. Formed in 1992 in an attempt to unify a resistance movement fractured by the marginalisation of the Uganda Democratic Christian Army, the group promotes a radical form of Christianity which it wants to make the foundation of a new Ugandan government. The group, led by Joseph Kony, has sought to achieve these objectives primarily through unbridled brutality. Rape, torture, and murder have become the group's hallmarks in the almost fifteen years that they have terrorised the citizens of Northern Uganda. The ranks of the LRA are filled in large part (approximately 80%) by children, who are kidnapped and brainwashed into service with the group. Human rights NGOs place the number of children currently fighting with LRA at around 3,000. LRA members also kidnap children, particularly girls, to serve as sex slaves; some have even been given as "gifts" to arms dealers in Sudan.

LRA attacks have been notable for both their brutality and their pointlessness. Two popular nightspots have been bombed, a bus full of people was attacked by club-wielding LRA soldiers who caused 22 fatalities, and an Italian priest was murdered. Other victims include World Food Program volunteers, the former President of Uganda, and mourners at a funeral, who were forced to cook and eat the body of the deceased. No discernible political program underlies these attacks aside from Kony's desire to cause extreme pain and suffering to all Acholi tribes that do not support the LRA.

In 2002, the Sudanese government reversed its longstanding policy of support for the LRA and began cooperating in efforts to eliminate the group's sanctuaries. Despite this declaration, the LRA continued to perpetrate its brutal attacks within Uganda, both in its longstanding operational area in the north, as well as on targets to the east.

The peace talks, which are taking place in the southern Sudanese town of Juba, are being mediated by south-Sudanese Vice-President Riek Machar. As the process gains momentum and there is increased participation from LRA leadership, other government leaders from Sudan, Uganda, and the Republic of the Congo are expected to join the talks. While the LRA leaders believe that coming out of hiding may result in their arrest on warrants issued by the International Criminal Court (ICC), government officials agree that a lasting ceasefire is contingent on the presence and participation from LRA's top-level.

The struggling peace process gained renewed attention in November 2006, when Jan Egeland, the UN Undersecretary-General for Humanitarian Affairs and Emergency Relief Coordinator, travelled to LRA camps near Ri-Kwangba along the Sudan-Uganda border. Egeland and Kony were scheduled to meet, each bringing their own objectives to the table. Egeland was particularly interested in obtaining the release of Acholi women and children abducted by the LRA and held in the camps, while Kony sought to gain an ally in his case with the ICC. The actual meeting, despite being cordial, was brief and did not produce the desired outcomes for either side. When confronted with the possibility of releasing the women and children, Kony denied their existence. However, the fact that the meeting took place without any problems, as well as generated publicity by the attendance of a UN official such as Egeland, creates a positive scenario for the tenuous peace talks. Additional visits from UN representatives may be a necessary tactic to foster stability in the surrounding region.

Loyalist Volunteer Force

Abbreviation: LVF
Continent: Europe
Country: United Kingdom
Background:
The Loyalist Volunteer Force (LVF) is a loyalist terrorist organisation fighting to protect Protestants from armed republican groups, such as the Real Irish Republican Army (RIRA), and resist efforts to unite Northern Ireland with the Republic of Ireland. In February 1997, the LVF publicly emerged as a splinter group of the loyalist paramilitary Ulster Volunteer Force (UVF) due to internal disputes.

Billy Wright, the group's founder and first leader (killed in prison by republican militants in December 1997), and subsequent LVF members disagreed with the UVF's participation in the Northern Ireland peace process and its ceasefire declared in 1994. Tensions within the UVF reached a boiling point when UVF leaders ordered its members to abstain from participating in the annual 12th July parades in 1996. July 12 parades commemorate the victory of Protestant Prince William of Orange's victory over Catholic King James II in the 1690 Battle of the Boyne and often pass through Catholic neighbourhoods, exacerbating sectarian tensions. UVF leaders were concerned that the participation of its members could possibly derail the ongoing and fragile peace process.

Since its formation, the LVF has engaged in bombings, killings, and kidnappings in retaliation for attacks on Protestants by republican groups. However, its attacks mostly have targeted civilians, often those with no connections to paramilitary organisations. The LVF has also been known to attack fellow loyalists, especially members of its founding group with whom the LVF has been involved in a feud since its 1997 formation.

In May 1998, the LVF declared a ceasefire and began to participate in peace negotiations following the Good Friday Agreement. However, there have been allegations that the LVF is solely motivated to participate in order to secure the early release of its incarcerated members. As part of the Good Friday Agreement, participants in peace talks are eligible to gain the early release of their members currently imprisoned.

Throughout its declared ceasefire, the LVF remained heavily involved in criminal dealings, especially in narcotics. In October 2001, due to its continued participation in criminal and violent activities, the British government no longer recognised its ceasefire. However, following a particularly violent summer in the LVF/UVF feud, the LVF declared it was standing down in 2005. The Independent Monitoring Commission, the independent body formed in 2004 to monitor paramilitary organisations, confirmed that violent attacks have ceased since the LVF ended its feud with the UVF, but stated that the LVF remained deeply entrenched in criminal activities.

Mahdi Army/Militia

Continent: Middle East

Country: Iraq

Background:

The Mahdi Army, also known as the Mahdi Militia or Jaish al Mahdi, is an Iraqi paramilitary force created by the Iraqi Shiite cleric Muqtada al-Sadr in June 2003.

The group rose to international prominence on the 4th April 2004 when it spearheaded the first major armed confrontation against the U.S.-led occupation forces in Iraq from the Shiite community in an uprising that followed the banning of al-Sadr's newspaper and attempts to arrest him, and lasted until the 6th June. The group is armed with various light weapons, including IEDs (improvised explosive devices, also called road-side bombs) during their attacks on Iraqi Security Forces and Coalition Forces. Many of the IED's used are extremely sophisticated infra-red trigger bombs, which were first used by the IRA in Northern Ireland.

The truce agreed to in June was followed by moves to disband the group and transform al-Sadr's movement into a political party to take part in the 2005 elections; Muqtada al-Sadr ordered fighters of the Mahdi army to go into a ceasefire unless attacked first. The truce broke down in August 2004 by provocative actions by the Mahdi Army, with new hostilities breaking out. The Mahdi Army's popularity has been strong enough to influence local government, the police, and cooperation with Sunni Iraqis and their supporters. The group is believed to have recently been popular in Iraqi police forces. National Independent Cadres and Elites party that ran in the 2005 Iraqi election was closely linked with the army.

The term Mahdi is actually in reference to the Army of the Mahdi, a prophetic army that will arise before the return of the "Hidden Imam" according to the Shiite Islamics.

Created by Muqtada al-Sadr and a rare portion of Religious Shiite Islamics. The Mahdi Army began as a small group of roughly 500 seminary students connected with Muqtada al-Sadr in the Sadr City district of Baghdad, formerly known as Saddam City. The group moved in to fill the security vacuum in Sadr City and in a string of southern Iraqi cities following the fall of Baghdad to U.S-led coalition forces on the 9th April 2003.

The group had been involved in dispensing aid to Iraqis and provided security in the Shiite slums from looters.

Gradually, the militia grew and al-Sadr formalised it in June 2003. The Mahdi Army grew into a sizable force of up to 10,000 who even operated what amounted to a shadow government in some areas. Al-Sadr's preaching was critical of the US occupation, but he did not initially join the Sunni Islamist and Baathist guerrillas in their attacks on coalition forces.

Sadr's position changed dramatically, however, by the beginning of April. Following the closure of the Sadr-owned newspaper al-Hawza and the arrest of one of his senior aides, Sadr gave an unusually heated sermon to his followers on Friday, 2nd April 2004. The next day, violent protests occurred throughout the Shiite south that soon spilled over into a violent uprising by Mahdi Army militiamen, fully underway by the 4th April 2004.

The Mahdi Army forces began an offensive in Najaf, Kufa, Kut, and Sadr City, seizing control of public buildings and police stations while clashing with coalition forces. The militants gained partial control of Karbala after fighting there. Other coalition forces came under attack in Nasiriyah, Amarah and Basra. Najaf and Kufa were quickly seized after a few fire fights with Spanish troops, and Kut was seized after clashes with Ukrainian troops soon afterwards.

After sporadic clashes, coalition forces temporarily suppressed most militia activity in Nasiriyah, Amarah, and Basra. Mahdi rebels expelled Iraqi police from three police stations and ambushed U.S forces in Sadr City, killing seven U.S troops and wounding several more. U.S forces subsequently regained control of the police stations after running fire fights with the fighters, killing dozens of Mahdi militiamen. Mahdi Army members still maintained some influence over many of the slum areas of Sadr City, however.

On the 16th April Kut was retaken by US forces, and several dozen Mahdi Army members were killed in the battle.

On the 4th May coalition forces began a counter-offensive to eliminate Mahdi Army in southern Iraq following a breakdown in negotiations.

On the 24th May after suffering heavy losses in weeks of fighting, Mahdi Army forces withdrew from the city of Karbala.

On the 6th June 2004, Muqtada al-Sadr issued an announcement directing Mahdi Army to cease operations in Najaf and Kufa. The militia have been defeated, or have left." The 6th June effectively marked the end of Shi'ite uprising. The total number of Mahdi Army militiamen killed in the fighting across Iraq is estimated at between 1,500 and 2,000.

The return of Najaf to Iraqi security forces following the cease-fire left Sadr City as the last bastion of Mahdi Army guerrillas still pursuing violent resistance. Clashes continued periodically in the district following the end of the Najaf-Kufa battles. On the 24th June Mahdi Army declared an end to operations in Sadr City as well, effectively ending militia activity, at least for the time being.

After the 4th June truce with the occupation forces, al-Sadr took steps to disband the Mahdi Army. In a statement, he called on militia members from outside Najaf to "do their duty" and go home. US forces in Najaf were then replaced by Iraqi police. Al-Sadr told supporters not to attack Iraqi security forces and announced his intention to form a party and enter the 2005 elections. He said the interim government was an opportunity to build a unified Iraq. Interim President Ghazi Yawer gave assurances that al-Sadr could join the political process provided he abandoned his militia. Iraqi officials also assured al-Sadr that he was not to face arrest.

On the 5th August, via his spokesman Ahmed al-Shaibany, al-Sadr re-affirmed his commitment to the truce and called on US forces to honour the truce. He announced that if the restoration of the cease-fire failed "then the firing and igniting of the revolution will continue". The offer was rejected by the governor of Najaf, Adnan al-Zurufi ("There is no compromise or room for another truce") and US officials ("This is one battle we really do feel we can win").

In the days that followed fighting continued around the old city of Najaf, in particular at the Imam Ali shrine and the cemetery. The Mahdi Army, estimated at 2,000 in Najaf, was outnumbered by some 2,000 US troops and 1,800 Iraqi security forces, and at a disadvantage due to the vastly superior American firepower and air cover, such as helicopters and AC-130 gunships. On the 13th August, the militia was trapped in a cordon around the Imam Ali shrine. While negotiations continued between the interim government and the Mahdi army, news came that al-Sadr had been wounded

On the 12th August, British journalist James Brandon, a reporter for the Sunday Telegraph was kidnapped in Basra by unidentified militants. A video tape was released, featuring Brandon and a hooded militant, threatening to kill the British hostage unless US forces withdrew from Najaf within 24 hours. Brandon was released after less than a day, following intervention by al-Sadr. At a press conference immediately after his release, Brandon commented on his treatment and thanked his kidnappers: "Initially I was treated roughly, but once they knew I was a journalist I was treated very well and I want to say thank you to the people who kidnapped me." A spokesman for al-Sadr said: "We apologise for what happened to you. This is not our tradition, not our rules. It is not the tradition of Islam."

The fact that American troops surrounded the Shrine became an impasse as the Mahdi army could not leave the shrine and US troops did not want to offend Islam by setting foot inside the shrine. The standoff did not end for three weeks until Sistani emerged from convalescence in London and brokered an agreement between the two forces.

The uprising seemed to draw an ambivalent reaction from the Iraqi population, which for the most part neither joined or resisted the rebels. Many Iraqi security forces melted away, wishing to avoid confrontation. In a sign of Mahdi Army's unpopularity in Najaf, however, which follows more traditionalist clerics, a small covert movement sprung up to launch attacks on the militants. The uprising did receive a good deal of support from Shiite radicals in Baghdad, however, who were galvanised by the simultaneous siege of the city of Fallujah.

Muqtada Sadr has close ties with the Islamic Dawa Party, which has ties to Iran. Many leaders of the Dawa Party fled to Iran, and elsewhere, after the Persian Gulf War where they remained in exile until the American invasion of Iraq in 2003. During this period, some of its factions moved to the SCIRI party. After the invasion, both al-Dawa and SCIRI returned to Iraq.

A New York Times report on the 9th February 2007, said that US intelligence has confirmed that Iran's Quds Force has provided Shia militants in Iraq with Iranian made explosively formed penetrators (EFP), which have been called the most effective improvised explosive device used against American troops. According to this article, many of these have been brought into Iraq at night at the border crossing at Mehran. Two days later US military commanders in Iraq gave a briefing to reporters, in which they displayed EFPs with what they said are Iranian serial numbers. According to them, these devices have killed over 170 Americans in Iraq. President Bush himself reaffirmed the information several days later. Despite this, some members of the US military and intelligence community are unsure if Iranian leaders are actually behind the delivery of weapons. On the 21st February Newsweek revealed that the US military briefer in Iraq had strayed from his script when he said that Iranians at the highest levels were involved in the weapons shipments.

These claims were denied by senior Iranian leaders. "They condemn us for making problems in Iraq, but they don't have any documentary proof," Iran Foreign Ministry spokesman Mohammad Ali Hossaini told reporters. "Lots of this evidence is fake, artificial. For example, when they wanted to start a war in Iraq, they made plenty of evidence that there were lots of weapons in Iraq, though the investigators of the International Atomic Energy Agency said they couldn't find any weapons in Iraq," he said. "Right now they're using weapons (with certain markings), but it doesn't prove where these weapons came from.

The Mahdi Army had also pledged military support to Iran if Iran were to be attacked by Western forces, and participated in attacks allegedly murdering innocent civilians in hospitals.

When reporting on an early October 2006 clash between the Mahdi Army and Coalition troops in Diwaniyah, BBC news suggested that currently the Mahdi Army is not a homogenous force, with local groups apparently acting on own orders.

In September 2006, a senior coalition intelligence official had remarked to reporters how there were political fractures within Al-Sadr's organisation in protest of his relatively moderate political course of action, with one coalition intelligence official claiming that at least six major leaders no longer answer to al-Sadr and as many as a third of the army was now out of his direct control

The name Jaysh al-Mahdī has apocalyptic connotations: in Shiite theology, the Mah'dī is an end-times figure who it is said will assist the Masīh to destroy the Dajjāl and establish a global Islamic khilāfah in preparation for the Yaum al-Qiyāmah; in more common terms, it is believed that the Mahdī will come to help the Messiah (i.e., Jesus, referred to in Islam as ʿĪsā ibn Mariyam) to defeat the Antichrist (literally, al-Masīh al-Dajjāl means "the Deceiving Messiah"), before establishing a just Islamic social order in preparation for Judgment Day.

In the Twelver school of Shia Islam, the Mahdī is believed to have been an historical figure identified with the Twelfth Imam, Muhammad al-Mahdī, and is therefore called al-Imām al-Mahdī. It is believed that he is still present on earth "in occultation" (i.e., hidden), and will emerge again in the end times. Those Shiʿites of this school believe that the Imām Mahdī is the rightful ruler of the whole Islamic community (ummah) at any given time, and he is therefore also called Imām al-Zamān, meaning "Imām of the Age/Time."

Also known as the Mahdi Militia or Jaish al Mahdi (JAM)

Martyr Abu Ali Mustafa Brigades

Continent: Middle East
Country: Israel, West Bank/Gaza
Background:
The "Martyr Abu-Ali Mustafa Brigades" is the military wing of the Popular Front for the Liberation of Palestine (PFLP). The group is named after Mustafa al-Zibri (Abu Ali Mustafa), the former leader of the PFLP who was killed in an Israeli air strike in August 2001.

The Abu-Ali Mustafa Brigades operates wholly under the direction of the PFLP. The PFLP is a Marxist-Leninist, Palestinian secular nationalist movement, and one of the most hard-line of the various Palestinian groups in the region. Opposed to the peace process in any form, the PFLP is dedicated to the destruction of Israel, and the Abu-Ali Mustafa Brigades is the military infrastructure set up to achieve these aims.

The Brigades have been responsible for dozens of attacks on both civilians and military targets in Israel and the Occupied Territories. Formerly known as the "Red Eagles," the Brigades can be said to be responsible for any violent action taken by the PFLP after the August 2001 killing of al-Zibri. These incidents include several suicide bombings in Israel, numerous attacks on Israeli settlements in Gaza, and the launching of rocket attacks on Israeli territory and settlements alike.

The Brigades, under the PFLP, enjoy widespread financial support from Syria. In addition, the organisation often cooperates with the al-Aqsa Martyrs Brigade, the Izz-al-Din al-Qassam Brigades, and the Al-Quds Brigades, the military wings of al-Fatah, HAMAS, and Islamic Jihad respectively.

Despite the Israeli withdrawal from Gaza in August 2005, and waning support when compared to HAMAS, the Abu-Ali Mustafa Brigades under the PFLP is an extremely active terrorist group. As most of the Brigades' attacks were cantered in Gaza settlements, before the Israeli disengagement, the Brigades can be expected to carry out more attacks in the West Bank and Israel in the future.

Also known as Red Eagles (former name). See the al-Aqsa Martyrs Brigade, the Izz-al-Din al-Qassam Brigades, Al-Quds Brigades

Mau Mau

Continent: Africa
Country: Kenya
Background:

The Mau Mau Uprising was an insurgency by Kenyan rebels against the British Empire administration that lasted from 1952 to 1960. The core of the resistance was formed by members of the Kikuyu ethnic group, along with smaller numbers of Embu and Meru. The uprising failed militarily, though it may have hastened Kenyan independence. It created a rift between the white colonial community in Kenya and the Home Office in London that set the stage for Kenyan independence in 1963. It is sometimes called the Mau Mau Rebellion or the Mau Mau Revolt, or, in official documents, the Kenya Emergency.

The name Mau Mau for the rebel movement was not coined by the movement itself- they called themselves Muingi ("The Movement"), Muigwithania ("The Understanding"), Muma wa Uiguano ("The Oath of Unity") or simply "The KCA", after the Kikuyu Central Association that created the impetus for the insurgency. Veterans of the independence movement referred to themselves as the "Land and Freedom Army" in English.

Also known as Muingi ("The Movement"), Muigwithania ("The

Understanding"), Muma wa Uiguano ("The Oath of Unity"), The KCA, Land and Freedom Army

Minutemen

Continent: North America
Country: United States of America
Background:

The Minutemen was a militant anti-Communist organisation formed in the United States in the early 1960s. The founder and head of the right-wing group was Robert Bolivar DePugh, a chemist from Norborne, Missouri. The Minutemen believed that Communism would soon take over all of America. The group, which saw themselves as new patriots, armed themselves and were preparing to take back the country if necessary.

According to "Traitors Beware: A History of Robert DePugh's Minutemen," by Eric Beckemeier, "The Minutemen were essentially a loosely organised band of guerrilla fighters who planned to defend the United States against what they considered to be an imminent Communist invasion."

The Minutemen organised themselves into small cells and stockpiled weapons for the counter-revolution. Some members would attempt to intimidate their enemies by mailing them a piece of paper with a crosshair on it. The implication was the person should be aware they were "in the Minutemen's gunsights". At times the Minutemen would infiltrate leftist and radical organisations in order to disrupt their activities and gather intelligence.

In February 1968, DePugh was indicted by a federal grand jury in Seattle, Washington for conspiracy to commit bank robbery. Also in 1968, he was arrested for violation of federal firearms laws. He skipped bail and went underground for over a year until he was caught in 1969 in Truth or Consequences, New Mexico. He was released from prison in May 1973. DePugh later wrote a survival manual, Can You Survive? and was associated briefly with Liberty Lobby. It has been suggested that the Minutemen were early forerunners of the Militia Movement.

Montana Freemen

Continent: North America
Country: United States of America
Background:

The Montana Freemen were a group of farmers and shysters who practiced Posse Comitatus theories of common law and sovereign citizenship. The

Montana Freemen refused to recognise the authority of the federal government and asserted their own right as "sovereign citizens" to print money and issue arrest warrants.

In September of 1995, two Freemen cells merged near Justus, Montana. Local tax protest leaders Leroy Schweitzer, Rodney Skurdal, and Daniel Peterson moved in with the Clark family. Schweitzer and Skurdal were infamous for teaching classes on how to pass fraudulent checks and file bogus liens. Earlier that year, the Clark family, who owed $1.8 million in mortgage payments and taxes, had convened a "common law court" and issued warrants threatening the life of the local sheriff and the county judge. When the two groups joined forces, they renamed the Clarks' farm, their base of operations, "Justus Township." They continued to threaten local authorities and teach seminars on how to execute classic Posse Comitatus scams.

Local law enforcement realised they would have to confront the Freemen, but Justus's sheriff didn't have the manpower to ensure that the confrontation went smoothly. The FBI, suffering from what the press dubbed "Weaver Fever" (the fear that a confrontation with militants would go as badly as the Ruby Ridge standoff had) was also reluctant to get involved. Local residents began to resent the apparent impunity with which the Freemen were flouting federal authority. "Call the IRS and ask them why they haven't seized their property," a local car dealer insisted. "Why do they get special treatment? I think the federal government has a responsibility to the people who are paying taxes."

Finally, on the 25th March 1996, the FBI arrested Leroy Schweitzer and Daniel Peterson, and demanded the dozen or so Freemen for whom they had arrest warrants leave Justus Township. The Freemen refused, and a standoff which was to last 81 days begun.

The FBI was determined not to make the same mistakes that were made at Ruby Ridge. The standoff was managed by the FBI's Critical Incident Response Group, which implemented lessons learned during the Ruby Ridge confrontation. Agents wore civilian clothes instead of camouflage and drove civilian vehicles instead of armoured cars. Federal officials made repeated, televised pleas to the Freemen to surrender peacefully. Instead of surrounding the Clark ranch, FBI agents merely stopped and questioned anyone who tried to enter or leave. Finally, the FBI notified paramilitary groups across the country before arresting a single Freeman, which pre-empted conspiracy theories and actually won the support of some militias. Several prominent figures in the militia community, such as the attorneys of Randy Weaver and families who died at Waco, actually served as negotiators in attempts to end the standoff.

At first, the Freemen showed no signs of willingness to compromise and deliberately made unreasonable demands to stall negotiations. For example, they insisted at one point that they would only negotiate if Supreme Court nominee Robert Bork acted as a mediator. They also issued a press release declaring independence from the "de facto corporate prostitute also known as the United States." The standoff dragged on for weeks, then months, without any sign of a breakthrough. On day 71, the FBI cut power to the Freemen Ranch. Finally, on the 13th June 1996, the remaining members of the Freemen surrendered peacefully, and the FBI arrested those for whom it had warrants, effectively ending the existence of the Montana Freemen.

Morzanist Patriotic Front

Abbreviation: FPM
Continent: South America
Country: Honduras, Nicaragua
Background:

The Morazanist Patriotic Front, or Frente Patriótico Morazanista (FPM), was a small, left-wing terrorist organisation responsible for a number of incidents in the late 1980s and early 1990s. Most of the group's attacks targeted Americans, both servicemen and civilians.

The FPM was sometimes linked to the Honduran Communist Party, and it aims are usually described as "leftist." However, while the FPM repeatedly made public statements claiming responsibility for attacks, it did not articulate a detailed set of aims. FPM's target selection indicates that its primary goal was combating the U.S. presence in Honduras, not fighting for a Marxist state.

The U.S. military presence in Honduras expanded in the late 1980s as a result of the civil war in neighbouring Nicaragua. The U.S.-backed Contras, right-wing rebels fighting the Sandinista government of Nicaragua, moved into Honduras in order to protect their forces. Attacks against the Sandinista government were launched from safe havens in Honduras. U.S. military personnel arrived in the country to coordinate material support to the Contras and to conduct training manoeuvres.

The presence of Contra forces and American military personnel provoked considerable animosity in many Hondurans. In fact, several groups associated with the political left formed to combat their presence with terrorism. Honduras, which had largely been spared the extensive terrorism associated with long civil wars in other Central American countries, saw an increase in terrorist bombings and assassinations in the late 1980s. These bombings were largely associated with the Contra crisis.

FPM was the most active group implicated in the upswing of attacks. The group's first reported attack was the fall 1988 slaying of American expatriate Leo Mills. Mills, a private businessman, was shot while jogging. Anti-American attacks claimed by the FPM would escalate over the next two years. The group claimed responsibility for an explosion at the U.S. Peace Corps in December 1988. The bomb caused no casualties but significant damage. FPM later targeted U.S. AID. The group's two most famous attacks both involved American servicemen. In July 1989, 7 U.S. soldiers were wounded when FPM terrorists threw a bomb at them as they left a night club. Seven more U.S. military personnel were wounded when their bus was attacked by snipers in March 1990.

The Contras departed Honduras after the Sandinista government lost out in a February 1990 election. While most of the Honduran terrorist organisations put down their arms after the Contras' left, FPM continued its terrorist attacks for several years. FPM was implicated in a rocket attack against a U.N. site in June 1991 and an assassination in February 1992. The group's last attack occurred in April 1995, when a leaflet bomb exploded near the offices of several foreign press agencies. No one was injured. The Morazanist Patriotic Front ceased its activities in the mid-1990s. It is no longer considered an active terrorist group.

Also known as Morazanista Liberation Front, Morazanista Patriotic Front, Morazano National Liberation Front

Morzanist Front for the Liberation of Honduras

Abbreviation: FMLH
Continent: South America
Country: Honduras, Nicaragua
Background:

In 1980, the Morazanist Front for the Liberation of Honduras (FMLH) split from the Party for the Transformation of Honduras (Partido para la Transformacion de Honduras, or PTH), itself an offshoot of the Communist Party of Honduras (Partido Comunista de Honduras, or PCH). Named after Honduran and Central American hero Francisco Morazan, who struggled to maintain the unity of the United States of Central America before it dissolved in 1840, the FMLH was a Communist movement that advocated the use of violent means to oppose the Honduran government.

Soon after the FMLH was created, the government in Honduras adopted very repressive measures designed to root out the leftist insurgencies that appeared in Honduras in the early 1980s. As a result, many leaders of these Marxist/Leninist/Communist groups fled the country and led their movements in exile, with the support of other leftist insurgencies in other Central American countries. During this period, the FMLH was administered from Nicaragua.

The 1980s witnessed a smattering of terrorist attacks in Honduras perpetrated by leftist groups, including the FMLH's attack on a Tegucigalpa disco that injured many. However, due to the lack of support from the relatively conservative people of Honduras and the harsh but effective measures undertaken by the Honduran government, the leftist movement never took hold.

The disco attack is the only incident ever attributed to the FMLH. FMLH is unrelated to the Morazanist Patriotic Front, a terrorist organisation that targeted U.S. servicemen stationed in Honduras up until the mid-1990s.

By the early 1990s, external support for the FMLH and most leftist groups in general waned as the Sandinista regime was voted out in Nicaragua and the leftist insurgency known as the Farabundo Martí National Liberation Front (FMLN) was successfully integrated into El Salvadoran politics. This downturn prompted the FMLH to seek political integration as well.

In 1992, the FMLH recreated itself politically as the Morazanist National Liberation Party (Partido Morazanista de Liberacion Nacional, or PMLN). The PMLN, along with three other groups, including the PTH, the Honduran Revolutionary Party (Partido Revolucionario Hondureno, or PRH), and Patriotic Renovation Party (Partido Renovación Patriótica, or PRP), merged into the Democratic Unification Party (Partido Unificacion Democratica, or PUD). The PUD, officially recognised by the government in 1993, is a very minor player in contemporary Honduran politics--its candidates take less than two percent of the vote in presidential, parliamentary, and municipal elections. Although the FMLH as a militant insurgency movement is inactive, its Communist ideals are marginally represented by the PUD in the contemporary Honduran political scene.

Mountaineer Militia

Continent: North America
Country: United States of America
Background:
The Mountaineer Militia is a right-wing militia group based in West Virginia which, in the mid-1990s, plotted to blow up federal buildings during an 'inevitable moment of confrontation' with the federal government. The leader of the Mountaineer Militia, Floyd Raymond Looker, became a vocal defendant of militias on a national scale before being arrested for organising a plot against an FBI building in West Virginia.

Initially, Looker and members of his militia were focused on protecting their constitutional rights. "Our common belief is that the U.S. government already has taken away many of our constitutional rights," Looker said. "And without the Constitution, we the people have nothing to protect ourselves against a government run amok, other than our guns." However, over time, Looker became more and more paranoid and radical. He became convinced that the government was dedicated to stripping Americans of their rights and staging a full takeover of the country, putting dissenters in concentration camps.

Like many militiamen, Looker believed that there would come a moment where they would be forced to face off with the government to protect their rights as citizens. Unlike most militiamen, Looker planned extensively for this moment. The main portion of his plan was the destruction of the Federal Bureau of Investigation Criminal Identification Centre in Clarksburg, West Virginia, a fingerprinting facility. Looker believed the government was using this facility to spy on all Americans, so he began plotting to blow it up. He and members of his group obtained blueprints of the building and began to stockpile an impressive amount of explosives – both made and acquired.

As Looker became increasingly convinced of the evil of the federal government, he became less willing to wait until the "moment of confrontation" to do harm. Instead, when approached by a FBI agent posing as a middle man wanting to sell explosives or intelligence to terrorists from the Middle East, Looker jumped at the opportunity. He saw it as a way to make money while ensuring that his plan would be put to action.

With the help of an FBI informant within the group, the FBI built a solid case against a number of members of the Mountaineer Militia, including Looker. The agent posing as the middle man completed the purchase of the blueprints; Looker was arrested immediately after on charges of conspiring to provide material support and resources with the intent to use them in the preparation for committing an injury or depredation against the FBI fingerprinting facility; conspiring to manufacture and deal in explosive materials; and transporting explosives across state lines. Looker was sentenced to 18 years in prison in 1997.

Six other militiamen were also arrested on charges of conspiracy and transportation of explosives across state lines. Four were convicted or pled guilty, and two were acquitted. One of the men was named James Johnson, sharing the name of well-known Ohio militia leader James "J.J." Johnson. This had led to the incorrect linkage of the Mountaineer Militia and J.J. Johnson's Ohio Unorganised Militia. There is, in fact, no connection between the groups.

The federal government has insisted that it did not investigate or arrest any of these men because of their associations with militia groups, which are entirely legal. Instead, they were arrested for plotting to destroy a federal building. Department of Justice officials have said there is no distinction in the law for a group plotting to destroy a federal building in response to some perceived injustice or attack.

Militia presence and membership dropped significantly in West Virginia after the 1996 arrests. It is believed that by 2004, however, interest was beginning to resurface. This does not necessarily indicate an increased likelihood of terrorist activity or plots. Most militia members deny any interest in violent action but are committed to defending their constitutional rights, especially the right to bear arms.

Movsar Baryayev Gang

Continent: Asia
Country: Chechnya, Russia
Background:
The Movsar Barayev Gang was a militant group based in the Russian state of Chechnya and dedicated to turning that state into an independent Islamic republic. Both the lineage and the rhetoric of the group's leader, Movsar Barayev, suggest a heavy influence of radical Islamic thought, common among Chechen separatists. Barayev had long been a member of anti-Russian militias led by his paternal uncle, the Islamic fundamentalist Arbi Barayev, killed by Russian forces June 2001. Arbi Barayev was especially fond of kidnappings for ransom, and gained notoriety in 1998 when he beheaded three Britons and a New Zealander captive. Movsar became a star of the Chechen resistance while still in his teens, leading a faction of rebels known as the "Islamic Regiment." However, it remains unclear whether Barayev was primarily driven by lofty goals, or was simply using faith as a cover for baser motives. One Chechen religious leader who knew Barayev claims that the terrorist was much more interested in making money than in fighting for Allah.

The Movsar Barayev Gang was largely made up of members from two other Chechen terrorists organisations, the Special Purpose Islamic Regiment (SPIR) and the International Islamic Brigade (IIB). Chechen rebel commander, Shamil Basayev, controlled both the SPIR and IIB, which has led many to conclude that he was also giving the Barayev Gang its orders. The "gang" conducted its first, and last, major attack when it took a theatre in Moscow and held patrons hostage on the 23rd October 2002. All of the terrorists (including Barayev), and a number of the hostages, were killed when Russian police retook the theatre by force three days later. In one of his many televised messages during the Moscow theatre crisis, he claimed that, "Each one of us is willing to sacrifice himself for the sake of God and the independence of Chechnya." Although the Barayev Gang technically went defunct when its leader died, its goals and methods still find acceptance among many Chechen separatists. In fact, it has been suggested by credible sources that the currently active and extremely dangerous Riyad us-Saliheyn Martyrs' Brigade was formed by remnants of the IIP and SPIR as a response to the Moscow theatre disaster.

Mudiad Amddiffyn Cymru

Abbreviation: MAC
Continent: Europe
Country: United Kingdom
Background:

Mudiad Amddiffyn Cymru (Welsh Defence Movement), abbreviated as MAC, was a Welsh freedom-fighting organisation, modelled to some degree on the Irish Republican Army, which was responsible for a number of bombing incidents between 1963 and 1969.

MAC was initially set up in response to the flooding of the Afon Tryweryn valley and the flooding of the village of Capel Celyn to provide water for Liverpool. Its founders were Owain Williams, John Albert Jones and Emyr Llywelyn Jones. On the 10th February 1963 a transformer at the dam construction site was blown up by three men, of whom one, Emyr Llywelyn Jones was identified, convicted and sentenced to one year's imprisonment. MAC blew up an electricity pylon at Gellilydan on the day of his conviction. This led to the arrest and conviction of Owain Williams and John Albert Jones.

The effective leadership of the organisation was later taken over by John Barnard Jenkins, a non-commissioned officer in the British Army. Under his leadership, MAC is widely suspected by British police to have been behind the bombing of the Clywedog dam construction site in 1966. In 1967 a pipe carrying water from Lake Vyrnwy to Liverpool was blown up. Later the same year MAC exploded a bomb at the Temple of Peace and Health in Cardiff's civic centre, close to a venue which was to be used for a conference to discuss the Investiture of Prince Charles as Prince of Wales. In 1968 a tax office in Cardiff was blown up, followed the same year by the Welsh Office building in the same city, then another water pipe at Helsby, Cheshire. In April 1969 a tax office in Chester was the next target. On 30th June 1969, the evening before the investiture, two members of MAC, Alwyn Jones and George Taylor, were killed when a bomb they had been intending to place on the railway line at Abergele, in order to stop the Royal Train from getting through to Caernarfon, exploded prematurely. In actuality, at the time the bomb was being placed, the Royal Train had already passed Abergele and was parked at a guarded remote site. In November 1969 John Jenkins was arrested, and in April 1970 was convicted of eight offences involving explosives and sentenced to ten years' imprisonment. Although there were further bombings, there is no evidence that MAC were involved.

Also known as Welsh Defence Movement

Mujahadi Bayt al Maqdis Brigades

Continent: Middle East
Country: West Bank/Gaza
Background:
The Mujahadi Bayt al-Maqdis Brigades, or the Fighters of Jerusalem Brigades, are a little-known Palestinian terrorist organisation whose members allegedly also belong to the Palestinian nationalist group, al-Fatah, and the more radical Popular Resistance Committees.

In the group's first known attack, members kidnapped human rights activist Kate Burton and her parents in Gaza near the Egyptian border in December 2005. The three hostages were released two days later, unharmed. Various motives for the attack have been reported including the demand for Israel to abolish its buffer zone in northern Gaza, the desire to draw attention to the plight of Palestinian prisoners held by Israel, and the condemnation of the historical role the British have played in the region.

The Burtons' kidnapping drew unprecedented criticism and condemnation by Palestinian resistance groups, including Hamas, al-Fatah, the Popular Resistance Committees, and the al-Aqsa Martyrs Brigades, due to Kate Burton's support for and humanitarian assistance to the Palestinians. One member of the al-Aqsa Martyrs Brigades was held in connection to the kidnapping although he was never charged for the attack. He was released on the 5th January after his followers attacked an Egyptian border fence with a bulldozer in protest. No further evidence has implicated the al-Aqsa Martyrs Brigades.

No recent attacks had been linked to the organisation, possibly because of the negative publicity generated among Palestinians by its first attack. While the group may have become inactive, its members are likely to remain active, conducting attacks on behalf of other Palestinian terrorist groups.

Also known as Fighters of Jerusalem Brigades, Mujahedeen Brigades Jerusalem Branch

Mujahedin e Khalq

Abbreviation: MeK
Continent: Europe, Middle East
Country: France, Iraq
Background:

The MEK is the primary opposition to the current Iranian government and acts as the focal point of the National Council of Resistance of Iran (NCRI), a coalition of Iranian opposition groups which claims to be the transitional parliament-in-exile with 570 members. The NCRI was headquartered in Iraq, with representative offices in other countries including a presence in Washington where it has previously received support from the US Congress. After the 9/11 attacks however, the US government actively courted cooperation from the government of Iran and further sidelined any unofficial support for the MEK. Worsening their reputation further, intelligence reports suggested that the MEK's military camps in Iraq might be hiding some of Iraq's weapons programs. The group surrendered to US forces following the US invasion of Iraq. In May 2003, US Central Command stated that the group was "complying fully with Coalition instructions and directives". The MEK began as a liberal nationalistic party supporting former Prime Minister Mossaddeq against the Shah. When a 1963 uprising against the Shah failed, more radical members split off to form the MEK. In 1971 the new group began its armed struggle against the Shah, whom it saw as a dictator and a puppet of the United States.

The group conducted a number of attacks on US military personnel and civilians in Iran in the 1970s. Although the group initially supported the 1979 revolution and the overthrow of the Shah, the group's secular perspective led to an eventual crackdown by the Khomeini regime following MEK's call for a mass demonstration after the 1981 impeachment of Abolhasan Bani-Sadr, the elected President and chairman of the Islamic Revolutionary Council. Thousands of MEK members were killed and imprisoned during the repression. The MEK's leaders fled to Paris and their military infrastructure moved to Iraq. The headquarters were relocated to Iraq in 1987, the MEK's military wing, the NLA was formed and began using Iraq as a base for cross-border raids into Iran. In 1991, it assisted Saddam Hussein in suppressing the Shia and Kurdish uprisings, and continued to perform internal security services for the Government thereafter. In April 1992, the MEK conducted near-simultaneous attacks on Iranian Embassies and installations in 13 countries. More recently, the MEK assassinated the deputy chief of the Armed Forces General Staff of Iran in April 1999, and was involved regularly in mortar attacks and hit-and-run raids on Iranian military and law-enforcement units and government buildings near the Iran-Iraq border throughout 2000 and 2001.

The MEK's goal is to overthrow the Iranian government and replace it with the NCRI. At a 1995 conference, the group outlined a 16-point plan:

1) Guarantee freedom of belief, expression and the press, without censorship; 2) Guarantee freedom for political parties, unions, groups, councils, forums, syndicates, except those loyal to either the Shah or Ayatollah

Khomeini, provided they stayed within the law; 3) Ensure governments would be elected; 4) Respect for the Universal Declaration of Human Rights; 5) Abolish courts, tribunals, security departments introduced by the Ayatollah Khomeini regime; 6) Ensure women enjoy the same social, political and cultural rights as men (including a ban on polygamy); 7) Abolish privileges based on gender, religion or ethnic group; 8) End discrimination against religious minorities; 9) Abolish compulsory religious practice; 10) Secure Iranian territorial integrity while recognising the right of Iranian Kurdistan to autonomy; 11) Safeguard all social, cultural and political rights for ethnic minorities; 12) Repeal what the MEK deems to be `anti-labour, anti-peasant laws'; 13) Encourage a return from exile for all who fled either the Shah or Khomeini regime; 14) Base the economy on the free market, national capitalism and private ownership; 15) Provide welfare needs to the poor; 16) Improve Iran's foreign relations with neighbouring and other states; to live in peaceful co-existence.

The Mujahedin-e-Khalq have periodically released information on Iran's developing nuclear weapons program, however the information cannot usually be verified. The group's information was, however, crucial in the 2002 revelation of Iran's uranium enrichment program. Its latest release came in February 2005, when the group passed on information to the International Atomic Energy Administration (IAEA) that Iran now possesses sources for polonium-210 and beryllium, crucial components in building an "initiator." The group claims that this is the last objective that Iran needed to fulfil and that they plan to have a nuclear weapon by the end of 2005.

Also known as Mojahedin Khalq Organisation, Mujahideen-e Khalq Organisation (MKO), People's Mujahideen of Iran (PMOI)

Mujahideen Message

Continent: Asia
Country: Afghanistan
Background:
Mujahedeen Message is held responsible for the August 2003 burning down of the Abu Sofial girls' school in Logar Province, south of Kabul Afghanistan. Another school for girls had also recently been burned down in this area. Under the Taliban's interpretation of Islamic Shari'a law, girls were prohibited from receiving education. Schools for girls opened across Afghanistan in the wake of the Taliban's fall in late 2001, yet certain Afghans remain opposed to the practice.

In addition to their opposition to female education, the group has threatened to kill anyone cooperating with the US-backed government led by Hamid Karzai. Mujahedeen Message has not claimed an attack since

2003; however, some reports suggest that it is linked to elements of the Taliban, which remain a deadly insurgent force.

Muslim Brotherhood

Continent: Africa
Country: Egypt
Background:

The Muslim Brotherhood was founded in 1928 by Hassan al-Banna, an Egyptian seeking to overthrow Egypt's monarchy, expel western influences and establish an Islamic theocracy. The Brotherhood has pursued these goals since its founding through political activity, ideological influence and acts of violence. The group became known for its extensive terrorist operations, including a failed assassination attempt on Egyptian leader Gamal Abdul Nasser. Its activities led to violent crackdowns by the governments of Egypt and Syria; it is banned in those countries and others. The brotherhood continues to enjoy a large following throughout the Muslim world. While forced to limit its violent activity, the group has influenced many terrorist leaders - including Osama Bin Laden - and its members have formed several radical and violent organisations. One of these, Egyptian Islamic Jihad - which was later absorbed into Al Qaeda - assassinated Egyptian president Anwar Sadat. Hamas, another spinoff, was formed by Palestinian members trying to increase the group's influence in the Israeli conflict. The organisation has praised and encouraged Palestinian and Iraqi suicide bombers and terrorists. Although it is headquartered in Egypt it has satellite groups throughout the Muslim world

The Muslim Brotherhood no longer openly conducts terrorist operations; it is primarily a political organisation that supports terrorism and terrorist causes. Many of its members, however, have engaged in terrorist activities and the group has spawned numerous terrorist groups, such as Hamas and Egyptian Islamic Jihad.

The Muslim Brotherhood's theology is based on the doctrine of salafiyya: the belief that present-day Muslims have been corrupted and must return to the pristine form of Islam practiced at the time of the Prophet Muhammad. Many Muslim Brotherhood members preach jihad. The group says: "Allah is our objective. The Prophet is our leader. Koran is our law. Jihad is our way. Dying in the way of Allah is our highest hope." Thus establishing theocracy in Egypt, the Middle East, ultimately worldwide, preaching, political agitation and advocating terrorism. The brotherhood participates in elections and attempts to gain influence through the political process. Although it is banned in Egypt, members of the brotherhood have been elected to the legislature there and in Jordan. It also promotes violence against the U.S. and Israel and sponsored through Saudi Arabia.

Muslims of the Americas

Abbreviation: MOA
Continent: North America
Country: United States of America
Background:

Muslims of the Americas (MOA) is a virulently anti-Semitic, Islamic extremist group with ties to Al-Fuqra, a terrorist organisation that has carried out firebombings and murders in the United States. MOA claims to have offices in six U.S. cities and Toronto and maintains secluded residential communities in New York, Virginia and California. The group's Web site and e-mails have featured writings by notorious anti-Semites and Holocaust deniers, including Michael Hoffman and former Klansman David Duke.

MOA was founded and is led by the radical Pakistani cleric El Sheikh Sayyid Mubarik Ali Jilani (commonly known as Sheikh Jilani or Sheikh Gilani). Based in Lahore, Pakistan, Jilani established MOA in 1980, after arriving in the United States for the first time. In the 1980s, Jilani, who claims to be a direct descendant of the Prophet Muhammad, actively recruited American Muslims to fight against the Soviet Union in Afghanistan.

The available evidence strongly suggests that MOA has served as a corporate front for another group founded by Sheik Jilani, the terrorist organisation Al-Fuqra, which has committed firebombings and murders on U.S. soil. Both Sheikh Jilani and MOA officials deny that Al-Fuqra even exists, and MOA claims to be a "peaceful" group. Though relatively few members of MOA have been arrested for criminal activity, two residents of the MOA community in Virginia were arrested for firearms violations, and a resident of the MOA community in California was arrested for the murder of a Sheriff's Deputy.

See Jamaat al Fuqra

Nation of Yahweh

Continent: North America
Country: United States of America
Background:

The Nation of Yahweh is a cult which believes that blacks are the true Jews and that their leader, Yahweh ben Yahweh, is the messiah. The Nation of Yahweh was the subject of an FBI terrorism investigation in the late 1980s that looked into the group's financial practices and links to multiple murders in the Miami area.

Founded by Yahweh ben Yahweh, born Hulon Mitchell, Jr., the Nation of Yahweh had a relatively large following in the Miami area in the early to mid-1980s. Many local leaders praised the group for revitalising poor, black neighbourhoods and preaching hard work and ambition in black communities. While not a terrorist group by traditional definition, the group quickly morphed from a black power, religious cult to a dysfunctional, violent community. According to many former cult members, Yahweh ben Yahweh began sleeping with women of all ages within the group and, soon after, began dispatching members of his inner circle to kill those who had left the cult and random "white devils."

While the FBI and local officials were never able to conclusively prove the link in court, at least 15 murders in the Miami area between 1981 and 1986 are associated with the Nation of Yahweh. Several Yahwehs were convicted of the murders, but prosecutors were unable to prove that the murders were issued by the group's leader.

Testimony given by several former cult members, however, indicates that the murders were committed at the direct order of Yahweh ben Yahweh, who advocated the murder of all his "enemies", namely white people and former followers who turned against him as the tone and practices of the cult became sinister. The first murder linked to the group was that of Aston Green, a Yahweh member who had left the cult but continued to visit friends in the community. On one of his visits, he was brutally beaten by members of Yahweh ben Yahweh's inner circle. After the beating, he was taken to a remote location and beheaded. The killers then reportedly brought Green's head back to Yahweh, who praised them for their accomplishment.

Several more murders followed – all of former cult members believed to be talking to the police about life inside the Yahweh community. As

Yahweh ben Yahweh become increasingly paranoid, those still within the group but believed to be disloyal to him were killed. Leonard Dupree was one such victim and testimony shows that Yahweh ben Yahweh forced every member of the group, regardless of age or gender, to take part in the beating murder in order to ensure that all were guilty and none would talk.

Finally, Yahweh ben Yahweh formed a group called 'The Brotherhood', responsible for violently keeping order within the community. In order to become a member of The Brotherhood, young men had to kill a "white devil" and bring a body part back to Yahweh ben Yahweh. One member alone admitted to killing seven people, saying he was fuelled by Yahweh ben Yahweh's praise. Authorities are unsure how many murders in the Miami area in the mid-1980s can be attributed to members and future members of the Brotherhood, who were told they were fighting the war against the nonbelievers by attacking random white people. Despite escaping murder convictions, Yahweh ben Yahweh was convicted of racketeering charges and sentenced to 18 years in prison. He was released in 2001 after serving 11 years. In May 2007, ben Yahweh died of cancer.

Since their leader's imprisonment, the members of the Nation of Yahweh attempted to remake their image, focusing on the religious aspects of the cult and insisting they are neither racist nor violent. Their primary area of operation has shifted from the Miami area to Montreal, which they call the "New Promised Land." A 2001 Yahweh meeting in Montreal attracted up to 1,000 members.

The group continues to emphasise that they are a nation of believers at war with nonbelievers but insist it is a war of words, not of violent action. Up to the point of his death in 2007, members still considered Yahweh ben Yahweh to be their leader. It is as yet unknown what effect his death will have on the group.

Also known as Yahweh

National Alliance

Continent: North America
Country: United States of America
Background:
The National Alliance is a white nationalist and a white separatist organisation. It was founded by William Luther Pierce, and was based in Hillsboro, West Virginia. Although it is based in the United States, the National Alliance claims to have members in various countries throughout the world. Membership is not based upon citizenship in any particular country, but on perceived white, gentile European ancestry. The National Alliance is often included in lists of neo-Nazi groups, in part due to its glorification of Adolf Hitler. For example, an article appearing in a 1989

issue of its magazine National Vanguard celebrated the 100th anniversary of Hitler's birth, declaring him "the greatest man of our era".

National Army for the Liberation of Uganda

Abbreviation: NALU
Continent: Africa
Country: Democratic Republic of the Congo and Uganda
Background:

The National Army for the Liberation of Uganda (NALU) is militant group that seeks to overthrow the long-standing Ugandan government led by President Yoweri Museveni. Since their formation in 1988, NALU forces have been engaged in armed conflict in the northern and western regions of the country with the Ugandan People's Defence Forces (UPDF), the military of the Ugandan government. NALU fighters have also staged attacks on civilian populations and small villages, a tactic consistently used by other Ugandan rebel groups. In 1998, a suspected suicide bombing claimed by NALU killed a busload of thirty people in Kampala, the capital of Uganda. Not only are innocent civilians targeted by groups like NALU, but they have also been occupied and displaced by the UPDF as they search for rebel fighters and supplies.

In 2005, the Ugandan government extended an amnesty to several rebel groups, including NALU. It was their hope that the majority of fighters would surrender and disarm in exchange for avoiding prosecution, but in reality less than fifty NALU members showed up. This failed attempt has increased the efforts of the UPDF to attack rebel groups.

Even though NALU activity has been minimal over the past five years, the group is still considered to be intact. The group has since merged with the Allied Defence Forces (ADF), a militant group with similar ideologies, and moved its base deeper into the Democratic Republic of Congo. Most recent accounts place these groups in North Kivu and the Rwenzori Mountains. Uganda and regions of the eastern Congo are hoping to develop a joint military operation that would serve to eliminate all militant groups that are based on the Ugandan/Democratic Republic of Congo border. This collaboration, which has not been approved mainly due to budgetary allocations, would allow the UPDF access to the Democratic Republic of Congo in order to seek out rebel bases.

Uganda's primary concern, however, remains the Lord's Resistance Army (LRA) and the tenuous peace talks that are in development with them. It stands to reason that if a lasting cease-fire and eventual disarmament can take place between the Ugandan government and the LRA, the other less powerful rebel groups may be compelled to follow suit.

National Council of Resistance of Iran

Abbreviation: NCRI
Continent: Middle East
Country: Iran
Background:

The National Council of Resistance of Iran (NCRI) is the parliament-in-exile of the Iranian Resistance, and is a broad-based political umbrella coalition of five opposition political organisations and parties and more than 550 political, cultural and social figures, specialists, artists, intellectuals, scientists, military officers and commanders of the National Liberation Army.

The President-elect of the NCRI is Maryam Rajavi. Massoud Rajavi is officially the President and official spokesman of NCRI but he has not been seen or heard since the 2003 invasion of Iraq. Alireza Jafarzadeh was its official representative in the USA until the Washington office was closed by the US State Department in 2002 on the grounds that it was only a front group for the People's Mujahedin of Iran (PMOI, also known as MEK or MKO), by then listed as a terrorist organisation in the United States. Most analysts believe the NCRI to be the political wing of the MEK though the NCRI and the MEK both claim that the MEK is simply a member of the NCRI. It has been alleged that the inclusion of NCRI and MEK in the list was a token offered to the theocratic regime of Iran rather than based the facts of the matter. According to Wall Street Journal: "Senior diplomats in the Clinton administration say the MEK figured prominently as a bargaining chip in a bridge-building effort with Tehran." The Journal added that: In 1997, the State Department added the MEK to a list of global terrorist organisations as "a signal" of the U.S.'s desire for rapprochement with Tehran's reformists, says Martin Indyk, who at the time was assistant secretary of state for Near East Affairs. President Khatami's government "considered it a pretty big deal," Mr. Indyk says. The MEK itself has been involved in several attacks, including bombings, on individuals and facilities (including government buildings) of the Islamic Republic of Iran, both within Iran and abroad. Some of these attacks have caused civilian deaths and both the MEK and NCRI are regarded by the Islamic Republic of Iran as being terrorists. The NCRI itself (if it is considered a separate entity to the MEK) is not an armed organisation and hence has not been involved in attacks on Iranian people and property.

The European Union in May 2004 implied that NCRI is part of the People's Mujahedin of Iran (rather than vice versa) and excluded the NCRI itself from a list of organisations considered to be terrorist organisations, including the People's Mujahedin of Iran "minus the National Council of

Resistance of Iran" on its list of terrorist organisations. The NCRI is classified as a Foreign Terrorist Organisation by the United States.

National Front

Continent: Europe
Country: Germany
Background:

Nationalistische Front (Nationalist Front) was a minor German neo-Nazi group active during the 1980s.

Founded in 1985 by Meinolf Schönborn the group, which had no more than 150 members, was characterised by its support for Strasserism rather than more usual forms of Nazism. The Nationalist Front - League of Social Revolutionary Nationalists had been formed in 1982 from the ashes of the banned Volkssozialistische Bewegung Deutschlands/Partei der Arbeit. This organisation was the basis for a merger with a number of smaller groups to form a new NF.

Based primarily in Bielefeld, the group had a largely Pagan membership, hosting fire rituals and similar ceremonies. The group also performed cross burnings and forged links with Dennis Mahon, the head of the White Knights of the Ku Klux Klan in Tulsa, Oklahoma.

The group also became noted for its armed wing, the National Task Force (Nationales Einsatzkommando - NEK) which was set up in 1991 with the help of Otto Ernst Remer and Herbert Schweiger. This group was blamed on a number of attacks, including burning a man to death in the mistaken belief that he was a Jew and the arson of an asylum seeker hostel in Dolgenbrodt, near Berlin. Firmly anti-Semitic, the NF was also associated with Jürgen Rieger, the well-known German Holocaust denier who was a speaker at a number of its events.

Its support for the Nazis led to the group being banned by the Federal Ministry of the Interior in 1992 along with the German Alternative of Michael Kühnen and the National Offensive of Michael Swierczek. The group was succeeded by a number of organisations including Direct Action Middle Germany and the Social Revolutionary Workers Front, all of which were banned.

National Front for the Liberation of Libya

Abbreviation: NFSL
Continent: Africa
Country: Libya, Sudan
Background:

The National Front for the Salvation of Libya (NFSL) was an opposition movement to Muammar Gaddafi's former regime in Libya. The NFSL was established on the 7th October 1981, when it publicly announced its formation in a press conference held in Khartoum, Sudan's capital. The NFSL launched a wide campaign to topple Gaddafi in Libya, establishing a short-wave radio station, a bi-monthly Arabic magazine "Al Inqad", along with a commando's military training camp. The NFSL's commando forces attempted to penetrate the barracks of Bab El-Azizia, where Gaddafi maintained his residence, in an attempt to assassinate the former Libyan ruler on the 8th May 1984. The effort was thwarted when the group's leader, Ahmed Ibrahim Ihwas, was captured in his attempt to enter Libya through its borders with Tunisia.

The NFSL continued its efforts to topple Gaddafi. The group formed the Libyan National Army, after a group of soldiers made prisoners by Chad during the Chadian-Libyan conflict defected from the Libyan Army and joined the NFSL in 1987. The Army was later evacuated from Chad after the President Hissène Habré was overthrown by one of his former officers, Idriss Déby, who was backed by Gaddafi.

The NFSL continued its campaign to topple Gaddafi, primarily through media campaigns and forming alliances with other political opposition groups. The National Conference for the Libyan Opposition (NCLO) was formed in June 2005 in London, which is composed of 7 opposition organisations, led by the NFSL and its leaders.

National Liberation Army (Columbia)

Abbreviation: ELN
Continent: South America
Country: Columbia
Background:
The ELN is a Cuban Revolution-inspired group, heavily influenced by the early actions and theories of Fidel Castro and Che Guevara. The ELN emerged following the overthrow of the Cuban government by Guevara and Castro in 1959. The National Liberation Army was founded by two distinct groups. The first group comprised of urban, left-wing intellectuals with strong ties to rural farmers. They co-founded the group with a radicalised group of oil sector unionists from Barrancabermeja's oil industry. Radical members of the Catholic clergy joined the group in late 1965. This was the first time that Christians and Marxists had joined together in a Colombian revolutionary movement.

The ELN's unique founding philosophy strongly emphasised socialism, mixing Castro-ism with the liberation theology of the Catholic Church.

More concretely, the ELN's self-appointed role was to represent the rural poor and decrease the foreign presence in Colombia. The ELN's goal was to take power from the Colombian government and replace it with a more egalitarian "popular democracy" that would represent all Colombians equally under the law. The ELN strongly opposed foreign investment, in part due to its location in an oil-rich area and its connections to trade unionists in the energy sector.

The Colombian Department of Administrative Security estimates that in 1998 alone, the ELN obtained U.S. $84 million from ransoms and U.S. $255 million from extortion. Employees of oil companies constitute a large percentage of the ELN's targets. The kidnapping and extortion of oil company employees is ELN's primary source of income. This is a natural legacy of ELN's formation in an area rich with oil wells and oil companies. A third, more recent source of income is the collection of a "property" tax from coca and poppy cultivators. It is not known whether the collection of property taxes is a centralised or decentralised activity.

Throughout its history, the National Liberation Army steadily gravitated towards violence and armed struggle as a means to attain a socialist Colombia. At the ELN's 1996 national conference, the group decided to decrease emphasis on creating a purely socialist Colombia. Instead, the ELN has returned to its founding objective: popular democracy for all Colombians, propagated at the local level. The ELN has not given up the use of violence in its efforts.

National Liberation Army (Macedonia)

Continent: Europe
Country: Albania
Background:

The National Liberation Army (Albanian: Ushtria Çlirimtare Kombëtare - UÇK ; Macedonian: - ___), also known as the Macedonian UÇK, was an insurgent guerrilla organisation that operated in the Republic of Macedonia in 2001. Although linked with the Kosovo Liberation Army (Ushtria Çlirimtare e Kosovës), with which it shared initials and a very similar name, it was officially a separate organisation. According to the National Memorial Institute for the Prevention of Terrorism (MIPT) of the United States (US), they are a nationalist/separatist organisation which, despite its name, is not an army but rather a loosely-organised terrorist group which calls for the unification of ethnic Albanian areas of the Western Balkans, including part of Macedonia and southern Serbia.

Following the 2001 Macedonian War, it was disarmed under the terms of the Ohrid Agreement, under which greater rights and autonomy were to be given to the country's Albanian minority population. However, in the disarmament of the organisation, mainly outdated weapons were returned, some even dating back to the First World War. The organisation also has ties to many public officials in Western Macedonia, Kosovo and Southern Serbia, and the threat of its re-emergence will be to the peril of the Balkans.

National Liberation Front of Corsica

Abbreviation: FLNC
Continent: Europe
Country: Corsica, France
Background:

The merger of two Corsican terrorist organisations: Ghjustizia Paolina and the Fronte Paesanu Corsu di Liberazione in 1976 resulted in the establishment of the FLNC and thousands of bombings in the 1970s and 1980s. The group was to split again, however, at the end of the 1980s and beginning of the 1990s due to political rivalry. The initial split into a 'canal historique' (historic channel) and the 'canal habituel' (usual channel) was followed by a further fracturing into a number of additional terrorist organisations: Resistenza, Fronte Ribellu, Front Arme Revolutionnaire Corse, etc. Some of the groups had only a brief existence, but others went on to later merge with each other or newer groups. Until the FLNC-canal habituel decided to end its activities in 1997, it and the FLNC-canal historique were considered the most important terrorist organisations in Corsica. The canal historique expanded its operations to include mainland France in 1996, targeting a series of senior government officials. They succeeded in assassinating Claude Erignac, the prefect of Corsica and the most senior representative of the French government on the island.

In 1999, yet another merger between the FLNC-canal historique and other smaller organisations resulted in the re-adoption of the name 'FLNC.' In December 1999, the FLNC declared a ceasefire. The three month ceasefire was eventually extended indefinitely and technically still exists; however, the conflict flared up again in 2000 with a series of bombings stemming from rivalries between the various separatist groups. The group is not considered to have a well-established ideology, although it generally supports leftist ideas and once claimed it was fighting the 'internal colonialism' of France. Women are not allowed to be members of the organisation.

The FLNC ultimately hopes to achieve self-determination for Corsica through independence and to preserve Corsican language and culture. In addition, the group would like for terrorist group members imprisoned in continental France to be moved to a Corsican prison or allowed amnesty. The group also wants for Corsica to become a tax-free zone in order to attract transnational companies. An influx of North African immigrants has led to some racist violence and discrimination; the FLNC has begun to advocate preferential treatment for Corsicans in the job market (over North Africans).

French Prime Minister Lionel Jospin was the first leader to engage in talks with the Corsicans and negotiated the 1999 ceasefire. In July 2000, he proposed that the island be allowed some elements of self-rule including local legislation and the ability to teach the local dialect in schools. In July of 2003, however, Corsicans narrowly rejected a French offer for greater autonomy from France in a referendum. In a 51% to 49% vote, Corsicans voted no on a plan to create a single regional assembly with the power to levy taxes and to hold greater control over public services.

Also known as Front de Liberation Nationale de la Corse, Fronte di Liberazione Naziunale di a Corsica

New African Freedom Fighters

Continent: North America
Country: United States of America
Background:

The New Afrikan Freedom Fighters were not a structured, hierarchical organisation. They have been treated as such by authorities, who have described them both as an offshoot of the Revolutionary Armed Task Force and as the military arm of the New Republic of Afrika. It is probably most accurate, however, to think of the term "New Afrikan freedom fighter" as the combination of two descriptive phrases, rather than a declaration of membership in a group.

New Afrikan: New Afrika is the separate black republic that some radical African-American activists hope to found within the United States. "We of the New Afrikan Independence Movement spell 'Afrikan' with a "k' because Afrikan linguists originally used "k' to indicake the "c' sound in the English language. We use the term "New Afrikan', instead of Black, to define ourselves as an Afrikan people who have been forcibly transplanted to a new land and formed into a "new Afrikan nation' in North America."

Freedom Fighter: The term "freedom fighter" is commonly used within Marxist circles to describe those who use force to struggle against the prevailing order. "We contend we are black freedom fighters. Fighters, because freedom has never come any other way." Omowale Clay (quoted in The New York Times, 5/21/85)

Those who used "New Afrikan freedom fighter" to describe themselves were, therefore, declaring themselves to be anti-capitalist and announcing a commitment to secede and form a black state, by force if necessary.

In October of 1984, nine New Afrikan freedom fighters were surrounded and arrested by over 400 New York City police officers and federal agents. The eight who eventually stood trial became known as "The New York Eight." Police found sawed-off shotguns, sub-machine guns, dynamite bombs, and bank blueprints in the apartment of ringleader Randolph Simms (Coltrane Chimurenga). The New York Eight were charged with conspiring to free black activists Kuwasi Balagoon and Sekou Odinga. Balagoon was imprisoned for participating in a 1981 robbery of a Brinks armoured car, which resulted in the death of two police officers and a guard. Odinga was convicted of conspiring to commit the same robbery. The prosecution also alleged that the New York Eight planned to rob banks in order to finance their activities.

The prosecution described the New York Eight as "a highly organised, dedicated cell of armed bandits. ... Their goal: robbery of armoured trucks and liberating their confederates from prison." (Quoted in the Associated Press, 10/22/84) The jury, however, saw things differently, and acquitted all 8 defendants of conspiring to free Balagoon and Odinga and to commit grand larceny. Coltrane Chimurenga, Roger Wareham, Robert Taylor, Yvette Kelley, Ruth Carter and Clay Omowale were all convicted of possessing illegal weapons, and Viola Plummer was convicted of falsely identifying herself to the police. All seven were sentenced to community service. The eighth defendant, Jose Rios, was acquitted of all charges.

Also known as New African Freedom Fighters, The New York Eight

New Order

Continent: North America
Country: United States of America
Background:

The New Order was a terrorist organisation operating in Illinois modelled after Robert J. Matthews' white supremacist group, the Order. Demmos McGiffen, former Grand Dragon of the Knights of the Ku Klux Klan (KKK), formed the organisation in May 1997 after determining that the KKK was "too wimpy." McGiffen is believed to have been heavily influenced by the Turner Diaries, a racist novel written by William Turner in 1978, and McGiffen's idol, Robert J. Matthews.

The New Order planned to ignite a race war through bombings, assassinations, and water supply poisonings. Members of the group selected several targets to bomb including: the Anti-Defamation League headquarters in New York (a Jewish anti-bigotry organisation), the Southern Poverty Law Centre in Montgomery, Alabama (a civil rights law firm), and the Simon Wiesenthal Centre headquarters in Los Angeles (an international

Jewish human rights organisation). Morris Dees, one of the founders of the Southern Poverty Law Centre, and a federal judge were selected as assassination targets. The group planned to finance their terrorist activities through bank and armoured car robberies.

Dennis McGiffen and two other members, Wallace Weicherding and Ralph Bock, were arrested on the 23rd February 1998 before they were able to conduct any attacks. Two other members, Glenn Lowtharp and Karl Schave, were also later arrested. These five individuals were believed to be the only members of the organisation and all were ultimately convicted and sentenced to various prison terms. During their trial, both McGiffen and Weicherding maintained that their terrorist plans were only "drunken ramblings." Although these five known members were previously members of the KKK and Aryan Nations, no known relationship existed between the New Order and these two other more-established racist organisations.

The New Order has never committed an attack in its history and has not been mentioned publicly in recent years, despite the fact that its indicted members have all been released from prison after serving their sentences. It seems likely that the group is inactive. Still, other violent white supremacist groups modelled after Robert J. Matthews' The Order, are likely to conduct violent activities against Jews and other racial minorities in the future as they continue their attempts to ignite a race war.

New Red Brigades/Communist Combatant Party

Abbreviation: BR-PCC
Continent: Europe
Country: Italy
Background:

The New Red Brigades is a splinter group of the Red Brigades, a terrorist group active in the 1970's and early 1980's. When the Marxist-Leninist Red Brigades folded in 1984, two successor groups emerged, the New Red Brigades/Communist Combatant Party (BR-PCC) and the New Red Brigades/Union of Combatant Communists (BR-UCC). The BR/PCC has unequivocally chosen to follow the violent Communist path of the Red Brigades. Specifically, the BR-PCC is opposed to NATO and Italy's policies on labour and foreign relations.

The New Red Brigades continue to target high-ranking Italian businessmen and politicians. These assassinations, coupled with other bombings and attacks, are ostensibly in pursuit of class struggle. The BR-PCC also justifies these continuing attacks as blows against imperialism, specifically as it is represented within Italian economic policies and the NATO system.

In March 2002, the New Red Brigades assassinated Marco Biagi, an adviser to the Italian labour minister. Following the assassination, the New Red Brigades published a statement claiming responsibility for the killing. Notably, the statement commends the perpetrators of the September 11 attacks in the United States. In their own words, the New Red Brigades express the "need for the forging of alliances between anti-imperialistic forces and revolutionary forces in the regions of Europe, the Mediterranean, and the Middle East".

Niger Delta Peoples Volunteer Force

Abbreviation: NDPVF
Continent: Africa
Country: Nigeria
Background:

The Niger Delta People's Volunteer Force is one of the largest armed groups in the Niger Delta region of Nigeria and is composed primarily of members of the region's largest ethnic group, the Ijaw. The group was founded in 2004 in an attempt to gain more control over the region's vast petroleum resources, particularly in Delta State. The NDPVF has frequently demanded a greater share of the oil wealth from both the state and federal government and has occasionally supported independence for the Delta region. Until 2005 the group was spearheaded by their presently incarcerated charismatic leader, Alhaji Mujahid Dokubo-Asari, who is viewed by many locals as a sort of folk hero.

The NDPVF's strongly Ijaw agenda has led to conflict with both the Nigerian state and federal governments, as well as with neighbouring ethnic groups, notably long-time rival the Itsekiri. . This rivalry precipitated a number of conflicts in the region, centred primarily around the cities of Warri and subsequently the 'oil capital' of Port Harcourt. The issue of local government ward allocation has proven particularly contentious, as the Ijaw feel that the way in which wards have been allocated ensures that their superior numbers will not be reflected in the number of wards controlled by politicians of Ijaw ethnicity. Control of the city of Warri, the largest metropolitan area in Delta State and therefore a prime source of political patronage, has been an especially fiercely contested prize. This has given birth to heated disputes between the Ijaw, the Itsekiri and the Urhobo about which of the three groups are "truly" indigenous to the Warri region, with the underlying presumption being that the "real" indigenes should have control of the levers of power, regardless of the fact that all three groups enjoy ostensibly equal political rights in their places of residence.

Prior to 2003, the centre of regional violence was Warri. However, after the violent convergence of NDPVF with the Niger Delta Vigilante (NDV) led by Ateke Tom (the NDV is also comprised primarily of Ijaws), conflict became focused on Port Harcourt and outlying towns. The two groups dwarf a plethora of smaller militias supposedly numbering more than one hundred. All of the groups are constituted mostly by disaffected young men from Warri, Port Harcourt, and their sub-urban areas. Although the smaller groups are autonomous from within, they have formed alliances with and are largely controlled from above by either Asari and his NDPVF or Tom's NDV who provided military support and instruction.

The NDPFV attempted control such resources primarily through oil "bunkering", a process in which an oil pipeline is tapped and the oil extracted onto a barge. Bunkering is illegal in the eyes of both the Nigerian state and the oil corporations, but is justified by the militias on the basis that they are being exploited and have not received adequate profits from the monstrously profitable but ecologically destructive oil industry. Bunkered oil can still however be sold for profit, usually to destinations in West Africa, but also abroad. Bunkering is a fairly common practice in the Delta but in this case the militia groups are the primary 'perpetrators'.

The intense confrontation between the NDPVF and NDV seems to have been brought about by Asari's political falling out with the NDPVF's financial supporter Peter Odili, governor of Rivers State following the April 2003 local and state elections. After Asari publicly criticised the election process as fraudulent, the Odili government withdrew its financial support from the NDPVF and began to support Tom's NDV, effectively launching a paramilitary campaign against the NDPVF.

See Niger Delta Vigilante (NDV)

Niger Delta Vigilante

Abbreviation: NDV
Continent: Africa
Country: Nigeria
Background:

The Niger Delta Vigilante (NDV) is an armed militia group in Niger Delta region of Nigeria. The NDV is led by Ateke Tom. The group is composed primarily by ethnic Ijaws from in and around Port Harcourt and their main goal is controlling the area's vast oil resources. They eventually precipitated a conflict with their rival Ijaw ethnic militia, the Niger Delta People's Volunteer Force (NDPVF). The two groups spent most of 2004 in an escalating conflict which was ended when the Nigerian government and military eventually intervened on the side of the NDV in summer of 2004.

The government's support of the NDV would eventually precipitate the Nigerian oil crisis, beginning in October 2004.

See Niger Delta People's Volunteer Force

November 25 Anarchist Group

Continent: Europe
Country: Greece
Background:

The November 25 Anarchist Group is responsible for one attack in its history, the bombing of a Wendy's fast food restaurant in Athens in 1996. It is unclear what the motivation behind this attack was, though it can be inferred that it was anti-American or at least Greek-nationalist in nature. November 25th could be a reference to the date that the ultranationalist Colonel Ioannides, once imprisoned under the rule of the Papadopoulus dictatorship, wrested power from the junta in 1973.

Like many other Greek nationalist terrorist groups, this group seems to have gotten together for one attack and then disbanded. Some or all of its members may have committed additional attacks under other group names, though there is no evidence to support this. As it has only been responsible for one terrorist attack that occurred some years back, November 25 Anarchist Group can be considered inactive.

Official Irish Republican Army

Abbreviation: OIRA
Continent: Europe
Country: United Kingdom and Ireland
Background:

The Official Irish Republican Army (OIRA) was a Marxist-oriented republican organisation that fought for an independent, united Ireland during the early 1970s. The founding group of the OIRA, the IRA, was formed over eighty years ago as a result of the British presence in Ireland. In 1969, the IRA split into rival factions, the OIRA and Provisional IRA (PIRA). Where the OIRA desired to transform the fight into a united class struggle and turn away from militant republicanism, the PIRA sought an escalated armed campaign against the British security forces stationed in Northern Ireland. The PIRA would later become the de facto IRA in Northern Ireland.

Following the split with the PIRA, members of the OIRA would continue to engage in small-scale armed attacks and bombings against British security forces. Many of these attacks were in protest of repressive policies, such as internment, in Northern Ireland. They also were known to launch attacks against their republican rivals and civilians. While the majority of its attacks occurred in Northern Ireland, the group did launch an attack in England in February 1972 against a military installation, killing five people. Members also participated in punishment beatings and internal killings against its own members and civilians.

In 1972, the OIRA declared an indefinite ceasefire. There have been several speculations regarding the declaration including: the group's desire to focus more attention on its class struggle and its negative reputation due to its perceived inability to protect Catholic civilians and several politically damaging attacks. The group also wanted to participate politically towards the establishment of a united Ireland ruled by a socialist government. While attacks against British security forces ceased, group members would continue to engage in "defensive" violence against rivals like the Irish National Liberation Army (INLA) and PIRA.

Following the OIRA ceasefire, the majority of its members would join the group's political wing, the Workers' Party, and largely cease to engage in violence. However, remnants remained active. Today, group members conduct mostly organised criminal activities as well as internecine attacks against the Official Republican Movement (ORM), which was established in 1996 by former members of the OIRA. The loss of operatives and the resulting feud between the two groups has substantially weakened the ORIA's capabilities. Even though the OIRA has never decommissioned its arsenal as part of the peace process, it is unlikely that they will re-emerge as a legitimate threat to stability in Northern Ireland.

Ogaden National Liberation Front

Abbreviation: ONLF
Continent: Africa
Country: Ethiopia, Somalia
Background:
Founded in 1984, the Ogaden National Liberation Front (ONLF) is an active insurgent group in eastern Ethiopia that seeks to establish an independent state for the Somali people in the Ogaden region of the Horn of Africa. Its members are largely drawn from the Ogaden and Darood ethnic groups, whose traditional lands stretch from eastern Ethiopia to central Somalia.

The ONLF accuses the Ethiopian government of widespread human rights abuses in the Ogaden, including illegally confiscating private property, interfering with relief work, and wrongfully expropriating international aid destined for the region. As such, they counter government influence in the region by staging ambushes and guerrilla-style raids on government forces. The ONLF is also known to kidnap foreign workers thought to be agents of the Ethiopian government or supporters of the regime in Addis Ababa. In the late 1980s, the ONLF grew to be the most dangerous insurgent group in Ethiopia, and it is widely believed that the group is directly responsible for the deaths of thousands of government troops. The abundance of religious and clan-affiliated regional terrorist groups makes it difficult to substantiate claims of responsibility for terror attacks committed in the area.

The ONLF was known to conduct joint operations with the Oromo Liberation Front (OLF), which represented a different clan whose indigenous territories lie in the western portion of the Ogaden. The OLF, once the dominant anti-Ethiopian force in the region, has seen its power dwindle significantly with the ascent of the ONLF and has been content to ally with the ONLF and other groups to fight the Ethiopian regime. In 2000, the OLF and ONLF joined with four other groups to form the United Liberation Front of Oromiya, which is thought to have existed in name only, as attacks continued to be unilaterally claimed by the ONLF.

It is suspected that the ONLF has bases in Somalia, and the Ethiopian government accuses neighbouring Eritrea of providing the ONLF with equipment and training. Ties between the ONLF and al-Qaeda have never been substantiated, though it is suspected that the Ethiopian government spread rumours to that effect to attract international assistance and attention.

Although the ONLF claims that its military actions are only undertaken by a separate military wing, the Ogaden National Liberation Army (ONLA), there is no proof that a formal separation exists between the two entities. Most attacks attributed to Ogaden insurgents are not claimed by the ONLA but rather by the ONLF through its propaganda mouthpiece, Radio Free Somaliweyn (Greater Somalia).

In June 2004, sources reported that the ONLF was discontinuing its violent campaign in the Ogaden. However, attacks on Ethiopian government troops continued. Efforts at peace failed again in July 2005, and in May 2006 the ONLF joined several political parties to form the Alliance for Freedom and Democracy (AFD), a coalition seeking to address the conflict in the Ogaden region through consultations with the Ethiopian People's Revolutionary Democratic Front (EPRDF), Ethiopia's ruling party. The EPRDF has yet to respond to the overtures of the AFD, and until substantive talks occur, the ONLF-led insurgency is expected to continue.

See the Oromo Liberation Front

Oklahoma City Bombing Conspirators

Continent: North America
Country: United States of America
Background:

On the 19th April 1995, at 0902 hrs, Timothy McVeigh committed one of the most heinous crimes in American history, the bombing of the Alfred P. Murrah Federal Building. 168 men, women and children were killed, and over 500 more wounded.

Timothy McVeigh was born in Pendelton, NY on the 23rd April 1968. Neighbours and friends remember McVeigh as a happy, likeable child. He developed a fascination with guns at a very early age, and was encouraged by his grandfather, Eddie, an avid outdoorsman. Timothy received his first rifle as a present for his thirteenth birthday, and would tell people who asked him what he wanted to be when he grew up that he planned to own a gun shop. His mother left the family the year McVeigh graduated from high school, and McVeigh appears to have been deeply resentful of her. McVeigh did well in school, and graduated with honours, but decided not to go to college.

Instead, he stayed home to devote his time to researching guns and the Second Amendment. He discovered the extremist militia movement, and the racist, anti-government propaganda he read resonated with him. The book that seems to have influenced him most was The Turner Diaries, an anti-government white supremacist fantasy in which the hero detonates a truck bomb outside FBI headquarters. He was also deeply impressed by Red Dawn, a movie in which Cuba invades the United States and the federal government immediately collapses. A small band of high school students led by Patrick Swayze, a survivalist who has been storing weapons and food in case of just such an emergency, organises a guerrilla resistance to the invasion and saves the day.

In May of 1988, McVeigh joined the Army. He thrived on the discipline and survivalist training he found there, and was described as an excellent soldier by his superiors. He met Terry Lynn Nichols and Michael Fortier, who would both play a role in the Oklahoma City Bombing, while all three were enlisted. McVeigh served in the Gulf War, and was awarded a Combat Infantry Badge and a Bronze Star. When he applied to become a Green Beret, however, he was rejected, reportedly because he didn't take time to recover his stamina after returning from the war. Disillusioned and disappointed, McVeigh left the Army.

Returning to civilian life deepened his resentment of the government. Instead of being treated as a conquering hero, McVeigh found himself back in a low-paying job as a security guard at Burke Armoured Cars. McVeigh's colleagues remember him constantly ranting about his hatred of the government, and boasting that he could easily steal guns from the Army. He spouted the same angry diatribe at women, which may explain why he never had a girlfriend. "He would talk about the Government a lot," says Catina Lawson, who met him at a party. "He also talked a lot about Hitler...From what I remember; he said he didn't necessarily agree with all those Jews being killed. But he said Hitler had the right plan... I didn't like him after that."

McVeigh began attending gun shows, where he made money and found likeminded people with whom to network. He became more and more deeply involved in the right-wing extremist movement, even attending the standoff at Waco to sell bumper stickers that read "A Man With a Gun Is A Citizen, A Man Without A Gun Is A Subject." He told a reporter who interviewed him there, "The government is continually growing bigger and more powerful, and the people need to prepare to defend themselves against government control."

The catastrophic end of the standoff at the Branch Davidian compound appears to have convinced McVeigh that it was time to take action. He wrote to Nichols and Fortier and invited them to participate in a bombing modelled on the one depicted in The Turner Diaries. Fortier refused, but allowed Nichols and McVeigh to stay at his house while preparing the attack. Nichols robbed Roger Moore, a contact McVeigh had made at a gun show, in order to finance the bombing. During the planning, McVeigh used his little sister's computer to send a letter to the Bureau of Alcohol, Tobacco, Firearms and Explosives (the organisation that initiated the government's confrontation with the Branch Davidians) warning, "all you tyrannical (expletive) will swing in the wind one day for your treasonous actions against the Constitution of the United States." McVeigh, according to the prosecution, chose the Murrah Building because "He thought the ATF agent, whom he blamed for the Waco tragedy, had their offices in that building."

After the bombing, many members of the media, the government and the public jumped to the conclusion that Islamic extremists were responsible. Militia experts at the FBI, however, noted the suspicious coincidence of the date: the bombing took place on the anniversary of the fire that ended the Waco standoff, and the battle of Concord, the opening battle of the American Revolutionary War. Both events are considered sacred by the militia movement. Tracing the truck axle and license plate back to the rental agency led the FBI to McVeigh, who had by that time already been arrested by an Oklahoma State trooper who had pulled him over for driving a car without licence plates.

McVeigh and Nichols were tried separately. Michael Fortier, his wife, and McVeigh's younger sister testified against them at trial, as did 138 other witnesses. Nichols, despite his insistence that he had been bullied into the bombing by McVeigh, was sentenced to life in prison. McVeigh was sentenced to death. His appeals were denied, and he chose not to petition the President for clemency. Six years after the bombing, McVeigh was executed. On his deathbed, McVeigh stated in writing, "I am the master of my fate: I am the captain of my soul."

Oklahoma Constitutional Militia

Continent: North America
Country: United States of America
Background:
The Oklahoma Constitutional Militia was a small, anti-government, anti-Semitic group whose only planned attack was foiled by an FBI informer. They believed that the New World Order existed and posed a direct and immediate threat to them. Militia leader Willie Ray Lampley expected Russia to invade the United States through Mexico during his lifetime, and he encouraged his followers to stockpile supplies and arms in preparation for the invasion. The Militia's members were all followers of the racist teachings of

Christian Identity, and the group was also known as the Universal Church of God. Lampley visited Elohim City, a compound at which the leaders of American white supremacy networked and discussed their shared beliefs.

The militia formed in 1994, when Lampley and Larry Wayne Crow met and forged a friendship based on their shared religious views. The two soon began to attend militia meetings, and published religious pamphlets. Lampley believed he was a prophet, and Crow, who testified for the prosecution at Lampley's trial, claims that Lampley thought it was his duty to act on God's alleged condemnation of supposedly sinful people such as homosexuals, abortion doctors, and civil rights activists.

Lampley, Crow, Lampley's wife Cicilia, and John Dare Baird were arrested in November of 1995 for conspiring to bomb several targets including gay bars, abortion clinics, and civil rights groups such as the Southern Poverty Law Centre and the Anti-Defamation League. Authorities found the supplies for an ammonium nitrate bomb in the Lampleys' home in Vernon, Oklahoma. Crow, who claims he had left the group, negotiated a plea bargain with the prosecution and testified against the other three group members. Lampley and his co-defendants claimed that they'd been entrapped by FBI agent Richard Schrum. Lampley insisted that it had been Schrum's idea to build the bomb. Cecilia Lampley, John Baird and Willie Ray Lampley were all convicted of conspiring to construct a homemade bomb. Willie Ray Lampley was also convicted on two additional counts. The Oklahoma Constitutional Militia ceased to exist after the arrest and trial of its only known members.

Also known as Universal Church of God

Omega-7

Continent: North America
Country: United States of America
Background:
Omega-7 was a violently anti-Castro Cuban group active from 1974 to 1983. The name Omega-7 comes from the group of seven revolutionaries who launched the group. Membership never rose above 20, but the group was financially supported by the Cuban exile community in Miami, New York and New Jersey. Their short-term goal was to harass the Castro regime, and their long-term goal was to raise and train an army of Cuban exiles to forcibly oust Castro. Omega-7 committed 18 major terrorist attacks, including the assassination of a Cuban diplomat to the UN on the 9th December 1980. The group's members had combat training and experience (some participated in the failed Bay of Pigs invasion), and their attacks were well planned and flawlessly executed. Their primary targets were

Cuban diplomatic and business interests and pro-Castro Cubans within the United States.

During the early 1980s, the Cuban exile community lost faith in efforts to overthrow Castro. Omega-7 turned to drug trafficking to raise funds. In 1982, six key Omega-7 leaders were arrested. The following year saw the arrest of Eduardo Arocena, the group's founder and leader. Arocena's arrest and the revelation during his trial that he had been working as an FBI informant, effectively destroyed Omega-7.

OPR-33

Continent: South America
Country: Argentina, Uruguay
Background:

The OPR-33 was an anarchist terrorist group that operated briefly during the 1970s. Despite the relatively small number of attacks and kidnappings it carried out, the group was high on the radar screen of both American and Uruguayan security forces during the period of Operation Condor, in which many operations were carried out against left-leaning groups in Latin America. The OPR-33 is believed by some to have been the clandestine armed wing of the Uruguayan Anarchist Federation.

According to declassified U.S. Defence Department documents, the OPR-33 was effectively destroyed in a raid carried out in Buenos Aires by Argentinean and Uruguayan security forces in September 1976.

Orange Volunteers

Abbreviation: OV
Continent: Europe
Country: United Kingdom
Background:

The Orange Volunteers (OV) is a loyalist paramilitary organisation operating primarily in Northern Ireland. Formed in the early 1970s, the group is closely associated with the Orange Order, a Protestant fraternal organisation.

As a loyalist organisation, the OV support the current political status of Northern Ireland. They support Northern Ireland's inclusion as part of the United Kingdom of Great Britain and reject any efforts to unite Northern Ireland with the Republic of Ireland. In the 1970s, the OV was the second largest loyalist organisation after the Ulster Defence Association (UDA). However, the OV was widely believed to have disbanded by the 1980s.

In July 1998, the OV re-emerged, issuing claims of responsibility for violent attacks in Northern Ireland. It is believed that the group was resurrected for the express purpose of destabilising the peace process and a political settlement with Irish republicans. The group is thought to be composed of disgruntled members of the UDA and Loyalist Volunteer Force (LVF) who opposed their groups' ceasefires. It is possible that the name was resurrected without any actual connection to the Orange Volunteers iteration founded in the early 1970s. Due to its emergence around the same time as the Red Hand Defenders (RHD), security forces believe the two groups share the same members. There have also been several instances where the RHD and OV have claimed responsibility for the same attack.

In addition to maintaining Northern Ireland's ties to the United Kingdom, the OV believe it to be their self-appointed duty to protect Northern Ireland's Protestant population, as well as the Protestant faith as a whole. To this end, in November 1998, the Orange Volunteers declared their first objective was to kill the Republican terrorist members who would be released as part of the peace process. However, the majority of its attacks have been pipe bombings, arson attacks, and assaults targeting Catholic civilian interests such as churches, residences, and businesses. Due to its selection of "soft" targets, there have been accusations that the OV is merely a cover name utilised by the UDA or LVF, enabling members to continue conducting attacks while their organisation publicly abide by ceasefires.

A major police operation in October 1999 led to the arrest of several leading members of the OV and its remaining leadership declared a ceasefire in September 2000. Despite the declaration, violent activities continued and the organisation issued a "Back to War" Statement in February 2001.

Another ceasefire was declared on the 31st December 2001 in an effort to distance the organisation from the narcotics and extortion activities of loyalist groups such as the UDA. However, in March 2003, the OV staged a show of strength to threaten to end its ceasefire if an unsatisfactory peace deal was revealed. Members of the OV are still considered active, engaging in the intimidation and assault of Catholics in Northern Ireland.

Orly Organisation

Abbreviation: OV
Continent: Europe
Country: France
Background:
The Orly organisation was a branch of the Armenian Secret Army for the Liberation of Armenia (ASALA), formed to intimidate French authorities into releasing ASALA terrorists held in France. The group was named after

France's Orly Airport, where one such Armenian terrorist was arrested in 1981 for carrying a false passport. The organisation attacked eight times in November of that year, striking a train station (twice), a McDonalds, the Eiffel Tower, a group of tourists sightseeing on the Seine River, and three French targets in Beirut (ASALA's home base). Attacks ceased for the month of December, but started again in January 1982, when Paris endured bombings at a bank, a convention centre, and a cafe. This wave of attacks, however, was apparently motivated by something other than the Orly arrest; it was claimed as a protest against the trial in Marseille of four ASALA terrorists who had attacked a Turkish Consular office in Paris. Bombings resumed in the mid-summer as the Orly Organisation attempted to force the French to designate the four Armenians as political prisoners and grant them asylum. Two further bombing attempts were made in Paris, one unsuccessful and one successful (in August and October respectively), this time on behalf of an Iraqi Armenian who had been arrested in Los Angeles for plotting to blow up Air Canada facilities. Though the Orly Organisation conducted 13 attacks in its 11 months of existence, they were not terribly dangerous, having caused no deaths and fewer than twenty injuries.

The Orly Organisation has not been heard from since October, 1982, and a rebirth is highly unlikely. With the collapse of the Soviet Union, Armenia has become an independent, sovereign state, fulfilling the major objective of most of the terrorists. Former terrorists now find themselves in the government or the military (or perhaps fighting the Azerbaijanis in the contested province of Nagorno-Kabakh), rather than conducting a campaign of international violence from the shadows.

See the Armenian Secret Army for the Liberation of Armenia (ASALA)

Palestine Islamic Jihad

Abbreviation: PIJ
Continent: Middle East
Country: Israel, Lebanon, Syria, West Bank/Gaza
Background:

The Palestinian Islamic Jihad (PIJ) is a violent offshoot of the Muslim Brotherhood, a Sunni, and Islamist, religious movement that originated in Egypt and seeks broad social, moral, and political reforms based upon Islam. The PIJ is one faction within a loosely organised, highly secretive group of Islamic Jihad movements that span the Middle East.

The PIJ was founded in the late 1970s by a group of radical Palestinian activists living in Egypt. This group of activists, led by Fathi Shaqaqi and Sheikh Abd al-Aziz Awda, believed that the Muslim Brotherhood movement had become too moderate and had abandoned the Palestinian cause. Inspired by the Shi'ia Islamic revolution in Iran; the PIJ blended Palestinian nationalism, Sunni Islamic fundamentalism, and Shi'ia revolutionary thought into its ideological agenda. PIJ believes that the annihilation of Israel and liberation of all of Palestine are prerequisites for recreating a pan-Islamic empire. PIJ stresses that the Arab-Israeli conflict is not a national dispute over territory but rather a fundamentally religious conflict. The group rejects any political arrangements or diplomatic activity to solve the conflict. PIJ believes that jihadist violence will inspire Palestinians to action and lead to the eventual destruction of Israel.

The PIJ initially operated out of Egypt, but after the assassination of Egyptian President Anwar Sadat in 1981 by Egyptian radicals, the PIJ leadership was exiled to the Gaza Strip. In the early 1980s, PIJ carried out a series of spectacular attacks on Israeli soldiers in Gaza. During the first Palestinian Intifada that began in 1987, the PIJ leadership was exiled to Lebanon. This allowed many PIJ leaders to establish direct contact with Iranian officials for the first time through the Islamic Republic's embassies in Beirut and Damascus. PIJ operatives soon began training at Hezbollah camps in Lebanon, under the supervision of Iran's Islamic Revolutionary Guard Corps. PIJ operatives stationed in Lebanon also carried out some joint operations with Hezbollah against Israeli forces in south Lebanon during the 1990s.

In 1989, Shaqaqi established PIJ's headquarters in Damascus, where it has remained since. While Syrian officials have continually stressed the informational character of the Damascus PIJ office, the office has directed PIJ funding and coordinated terrorist operations in the West Bank and Gaza. In addition, it is widely believed that Syria allows Iranian weaponry to pass through its territory in route to Palestinian militant groups in the Palestinian territories, such as PIJ.

PIJ strongly opposed the 1993 Oslo Accords and attempted to derail the peace process by committing a number of terrorist attacks against Israel. Israel dealt PIJ a severe blow in 1995 with its assassination of Shaqaqi in Malta. However, with the beginning of the al-Aqsa Intifada in September 2000, PIJ sprang back to life. Since 2000, it has claimed responsibility for scores of terrorist attacks in Israel. In part, this has reflected the group's greater coordination with other Palestinian militant groups such as Hamas and the Palestinian security services. Another critical factor in PIJ's revival has been an increase in Iranian funding.

PIJ remains a relatively small organisation with a limited base of support. This limited support partly stems from PIJ's exclusive focus on terrorist attacks and unwillingness to offer impoverished Palestinians a network of social services like Hamas does. The PIJ's prominence also has fallen since 1995, when Shaqaqi was gunned down, purportedly by Israeli Mossad agents. Ramadan Shallah, who replaced Shaqaqi as PIJ's leader, lacks the charisma of Shaqaqi. The PIJ's worldwide activities have further been hampered by a series of arrests and indictments in the U.S. following the September 11, 2001 attacks. Also, the construction of security fences by Israel along both the West Bank and Gaza border has made it more difficult for PIJ to execute terrorist attacks in Israel proper. Still, PIJ remains dedicated to the violent destruction of Israel, shows no interest in joining the political process, and will likely continue its attempts to injure Israeli civilians and military personnel through acts of terrorism.

Also known as Harakat al-Jihad al-Islami Fi Filastin

Palestine Liberation Front

Abbreviation: PLF
Continent: Middle East
Country: Iraq, Lebanon, Libya, Tunisia
Background:

The Palestine Liberation Front (PLF) was first established in 1959 by Ahmad Jibril, but by 1968 had been absorbed into Jibril's Popular Front for the Liberation of Palestine – General Command (PFLP-GC), after his group split from the main PFLP faction. The PLF became a separate entity again, remaining focused on the destruction of Israel, in 1977, when

Muhammad Zaidan (Abu Abbas) broke from the PFLP-GC. The group split again in 1983 into pro-PLO and pro-Syrian factions, with the pro-Syrian bloc undergoing another split in 1984, which resulted in one faction moving to Libya. All factions retained the name Palestine Liberation Front and claimed to act for the group as a whole. The majority of the PLF's attacks against Israel were carried out from Southern Lebanon.

Abbas's Tunisia-based pro-PLO faction became the most well-known in 1985 with the hijacking of the Italian cruise ship Achille Lauro. During the hijacking, PLF terrorists murdered and dumped overboard the elderly Jewish American citizen Leon Klinghoffer. Four PLF members were imprisoned in Italy and Abbas, who was not aboard the ship, was sentenced to life imprisonment in absentia, although he was briefly held and then released by Italian authorities. Following the Achille Lauro affair, Abbas's PLF faction was expelled from Tunisia and took up residence in Iraq.

The PLF continued to carry out attacks against Israelis through the 80's and 90's, often employing unique techniques such as hand gliders, and even claimed a naval unit. Abbas and the PLF did, however, support the signing of the 1993 Oslo accords, and officially renounced terrorism against Israel. Abbas was permitted to move back to Gaza in 1996 under an Oslo-related Amnesty program. PLF involvement in terrorism was still suspected after 1993 due to the group's distribution of Iraqi funds to Palestinian suicide bombers.

Abbas, who had moved back to Baghdad in 2000, also denounced the 9-11 attacks on the US, claiming that the Palestinian struggle is separate from al-Qaeda's holy war. He was captured by US Special Forces in April, 2003, and died in US custody in March, 2004, from natural causes.

See the Popular Front for the Liberation of Palestine – General Command (PFLP-GC)

Palestine Liberation Organisation

Abbreviation: PLO
Continent: Middle East
Country: West Bank/Gaza
Background:

The Palestine Liberation Organisation (PLO) is a Palestinian umbrella organisation dedicated to creating an independent Palestinian nation-state. The PLO umbrella includes many of the key Palestinian political groups and terrorist organisations. According to one of its original leaders, circa 1964, the PLO's goal was to "drive the Jews into the sea." Thus, the group's original goals were to destroy the Israeli state. Since its founding, the PLO has significantly altered its rhetoric and goals. The current view of the PLO is that Israel has the right to exist if an independent Palestinian state is established on part of the "historic lands of Palestine." While the PLO is an umbrella organisation, it does not necessarily support the goals of all its constituent members, which include terrorist organisations devoted to Marxist goals, world-revolution objectives, and the destruction of Israel. However, the PLO is a nationalist organisation that has used terrorism in pursuit of its goals.

The PLO was originally formed by the Arab League in 1964. Consequently from 1964 to 1967, the PLO was largely under the control of the founding Arab states. Following the six-day war in 1967, the Arab states controlling the PLO lost much of their legitimacy. Yasir Arafat, of the terrorist organisation al-Fatah, took advantage of the resulting power vacuum and was elected chairman of the PLO in 1969. In addition to al-Fatah, several other guerrilla organisations also gained power within PLO at this time. The PLO umbrella contains several significant terrorist organisations, such as al-Fatah, Palestine Liberation Front (PLF), Popular Front for the Liberation of Palestine (PLFP), Hawari Group, and Force 17.

With the signing of the 1993 Oslo peace accords, Yasser Arafat publicly denounced terrorism. As chairman of the PLO, Arafat also oversaw the official annulment of several sections of the PLO charter which had called for the destruction of Israel. While the PLO ostensibly renounced terrorism some years earlier, it has, in the past, utilised terrorist attacks to further its goals. In addition, the PLO umbrella contains both political and guerrilla constituencies, some of which are actively engaged in terrorism.

See al-Fatah, Palestine Liberation Front (PLF), Popular Front for the Liberation of Palestine (PLFP), Hawari Group, Force 17

Palestinian National and Islamic Forces

Continent: Middle East
Country: Israel, West Bank/Gaza
Background:

The National and Islamic Forces group was formed shortly after the outbreak of the second intifada in 2000. It is a committee comprised of representatives from each of the most important Palestinian political factions, both mainstream and radical, including Hamas, the PFLP and the PLFP-GC. It was formed with the authorisation of former Palestinian leader Yasser Arafat and was led by Marwan Barghouti, who was incarcerated in 2002. The National and Islamic Forces coordinates the agenda of its members and helps plan and execute joint terror operations against Israel. While the group enjoyed significant influence during the second intifada, it has been less visible since the election of Mahmoud Abbas in 2005.

Although it has carried out no major attacks that are known it facilitates but does not conduct attacks. The group was authorized by Yasser Arafat; led during the second intifada by Marwan Barghouti. Whose ideology was Palestinian Nationalism by organising a unified effort among major Palestinian factions to oppose Israel and coordinate terror attacks.

Palestinian Popular Struggle Front

Abbreviation: PSF
Continent: Middle East
Country: Lebanon, Syria, West Bank/Gaza
Background:

The Palestinian Popular Struggle Front (PSF) is a relatively small member of the Palestinian terrorist scene. Originally founded as an ideological splinter group of al-Fatah, the PSF has re-joined and then split from al-Fatah and the PLO many times since its inception in 1967. The PSF's original leaders were Dr. Samir Ghosheh (Ghawshah) and Bahjat Abu Gharbiah, who founded the group in the West Bank before the 1967 war.

The PSF has held its headquarters in Jordan, Lebanon and Syria. Generally following the PLO, the group was centred in Jordan until the events of September 1970 and then in Lebanon until the Israeli invasion of 1982, after which the group relocated again to Damascus. The group's most prominent attack was the 1970 hijacking of an Olympic Airways jet to Cairo. With the Red Cross mediating, the group successfully negotiated for the release of a number of terrorists, including PSF member Mildos Dergarabedian, who carried out the group's earlier attack on Israeli Airline El Al's offices in Athens and Mansour Marad, who later became a member of the Jordanian parliament.

Although it has not initiated a significant terrorist attack since 1989, the PSF is reported to have moved its base of operations back to the Bekaa Valley of Lebanon. Its presence and support in the Occupied Territories, however, remains minimal. In 1999 Syrian leaders claimed to have told a number of Palestinian terrorist groups, including the PSF, to "get used to confining their role to a political one," although U.S. officials said that they had no independent confirmation of this claim.

In recent years the PSF has indeed appeared to have rejected violence in favour of political means. The group has taken part in Palestinian legislative elections (garnering little support) and appears to have given up terrorism tactics permane

Also known as Popular Struggle Front

Party for the Liberation of the Hutu People

Abbreviation: PALIPEHUTU

Continent: Africa

Country: Burundi

Background:

The Party for the Liberation of the Hutu People (also known as PALIPEHUTU, the acronym of its French name Parti pour la liberation du peuple hutu) is a rebel group in Burundi which fought in the Burundi Civil War for the Hutu ethnic group. The armed wing of PALIPEHUTU is the National Forces of Liberation (FNL or Forces nationales de liberation). The FNL is led by Agathon Rwasa and is estimated to have around 3,000 combatants.

PALIPEHUTU was founded in 1980 in refugee camps in Tanzania, where Hutus had fled following persecution by the Tutsi-led government. PALIPEHUTU advocated armed struggle and established its armed wing, the FNL, in 1985. The National Liberation Front (FROLINA) split from PALIPEHUTU in 1990, and the armed wing PALIPEHUTU-FNL, led by Cossan Kabura split from the political wing of PALIPEHUTU in 1991. The political wing of PALIPEHUTU was renamed the Party for the Liberation of People-Agakiza and is led by Etienne Karatasi. In 2002 PALIPEHUTU-FNL split into two factions, one led by Kabura and one by Agathon Rwasa.

Generally, PALIPEHUTU's support comes more from the central region of Muramvya and Lake Tanganyika, whereas the main Hutu political party CNDD derives its support from the southern Bururi region.

During the civil war, PALIPEHUTU-FNL was linked to the killing of Monsignor Michael Courtney, the Catholic Church's chief representative in Burundi, the Titanic Express massacre and the Gatumba massacre in which over 150 Banyamulenge Congolese refugees were killed.

PALIPEHUTU also fought in the Second Congo War alongside the Congolese army, the Army for the Liberation of Rwanda and the Mai-Mai against the Burundian army.

Following the Gatumba massacre, the Great Lakes Peace Initiative declared PALIPEHUTU-FNL to be a terrorist organisation, and the South African President, Thabo Mbeki called on the International Criminal Court to prosecute. PALIPEHUTU-FNL was the last Hutu rebel group to sign an agreement with the Burundi government, which it did in September 2006.

Patriotic Resistance Army

Continent: Central America
Country: Honduras
Background:

Little is known about the Patriotic Resistance Army. The group claimed responsibility for a small bombing at a shopping centre in the Honduran city of Tegucigalpa on the 15th March 1990. The blast injured three people, including one American.

When compared to other Central American countries, Honduras suffered fairly low levels of political violence and terrorism in the second half of the 20th century. Full-scale leftist insurgencies did not materialise in Honduras as they did in Guatemala and El Salvador, and, consequently, neither did the rightist paramilitary groups that combated them. The 1980s, however, saw an increase in political violence in the country, though not to the levels of its neighbours. A few leftist groups did emerge, such as the Morazanist Patriotic Front, but their attacks remained few in number and small in scope. Small but dangerous attacks like the 15th March bombing, which were frequent in other parts of the region, were less common in Honduras.

One of the policies that Honduran leftist groups specifically denounced was the presence of several thousand Nicaraguan Contras in the 1980s. The Contras, who were supported by the United States, were fighting the Nicaraguan Sandinista regime in a vicious civil war. Many Hondurans opposed hosting the Contras. Opposition was occasionally violent: several American targets were hit in the late 1980s, including offices of the Peace Corps and U.S. AID, a bus carrying American military personnel, and an American businessman. However, the conflict between the Contras and the Sandinistas ended in the electoral defeat of the Sandinistas in February 1990. Contra forces began to withdraw from Honduras and return to Nicaragua.

Given the political context, it is difficult to ascertain the key motivations of the Patriotic Resistance Army. While opposition to the Contras was the most common motivation for this type of incident in Honduras during that era, the bombing occurred after the crisis was effectively over. And, though an American woman was injured in the bombing, it is not known if she was specifically targeted, or if she was another unfortunate victim. The group's name and target do not indicate anything concrete about the group's aims. The Patriotic Resistance Army did not publicly articulate its goals, nor did it claim credit for any other attacks. It is not known what political affiliations they held.

Patriotic Union of Kurdistan

Abbreviation: PUK
Continent: Middle East
Country: Iraq
Background:

The Patriotic Union of Kurdistan (PUK) is a splinter group of the Kurdistan Democratic Party. Under the leadership of Jalal Talabani (also known as Mam Jalal, "Uncle Jalal"), the PUK was formed in June 1975. It remains unclear why Talabani left. The PUK is a coalition of five separate factions, the leading factions being the Komala ("group") and Shorish Geran ("revolution spreaders"). Like the majority of Kurdish groups, the PUK seeks the establishment of an independent Kurdish state. Kurds are indigenous to a geo-cultural region commonly referred to as Kurdistan that is composed of territory from Iran, Iraq, Syria, and Turkey. Estimated at about 30 million people, the Kurds comprise one of the largest stateless ethnic groups in the world.

Throughout its history, the PUK has engaged in several different forms of terrorist activities. The group often targets their Kurdish rivals in the Kurdish Democratic Party (KDP) and is also often the victim of KDP attacks. In 1998, however, the two groups signed a peace agreement and now share control of the Kurdistan Regional Government.

During the 1980s, the PUK was also involved in numerous kidnappings of foreign nationals. The kidnappings were part of a campaign by the PUK to curb foreign support for Saddam Hussein's government and his oppressive policies towards the Kurds. In these situations, hostages were later released unharmed. In addition, members of the PUK launched frequent, often devastating attacks against Iraqi forces during the Iran-Iraq War as a result of the group's alliance with Iran. However, Talabani and the PUK also entered into talks with the Iraqi government regarding an agreement during the war to help repel Iranian troops in return for autonomy. These talks eventually fell through and the PUK continued its attacks on Iraqi soldiers. Throughout the 1980s and 1990s, Syria was one of the principal supporters of the PUK, even hosting leader Jalal Talabani after he was exiled from Iraq for his cooperation with Iran.

During the Gulf War of 2003, forces from the PUK assisted the US-led coalition in its overthrow of Saddam Hussein and, together with the KDP, were the principal US allies fighting in the north. Recently PUK militiamen, allied with US coalition forces, have also been involved in the expulsion of Kurdish Islamist groups (such as Ansar al-Islam) from their territory in Sulaymaniyah. Kurdish Islamists oppose the PUK's secular policies and seek to establish an independent, Islamic state for Kurds.

In June 2005, Jalal Talabani, Secretary General of the PUK, was elected president of Iraq by the Iraqi Provisional Council and re-elected in April 2006 by the Iraqi National Assembly. In addition, as a result of the 1998 peace agreement, the PUK and KDP now share control of the Kurdish Regional Government, which administers the semi-autonomous region in Iraq established by the Kurds after the fall of Saddam Hussein in 2003. The semi-autonomous government includes an elected parliament, police force, schools, tax collectors, and an army. As an organisation, the PUK has evolved into a political party representing Kurds in the current Iraqi government. The group now maintains that it will peacefully work for an independent Kurdistan. However, as an independent Kurdistan has yet to be established, there still exists the possibility that members of the PUK will commit violent acts in the future.

People's Command

Continent: Central America
Country: Bolivia
Background:
The People's Command claimed responsibility for a minor attack on the U.S. Embassy in La Paz, Bolivia on the 27th March 1986. A small dynamite bomb was thrown at the embassy from a nearby building. The bomb caused minor damage but no injuries. A message identifying the People's Command (previously unknown) as the attacker threatened further incidents and cited U.S. policy towards Libya as the primary motivation for the attack. Tensions had been rising between the United States and Libya for some time. The U.S. ran a provocative naval drill off of the Libyan coast in March 1986. Shortly thereafter, terrorists connected to Libya bombed a Berlin discotheque popular with American soldiers. One U.S. serviceman was killed. The U.S. launched a retaliatory air strike against Libya on the 15th April.

The U.S.-Libya crisis inspired a similar bombing attack outside the U.S. Embassy in Mexico City in May 1986. The bomb, placed in a car parked outside the embassy, was defused following an anonymous tip. A previously unknown group called the Commando Internacionalista Simon Bolivar claimed credit for the attack. The group later claimed credit for an attack against a General Motors factory on the one-year anniversary of the Libya air strike.

It is highly unlikely that the Mexico City embassy car bomb and the dynamite attack in La Paz are connected. However, they are both indicative of the type of minor, non-lethal incident at a U.S. facility that occurs with some frequency in Latin America. Notes or phone calls claiming these attacks frequently identify a group name. However, these groups are usually never heard from again. More active Latin American terrorist groups occasionally claim attacks under front names, such as the Shining Path's assassination of a Peruvian military attaché in Bolivia under the name "Workers' Revolutionary Party" in December 1988. However, this is not likely the case in this instance. More likely, the dynamite toss was a one-time statement made by an individual or small group.

The People's Command has not claimed credit for any other terrorist attacks since May 1986. The embassy attack was most likely the work of an individual or small group wishing to make an anti-American statement, not a working terrorist organisation.

Peoples Liberation Forces (Columbia)

Abbreviation: FPL
Continent: South America
Country: Columbia
Background:

The People's Liberation Forces (FPL) was a small terrorist organisation that operated in Medellin, Colombia during the late 1990s. Due to the group's limited activity, little information is available for the People's Liberation Forces. The group was most likely a small urban faction of the larger Colombian terrorist organisation, the National Liberation Army (ELN). Due to the FPL's close association and joint operations with the socialist terrorist organisation ELN, the FPL is assumed to share ELN's socialist ideology. The People's Liberation Forces operated exclusively in the city of Medellin.

By 2000, Colombian authorities announced that they had eliminated all remnants of the People's Liberation Forces. However, the People's Liberation Forces was most likely either a faction of the ELN or simply a cover name used by the ELN. While the People's Liberation Forces is currently inactive, the ELN is actively engaged in terrorism.

Peoples Liberation Forces (El Salvador)

Abbreviation: FPL
Continent: Central America
Country: El Salvador
Background:

The People's Liberation Forces (FPL) was one of the first Salvadoran terrorist groups to emerge in the 1970s. Opposed to foreign investment, "Yankee imperialism," and the Salvadoran oligarchy, these terrorist organisations spurred the existing Communist Party of El Salvador (PCES) to form new terrorist insurgency groups. The Popular Forces of Liberation was actually formed by then-secretary general of the PCES, Salvador Cayetano Carpio. Cayetano hoped his new organisation would begin a "prolonged popular war" that would eventually lead to a communist El Salvador. The Marxist group would emerge as the largest of the Salvadoran terrorist groups of the 1970s.

The Popular Forces of Liberation included a radical militant faction and a more liberal group devoted to grassroots political work. The two elements of the group would cause internal divisions, especially as some members moved towards conciliatory government negotiations. FPL continued its terrorist actions throughout the 1970s. In 1980, the group joined Farabundo Marti National Liberation Front (FMLN), an umbrella terrorist organisation. Reflecting the strength of FPL, the existing FPL leadership would heavily influence the direction of the newly-formed insurgency group.

In April 1983, FPL members killed their own deputy leader because of her perceived openness to government negotiations. In an apparent reaction to the death of his deputy, FPL's leader Salvador Cayetano Carpio committed suicide less than a week later. The death of its top two leaders decreased FPL's influence within the larger umbrella group. The Farabundo Marti National Liberation Front continued its terrorist attacks throughout the 1980s but finally reached a peace settlement with the Salvadoran government on the 31st December 1991. The Marti National Liberation Front (FMLN) is no longer an active terrorist organisation. Today, FMLN is a legal political party in El Salvador.

Also known as Farabundo Marti Popular Liberation Forces, Popular Forces of Liberation, Popular Liberation Forces

People's Revolutionary Party

Abbreviation: PRP
Continent: Africa
Country: Democratic Republic of the Congo, Tanzania, Zaire (Belgium Congo)
Background:
The People's Revolutionary Party (PRP) was an anti-Mobutu movement based in the Democratic Republic of the Congo (known as Zaire from 1971 to 1996). Their stated mission was the "liberation of all people of the Congo from the government of President Mobutu," and they sought to pressure the U.S. and Tanzania to force regime change in the Congo. Following the chaos that characterised the first five years of Congolese independence, Mobutu Sese Seko seized power from the first Prime Minister of the Republic of the Congo, Patrice Lumumba, in a 1965 military coup backed by the Central Intelligence Agency (CIA).

PFP membership was comprised of a combination of Marxist extremists, pro-Lumumba rebels disgusted with the Mobutu regime, and former witchdoctors, sorcerers, and tribesmen left over from the anti-regime Simba Uprising of June 1964.

The PRP's only attack on record was a high-profile 1975 raid of British scientist Jane Goodall's Gombe Stream Research Centre in Tanzania, during which three Stanford University students and one Dutch research assistant were taken hostage. In return for the release of the hostages, PRP terrorists demanded $460,000, American-manufactured weapons, and the release of four of their leaders being held in a prison in Zaire. One hostage was released to carry the demands to Tanzanian and U.S. authorities, and later, the rest of the hostages were released in intervals, the last one in July 1975. Stanford claimed that it did not pay any ransom, but Newsweek reported that the university contributed $400,000 towards the release of the hostages when the Tanzanian government refused to negotiate with the PRP.

Following the massive surrender of hundreds of PFP rebels in 1986, the PFP has been quiet, only issuing one joint communiqué with two other outlawed movements denouncing Mobutu in 1988. The Democratic Republic of the Congo (or Congo-Kinshasa) has undergone major political change since. In 1997, Mobutu's regime fell to a rebellion led by Laurent Kabila, who was assassinated after only four years in power and succeeded by his son, Joseph Kabila. Hence, it is unlikely that the PFP, originally formed to oppose Mobutu specifically, still exists as a terrorist organisation.

Also known as Popular Revolutionary Party (PRP), Zaire's People's Revolutionary Party

Phineas Priests

Continent: North America
Country: United States of America
Background:
Phineas Priests are members of a terrorist organisation operating inside the United States. The group derives its name and convictions from the Biblical story of a priest named Phineas who, by slaying an Israelite and his 'heathen' wife, saved the people of Israel from a plague from God. Phineas Priests are described as Christian white supremacists who are strongly anti-Semitic, anti-racial mixing (as was the original Phineas), and anti-abortion. Members following its ideology desire a Christian-only, white-only state in North America.

Similar to other white supremacist organisations in the United States, the Priesthood operates in extreme secrecy and believes in 'leaderless resistance,' tactics that ensure members escape detection and the organisation is protected from infiltration. Although individual action is paramount, Priests desire to ignite a racial revolution, rather than merely gain members for the organisation. As a result of the secrecy employed, it is difficult to determine exactly when the group was formed or obtain an accurate accounting of its membership and supporters. In part, this is because, unlike other supremacist or extremist organisations in the United States, the Phineas Priests is not a membership organisation in the traditional sense: there are no meetings, rallies or newsletters. Rather, extremists become 'members' when they commit 'Phineas acts,' any violent activity against 'non-whites.'

The Priesthood is commonly referred to as a terrorist, paramilitary arm of Christian Identity, a radical, Eurocentric interpretation of Christianity that maintains white Europeans are the true Chosen people. The Phineas Priesthood cross and the inscription '25:6', the chapter and verse in the Book of Numbers telling the Phineas story, are Priesthood symbols often present at the meetings and rallies of Christian Identity, Aryan Nations, and other white-supremacist, extremist organisations.

As a group, the Phineas Priests has not conducted any major attacks. However, individuals professing to be Phineas Priesthood members have engaged in terrorist activities such as bombing, robbery, murder and arson. Convicted bank robbers and bombers, Charles Harrison Barbee, Verne Jay Merrell, Robert Sherman Berry, and Brian Edward Ratigan, are several self-professed members of the Phineas Priesthood. Operating as individuals or in small groups of two or three individuals, Priests carry out attacks targeting Jews, racially-mixed individuals, non-white ethnicities, abortion clinics and their personnel, banks, and the government, whom they view as being run by Jews and other 'undesirables.'

As the organisation has no formal infrastructure, Priests can attack indiscriminately without orders, another benefit of leaderless resistance. Attacks against various targets continue to be conducted; violence from both the organisation and its followers is expected to continue in the future.

Also known as Phineas Priesthood

Popular Front for the Liberation of Palestine

Abbreviation: PFLP
Continent: Middle East
Country: Palestine
Background:
The PFLP is a Marxist-Leninist, Palestinian secular nationalist movement. The PFLP was founded in 1967 by George Habash after the crushing defeat of the Arabs in the 1967 Arab-Israeli War. This defeat largely discredited

the pan-Arab movement and focused attention towards Palestinian nationalism. Inspired by revolutionary Marxist-Leninist ideology, Habash and the PFLP saw the Palestinian nationalist movement as part of a broader movement to transform the Arab world along Marxist-Leninist lines. The PFLP joined the PLO in 1968 and quickly became the organisation's second-largest faction (behind Arafat's Fatah faction). Though the PFLP is committed to destroying Israel, it also opposes conservative Arab regimes, seeking to replace them with Marxist-Leninist states.

Throughout the 1960s and 1970s, the PFLP conducted a series of high-profile terrorist attacks around the world, pioneering the use of airplane hijackings to bring attention to the Palestinian cause. In 1970, the group hijacked 4 commercial airliners, forcing them to land in Jordan, and eventually blowing them up after evacuating the hostages. This attack led to the "Black September" of 1970 in which King Hussein expelled all Palestinian organisations from Jordan. In 1976, despite a PLO agreement to end terrorism outside of Israel, PFLP operatives and German Baader-Meinhof terrorists hijacked an airliner that was famously rescued by Israeli commandos in Entebbe, Uganda. Faced with decreasing support from the Soviet Union in the late 1970s and early 1980s, the PFLP became an increasingly marginalised player in the Palestinian nationalist movement.

The PFLP vehemently opposes the peace process with Israel and continues to espouse the use of violence against Israeli targets. It believes that Fatah, the PLO, and the Palestinian Authority effectively sold out the Palestinian people by agreeing to negotiate with Israel. In 1999, the PFLP leadership reconciled with Arafat and his Fatah faction in an effort to increase the group's role and visibility in the Palestinian cause. In 2002, in an effort to crack down on militants, the Palestinian Authority arrested the PFLP's Secretary General, further straining the relationship between Arafat/Fatah and the PFLP.

The PFLP has continued to conduct limited operations against Israel, including the assassination of Israel's tourism minister in 2001. Despite these operations, the PFLP continues to be a marginal player in the Palestinian movement, losing ground to both Islamist (Hamas and Palestinian Islamic Jihad) and secular (Fatah) rivals.

Also known as al-Jabha ash-Sha'abiya li-Tahrir Falastin

Popular Liberation Army

Abbreviation: EPL
Continent: South America
Country: Columbia
Background:

The Popular Liberation Army grew out of the Colombian Communist movement of the 1960s. In 1967, the Marxist-Leninist Communist Party (ML-CP) broke off from the larger communist political party, the Colombian Communist Party. Dissatisfied with the political chaos of 1960's Colombia, the ML-CP augmented its political organisation with an armed wing in 1967. The new group soon embarked on terrorist activities under the name People's Liberation Army. Both the ML-CP and EPL advocated the Maoist ideology of sparking a national socialist revolution by beginning in the countryside. Efforts to indoctrinate the peasantry largely failed and the EPL never reached the size of larger Colombian terrorist insurgencies such as the FARC and ELN. In an effort to expand their support base, the EPL abandoned strict Maoism in 1980. The group continued, however, to work toward the goal of overthrowing the democratically elected Colombian government and replacing it with a communist state. Furthermore, the EPL continued to pursue these insurrectionist goals through terrorist activities.

The EPL was one of the principal groups that pushed for a peace accord with the Colombian government in the early 1980s. With the signing of the peace accord in 1984, the EPL attempted to join mainstream Colombian politics. Their efforts were blocked, however, by the newly formed right-wing paramilitary groups, such as the ACCU. In an effort to derail the efforts to grant the politicisation of the EPL, the right-wing paramilitary groups attacked political representatives of the EPL. The peace accord soon unravelled as other leftist groups, the paramilitaries, and the Colombian Army continued their attacks on one another.

Following the failure of the peace accord, the EPL attempted to rejoin the violent fray involving the guerrillas and Colombian security forces, but this attempt proved futile. The EPL essentially disbanded in 1991, when it signed a truce with the Colombian government, although a breakaway faction operating under the same name refused to accept the truce. This breakaway faction continues to operate today, despite the arrest of its co-founder and principal leader, Francisco Caraballo, in 1994.

Popular Movement for the Liberation of Angola

Abbreviation: MPLA
Continent: Africa
Country: Angola
Background:
The Popular Movement for the Liberation of Angola (MPLA) is the ruling political party in Angola. It was founded in 1956 by a student movement led by Agostino Neto. MPLA was one of three major independence movements to arise in response to Portuguese rule. Initially influenced

by Marxism, MPLA enlisted the aid of the Cuban government and used Cuban military assistance to take over the capital city of Luanda in 1975. In 1983 MPLA became the MPLA-PT (Popular Movement for the Liberation of Angola-Party of Labour).

In November 1975, Agostino Neto became the first president of Angola. Over the next fourteen years, MPLA fought a protracted civil war with the other two independence movements that vied for power during the days of Portuguese rule-the National Union for the Total Independence of Angola (UNITA) and the National Front for the Liberation of Angola (FNLA). 1989 peace talks helped bring about elections in 1992 which MPLA-PT won. Another period of fighting emerged which came to an end with the death of UNTIA's leader, Jonas Savimbi, in 2002.

MPLA has traditionally used conventional weapons and military means against its rivals UNITA and FNLA. On one occasion the group kidnapped two Americans, teacher Patricia Thornton and cattle rancher Jose Diaz. However, MPLA has not shown a pattern of terrorist action throughout its history.

MPLA-PT is currently focusing on winning upcoming national elections (as of 2005) and fending off political pressure from a gradually strengthening UNITA. There is no reason to believe it will engage in terrorist activity.

Also known as Popular Movement for the Liberation of Angola-Party of Labour

Popular Resistance Committees

Abbreviation: PRC
Continent: Middle East
Country: West Bank/Gaza
Background:

The Popular Resistance Committees (PRC) is a radical Palestinian terrorist organisation based in the Gaza Strip. The PRC was founded by Jamal Abu Samhadana (killed in an air strike in June 2006), a former member of al-Fatah and the Tanzim. Samhadana was a Rafah resident, but the bulk of the group's support appears to be in the Jabaliya refugee camp.

The membership of the PRC encompasses both the secular and fundamentalist Palestinian movements – terrorists from Hamas, the PFLP, al-Fatah and the Tanzim are all in the ranks of the group. Ex-members of the Palestinian Preventive Security apparatus, part of the security forces of the Palestinian Authority, are also reported to be active in the PRC. The group is also suspected of being under the influence of Hezbollah, but no definitive connections between the groups have been discovered yet. The group maintains its "armed wing" under a separate name, the Salah al-Din Battalions/Brigades, although the PRC as a whole does not have any focus beyond armed terrorism.

The PRC continue to be an active terrorist force in the Occupied Territories, where their main method of attack has been firing rockets from the Gaza Strip into towns in southern Israel and Jewish settlements inside Gaza.

The group has also been implicated in the 15th October 2003 attack that killed a number of U.S. diplomatic security personnel in the Gaza Strip. The attack, a roadside bomb that destroyed the van the men were travelling in, was claimed then later denied by the PRC. Israeli suspicions remain focused on Hamas, although PFLP involvement has also been suspected.

After the death of their leader Samhadana in June 2006, the PRC (with Hamas) launched a daring raid on an Israeli army post near the Gaza strip. The group killed two Israeli soldiers and managed to capture another soldier named Gilad Shalit.

In return for Shalit's freedom, the perpetrators have demanded that Israel free all Palestinian women and minors in Israeli jails. As yet, the Israelis have rejected any demands for a prisoner swap. Several days after the kidnapping of Shalit, the PRC announced that they had kidnapped a Jewish settler in the West Bank. The claim had not been confirmed.

At the present time it is unclear whether or not PRC or Hamas were the main group behind those high-profile kidnappings. PRC has said the raids were revenge for Samhadana's death, but Hamas has been mainly blamed by the Israelis. In any case, these events will no doubt provoke a strong response from the Israeli military, likely involving the targeting killings of PRC members.

See the Salah al-Din Battalions/Brigades

Popular Revolutionary Army

Abbreviation: EPR
Continent: Central America
Country: Mexico
Background:

The Popular Revolutionary Army (EPR – Ejercito Popular Revolucionario) was a Mexican guerrilla organisation supporting armed struggle against the country's government. The group first appeared with a series of coordinated attacks on policemen in six Mexican states in the summer of 1996. More than a dozen people were killed. Though EPR splintered in 2000, several successor organisations have continued to conduct sporadic, small-scale attacks in Mexico's south ever since.

Formed as a merger of 14 smaller groups, EPR's primary aim was to overthrow the government of Mexico. In its first public statement, which came on the 28th June 1996 at a memorial service for 17 citizens killed by police in Guerrero state, the group claimed that the Mexican government was "anti-popular" and "anti-democratic." They pledged armed struggle to establish a government representative of the people, denouncing Mexico's wealthy and the "foreign capital" interests dominating the country. The group published many of its statements through a political arm called the Partido Democratico Popular Revolucionario (PDPR), or the Democratic Popular Revolutionary Party in English.

The group's ideology is congruent with that of many popular movements and guerrilla groups in Latin America. EPR expressed some Marxist ideas, but its professed program is better understood in the context of Latin American populism. In both Central and South America, political leaders and armed, anti-government rebels have fought for the interests of rural villagers against perceived economic oppression by the wealthy classes and foreign businesses, who own most of the land and natural resources. Like these groups, the EPR preached that foreign corporations pillage Mexico at the expense of the country's "campesinos," or villagers. Group members were active mainly in the states of Guerrero, Oaxaca, and Chiapas and generally limited their targets to government forces or assets.

Internal squabbling eventually caused a splintering of the EPR in 2000. Former members created the Insurgent People's Revolutionary Army, Revolutionary Armed Forces of the People, and other small groups. Several other groups with similar agendas are still active in Mexico's southern regions, though their footprints are small.

Newly elected Mexican President Vicente Fox offered the EPR an amnesty in December 2000 as part of an effort to calm down the insurgency in southern Mexico. The group has continued to issue public statements, including condemnations of the 9/11 attacks and the U.S.-led war in Iraq, and there have been recent allegations that the group is remerging. Mexican police officials contend the group played a role in the 2006 mass protests in Oaxaca and a November 2006 bombing in Mexico City. Due to numerous claims of responsibility for the bombing, it remains unclear which group was the actual culprit. Given the continued economic and political tensions in Mexico, it remains a possibility that the EPR could engage in future, small-scale attacks.

Also known as Ejercito Popular Revolucionario

Popular Self-Defence Forces

Abbreviation: FAP
Continent: Africa
Country: Democratic Republic of the Congo
Background:

The Forces Autodefense Populaires (FAP), or Mai-Mai, is not so much a single organised terrorist group as it is a confederation of militias operating in the Democratic Republic of Congo. Made up of Congolese natives favouring national unity and opposed to outside interference in Congo's brutal civil war, the Mai-Mai have fought Rwandan and Ugandan army elements, rebel groups, and multinational-corporations. The government and army of the DRC, led first by Laurent Kabila and subsequently by his son, Joseph, are suspected of directly supporting the Mai-Mai, in large part because central authorities were incapable of preventing foreign incursions. However, the Mai-Mai's guns had increasingly been turned on government forces in recent months. On a similar note, while the Mai-Mai often relies on popular support from the villages, they are also known to prey on those same villages when they need food, shelter, or money. Known previously for terrorist attacks on Congolese civilian targets, such as markets and public transportation, the FAP gained international notoriety after taking 26 hostages from a Thai-Ugandan logging company operating in the Northeast of the country. The hostages, who included one Kenyan, one Swede, and 24 Thai nationals, were abducted from their company's compound on the 15th May 2001. The FAP claimed that it was acting out of anger at the looting of Congolese resources by foreigners, and demanded that any negotiations for the hostages' release be observed by both UN representatives and officials from the embassy of either the US, France, Belgium, Sudan, Libya, Angola, or Zimbabwe. The group eventually released the hostages without receiving any significant concessions.

The fighting in the DRC continues and the Mai-Mai are as active as ever. However, much of the FAP's recent activities have been with the Congolese Armed Forces (FAC), rather than anti-government rebels. The Mai-Mai apparently feel that, while they have been risking their lives for the Kabila regime, the army had been looting their villages and abusing their families. The FAP now appears to have aspirations beyond simply protecting the country from foreign influence. Some Mai-Mai spokespeople have announced that the FAP would be capable of running a united DRC, or would defer to the international community if some sort of peace deal were brokered, but they are unwilling to playing a significant part in a coalition government. The group claims that it would be willing to turn in its weapons and negotiate directly with the Kabila government.

Also known as Mai-Mai, May-May, Mayi-Mayi

Portland Seven

Continent: North America
Country: United States of America
Background:

The Portland Seven was a group of American Muslims from the Portland, Oregon area arrested in October 2002 as part of an FBI operation attempting to close down a terrorist cell. The seven were attempting to join Al Qaeda forces in their fight against the United States military and coalition forces in Afghanistan, or aiding in that attempt.

Originally referred to as "The Portland Six", Patrice Lumumba Ford, Jeffrey Leon Battle, October Martinique Lewis (Battle's ex-wife), Muhammad Ibrahim Bilal, Ahmed Ibrahim Bilal, and Habis Abdulla al Saoub made up the original six members arrested in October 2002. In April 2003, Maher "Mike" Hawash was arrested, and the name became "The Portland Seven".

The members of the Portland Seven "were all named in the 15-count superseding indictment that included charges of conspiracy to levy war against the United States, conspiracy to provide material support and resources to al Qaeda, conspiracy to contribute services to al Qaeda and the Taliban, conspiracy to possess and discharge firearms in furtherance of crimes of violence, possessing firearms in furtherance of crimes of violence and money laundering."

Proletarian Action Group

Continent: South America
Country: Chile
Background:

Proletarian Action Group was a Chilean terrorist group which claimed responsibility for the bombing of the repair facilities of a French firm north of Cologne, Germany in May 1985. The bombing occurred while President Ronald Reagan was visiting Germany. Proletarian Action Group's attack is thought to have been in protest of Reagan's visit. Proletarian Action Group is also thought to be responsible for an October 1973 bombing attempt at the U.S. consulate general in Genoa, Italy. The attack was thought to be related to Chilean politics. Proletarian Action Group is no longer active.

Proletarian Combat Groups

Abbreviation: PCC
Continent: Europe
Country: Italy
Background:

The Proletarian Combatant Groups is an ally/suspected alias for the newly formed yet dangerous Proletarian Nuclei for Communism (NPC). This is the name used for the initial claim of responsibility for the August 2004 attempted bombing of Italian Prime Minister Silvio Berlusconi at his villa in Sardinia. With Italian authorities claiming that the NPC now has members of the Red Brigades (BR) acting as mentors, links between the various Marxist/anarchist Italian terrorist groups have become murky.

Due to the tracing of a cell phone call, Italian authorities originally believed they had a solid lead on the terrorists of the NPC/Proletarian Combatant Groups after the bombing of Berlusconi's villa. The perpetrators, however, still remain at large. Whatever the exact nature of the relations between the Proletarian Combatant Groups and the rest of the Marxist/anarchist Italian terrorist scene, these groups remain active and dangerous.

Q

Quintin Lame Command

Continent: South America
Country: Columbia
Background:

In 1984 was a new guerrilla group emerged in Colombia: the Movimiento Armado Quintín Lame (Quintin Lame Armed Movement), named after a NASA tribe leader (Manuel Quintín Lame Chantre), it was a guerrilla group, thus an illegal armed organisation. It entered peace talks with Colombia's government and laid down its weapons in May 1991.

Quranic Open University

Continent: North America
Country: United States of America
Background:

Though primarily based in Lahore, Pakistan, Jamaat ul-Fuqra has operational headquarters in the U.S. The group seeks to counter "excessive Western influence on Islam" through any means necessary, publicly embracing the ideology that violence is a significant part of its quest to purify Islam. The enemies of Islam, the group says, are all non-Muslims and any Muslim who does not follow the tenets of fundamentalist Islam as detailed in the Quran.

Jamaat ul-Fuqra openly recruits through various social service organisations in the U.S., including the prison system. Members live in compounds where they agree to abide by the laws of Jamaat ul-Fuqra, which are considered to be above local, state and federal authority. According to the report, there appear to be more than two dozen "Jamaats," or private communities, loosely connected and scattered throughout the U.S. with an estimated 5,000 members.

An investigation of the group by the Colorado Attorney General's office in the early 1980s found several of the communities operate covert paramilitary training compounds, including one in a mountainous area near Buena Vista, Colorado.

Muslims of the Americas Inc., a tax-exempt organisation formed in 1980 by Gilani, has been directly linked by court documents to Jamaat ul-Fuqra. The organisation operates communes of primarily black, American-born

Muslims throughout the U.S. The investigation confirmed members commonly use aliases and intentional spelling variations of their names and routinely deny the existence of Jamaat ul-Fuqra.

Members have been known to go to Pakistan for paramilitary training, but the investigation found evidence the U.S. encampments offer such training so members don't need to risk travelling abroad amid increased scrutiny following the 9-11 attacks. The report stated Jamaat ul-Fuqra members had "purchased isolated rural properties in North America to live as a community, practice their faith, and insulate themselves from Western culture. The group had established rural encampments that U.S. authorities allege are linked to murder, bombings and other felonies throughout North America."

U.S. authorities have probed the group for charges ranging from links to al-Qaida to laundering and funnelling money into Pakistan for terrorist activities. The organisation supports various terrorist groups operating in Pakistan and Kashmir, and Gilani himself is linked directly to Hamas and Hezbollah. Throughout the 1980s, JF was responsible for a number of terrorist acts across the United States, including numerous fire-bombings.

Gilani was at one time in Pakistani custody for the abduction of American journalist Daniel Pearl. Intelligence sources have determined Pearl was attempting to meet with Gilani in the days before he disappeared in Karachi. Intelligence sources also suggest a link between Jamaat ul Fuqra and Richard Reid, the infamous "shoe bomber" who attempted to ignite explosives aboard a Paris-to-Miami passenger flight on the 22nd December 2001.

See Jamaat ul-Fuqra

Rabha National Security Force

Abbreviation: RNSF
Continent: Asia
Country: India
Background:

Rabha National Security Force (RNSF) was formed by a group of youth belonging to the Rabha tribe to carve out a separate Rabha hasong (Rabhaland), comprising Goalpara, Bongaigaon and Dhubri districts, outside Assam through armed struggle. When the RNSF was still in a nascent stage it had established close ties with the most active militant groups of Assam, United Liberation Front of Asom (ULFA). Reports indicated that the RNSF was also trying to forge links with other insurgent groups operating in India's Northeast. The organisation had a cadre strength of about 120, of whom 40 are being imparted arms training by ULFA along the border of Meghalaya. The RNSF had recently launched an extortion drive in a number of districts in lower Assam. Reports suggested at the time that its leadership had made concerted efforts to procure modern weapons with the help of ULFA. Its activities were mainly confined to lower Assam. However, in the face of intensified counter-insurgency operations in Assam, the RNSF was trying to set up camps in the forest areas of Coach Behar district in neighbouring West Bengal.

Real Irish Republican Army

Abbreviation: RIRA
Continent: Europe
Country: United Kingdom and Ireland
Background:

The Real Irish Republican Army (RIRA) is a splinter group of the Irish Republican Army (IRA). While the IRA and its political wing, Sinn Fein, pursued negotiations for a cease-fire in Northern Ireland, an internal rift grew within the IRA itself. Members of the IRA who opposed the ceasefire negotiations broke off in early 1998 to form the RIRA.

The creation of the RIRA was instigated by the 1994 and 1997 ceasefires declared by the IRA, as well as Sinn Fein's agreement to the Mitchell Principles on democracy and nonviolence. Some hard-line members of the

IRA objected to the policy of cease-fires and negotiations. The final catalyst was the signing of the Good Friday Agreement reached in 1998. While much of the world heralded the Good Friday Agreement as an enormously positive step towards peace, some members of the IRA chose to continue their brutal terrorist attacks throughout Ireland and Northern Ireland. These members broke from the IRA and created the RIRA.

As a paramilitary organisation, the RIRA remains devoted to terrorist tactics to attain the goal of unifying Ireland's 32 counties under an independent Republic of Ireland. Currently, six counties in Northern Ireland remain part of the United Kingdom. The RIRA believes that armed struggle is the best method through which to rid Northern Ireland of any British troops. They have consistently attempted to derail peace prospects in Ireland through bombings, assassinations, and robberies. Traditional targets have been British military forces and Northern Ireland's police and Protestant communities. Members of the group have also conducted bombings in London against British government targets and the British Broadcasting Corporation (BBC).

On the 15th August 1998, the RIRA carried out the single largest terrorist attack in Northern Ireland's history. Using a car bomb, the RIRA killed 29 people in the town of Omagh. After the attack, the organisation claimed responsibility for the incident, and apologised, saying that it was not the group's intent to kill civilians and that prior warning had been given. The group also committed to a cease-fire, which was never implemented. Members of the Irish National Liberation Army (INLA), a related Irish republican terror group, were also suspected of providing supplies and transportation for the bombing.

On the 7th August 2003, the group's founder and leader, Michael McKevitt, was sentenced to a 20 year prison term on charges of directing terrorism. Since his detainment, McKevitt has called for the disbandment of the RIRA. However, despite his calls for disbandment and the imprisonment of approximately 40 other members of the RIRA, the attacks continue. Members of the RIRA remain committed to the unification of Ireland and the use of violence to attain this goal.

The RIRA was one of two republican groups to disavow the disarmament process initiated by the Irish Republican Army in the summer of 2005 (the Continuity IRA was the other) and continues to affirm its commitment to armed struggle. In June 2006, 10 members of the group were arrested for buying small arms and heavier weaponry (including SAM-7 rockets) as the result of a sting operation by British security services.

Some reports indicate that RIRA groups are splintering. Moreover, much of their current activity may have more to do with organised crime, particularly protection rackets, targeting pubs and other businesses, and smuggling rings, than political goals. At the least, the dissident republican community has remained small and fractious since the 2005 disarmament process began. Intelligence operations involving moles and informants, such as the June 2006 arms sting, may sow distrust in the community and serve to atomise it. However, a small number of republicans dedicated to armed struggle persist and the RIRA is expected to remain active.

Red Army Faction

Abbreviation: RAF
Continent: Europe
Country: Germany
Background:

The Red Army Faction is the name assigned to the terrorist successors of the Baader-Meinhof Group. In a confusing interplay of names, the Red Army Faction was the original name of the Baader-Meinhof Group. However, Baader-Meinhof Group became the organisation's assigned name for the period 1968-1977. The Baader-Meinhof Group essentially ceased to exist in 1977 with the multiple suicides of its original leaders. Following the deaths, the remaining followers of the Baader-Meinhof Group reverted to its original name, the Red Army Faction. The Red Army Faction would terrorise Germany from 1978 until 1992.

The Red Army Faction loosely followed a Communist ideology. The group targeted German business and political leaders, as well as U.S. military facilities. While the group's membership at any given time was estimated at only 10 to 20 people, the Red Army Faction carried out numerous deadly terrorist acts. The group was never successful in its goal of creating additional socialist states in Europe

By the early 1990s, the Red Army Faction had largely run out of steam. On the 10th April 1992, the group issued a communique that declared a conditional cease-fire. Six years later, on the 20th April 1998, the Red Army Faction officially announced the dissolution of their group.

Also known as Baader-Meinhof Gang, Baader-Meinhof Group

Red Brigades

Continent: Europe
Country: Italy
Background:

The Red Brigades were founded on rigidly Marxist-Leninist principles. This radical leftist group advocated violence in the pursuit of class warfare. Concentrated in Italy, the Red Brigades targeted businessmen and politicians and were a notable terrorist threat in Italy during the 1970s and early 1980s. Due to developments during its existence, the Red Brigades took on some qualities of anarchist groups while still propagating its especially virulent and violent Communist philosophy. In the end, the Red Brigades' increasingly brutal attacks eroded the support of those sympathetic with the group's Communist ideals.

In April 1984, four of the Red Brigades' key leaders wrote a communique from their jail cells. In the open letter, the leaders proclaimed further armed combat as futile. The Red Brigades essentially ceased to exist with this letter. In their words, "The international conditions that made this struggle possible no longer exist." (Xavier Raufer, "The Red Brigades: Farewell to Arms," Studies in Conflict and Terrorism, 1993, Vol.16)

However, the legacy of the Red Brigades continues to this day. Following the release of this letter, two splinter groups broke off from the Red Brigades: the New Red Brigades/Communist Combatant Party (BR/PCC) and the Red Brigades/Union of Combatant Communists (BR/UCC). The BR/PCC specifically has chosen to continue in the ideological and violent path of the Red Brigades.

Also known as Armed Communist Combatants, Italian Red Brigade, Red Regiments

Red Guerrillas

Continent: Asia
Country: Russia
Background:
Very little information is available concerning the Russian terrorist organisation, Red Guerrillas. In taking responsibility for their lone terrorist attack, a 2002 bombing of the offices of "Marching Together," a youth group supportive of Russian President Vladimir Putin; the Red Guerrillas espoused no ideology and identified no objectives to their activity. The silence of the Red Guerrillas, both before and after the 2002 bombing, leave people more or less in the dark about their motives and membership. From their name and their choice of targets, however, once might guess that the Red Guerrillas are pro-Communist militants opposed to Putin's rule.

Longing for a return to Communism is not uncommon in Russia, and Communist parties regularly perform well in local and national elections. However, the majority of citizens continue to support President Putin and his allies, especially given the improving economic picture throughout most of the country as well as the escalating incidences of Chechen terrorist attacks on Russian soil. It remains to be seen whether the Red Guerrillas will resurface in the near future, or if other Communist groups will be drawn to violence as a means of circumventing the democratic process which continues to keep their opponents in power. The first and last attack by the Red Guerrillas took place in September 2002. No further activity is predicted.

Red Hand Commandos

Abbreviation: RHC
Continent: Europe
Country: United Kingdom
Background:
The Red Hand Commandos are a Northern Ireland loyalist paramilitary group closely linked to the Ulster Volunteer Force.

The RHC were formed in 1972 in the Shankill area of West Belfast by John McKeague. Membership was strong in the Sandy Row and Shankill Road areas of Belfast, as well as East Belfast and parts of County Down. In 1972 the RHC agreed to become an integral part of the UVF. It retained its own structures but in 'operational' matters agreed to take their lead from the UVF and share arms and personnel. The group was declared illegal in 1973.

The RHC were part of the Combined Loyalist Military Command (CLMC). The Loyalist Retaliation and Defence Group (LRDG) were believed to be associated with the RHC. The UVF and Red Hand Commando supported the signing of the 1998 Good Friday Agreement and maintained a ceasefire from 1994 until the autumn of 2005. On the 3rd May 2007, along with the UVF, the Red Hand Commandos declared they were renouncing violence and ceased to exist as a paramilitary organisation. The organisation stated that they would retain their weapons but put them "beyond reach" and "under the control of the UVF leadership, but not accessible for use by members". The Independent International Commission on Decommissioning stated this was not acceptable.

According to the Sutton database of deaths at the University of Ulster's CAIN project, the RHC have killed 13 people, including 12 civilians and one of its own members.

See the Ulster Volunteer Force

Red Hand Defenders

Abbreviation: RHD
Continent: Europe
Country: United Kingdom
Background:
The Red Hand Defenders (RHD) is a little known loyalist terrorist

organisation in Northern Ireland that is believed to be a cover organisation for members of the Ulster Defence Association (UDA) and Loyalist Volunteer Force (LVF). The red hand of Ulster, a symbol commonly associated with Protestants, is utilised by unionists and loyalists to symbolise the six counties of Northern Ireland.

First emerging in 1998, the RHD is believed to be used by larger loyalist groups to enable members to continue to conduct attacks while their organisations observe ceasefires. The RHD emerged at the same time as the Orange Volunteers and is believed to share the same members. There have also been several instances where the two organisations claimed responsibility for the same attack.

Opposed to the Good Friday Agreement, the RHD seeks to derail the peace process by attacking Catholic civilians through the use of pipe bombings, arson attacks, and bomb hoaxes on 'soft' targets such as residences, businesses, and, notoriously, Catholic school staff and postal workers in Belfast.

As a cover name for larger loyalist groups, the Red Hand Defenders are expected to remain active in Northern Ireland, committing violent attacks on Catholic civilians, while the UDA and LVF publicly commit to ceasefires. Members of the RHD pose a particular danger to peace in Northern Ireland as their attacks could ignite sectarian tensions and damage the peace process.

See the Ulster Defence Association (UDA), Loyalist Volunteer Force

Republic of New Africa

Abbreviation: RNA
Continent: North America
Country: United States of America
Background:
Republic of New Africa (RNA) is a movement which began in 1968 as a result of a Detroit conference of militant African American nationalists. Two brothers, Milton and Richard Henry, founded the RNA and changed their names to Gaidi Obadele and Imari Abubakari Obadele respectively. Imari Obadele then became president of RNA.

RNA was the first group to seriously demand reparations for American slavery prior to the civil war. The group demanded control of Louisiana, Mississippi, Alabama, Georgia, and South Carolina. These states would constitute the Republic of New Africa, which would make cooperative economics and community self-sufficiency central to its economic model. RNA also demanded $400 billion dollars from the government as reparations. RNA's message particularly resonated with students at Tougaloo

College in Jackson, Mississippi. Tougaloo college papers were often used as a way of disseminating the RNA's statements.

RNA was involved in a small number of shootouts with police and FBI agents. Three people who hijacked a TWA flight in 1971 claimed to be members of RNA. The group's militancy led FBI officials to raid RNA bases. A 1971 raid in Jackson, Mississippi led to the death of one policeman and the arrest of Imari Obadele for murder of the police officer. Six other prominent RNA members were arrested. The group's militant activities decreased in the following years and Obadele focused on establishing a political movement after his release from prison in 1980.

RNA is now a non-militant organisation which views itself as a provisional government for the Republic of New Africa. Its leaders aim to hold a plebiscite for African-Americans to gauge support for self-determination. The group claims to have more than 10,000 members but, lacking any registry of RNA members, such claims are highly dubious.

RNA is currently a political organisation still attempting to achieve an independent nation in 5 American southern states. The group's radical militancy has abated and there is no indication that it will perform terrorist acts in the future.

Republic of Texas

Abbreviation: RoT
Continent: North America
Country: United States of America
Background:

The Republic of Texas (RoT) is a group of people who believe that the United States never legally annexed the state of Texas and that Texas is therefore an independent nation. In 1995, the RoT declared the state of Texas to be an independent Republic, and RoT "citizens" have been behaving as if that were the case ever since. RoT members believe that they are not legally bound to obey the federal government or the state government of Texas, and they resent both for taking away their freedoms. The RoT is part of the common law movement. (The common law movement declares that its members are exempt from the laws of the United States, and cite pseudo-legal theories that justify their illegal activities, which typically involve issuing phony legal documents such as liens and money orders.) RoT also teaches its members to practice redemption (a complicated set of bank fraud techniques, morally justified in the eyes of its practitioners by elaborate conspiracy theories) and paper terrorism (using fraudulent legal documents and filings to harass the government). They do not consider the money orders or comptroller's warrants they issue to be fraudulent, because they believe the United States government has no legal authority to print money, let alone the legal authority to forbid the Republic of Texas from printing its own money.

In 1996, the RoT split into three factions: one led by David Johnson (later replaced by Jesse Enloe), one led by Archie Lowe (later replaced by Daniel Miller) and one led by Rick McLaren. Two of the three factions have been involved in terrorist activity. In the spring of 1997, several RoT members led by McLaren stormed the house of Joe and Margaret Ann Rowe, who they held for 12 hours as "prisoners of war." McLaren demanded the release of two RoT members (Ann Turner and Robert Scheidt) in exchange for his hostages, but he eventually released them in exchange for Scheidt alone. McLaren's wife, Evelyn, convinced him to surrender peacefully after a week-long standoff with police. McLaren and five of his followers (Evelyn McLaren, Richard "White Eagle" Otto, Greg Paulson, Karen Paulson, and Richard Keyes) were sent to prison following the incident, which effectively destroyed the McLaren faction of the RoT.

The other terrorist act committed by the RoT involved members of three Jesse Enloe's faction, Jack Abbot Grebe Jr. and Johnie Wise. (Oliver Dan Emigh was tried as a co-conspirator, but acquitted.) Grebe and Wise were convicted in 1998 of threatening to assassinate several government officials, including President Clinton. Their plan was to build a cigarette lighter that would shoot cactus thorns dipped in biological agents such as anthrax, rabies, botulism, and AIDS. The conviction was largely based on evidence provided by undercover FBI informant John L. Cain. Cain, a computer consultant, was approached by Grebe and Wise, who wanted him to help them send threatening e-mail messages to government officials. Cain contacted the FBI, and collaborated with the agency by secretly taping meetings he had in his trailer with Grebe and Wise.

Many members of the Republic of Texas were upset by and openly critical of the criminal activities of McLaren, Grebe and Wise (although all three are listed as prisoners of war on the group's website). The group appears to have decreased in size and become more moderate since the late 90s. Chris Berlet, senior analyst at Political Research Associates, a Boston group that monitors the far right, says the group is no longer a threat to anyone. The RoT has demonstrated a willingness to support the government it despises, albeit in ways that government officials don't necessarily approve of. After September 11, its members drilled in preparation for assisting the government during a terrorist attack. The RoT has also been organising border patrols to collect and forcibly deport Mexican immigrants illegally crossing the border, despite the fact that the INS strongly discourages private citizens from patrolling the border. President Daniel Miller told the Boston Globe, "The American people are our brothers...We extend a helping hand." Despite its increased cooperation with the state and federal government, the RoT remains committed to its vision of Texas as an independent nation.

Revolutionary Army

Continent: Asia
Country: Japan
Background:

Kakumeigun, Japanese for "Revolutionary Army," is a terrorist organisation that has been active since 2000. Kakumeigun has strongly protested against the deployment of Japanese troops to Iraq. The groups also criticised any potential plans of Japan, South Korea, or the U.S. to attack North Korea. However one feels about this group's ideological beliefs, these anti-war terrorists went beyond legal protest when they bombed government facilities. The group claimed these violent actions were carried out to dissuade the Japanese government from pursuing military actions against Iraq or North Korea.

In addition to targeting government facilities, Kakumeigun also targeted an educational organisation. The group attacked the offices of the Japanese Society for History Textbook Reform, an organisation that has authored recent school textbooks. The textbook reform group was targeted because of their supposedly right-wing and excessively nationalistic descriptions of Japanese history. Specifically, the educational group was criticised for insensitivity towards neighbouring countries that Japan had previously invaded, such as South Korea and China.

U.S. intelligence reports from 2000 posited that Kakumeigun could potentially be a cover name for another terrorist organisation, Kakurokyo. However since 2000, continued terrorist actions have been claimed by Kakumeigun and definite evidence of its use as a cover name has not been proved. Kakumeigun continues to protest the deployment of Japanese troops to Iraq.

Also known as Kakumeigun

Revolutionary Armed Forces of Columbia

Abbreviation: FARC
Continent: South America
Country: Columbia
Background:

The Revolutionary Armed Forces of Colombia (FARC) grew out of the Colombian Communist Party of the 1960s. Unsurprisingly, the FARC was founded as a Communist organisation. The FARC leaned towards the Marxist strain of Communism and received a limited amount of funding from the Soviet Union during the Cold War. The FARC's stated goal is to overthrow the current democratic government of Colombia and replace it with a Communist government.

While the FARC is undoubtedly the largest and oldest of the Communist insurgent groups of Colombia, it is not necessarily the most dogmatic in its devotion to the Marxist ideology. In fact, the FARC's growing hand in cocaine trafficking, and even production, coupled with its on-again, off-again peace talks with the Colombian government, indicate that the ideological backbone of the FARC is at best, ill-defined. However, a significant portion of the FARC's leadership, including FARC chief Manuel Marulanda, have been part of the organisation since its founding and are presumably still dedicated to its Marxist ideology. The FARC continues to wage a war of words devoted to Marxist principles, despite the fact that many of its battles are fought with the less idealistic motive of controlling the illicit drug industry.

Today, the FARC's primary goal is territorial control within Colombia. The FARC has several sources for the money it needs to pursue this goal. The majority of its funding comes from the cocaine trade, but the FARC also pursues kidnapping, extortion, and hijacking. In addition to these operations, the FARC also attacks Colombian political and military installations. Its activities frequently disrupt economic activity in Colombia, particularly when conflicts with Colombia's rightist paramilitary groups break out. Ordinary Colombian citizens are often caught in the middle of this violent and bloody struggle.

The FARC's larger goals are a matter for speculation. For four decades the FARC has struggled to overthrow the Colombian government. This does not seem likely unless the FARC dramatically shifts its approach and increases its strength. The more likely outcome is that the FARC will continue to destabilise Colombian democracy but never actually overthrow the government. Furthermore, the FARC's recent participation in peace talks demonstrates a certain willingness to negotiate with its ideological enemies. The FARC's ideological commitment is in doubt, but its immediate goals are not. The FARC aims to maintain its significant financial and territorial power. From all indications, the FARC will continue its violent criminal action for the foreseeable future.

Also known as Fuerzas Armadas Revolucionarias de Colombia - Ejercito del Pueblo (FARC-EP)

Revolutionary Armed Forces of the People

Abbreviation: FARP
Continent: Central America
Country: Mexico
Background:

The Revolutionary Armed Forces of the People, known by its Spanish acronym FARP, emerged in February 2000 as a splinter group of the Popular Revolutionary Army (EPR). Citing political, ideological, and strategic differences, FARP is believed to have split from the EPR as early as June 1999. FARP follows its founding group's Marxist-oriented ideology, staunching opposing the neo-liberal economic policies of the Mexican government and globalisation and its link to the United States. Group members seek to establish a popular democratic republic complete with a new constitution and a more conservative economic system.

One of the group's most publicised attacks occurred when homemade incendiary devices exploded at three Banamex bank branches shortly after the bank was acquired by the U.S. company, Citigroup, in 2001. As the devices were engineered to garner media attention rather than inflict injury, only one minor injury was reported. FARP claimed responsibility by spray-painting its initials at two of the branches. The group has also launched attacks on the Mexican government and police forces and as part of the umbrella organisation, the Group of Guerrilla Combatants of Jose Maria Morelos y Pavon (CGNJMMP).

No recent attacks have been claimed by FARP. However, the group continues to issue communiqués and should be considered active and capable of future attacks given the continued economic and political tension in southern Mexico.

Revolutionary Army of the People

Abbreviation: ERP
Continent: Central America
Country: Dominican Republic
Background:

The Dominican Republic's Revolutionary Army of the People (Ejército Revolucionario del Pueblo -- ERP) was a short-lived group that only carried out two attacks in its history, both on the same day and both on American business targets. From its name, tactic and choice of targets, it can be assumed that this group's ideology was similar in nature to that of Latin America's other left-wing insurgent groups, who resented American "neocolonialism" and support for right-wing regimes.

At the time of the attacks the Dominican Republic was in the midst of an economic crisis and widespread opposition to long-time president Joaquín Balaguer. Elsewhere in Latin America in 1989, however, most violent insurgent conflicts were boiling down due to the end of the Cold War. It remains unknown if the ERP of the Dominican Republic was comprised of Dominicans or other Latin American revolutionaries spilling over from abroad as their insurgencies came to the end. Regardless, the Revolutionary Army of the People is now inactive.

Revolutionary Cells

Abbreviation: RZ
Continent: Europe
Country: Germany
Background:
Revolutionary Cells (German: Revolutionäre Zellen or RZ) was perhaps the most successful (based upon the number of attacks and the limited number of arrests) of the left-wing West Germany-based urban guerrilla organisations, although certainly not the most well known.

Different in group organisation from the much more well-known Red Army Faction, they were very loosely organised into tight-knit cells, making them much harder to capture. The group believed that their organisation members should be regular members of society, again in contrast to the Red Army Faction, who believed that revolutionaries should truly be underground, or outside the system. The group is assumed to have broken up and merged back into society after the collapse of the Soviet Union. Two of its members hijacked an airline with numerous Israelis and were killed in Operation Entebbe.

Revolutionary Cells

Continent: North America
Country: United States of America
Background:
The Revolutionary Cells-Animal Liberation Brigade is an unusually violent animal-rights terrorist movement. The group has claimed responsibility for two bombings in 2003. One bombing occurred in August 2003 on the grounds of Chiron, an Emeryville-based biotechnology firm. The other bombing occurred a month later when the Revolutionary Cells-Animal Liberation Brigade planted a nail bomb at the headquarters of the Shaklee Corporation, which manufactures health foods, vitamins and cosmetics.

Both groups were targeted for their association with Huntingdon Life Sciences, an animal-testing contractor.

The Revolutionary Cells-Animal Liberation Brigade is an unusual group because its tactics are more violent than those employed by other animal-rights extremists. In an e-mail message following the Shaklee bombing, the group specifically threatens certain individuals in particularly menacing ways. The group also claims that its attacks will grow larger and larger until either Huntingdon Life Sciences is shut down or American cities lie in rubble.

The Revolutionary Cells-Animal Liberation Brigade also claims to be a front for a diverse number of groups and claims to be an international coalition fighting injustice. The group's e-mail voices its solidarity with a disparate group of international terrorists. Yet despite such claims, Revolutionary Cells-Animal Liberation Brigade is undoubtedly a small terrorist group concerned with animal rights and with a penchant for hyperbole and casting about pretensions of power and importance.

Considering the group's failure to follow up a threat of an imminent increase in its activities following the Shaklee bombings, it is safe to say that the Revolutionary Cells Animal Liberation Brigade lacks the means to continue its terrorist activity. The prime suspect in the Emeryville bombings, Daniel Andreas San Diego, has been identified and is currently hiding from law enforcement officials. It is highly likely that this is a significant blow to the Revolutionary Cells Animal Liberation Brigade's ability to conduct further attacks.

Revolutionary Front for Proletarian

Abbreviation: FRAP
Continent: Europe
Country: Belgium
Background:

The Revolutionary Front for Proletarian Action (Front Révolutionnaire d'Action Prolétarienne – FRAP) was a Belgian terrorist group that operated briefly during the 1980s. Like most of Europe's left-wing terrorist groups of the mid to late 20th century, the FRAP targeted what they felt were symbols of "imperialism" – in this case, a NATO installation and a West German corporation.

Some sources maintain that the FRAP was a cover name used for an ally of Belgium's principal group operating at this time, the Communist Combatant Cells (Cellules Communistes Combattantes – CCC). These links were originally confirmed by Belgian police, but later allegedly denied. CCC members also refuse to be associated with the FRAP, and have claimed that the FRAP was a creation of the French group Action Directe. CCC and Action Directe were generally politically allies, but differed on the issue of forming a "West European Guerrilla Front," which the CCC opposed. Whether it was an alias for Action Directe or the CCC or truly an independent group, the FRAP is now inactive.

Revolutionary Force Seven

Continent: North America
Country: United States of America
Background:
Both the origin and political orientation of Revolutionary Force Seven remain unknown. The group was evidently formed solely for the purpose of carrying out four attacks, all on the 2nd June 1970, against various Latin American embassies in Washington, DC.

Historical context can shed some light on the group. The four nations whose embassies were attacked – Argentina, The Dominican Republic, Uruguay and Haiti – were all Cold War allies of the United States and all ruled by right-wing military dictatorships at points in their history. The exact philosophy of Revolutionary Force Seven is unknown, but two likely possibilities are that the group was comprised of Latin Americans opposed to their own governments and to the American presence there, or the group was comprised of United States citizens. Revolutionary Force Seven is presumed to be inactive.

Revolutionary Offensive Cells

Abbreviation: COR
Continent: Europe
Country: Italy
Background:
Revolutionary Offensive Cells (COR) is an Italian terrorist group based in Tuscany which focuses its attacks primarily on Pisa though it has struck in many different locations. Investigators believe that the group is comprised primarily of former members of the anarchic club "Il Silvestre" as well as Tuscan soccer hooligans. The group's symbol is a 5-pointed black-circled star.

The ideology of the Revolutionary Offensive Cells is an amalgamation of anarchism, Marxism, and environmentalism. Although the Italian press ordinarily refers to the group as anarchist, the language found in its communiqués is laced with Communist overtones as it disparages capitalist and bourgeoisie influences in the mainstream media and society. Revolutionary Offensive Cells aims to "act as a link between various fighting Communist revolutionary components, and insurrectional anarchist and anti-imperialist groups" across the world.

Revolutionary Offensive Cells is responsible for between twenty and thirty bombings in mid-2003. The group targeted Italy's major union headquarters as well as members of three major political parties: the National Alliance (AN), Forza Italia, and Italia dei Valorias. The group also attacked the barracks of the military group, Carabinieri, as well as newspapers and temporary job agencies. These attacks and a pattern of death threats upon journalists and politicians increased the emphasis placed by Italian police agencies upon finding the group. Although some of its key members have been arrested, in December 2004 COR announced its resolve to continue attacks in Italy.

Although the COR has been quiet since late 2003, the group is still active and it is impossible to rule out the possibility that COR will launch a string of attacks in the future. Italian police do not think they have crippled the group, and COR's relative inactivity is quite inexplicable. The ultra-violent language employed by COR and the wide range of targets it has chosen indicate that COR is not likely to lose its fervour for future action.

Revolutionary Organisation of Armed People

Abbreviation: ORPA
Continent: Central America
Country: Guatemala
Background:
Revolutionary Organisation of the People in Arms (Spanish: Organización Revolucionario del Pueblo en Armas) was one of the four groups of armed resistance during the Guatemalan Civil War.

In the 1970s, a new organisation installed itself in the mountains and the forests above the coffee estates. The Revolutionary Organisation of Armed People (ORPA) was started by local youth and university intellectuals. Of the various Guatemalan guerrilla groups, ORPA seemed the least violent, partly because it was led by the urbane Rodrigo Asturias, the son of Miguel Angel Asturias, Guatemala's Nobel Laureate in literature. ORPA was also a group to which, with a few horrifying exceptions, the army did not respond with its trademark village massacres. Why this was so is an interesting question. One possibility is ORPA's decision not to organise villages as publicly declared support bases. Another possible explanation is that planters needed their workers' labour too much for the army to slaughter them en masse.

See Guatemalan National Revolutionary Unity (URNG), Guerrilla Army of the Poor (EGP), Rebel Armed Forces (FAR), National Directing Nucleus of PGT (PGT-NDN)

Revolutionary Organisation of Socialist Muslims

Abbreviation: ROSM
Continent: Middle East
Country:
Background:

The Revolutionary Organisation of Socialist Muslims is one of many factions/suspected cover names of the Abu Nidal Organisation (ANO). Other allies/cover names of ANO include: Fatah Revolutionary Council, Arab Revolutionary Council, and Arab Revolutionary Brigades. The Revolutionary Organisation of Socialist Muslims was used to claim credit for attacks on British targets. Sabri l-Banna aka Abu Nidal, the leader of the Abu Nidal Organisation (ANO), died in Baghdad, Iraq in August of 2002. His death has been labelled a suicide by the Iraqi authorities; many sources believe he was assassinated by an Iraqi intelligence agent. The Revolutionary Organisation of Socialist Muslims has not attacked Western targets since the 1980s, and is now not considered a terrorist threat. Financial Sources are thought to be from Syria, Libya and Iraq.

See the 15 May Organisation, Abu Nidal Organisation, Arab Revolutionary Brigades (ARB), Black September Organisation (BSO).

Revolutionary Organisation 17 November

Abbreviation: RO-N-17
Continent: Europe
Country: Greece
Background:

17 November takes its name from the date of a 1973 student protest against the military dictatorship of Greece. 17N's campaign of bombing and assassinations did not, however, begin during the military dictatorship, but rather during the metapolitefsi, the founding of Greece's democratic Third Republic. 17N believes the democratic government of Greece to be nothing more than a placebo designed to pacify the Greek people and delay the inevitable communist revolution. 17N has declared itself to be Marxist-Leninist as well as anti-American, anti-Turkey, anti-NATO, anti-EU, anti-Greek establishment, anti-colonial, and anti-capitalist. They seek the expulsion of the Turkish military from Cyprus and the closure of American bases in Greece, as well as the withdrawal of Greece from NATO and the EU. They are fanatically nationalist, and they believe all of the groups they target to be responsible for the underdevelopment or exploitation of Greece.

A failed bombing attempt in June of 2002 led police to the first ever arrest of a 17N member, Savvas Xyros (Xiros). Documents in Xyros's apartment led police to the arrest of 18 other suspects. Greek police say all core members of 17N are now in custody. Xyros, however, has claimed that 10 members of 17N remain at large. An unknown individual or group claiming to be 17N has issued a communique insisting that the group is still active and threatening to take hostages with which to bargain for the release of its imprisoned members. Their trial began in March of 2003. Some suspects have confessed to participating in assassinations, others have confessed to limited participation, and many, including the group's alleged leader Alexandros Giotopoulos, have insisted that they are innocent of all charges. In December of 2003, all but 4 of the 19 defendants were convicted. Several, including Giotopoulos, were sentenced to life in prison. 17N has been inactive since the arrest of its only known members, but some believe that the new group Revolutionary Struggle is composed of unapprehended members of 17N.

Also known as the November 17. See the Revolutionary Struggle

Revolutionary Socialists

Continent: Europe
Country: Sweden
Background:

The Revolutionary Socialists has been linked to one incident since it was first heard from in 1999. The group first announced its presence when it distributed fliers in Malmo, Sweden. It was not until the next year that the group expressed itself violently, once again in the city of Malmo. Based on its choice of name, the group is assumed to follow a socialist ideology. However, due to its limited activity and the little available literature on the organisation; the group's ideological rigidity is not known.

From all appearances, the Revolutionary Socialists perpetrated its one and only attack to protest a specific political development. The attack occurred after the conservative political party, the Freedom Party, joined the Austrian government. The political gain of a conservative political party is viewed as the Revolutionary Socialists' justification to engage in terrorism.

Like many groups that have been implicated in a small number of attacks, it is possible that the Revolutionary Socialists never existed as an independent terrorist organisation. It is possible that the name, Revolutionary Socialists, was used as a cover name by a larger terrorist organisation. However, no linkages between the Revolutionary Socialists and any other terrorist entity have ever been made public. Since the group has not been heard from since 2000, it is presumed to be inactive.

Riyad us Saliheyn Martyrs Brigade

Continent: Asia
Country: Chechnya, Russia
Background:

The Riyad us-Saliheyn Martyrs Brigade is a relatively young terrorist organisation, dedicated to the creation of an independent Islamic republic in Chechnya (and other primarily Muslim parts of Russia such as Dagestan, Kabardino-Balkaria, Ingushetia, Ossetia and Tataria). The group, whose name translates to "requirements for getting into paradise," espouses radical Islamic doctrine (Wahabbism), and is believed to have strong ties to Al-Qaeda. However, most experts agree that the primary inspiration behind Riyad's activities is a desire for the independence of "Chechen lands," rather than religious zealotry. Before his death in July 2006, Riyad was led by the rebel commander, Shamil Basayev, who briefly served as President of Chechnya. Riyad is believed to be descended from two other Chechen terrorist organisations led by Basayev, the Special Purpose Islamic Regiment (SPIR) and the International Islamic Brigade (IIB). It has even been suggested that Riyad is simply the result of the marriage of these two groups

Riyad terrorists have intensified their attacks in recent years, claiming responsibility for some of the worst terrorist incidents in Russia's history. Their first attack, in December 2002, destroyed the headquarters of the pro-Russian Chechen government, killing 72 and injuring 280 people. According to Basayev, the perpetrators of the attack were an ordinary Chechen father and his two teenage children. In August 2003, a similar attack was made on Russian territory, but this time the target was a hospital housing both civilian and military patients. The attack resulted in the death of 52, while injuring 72.

The group has also used "Black Widow" suicide bombers to carry out attacks, such as the August 2004 airline and subway bombings. As long as the Russians press their claims in Chechnya and as long as Chechens are willing to give their life to resist control from Moscow, the Riyad us-Saliheyn Martyrs' brigade will most likely remain in business. While the death of Shamil Basayev in July 2006 is seen as a large setback for the brigades, the group remains an active security threat in the region.

Also known as Riyadh-as-Saliheen, Riyadus-Salikhin Reconnaissance and Sabotage Battalion of Chechen Martyrs. See the Special Purpose Islamic Regiment

S

Sa'ad bin Abi Wagas Brigades

Continent: Middle East
Country: Iraq
Background:

The Saad bin Abi Waqas Brigades is an offshoot of al-Qaeda affiliate Ansar al-Islam, a terrorist organisation dedicated to the establishment of an Islamic state in Iraq. The group takes its name from an uncle of the Prophet Mohammed, who was one of the earliest known converts to Islam.

The Brigades opposes the "American occupation" in Iraq and is known to attack Shia and American targets. It has demonstrated a range of tactics and methods in the short time it has been active. Its first operation took place in January 2005 and was an armed attack that killed Mahmud al-Madahaini (a prominent aide to Shia Grand Ayatollah Sayyid Ali Husaini al-Sistani), al-Madahaini's son, and several bodyguards. This was part of a wave of anti-Shia violence that occurred before the January 2005 legislative elections in Iraq, which various Sunni groups attempted to render illegitimate through a general boycott. In November of that year, the Saad bin Abi Waqas Brigades kidnapped six Iranian Shia pilgrims and their Iraqi guide near Balad. The purpose of the attack appears to be to terrorise Shias, as no motives or demands were given in the video claiming the attack.

The Saad bin Abi Waqas Brigades' last attack occurred in December 2005 and targeted an American base with a Katyusha rocket. Given the level of sectarian strife in Iraq, growing frustration with American and coalition post-war reconstruction efforts and general discontent of Shia Iraqis with the democratically-elected government of Iraq, the group is expected to remain active.

Also known as Sa'ad ibn Abi-Waqqas. See the Ansar Al-Sunnah

Sabaot Land Defence Force

Abbreviation: SLDF
Continent: Africa
Country: Kenya
Background:

The Sabaot Land Defence Force (SLDF) is a guerrilla militia operating in the Mount Elgon District of Kenya since 2005. It has been accused of killing more than 600 people, and of committing a variety of atrocities including murder, torture, rape, and the theft and destruction of property. More than 66,000 have been displaced in an 18 month period. The group draws its members from the Sabaot people, who are a sub-tribe of the Kalenjin, an ethnic group which forms only 11% of the Kenyan population, but a much larger percentage in the Rift Valley and Western Uganda. They were led by a former bodyguard to the President, who has now been killed by security forces. Wycliffe Matakwei Kirui Komon is the deputy commander; he commands an estimated force of 35,000 soldiers and scouts. Unusually for groups in the area, they wear jungle camouflage uniforms and have access to ammunition - although AK47s and other guns are easily accessible from bordering nations such as Somalia, costing around 500,000 UGX, ammunition is more difficult to acquire. The SLDF is funded by unofficial "taxation" of the local residents, and has implemented a parallel administration system.

Commentators have attributed the outbreaks of violence and rise of the militias to several factors: conflict over scarce land resources, widespread unemployment among young men, and a fast growing population (50% of the Kenyan population is aged below 16). In local tradition it has been considered good for a man to have as many children as possible, and international aid agencies which receive any portion of funding from the US federal government have been prohibited from providing advice on family planning. This has resulted in a fast growing population which is stressing agricultural resources. Tensions between different ethnic groups were also manifested in the 2007–2008 Kenyan crises.

The government initially treated the SLDF as common criminals, but has begun to treat them as an organised group. An amnesty offered 10,000 Ugandan shillings to fighters surrendering their weapons, but no weapons were surrendered. Security forces have found it difficult to gain information on the group, due to intimidation and the threat of violence towards the families of those who might come forward with information. A large scale military assault in March 2008 has resulted in allegations of serious human rights abuses by the Kenya Army, including murder, torture, rape, and arbitrary detention. Wycliffe Matwakei Komol, the leader of SLDF was killed by Kenyan army on the 16th May 2008.

Saif ul Muslimeen

Continent: Asia
Country: Afghanistan
Background:
Saif-ul-Muslimeen (Sword of Muslims) is a terrorist group that has operated

in eastern Afghanistan. Although officially held responsible only for the April 2003 rocket attack on a military airport in Jalalabad, the group has claimed a number of other attacks, including the bombing of UNICEF's Jalalabad office. As the group's attacks have focused on the new Afghan government and Western institutions, it is presumed that the group is oriented both religiously and politically, opposing the post-Taliban situation in Afghanistan in which a secular regime governs from Kabul with U.S. support.

Saif-ul-Muslimeen has not claimed an attack since 2003 although it is not assumed that they are no longer active. Many areas of Afghanistan remain restive and out of the control of either coalition or Afghan troops, with the Taliban and al-Qaeda remaining potent forces across the country.

Also known as Saif-ul-Muslimeen, Lashkar Jihad, Sword of Muslims

Salafia Jihadia

Continent: Africa
Country: Morocco
Background:

Established in the mid to late 1990s, Salafia Jihadia is an Islamist terrorist organisation based in Morocco. The group's goals are to overthrow "impious" Arab governments, pressure the West to stop support of "corrupt" Arab regimes, and achieve these objectives through violent jihad. Salafia Jihadia recruits mainly from Morocco's suburbs, rife with poverty and poor social conditions. This group is one of the largest terrorist groups in Morocco, and it is a close ally and offshoot of the Moroccan Islamic Combatant Group (GICM), which was one of the original fundamentalist terrorist groups in Morocco. Salfia Jihadia is compartmentalised, fairly decentralised, and "more of a doctrine than an organisation", lending credence to the belief that the organisation is actually a network of loosely-affiliated Moroccan fundamentalist groups which may include al Hijra Wattakfir, Attakfir Bidum Hijra, Assirat al Mustaqim, Ansar al Islam, and the Moroccan Afghans.

In a Senate Armed Services Committee hearing, former Director of Central Intelligence George Tenet commented that Salafia Jihadia is made up of many small, local, and autonomous cells. It is alleged that some of these cells receive operational help from the Salafist Group for Call and Combat (GSPC) and strategic guidance from al Qaeda in Iraq's leader Abu Musab al-Zarqawi. This suggests that Salafia Jihadia is responsible for operational planning and the delegation or execution of actual attack plans. Some also allege that to facilitate terrorist suspect processing and conviction, the name "Salafia Jihadia" was created by the Moroccan government as a catch-all categorisation for the many different Salafist groups that operate in Morocco. In fact, Salafia Jihadia is also the name of the larger Wahabi jihadist doctrine exported to the rest of the Arab world by Saudi Arabian radicals following the Gulf War of 1991. In contrast, most Moroccans follow the moderate Malekite version of Islam.

Members of Salafia Jihadia have been charged with arson, petty crime, kidnapping, drug dealing, and murder, though the group best known for planning and executing a massive coordinated suicide bombing in Casablanca on the 16th May 2003 that resulted in 45 casualties. The attack targeted a private Spanish club (Casa de España) near the Spanish consulate, the Israeli Alliance Club, a Jewish cemetery, the Belgian consulate, and a hotel popular with businesspeople. All 14 suicide bombers, including the two who backed out at the last minute, were from the same downtrodden suburb of Casablanca, Sidi Moumen. This attack led to a surge in general membership as well as an influx of "religious theorists" into the group, mostly from the Assirat al Mostaquim (Straight Path) religious association. In all, 31 Salafia Jihadia members were found to be responsible, 10 of which were given the death penalty (Yussef Fikri, Mohamed Damir, Saleh Zarli, Abderrazak Faouzi, Kamal Hanuichi, Bouchaib Guermach, Lakbir Kutubi, Buchaib Mghader, Omar Maaruf and Laarbi Daqiq). Salafia Jihadia's spiritual leader, Mohamed Fizazi, was given a sentence of 30 years in prison.

The investigations following the March 2004 Madrid bombings (claimed by the al Qaeda-affiliated Abu Hafs al-Masri Brigade) uncovered several pieces of evidence that suggest elements of Salafia Jihadia played at least a minor role in the attack. In fact, Spanish authorities working with their Moroccan counterparts questioned many Moroccans, including several members of Salafia Jihadia, regarding their involvement in the attack. One of the investigation's prime suspects is Jamal Zougam, a Moroccan who was spotted on one of the trains shortly before the bombs were detonated. A member of al-Qaeda's Spanish cell led by Abu Dahdah (indicted in Spain on charges of aiding preparations for the September 11th attacks), Zougam is alleged to have planned the Madrid attacks and planted at least one of the bombs himself.

Zougam had close ties with Salafia Jihadia elements and reportedly shared a safehouse with Salafia Jihadia terrorist Abdelaziz Beyaich, who took part in the Casablanca attack. A wiretap obtained by a French private investigator also revealed that Zougam participated in a meeting with Salafia Jihadia leader Mohamed Fizazi in 2001. Fizazi is known to have preached at a Hamburg Islamic centre frequented by 9/11 operational leader Mohammed Atta.

Though much of Salafia Jihadia's top leadership was captured soon after the Casablanca attacks, the group still poses a threat to regional stability due to its flattened organisational structure and substantial base of contacts with other fundamentalist groups in the region.

Sami al Ghul Brigades

Continent: Middle East
Country: Israel, Palestine
Background:

First mentioned in March 2006, the Sami al-Ghul Brigades is one of several active armed factions of the Palestinian nationalist organisation al-Fatah. Though al-Fatah has never publicly acknowledged any connection to these groups, it is believed that al-Fatah uses these splinter factions to simultaneously terrorise Israel while participating in legitimate politics under the premise that it does not use violent means to achieve its objectives.

Many Palestinian nationalist organisations employ the use of "armed wings" in an attempt to draw a distinction between their political cause and their terrorist tactics. The Sami al-Ghul Brigades is related to al-Fatah in much the same way as the al-Quds Brigades is related to Palestinian Islamic Jihad, the al-Aqsa Martyrs Brigades is related to al-Fatah, and the Salah al-Din Battalions is related to the Popular Resistance Committees. Though no evidence exists that decisively proves that the Sami al-Ghul Brigades is under the direct control of al-Fatah, it is assumed that the group shares al-Fatah's secular Palestinian nationalist ideology.

The Sami al-Ghul Brigades is known to conduct rocket attacks against Israeli targets, often in collaboration with other armed Palestinian factions, such as the al-Aqsa Martyrs Brigades or the Abu al-Rish Brigades.

With Israel's July 2006 incursion into the Gaza Strip, the political situation surrounding the Palestinian territories is all but certain. The Sami al-Ghul Brigades had conducted several attacks in the last several months and it is assumed that the group will continue to actively operate.

Sandinistas

Continent: Central America
Country: Nicaragua
Background:

The Sandinistas is an anomaly among terrorist organisations. The group began as a terrorist guerrilla organisation devoted to Marxist-Leninist beliefs. Partly because of its adherence to communist ideology, the Sandinistas received assistance from its Western Hemisphere neighbour, Cuba. In addition, Costa Rica and the terrorist organisation, the Popular Front for the

Liberation of Palestine (PFLP), were supportive of the Sandinistas. The Sandinistas existed from 1960 to 1979 as a state-sponsored terrorist organisation. During this time, the group carried out numerous terrorist activities against the ruling Somoza regime in Nicaragua.

The Sandinistas' primary goal was to overthrow the Somoza regime and replace it with a communist government. Taking advantage of public unrest and massive demonstrations against the dictatorial Somoza regime, the Sandinistas successfully ousted the Somoza regime in 1978-79. The Sandinistas ruled Nicaragua until democratic elections forced them out in 1990. During their rule, the Sandinistas re-shaped their terrorist cells into their own party-controlled standing army. As of 1979, the Sandinistas ceased to exist as a terrorist organisation. However, the Sandinistas remained a terrorist threat; only now they were the state sponsors of terrorism abroad.

In 1990, the Sandinistas lost the general election for the Nicaraguan presidency. The Sandinista regime was over but the group did not disappear. The Sandinistas retained control of their own army and maintain a substantial political presence even today. Terrorist activities have been perpetrated since 1990 by people wearing Sandinista uniforms. In addition, terrorist organisations have formed with pro-Sandinista views. The relationship between the Sandinista political party and these terrorists is not fully known. Nevertheless, government officials have accused the Sandinistas of using terrorists to influence election results.

Also known as Sandinista National Liberation Front

Sardinian Autonomy Movement

Abbreviation: MAS
Continent: Europe
Country: Italy
Background:
Little is known about the Sardinian Autonomy Movement (MAS) other than the name they chose for themselves and the circumstances of their only attack. The name, Sardinian Autonomy Movement, first appeared in the 1970s. However, because of the significant time gap, it is not suspected that any MAS associates from the 1970s were involved in the attack of 2002. It is more likely that the name was resurrected by a new set of terrorists. When the group re-emerged in July 2002, the Sardinian Autonomy Movement claimed that its terrorist bombing was in the name of an independent Sardinia. In the words of the terrorists, they fight for a "Sardinia for the Sardinians." The message was written both in Italian and the Sard language.

Since 1948, the island of Sardinia has maintained a special status within the Italian Republic. With this special status, Sardinia enjoys more autonomy than the mainland regions of Italy. While Sardinia is, in many ways, a positive example of an autonomous region within a republic, there has been some terrorist activity in the name of a fully independent Sardinia. However, the terrorist activity has been limited. In fact, the terrorist activity in Sardinia is more often connected to anarchist terrorists from the Italian mainland that uses the informal Sardinian economy as a way to launder money. It is suspected that this arrangement might have put Italian anarchist terrorists in contact with the smaller Sardinian separatist groups. The Sardinian Autonomy Movement has not been involved in an attack since July 2002 and is presumed inactive.

Scottish National Liberation Army

Abbreviation: SNLA
Continent: Europe
Country: United Kingdom
Background:

The Scottish National Liberation Army (SNLA) is a militant group, with aims to bring about Scottish independence. The SNLA has been a proscribed organisation by the government in the United Kingdom. In all likelihood, it is a catch-all term used by any group of disgruntled Scottish troublemakers.

The group has been reported to have been founded by Adam Busby, a former soldier from Paisley, Scotland, after the 1979 devolution referendum, which the organisation claimed was fixed. There have been claims that the SNLA are a false flag organisation, designed to blacken the name of Scottish independence.

In January 2008 two men, Wayne Cook and Steven Robinson were convicted in Manchester of sending miniature bottles of vodka contaminated with caustic soda and threatened to kill English people 'with no hesitation or compunction' by poisoning the country's water supply, echoing a previous threat in 2006. The accompanying letters were signed 'SNLA'. Cook Robinson was sentenced to 6 years for each of these offences.

The previously most high profile act occurred in 1983 when letter bombs were sent to Lady Diana Spencer and to the Prime Minister, Margaret Thatcher. The device sent to Thatcher was active and was opened by parliamentarian Robert Key: there was no explosion. Busby fled to Dublin in 1983 after the letter-bombing campaign; he was jailed in connection with that campaign in 1997.

In 1993, Andrew McIntosh was jailed for 12 years for conspiring to coerce the government into setting up a separate government in Scotland. The High Court in Aberdeen heard McIntosh had masterminded a campaign of disruption and fear which included placing hoax bombs outside oil industry offices and sending letter bombs to the Scottish Office in Edinburgh. McIntosh served six years and was released in 1999. He died in 2004 after being arrested on firearms charges.

In 2002 Cherie Blair became a target of a renewed campaign by the SNLA when she was sent an anonymous parcel containing a vial that was crudely labelled as containing 'Massage Oil', but which on investigation actually proved to contain caustic acid. In addition to this attempted attack a renewed letter bomb campaign was waged against Scottish politicians the same year. The parcels were recovered after a man claiming to be from the Scottish National Liberation Army made an anonymous phone call to Scotland Yard. Police have never confirmed that the parcels were associated with the SNLA and declared that they might have been the work of an individual. Professor Paul Wilkinson, opined at the time: "The SNLA has surfaced from time to time. It's obviously very tiny; in fact I understand the police are working on the theory it may have been just one individual behind this."

In September 2006, an e-mail from the SNLA was sent from a Canadian server to the offices of The Sunday Times in Glasgow which stated: "Our aim is to poison water supplies in England, not in the entire UK. We have the means to do this and we shall. This is a war and we intend to win it... This will permanently contaminate the drinking water supplies on which all urban society is totally dependent, killing and injuring thousands of people." The email is currently the subject of a Strathclyde Police investigation. Meanwhile, Busby may be targeted for extradition to America to face terror charges following a series of e-mails to America about how to contaminate US water supplies.

In February 2007, SNLA involvement was claimed in the fatal Grayrigg derailment of a Virgin train travelling from London to Glasgow. A point's failure was later found to be responsible.

The Scottish Separatist Group (SSG) has been described as the political wing of the SNLA. The SSG was formed in 1995 by former members and supporters of the SNLA. Both groups want to reverse English immigration into Scotland and restore Gaelic as the country's national language.

Secret Organisation of al Qaeda in Europe

Continent: Europe
Country: United Kingdom
Background:

The Secret Organisation of al-Qaeda in Europe claimed responsibility for the July 2005 London subway bombings, although it remains unclear whether they actually committed the attacks. Little is known about the group's size and structure, capabilities or leadership, which fosters the possibility that they may not be a legitimate organisation at all. However, the group may consist of al-Qaeda-inspired individuals who have no direct ties to the organisation, or a wing or an alias of a wing of al-Qaeda.

On the 7th July 2005, four suicide bombers coordinated an attack targeting the London public transport system. Bombs exploded on three subway trains and one double-decker bus, killing 53 people.

On the day of the attack, a claim was made on a well-known Islamist website forum, Al-Qal3ah or "the castle." The claim stated that the attack had been carried out in retaliation for the "massacres" committed by British forces in Iraq and Afghanistan and warned of attacks against other countries, specifically Denmark and Italy, who also had troops fighting in those regions. Due to an error in one of the quoted Koran verses and the fact that the claim has never been independently verified, it is widely believed to be a hoax.

Speculation as to the nature and legitimacy of the Secret Organisation of al-Qaeda in Europe continues. It remains unclear how the four London suicide bombers are connected to the group, if at all. Two of the bombers are known to have visited Pakistan and studied at Islamic learning centres. In a video released a year after the attack, al-Qaeda deputy Ayman al-Zawahiri claimed the two men had trained at al-Qaeda camps; however, their presence at the training camps has never been verified.

The Secret Organisation of al-Qaeda in Europe was not the only group to claim responsibility for the London bombings. On the 9th July 2005, the Abu Hafs al-Masri Brigade also issued a statement claiming responsibility. The al-Masri Brigade is closely linked to al-Qaeda, though it is not clear if it is simply the European division of al-Qaeda or an alias for another existing organisation. The Brigade has issued false claims of responsibility for previous events including the 2004 Madrid bombings and the summer 2003 blackouts in North America. On the 1st September 2005, al-Qaeda released a video showing the London bombing mastermind, Muhammad Sadiq Khan, and al-Zawahiri separately addressing the London attack. The video was edited to suggest a direct link between the two men, but there is no indication that they had ever met or communicated. Many took the video as proof that al-Qaeda was responsible for the attack while others saw it as merely an endorsement of the attack.

Based on the information available, it is unlikely that the Secret Organisation of al-Qaeda in Europe is responsible for the July 2005 London bombings. It is far more plausible that the London bombers, inspired by al-Qaeda and espousing a similar ideology, acted independently while others sought recognition for the attack. Even though no evidence lends credence to the legitimacy of the Secret Organisation of al-Qaeda in Europe, additional intelligence would aid in determining any future threat the group may pose to the region.

Secret Organisation Zero

Continent: North America
Country: United States of America
Background:

Secret Organisation Zero is the organisation involved in the assassinations of Jose Elias de Torriente, Ricardo Morales Navarrete, and Rolando Mansferrer. The group would place dark sheets of paper with their victim's initials and a symbol of a zero on the scene of the assassination. Secret Organisation Zero dedicated itself to the liberation of Cuba from Fidel Castro's rule and appeared to be focused on killing the leaders of rival anti-Castro groups. The group is highly secretive and its existence was fleeting as it is likely a temporary name employed by a faction of the Cuban mafia for the purposes of carrying out its assassinations.

However, what little evidence there is indicates that the man behind Secret Organisation Zero was Orlando Bosch, an infamous Cuban terrorist who fought to bring down Fidel Castro. Navarrete was an informant who testified against Bosch. Torriente was the head of a rival group, the National Front for the Liberation of Cuba (FLNC) and a letter released after his death accused him of being insufficiently dedicated to bringing down Fidel Castro. Mansferrer was similarly believed to be a detriment to the anti-Castro cause as he was at the head of "30th of November," an anti-Castro organisation that was quickly proving ineffective. All of these facts increase the plausibility of the claim that Bosch, a rabid anti-Castro militarist, was attempting to consolidate control over anti-Castro forces in Miami. The F.B.I., although it did not reach any conclusions, viewed Guillermo Novo as the prime suspect in the murder of Mansferrer. Novo was a close associate of Bosch. Secret Organisation Zero is no longer active.

Also known as Group Zero, Zero

Shariat Jamaat

Continent: Asia
Country: Dagestan
Background:

Shariat Jamaat, officially the Islamic Jamaat of Dagestan Shariat, is a militant Islamist organisation connected to numerous attacks against the local and federal security forces in Russian region of Dagestan in the North Caucasus. It's part of the Caucasian Front of the Second Chechen War. The Jamaat is thought to be responsible for the deaths of hundreds of policemen, military personnel and local officials.

Shariat Jamaat, closely associated with the separatist conflict in nearby Chechnya, was established by Rasul Makasharipov following the destruction of his Dzhennet group (Arabic: Paradise). After moving to Chechnya, Makasharipov went back to his home-land Dagestan and organised the Dzhennet group which, since 2002, had been killing policemen, judges and prosecutors in Dagestan, in favour of Chechnya's independence during the Second Chechen War. Makasharipov replaced Dzhennet group with the Shariat Jamaat, which in May 2005 became part of the Caucasian Front established by then president of the Chechen Republic of Ichkeria Abdul-Halim Sadulayev after the death of Aslan Maskhadov.

The leader of the Shariat Jamaat, Makasharipov, was killed during a shootout with Russian troops on the 6th July 2005. He was succeeded by Rappani Khalilov, who was killed on the 17th September 2007. With the statements of Dokka Umarov published by Kavkaz Centre on the 1st October 2007, Khalilov has been replaced by his deputy, Abdul Madzhid who is now leading the Shariat Jamaat.

The Shariat Jamaat is involved in hundreds of attacks against the local politicians, officers of the MVD (Russian Interior Ministry) and the FSB (Federal Security Service), prosecutors, and court officials in Dagestan. They were seen as responsible for the assassination of the deputy Interior Minister for Dagestan Magomed Omarov in February 2005.

Shining Path

Continent: South America
Country: Peru
Background:

In the 1960's, Sendero Luminoso grew out of the Communist movement in Peru. Sendero Luminoso's radical Marxist ideology was shaped by its founder and long-time leader, Abimael Guzmán Reynoso. Abimael Guzmán, a former university professor, was able to use his position within academia to gain credibility and entice students to his fledgling Communist movement. In fact, for a decade and a half, Sendero Luminoso primarily waged a war of militant Maoist ideas and propaganda. It was not until 1980 that Sendero Luminoso turned to violence. Once Shining Path turned to violence, the group unleashed a brutal terrorist campaign within Peru. The group has been implicated in countless deaths of Peruvian citizens.

Sendero Luminoso's stated goal is nothing short of an entire re-ordering of Peruvian society and institutions. Under Guzmán, Sendero Luminoso pushed for the destruction of all existing Peruvian institutions. SL will then, theoretically, replace the destroyed institutions with organisations based on communist ideals. At times, Sendero Luminoso imposed rigorous regulations on the rural populations it has sporadically controlled. This has included the prohibition of alcohol and capitalist ventures. In addition, Sendero Luminoso is opposed to influence by any foreign governments within Peru.

In 1992, Abimael Guzmán, Sendero Luminoso's founder and architect, was captured in Lima. Guzmán has been imprisoned since this time. Shortly after his arrest, Guzmán called for a ceasefire from jail. The combination of the Peruvian government's crack-down, Guzmán's arrest, and his subsequent calls for ceasefire caused Sendero Luminoso's to shrink drastically. SL membership has fallen from a one-time high of 10,000 to around 500.

Following Guzmán's arrest, one of SL's long-time commanders, Oscar Ramírez Durand, continued to espouse violence under the banner of Sendero Luminoso. Ramírez continued to lead this break-off faction of Sendero Luminoso until his capture in 1999. Despite Ramírez's arrest, his faction of Sendero Luminoso is still active, although it has scaled back its activities. While still pushing for an overall Peruvian government overthrow, Sendero Luminoso's efforts are largely directed towards controlling Peru's coca-producing rural regions.

Also known as Sendero Luminoso (SL)

Socialist National Front

Abbreviation: SNF
Continent: Europe
Country: Switzerland
Background:
Little is known about the Socialist-Nationalist Front (SNF) aside from their name and the circumstances surrounding their claim of responsibility for a November 1988 bombing in Switzerland. The bombing took place outside a building in Geneva which housed offices for Soviet airline Aeroflot, several banks (two Arab, one French), and a jewellery store. The bomb was reportedly hidden in a rubbish bin, and caused a great deal of damage, as well as five serious injuries.

Later that day, an anonymous caller claimed responsibility for the attack on behalf of the previously unknown Socialist-Nationalist Front, saying that the bomb had targeted "communist, capitalist and Jewish interests." Although Swiss officials publicly doubted the claim made by the organisation, no other group claimed responsibility, and the perpetrators of the attack were never caught.

Although the group's name and stated targets (communists and Jews) could imply that the SNF had ties to the neo-Nazi movement, there is no evidence to confirm this assumption. Furthermore, neo-Nazi and extreme right-wing organisations are generally not anti-capitalist, the other target mentioned in SNF's claim. In any case, the SNF did not claim responsibility for any other attacks, and was never heard from again. The Socialist-Nationalist Front is inactive.

Sons of Glendower

Continent: Europe
Country: United Kingdom
Background:

A clandestine group calling itself the Sons of Glendower stepped up a 9-year-old arson campaign against English-owned property in Wales, increasing fears that the attacks would begin to claim lives. The group chose violence to fight what many Welsh oppose was the increased immigration of the English into Wales. Celtic Wales had been united with Saxon England for 452 years, but nationalism remains a strong undercurrent in Wales, and the English influx was widely blamed for diluting the Welsh language and culture and inflating house prices beyond reach of the local people. Such themes are not confined to Wales. Regional nationalism flourished, often divisive force in this United Kingdom of England, Scotland, Wales and Northern Ireland, not to mention subdivisions like Cornwall and the Isle of Man, where outsiders' vacation homes are also a target of local nationalists.

But in this western, coastal region of Britain, the Welsh extremists had struck more frequently and had pushed across the border to burn down property in England. The arsonists, who had their supporters but were shunned by the nationalist mainstream, also had expanded their targets from mostly vacation homes to commercial property like real estate offices, and they had began using more sophisticated incendiary time-bombs. Nobody expected the attacks to escalate into a conflict like Northern Ireland's. But the time-bombs, which could go off at the wrong time or in the wrong hands, were causing serious concern.

Wales, brought under English rule by King Edward I in 1282 and united with England in 1536, has a long history of protest against its conquerors. In the 1960s, for example, a group called the Free Welsh Army waged a violent anti-English campaign. The Welsh Language Society for years has waged non-violent protest against English immigration, staging sit-ins in real estate offices and gluing their locks. Non-violent nationalists support measures such as limiting property sales to English newcomers and imposing higher taxes on second homes. The Sons of Glendower, or Meibion Glyndwyr, take their name from Owen Glendower, a 15th-century Welsh rebel leader. The group is believed to have been responsible for most of the 150 arson incidents, counted primarily in rural, picturesque north Wales since the first attack, on a cottage in Mynydd Nefyn on the 13th December 1979. The group, which initially broke into empty homes and built simple fires, had made erratic phone calls and delivered letters claiming responsibility. ``The target now the colonists and the capitalists," said a letter delivered to HTV, the Welsh television station, after recent attacks on a tackle shop and canoe gear store in Wales. ``They are the enemies of the people. Their free markets are killing Wales. We demand justice." The group is thought to be inactive.

Also known as Meibion Glyndwyr

Sons of the South

Continent: Middle East
Country: Lebanon
Background:

"Sons of the South" is the name of a pro-Israel Christian militia from southern Lebanon. The group adopted their name during the Lebanese civil war; "sons of the south" is a familiar and popular term for any inhabitant of southern Lebanon.

The group emerged in July 1984, when its members kidnapped Sheikh Mohammed Hassan Amin, a well-known Shiite religious figure in Southern Lebanon. According to news reports, Amin was kidnapped because he had been suspected of inciting attacks against Israeli soldiers. Amin was taken by the militia to an Israeli interrogation centre, where he was released and told to not return to southern Lebanon.

Since the Amin kidnapping, the Sons of the South have not been responsible for further terrorist incidents. Although the term "sons of the south" is often employed by Lebanese politicians and militias alike, the pro-Israeli group of that name has remained inactive.

South Londonderry Volunteers

Abbreviation: SLV
Continent: Europe
Country: United Kingdom
Background:

The South Londonderry Volunteers (SLV) is a little-known Loyalist terrorist organisation operating in Northern Ireland that is widely believed to be a cover name for a larger Loyalist group such as the Ulster Defence Association (UDA) or the Ulster Volunteer Force (UVF). Londonderry is the second largest city in Northern Ireland, located in the northwest with a slight Catholic majority according to a 2001 census.

As the group first emerged after the 1998 Good Friday Agreement, it is suspected that members of the UDA or UVF utilise the cover name in order to publicly appear to be abiding by its ceasefire declaration while continuing to engage in terrorist acts. As a Loyalist organisation, the SLV is engaged in an armed struggle to prevent the unification of Northern Ireland and the Republic of Ireland, ensuring it remains part of the United Kingdom, and to protect Protestants from armed Republican groups such as the Real Irish Republican Army (RIRA). To this end, the UDA and other Loyalist groups will often conduct retaliatory attacks against Catholics, including civilians.

The SLV was first mentioned in 2000 when it claimed responsibility for planting a small bomb hidden inside a cigarette package which was safely defused by police. In 2001, the group conducted several homemade pipe bombs attacks, mainly against targets associated with the Gaelic Athletic Association (GAA). In addition, the group has been known to issue threats against businesses associated with the GAA. All of its targets have been civilian, Catholic-affiliated ones.

No public claims of responsibility have been issued by the group since 2001. However, the group is likely to have remained active, engaging in petty crimes and the intimidation of Catholics. The group continues to pose a threat in Northern Ireland as its actions could exacerbate sectarian tensions in the area, leading to the end of declared ceasefires and the fragile peace process.

Also known as South Londonderry Protestant Volunteers

South Maluku Republic

Abbreviation: RMS
Continent: Asia, Europe
Country: Indonesia, Netherlands
Background:

The South Maluku Republic (Republik Maluku Selatan or RMS) is an Indonesian Christian separatist group that seeks independence for the Maluku (Molucca) Islands province in eastern Indonesia. Although Indonesia is around 90% Muslim, Christians make up about half the population in Maluku. The history of Christian-Muslim fighting in Maluku stretches back hundreds of years, and it is from this violence that the South Maluku Republic group has emerged.

Under Dutch colonial rule, the Christian population of Maluku was favoured, but the tide quickly turned after Indonesia gained independence following World War II. In 1950, Christian separatists attempted to establish the independent "South Maluku Republic," but the rebels were quickly crushed by Indonesian armed forces, and the separatist movement was banned. Tensions between Muslims and Christians in Maluku have been strained ever since. The Maluku Islands were a single province until 1999, when the province split into a majority Muslim "North Maluku" province, and a second province in South Maluku, now simply referred to as Maluku.

Since the late 1990s, violence and rioting has killed thousands of Christians and Muslims in Maluku, despite repeated attempts by the Indonesian government to broker an end to the conflict. Destroyed in the 1950s, the new RMS group re-emerged in 1998 in the wake of renewed sectarian violence. The RMS can best be described as a gang of Christian extremists who have adopted the name of a long-extinct independence movement to lend credibility to their organisation. Although the RMS is clearly fighting for an independent Christian Maluku state, it is difficult to distinguish between RMS actions and General Christian-Muslim violence. To that end, the RMS has been blamed for numerous small bombing attacks and other terrorist events in Maluku, but it is unclear whether these events were sanctioned by the RMS or simply an outgrowth of sectarian strife in Maluku. In a more significant event, the RMS is suspected of bombing the Maluku Governor's office in spring 2002, killing four people and wounding 63 others.

The Indonesian government has taken a hard line against separatist movements in Indonesia, and the RMS is certainly no exception. Officially banned by the government with many of their members exiled to the Netherlands, suspected RMS members face arrest for as little as demonstrating in public or raising the former flag of the short-lived "South Maluku Republic." Despite this crackdown, as long as violence between Muslims and Christians is prevalent in Maluku, the RMS will actively pursue an independent Maluku state through both violent and non-violent means.

South-West Peoples Organisation

Abbreviation: SWAPO
Continent: Africa
Country: Angola, Namibia, Namibia SWAF
Background:
Like the African National Congress (ANC) in South Africa and Zimbabwe

African Nationalist Union (ZANU) in Zimbabwe, the South West Africa People's Association (SWAPO) has undergone the transition from armed liberation movement to governing party. Namibia, formerly South West Africa, has a history of colonisation. It was a German colony until 1915 when it was transferred to South African control, first under a League of Nations and then a United Nations (UN) mandate. South Africa retained hold over Namibia after their mandate was withdrawn in 1966. The SWAPO, formed in 1960, launched its armed struggle in 1966 with the goal of liberating the nation from South African control.

Despite pledging to settle the "Namibian" problem in 1978, South Africa continued to administer the territory until 1989 and continued to clash with SWAPO forces, which operated mainly from bases within Angola. SWAPO participated in occasional terrorist attacks against citizens in addition to fighting the South African Defence Force (SADF) and its Namibian proxies. In 1989, South Africa agreed to allow Namibian independence in exchange for the withdrawal of Cuban troops from Angola. After a brief transition period, elections were held in 1989 and SWAPO won 57% of the vote.

SWAPO has been the ruling party in Windhoek since the 1989 elections; SWAPO is no longer operating as a terrorist organisation. In fact, democracy in Namibia is more multi-party in nature than in most southern African states, although SWAPO continue to dominate the political spectrum. Despite their historical espousal of socialist liberation philosophy, SWAPO-run Namibia is essentially a liberal capitalist society.

After a resounding victory in Namibia's 2005 presidential and parliamentary elections, SWAPO's winning candidate Hifikepunye Pohamba declared that "Our doors will remain open for foreign investors to invest in our country and assist our economy." Namibia's main opposition party criticised the elections as flawed, leading them to peacefully but, as of late April 2005, unsuccessfully challenge the results in court.

Southern Sudan Independence Movement

Abbreviation: SSIM
Continent: Africa
Country: Sudan
Background:
The Southern Sudan Independence Movement (SSIM) was a militant rebel army in southern Sudan opposed to the Khartoum government, which is perceived to favour the minority northern Arab Muslim population over the southern Sudanese animist/Christian people. SSIM fighters were mainly of Nuer descent and came from the oil-rich region of the Upper Nile.

This organisation focused on conducting combat operations against the Sudanese military, though at times it resorted to terrorist tactics against non-combatant targets, as seen in its 1995 kidnapping of 12 Medicins Sans Frontieres (MSF) workers.

Originally called the SPLM/A-United, the SSIM was created by Dr. Riak Machar in August 1991 when it split from John Garang's mainly ethnic-Dinka Sudan People's Liberation Army (SPLA) over philosophical differences. As their names would suggest, the SPLA envisioned a unified and democratic Sudan as their goal, whereas the SSIM faction was willing to secede from Sudan if the government would not meet their demands for equal treatment. Ironically, it was the SSIM that would merge with government forces in April 1996, when Khartoum and six rebel groups from the south, including the SSIM, signed a peace agreement. In April 1997, the agreement was formalised in the Sudan Peace Agreement, which created the United Democratic Salvation Front (UDSF), a political body that served to merge elements of the militant groups into the government and internal security forces of the state. The military wing of this body, used to patrol Southern Sudan on behalf of the government, was called the Southern Sudan Defence Forces (SSDF) and was led by Machar. In August 1997, the Khartoum government appointed Machar to the Presidency of the Coordinating Council of the Southern States and Assistant of the President of the Republic, a cabinet-level position.

The SSIM never recovered from Machar's decision to integrate into the government, and for all intents and purposes, became inactive after it merged into the SSDF, though some ex-SSIM fighters have since merged into both anti- and pro-government forces in Southern Sudan.

Also known as Movement of Riak Machar, Southern Sudan Independence Army, Southern Sudan Independence Movement/Army (SSIM/A), Sudan People's Liberation Army United (SPLA United)

Spanish Basque Battalions

Abbreviation: BVE
Continent: Europe
Country: France, Spain
Background:

The Spanish Basque Battalion (BVE) was a paramilitary organisation active from 1975 to 1981. Despite its misleading name, the Spanish Basque Battalion was primarily active in the Basque region of France, not Spain. The group's modus operandi were assassinations and attacks against suspected members of Basque separatist terrorist groups, specifically ETA. The BVE was one of a number of terrorist groups formed to counter the continuing terrorist actions of Basque separatists. The counterrevolutionary Spanish Basque Battalion instigated attacks in the Basque region of France with the intent to decrease ETA's ability to attack Spanish citizens and facilities.

Despite the ongoing terrorism in the Basque region today, the more potent counterrevolutionary paramilitary groups have been inactive since the late 1980s. The Spanish Basque Battalion has been inactive since 1981.

Spanish National Action

Continent: Europe
Country: France, Spain
Background:

Spanish National Action is responsible for two acts of terrorism, both directed against the terrorist group Basque Fatherland and Freedom (ETA). ETA caused a reign of terror throughout France and Spain and, in retaliation, a number of groups formed to retaliate. Their actions, however, often indiscriminately targeted civilians with no links to the ETA. Some of these groups, including Spanish National Action, were believed to have been funded and organised by the Spanish government and security forces. One of these groups, the Spanish Basque Battalion (BVE) is held responsible for one of the attacks also claimed by Spanish National Action. It remains unknown precisely whether there were two distinct groups or if Spanish National Action was an alias for the BVE. Spanish National Action is inactive.

Strugglers for the Unity and Freedom of Greater Syria

Continent: Middle East
Country: Lebanon
Background:

The Strugglers for the Unity and Freedom of Greater Syria first surfaced in June 2005 when they claimed responsibility for the assassination of Lebanese journalist Samir Kassir. In December 2005, the group also claimed responsibility for the assassination of prominent Lebanese journalist Gebran Tueni. Both Tueni and Kassir were well known for their anti-Syrian views and both had made public calls against continued Syrian presence in Lebanon. In a statement issued following the Tueni assassination, the group threatened future attacks against those who espoused similar anti-Syrian rhetoric.

Little is known about the group beyond its claims of responsibility for these attacks. Some allege this organisation is merely a front for Syrian Intelligence, although this claim is thus far unsubstantiated. However, it appears unlikely that an attack characterised by this degree of sophistication could have been carried out by a previously inactive group such as the Strugglers.

The attacks claimed by this group came amidst a backdrop of growing Syria-Lebanon tensions. Syrian authorities have exerted increased influence over Lebanese political affairs since first sending troops to the country during the Lebanese civil war in 1976. A 2004 United Nations Security Council resolution calling for Syria's withdrawal of troops fuelled the escalation of tensions and provided a motive for Syrian hostility towards outspoken Lebanese critics. In February 2005, Rafik Hariri, a former Lebanese Prime Minister and outspoken critic of the Syrian regime was assassinated and a United Nations report issued the day of the Tueni assassination implicated Syrian officials in the attack.

On the 27th December 2005, a Syrian national named Abdel-Qader Abdel-Qader was arrested and accused of having a role in the Tueni assassination plot. Abdel-Qader was allegedly in close proximity to the attack and made suspicious telephone calls before and after the attack on Tueni's motorcade. As yet, a formal link between Abdel-Qader and The Strugglers for the Unity and Freedom of Greater Syria has not been established.

Based on their statements and actions, the objective of the Strugglers for the Unity and Freedom of Greater Syria is to support Syrian influence in Lebanese affairs and silence critics of this policy. As long as tensions remain high between the two countries, this group, whether or not they were actually perpetrators of their claimed attacks can be considered a threat.

Sudan People's Liberation Army

Abbreviation: SPLA
Continent: Africa
Country: Sudan
Background:

The Sudan People's Liberation Army (SPLA) was formed in 1983 to oppose the implementation of shari'a law, or strict Islamic law, by Sudanese President Nimeiri. While the largely Muslim population of Sudan's Northern provinces generally welcomed the change, the Christians and Animists of southern Sudan were alarmed. According to the treaty that had ended the country's first civil war in 1972, the South was to maintain its autonomy from the North. Nimeiri's attempt to implement shari'a nationwide violated that agreement and created widespread resentment among the Southern population. Sent by the Army to quell a mutiny in the South, Lt. Colonel John Garang instead embraced the insurrection and became its leader, forming the SPLA. From an initial nucleus of 500 soldiers in 1983, Garang's rebel army grew rapidly, hitting an estimated 50,000 to 60,000 by 1991. The group's stated goal is the formation of a secular, democratic Sudan. In the mid-nineties, the SPLA became the vanguard element of a rebel umbrella organisation, the National Democratic Alliance, which even contained some moderate Muslim parties. The SPLA's success, however, cost the citizens of Sudan dearly. It is estimated that the civil war, which did not cease until 2002, took some 1.5 million lives.

Although the SPLA was primarily designed to perform military operations against the Sudanese Army, it also engaged in a few acts of terrorism against westerners and western interests in the country. In 1999, the SPLA took six Red Cross workers hostage, four of whom died in captivity. Although SPLA spokespeople claim that the deaths occurred during a botched rescue attempt, the Sudanese government claims that they were executed. Two years later, the SPLA claimed responsibility for one successful bombing and one unsuccessful bombing attempt against oil companies operating in Southern Sudan. The SPLA specifically targeted the oil industry to prevent oil proceeds from strengthening the government forces. In 2002 the Khartoum government and the rebels were able to hammer out a power-sharing agreement that has ended, or at least significantly lowered the ferocity of, Sudan's civil war. As part of the implementation of this agreement, John Garang was named Vice-President of Sudan in 2004.

As the SPLA has become a mainstream political force within Sudan, its interest in using terrorism as a means of achieving its goals has waned. On the 9th January 2005, the SPLA signed a peace agreement with the Khartoum regime, officially ending the Civil War that had ravaged Sudan since 1983. Under the terms of the agreement, southern Sudan will gain religious autonomy and a share of the nation's oil wealth. After the 6-year period of autonomy, residents of the South will vote on a referendum on whether to remain a part of Sudan or form an independent nation. Observers both inside and outside of Sudan hope that this peace agreement can also help resolve the violent humanitarian crisis going on in the Darfur region of western Sudan.

Also known as Sudan People's Liberation Movement

Supporters of Horst Ludwig Meyer

Continent: Europe
Country: Denmark
Background:

The Supporters of Horst Ludwig Meyer were formed to protest the shooting of Mr. Meyer, a notorious terrorist of the Red Army Faction. The communists of the Red Army Faction were active between 1978 and 1992, killing sixty three people in attacks on military and industrial facilities across Europe. Although the group ceased operating after 1992, authorities continued hunting RAF members. In September 1999, Meyer, and his terrorist girlfriend, Andrea Klump, were finally tracked down by Austrian police in Vienna. The exchange of fire that ensued left Klump in custody, a policeman injured, and Horst Ludwig Meyer dead. Red Army Faction sympathisers immediately began questioning the official version of events, claiming instead that Meyer had been shot by police in cold blood. The Supporters of Horst Ludwig Meyer went beyond verbal protestation, lobbing four Molotov cocktails at the Austrian embassy in Denmark. Fortunately for the embassy staff, three of the homemade devices failed to burst into flames. The fourth Molotov cocktail did explode, causing some damage to the embassy but no injuries. Although Horst Ludwig Meyer is still dead, his supporters have not engaged in any acts of protest since the first one in 1999. No further activity is expected.

Sword of Righteousness Brigades

Continent: Middle East
Country: Iraq
Background:
Swords of Righteousness Brigades is a previously unknown Iraqi insurgent group that made headlines for claiming responsibility for the November 2005 kidnapping of four Christian peace activists.

The four hostages worked for Christian Peacemaker Teams, an aid group that opposed the US invasion of Iraq. The men were identified as Tom Fox from the United States, Norman Kember from Great Britain, and James Loney and Harmeet Singh Sooden from Canada.

Over the course of several months the group released videos of the hostages and accused the four men of being spies. At various times the group demanded the release of all Iraqi prisoners from US custody and the removal of US and British troops from the country or else the hostages would be killed. Deadlines were set but were often extended or changed.

The kidnapping of these men provoked great outrage throughout the world, including amongst Muslims. Several prominent Muslim groups and clerics called for the release of the men, including Abu Qatada, an imprisoned cleric with alleged ties to al-Qaeda.

In March 2006, after numerous deadline extensions, the body of Tom Fox was found in Baghdad. He had been tortured and shot. Although this raised fears for the fate of the other hostages, some two weeks later the remaining abductees were freed in a joint military operation in a town near Baghdad. However, at the time of the operation, the Swords of Righteousness Brigades were apparently "nowhere to be seen," raising the possibility that ransom had been paid for the three men. Despite Canadian and British denials, Sooden remarked after his release that it was "highly likely" that ransom had been given to his captors.

Despite demanding the removal of troops and the freeing of all Iraqi prisoners from custody, the Swords of Righteousness Brigades did not espouse any specific ideology or aims.

Kidnapping of foreigners is common in post-war Iraq, although the motives behind such abductions vary greatly. Sometimes the perpetrators have concrete demands, such as the removal of troops or the freeing of prisoners from U.S. custody. In other cases the perpetrators simply want to kill their hostage to invoke fear and to deter further foreign involvement. Oftentimes the kidnapping is a simple criminal act in order to extract ransom money.

Although this particular group did make concrete demands, it is likely that money was the motivating factor. The complete removal of US troops is an unreasonable demand and was probably not expected to be met. However, no evidence exists that ransom was paid and the actual motives of the Swords of Righteousness Brigades remain unknown.

As the insurgency rages in Iraq, the kidnapping of foreign nationals continues at a steady clip. It is likely that the Swords of Righteousness Brigades remains an active organisation and that further kidnappings are possible, either for monetary or ideological reasons.

Also known as Swords of Truth Brigades

Syrian Mujahideen

Continent: Europe
Country: Belgium
Background:

Syrian Mujahideen was the name of a terrorist organisation that operated in Belgium in the 1980s. It is unclear whether or not the group actually existed. In its history, Syrian Mujahideen was only associated with one attack, the assassination of Antanios Hanna, the First Secretary of the Syrian Embassy in Brussels, on the 7th October 1987.

A group by the name of People's Mujahideen also claimed the attack. It is likely that People's Mujahideen were the actual perpetrators of the attack, given their failed attempt to assassinate another Syrian diplomat in December 1989. However, it is also possible that Syrian Mujahideen and People's Mujahideen were one in the same, as their claims of responsibility contained similar language alleging that Hanna was a Syrian intelligence officer. Given the group's name and information divulged in their claim of responsibility, it appears that Syrian Mujahideen opposed the secular Ba'ath government of Syria and its intelligence services, renowned for crushing government opposition brutally.

Syrian Mujahideen received no public mention before or after the only attack it claimed to have perpetrated. Given the lack of subsequent attacks and the ambiguity regarding its involvement in Hanna's assassination, it is unlikely that Syrian Mujahideen is still active.

Syrian Social Nationalist Party

Abbreviation: SSNP
Continent: Middle East
Country: Lebanon, Syria
Background:

The Syrian Social Nationalist Party (SSNP) was founded in the early 1930s by Antun Sa'adeh. Sa'adeh, a Greek Orthodox Syrian, founded the SSNP with the goal of creating a "Greater Syria" encompassing Syria, Lebanon, Jordan and Israel (then the British territory of Palestine). The SSNP's stated goals also included the separation of church and state, the distribution of wealth and labour and the establishment of a strong army for the "destiny of the nation and the homeland." Sa'adeh's adherence to the rule of law was suspect from the beginning, as he declared that he chose a "clandestine format for the party to shield it from the onslaught of the various factions in society."

The SSNP's extreme nationalist ideology was influenced by the growing fascist movement of the time. Between 1949 and 1961, the SSNP attempted two coups and successfully assassinated Syrian Prime Minister Riyad al-Sulh. As a result, almost 3,000 members were imprisoned. During their time in prison, many of the group's members were exposed to Marxist and pan-Arab ideologies, shifting the group's ideology to the left. Many members even joined the Lebanese National Movement and fought with the Palestine Liberation Organisation (PLO) during the Lebanese Civil War. The SSNP was also heavily involved in politics in Lebanon, where Syria has maintained troops since the Civil War.

The SSNP no longer operates as a terrorist organisation. The group has descended into infighting and is not a major player in either Lebanese or Syrian politics, although it remains an organised party. Its ideology of pan-Syrianism has also fallen out of favour and is not a serious political force in the Middle East.

Also known as al-Hizb a-Suri al-qawmi al-ijtima'ee

Takfir Wa Hijra

Continent: Africa, Europe, Middle East
Country: Algeria, Egypt, France, Germany, Italy, Lebanon, Morocco, Netherlands, Spain, United Kingdom
Background:

Takfir Wa Hjira, whose name means "rejection of sins and exodus" in English, is regarded as one of the most fundamentalist of the Islamist groups operating today. Claims differ as to the origin of the group. Some suggest that the group was founded in the early 1970s in Egypt under the leadership of Mustafa Shukri. In Egypt, the group targeted secular institutions such as cafes as well as government ministers, and set up a commune in the desert to separate themselves from Egyptian society. Others assert that Takfir Wa Hjira grew out of the al-Zawahiri faction of the early 1980s split in Egyptian Islamic Jihad (EIJ), a claim that fits with evidence that Takfir members were involved in the EIJ-linked 1981 assassination of Egyptian President Anwar al-Sadat. Official Dutch government reports claim that Takfir is now under the guidance of a UK-based Palestinian, "Caliph" Abdallah al-Rifai.

Takfir Wa Hijra is best analysed as a pan-Islamic religious sect or cult, whose membership allegedly includes al-Qaeda deputy Ayman al-Zawahiri and Iraqi terrorist leader Abu Musab al-Zarqawi, rather than an organised terrorist group. Its members, who reportedly can never leave the sect once joining, attempted to assassinate Osama bin Laden in 1995 in Sudan for his "liberal" views.

Takfir Wa Hjira, whose membership includes Egyptians, Syrians, Palestinians, Lebanese and other Arabs, operates throughout the Arab and Muslim world and also has cells in Europe. The group suffered a setback in 1999 and 2000 when Syria-backed Lebanese troops crushed one of its strongholds in northern Lebanon, capturing and killing a number of its members. Authorities in a number of Arab countries have arrested members of the group, however Takfir Wa Hjira remains active, and has recently been linked to the November 2004 murder of Dutch filmmaker Theo van Gogh. Moroccan sources have asserted that Takfir members in Morocco have formed an operational alliance with the Armed Islamic Group (GIA) in neighbouring Algeria.

Also known as Martyrs for Morocco, Rejection of sins and exodus

Taliban

Continent: Asia
Country: Afghanistan
Background:
The Taliban is an infamous organisation, having ruled Afghanistan under strict Islamic rule for five years, between 1996 and 2001. The Taliban is also notorious for harbouring the international terrorist Osama bin Laden during its rule of Afghanistan. Today, the Taliban has been ousted from power but has re-surfaced as a non-state terrorist entity within Afghanistan. The Taliban first emerged as a significant force in 1994. The group was principally comprised of Afghanistan's ethnic Pashtun tribesmen, who had found refuge in Pakistan. The refugees studied in Pakistan's madrassas (religious schools) and received assistance from Pakistan, specifically from the Inter-Services Intelligence (ISI). The Taliban's membership also included Mujahideen veterans who had fought the Soviet Union in the 1980s.

In 1994, per the request of the Pakistani government, the Taliban served as a security force for a Pakistani convoy, which aimed to open up trade between Pakistan and Central Asia. The convoy trip would prove to be the first step towards the Taliban's overthrow of the Afghan government. The Taliban's initial territorial possession was the city of Kandahar, which it wrested away from a Mujahideen group. The Taliban continued to expand its territorial control, sometimes through armed conflict but also through negotiations and payouts to regional warlords. In 1996, the Taliban took control of Kabul, Afghanistan's capital city, thus becoming the de facto government of Afghanistan. By the time the Taliban was ousted in late 2001, they would control 95 percent of the country.

The Taliban government immediately imposed a strict interpretation of Islamic law throughout Afghanistan. The group's goal was to establish the most pure Islamic state in the world. One by product of this was the restriction on women to either work or go to school. The Taliban also enforced amputations and public executions for violating Islamic law. The Taliban curtailed the flow of information by banning the Internet, television, and radio. The group forced Hindus and other religious minorities to wear symbols that identified them as non-Muslims and forced Hindus to wear veils as all Muslim women were required. There was, of course, a certain amount of resentment created by these restrictions, especially the Taliban's arrest of foreign aid workers who were assisting the poor Afghani population. However, the Taliban did enact certain reforms that garnered support among the people. First, the Taliban greatly reduced the rampant corruption that had taken hold within the government. Second, the Taliban stabilised Afghanistan, by reducing the internal fighting between warlords and diminishing the warlords' control of Afghan's civilian population.

The Taliban is perhaps most infamous for providing safe haven to the terrorist leader Osama bin Laden. Not only was bin Laden allowed to roam freely within the country, he also established training camps for legions of future terrorists. The decision to host bin Laden destroyed the Taliban's chance of attaining international credibility. Only three countries (Pakistan, Saudi Arabia and the United Arab Emirates (UAE)) recognised the Taliban government. The United Nations did not recognise the government, and in fact, applied multiple sanctions on the Taliban government.

Despite the pressure on the Taliban, they continued to rule the country under strict Islamic law and to allow bin Laden safe haven from 1996 to 2001. Following the September 11, 2001 attacks on the World Trade Centre and Pentagon, which were orchestrated by Osama bin Laden and al-Qaeda, the Taliban's support of bin Laden could no longer be tolerated. The Taliban was overthrown by an international coalition and by the 22nd December 2001, the Afghan Interim Authority (AIA) had replaced the Taliban government.

Following the Taliban's ouster in late 2001, the group re-emerged as a non-state terrorist entity. Since 2001, the Taliban has murdered NGO workers, Afghan civilians, government officials, and policemen, among others.

Tanzim

Continent: Middle East
Country: Israel, Gaza/West Bank
Background:

The origins of the Tanzim ("Organisation" in Arabic) lie in the leadership group of al-Fatah that remained in the Occupied Territories while the mainstream branch of al-Fatah, led by Yasser Arafat, was based in Jordan, Lebanon and finally Tunisia. After the 1993 Oslo Accords brought the al-Fatah and PLO leadership back to the Occupied Territories, tension rose. The Tanzim held political and military sway on the ground but were not included in the Palestinian Authority (PA) leadership, which was dominated by the mainstream faction of al-Fatah. Marwan Barghouti emerged as the leader of this group that soon found itself in opposition to the "Tunisians" who excluded them from positions of leadership. Barghouti originally acted as a reformer, crusading against corruption in the PA and advocating peaceful negotiations with Israel.

As he realised that the time and political climate were not ripe for reform in the territories, Barghouti and his group resorted to terrorism, with the

Tanzim rising to public prominence during the beginning of the al-Aqsa intifadah in September 2000. The exact nature of the relationships between the Tanzim, the al-Fatah leadership and the al-Aqsa Martyrs Brigades (another group linked to al-Fatah) remains unclear. Al-Fatah's leadership has publicly renounced terrorist activity and claims that the Tanzim and the al-Aqsa Martyrs Brigades operate independently. Many terrorist attacks within Israel and the Occupied Territories, however, were still reported as being the work of al-Fatah in general.

The February 2005 summit in Egypt between Ariel Sharon and Mahmoud Abbas, the first post-Arafat leader of the PLO, had brought hopes for peace to the region. At this time it appeared that all PLO factions, among them those linked to al-Fatah, were heeding the cease fire. It remains unknown if the Tanzim will be integrated into the newly strengthened PA Security Forces or if they will remain an opposition force.

Tawhid Islamic Brigades

Continent: Africa
Country: Egypt
Background:

The Tawhid Islamic Brigades have only been associated with one attack in their history. On the 7th October 2004, three nearly-simultaneous car bombings occurred in the Sinai Peninsula, killing 36 and injuring 171. Egyptian authorities stated that Egyptian-born Palestinians, Ayad Said Saleh and Suleiman Ahmed Saleh Flayfil were responsible for the suicide car bombing that killed 34 and injured 159 at a Hilton Hotel in Taba. The other two car bombs were detonated remotely in campgrounds in Ras al-Shitan by Hammad Gaman Gomah and Mohamed Ahmed Saleh Flayfil, the brother of Suleiman Ahmed Saleh Flayfil. Thus far, both of these men have managed to avoid capture. A spokesperson for the Egyptian government speculated that these attacks were carried out in response to an Israeli offensive in Gaza that killed 84 Palestinians.

Three terrorist organisations claimed responsibility for this attack, two of which were previously unknown (the Tawhid Islamic Brigades and Jammaa Islamiya) and one of which is a fairly well established group with known ties to al-Qaeda (the Battalions of the Martyr Abdullah Azzam, al-Qaeda in the Levant and Egypt). Though all three claims neglected to give details about how the attacks were carried out, a common feature of most legitimate claims, the Tawhid Islamic Brigades' claim is most interesting because it correctly identifies that four men were involved in the attack.

The Tawhid Islamic Brigades' claim was announced on a website normally used for claims originating from Saudi Arabia and Iraq, fuelling suspicion that the group has ties with Abu Musab al-Zarqawi's Tawhid and Jihad and its successor organisation, al-Qaeda Organisation in the Land of the Two Rivers, which seeks to create an Islamic state in Iraq. Zarqawi, like the men who were behind the Sinai attacks, is Palestinian.

Since the Sinai attacks, this organisation has neither claimed nor been implicated in any terrorist activity. It is likely that Tawhid Islamic Brigades is an alias for another group or the name of a small group with close ties to larger organisations.

Terra Lliure

Abbreviation: TL
Continent: Europe
Country: Spain
Background:

Terra Lliure (TL) was a terrorist organisation active in Spain from the 1970s until it publicly renounced terrorism in July 1991. Terra Lliure, which means Free Land, was a separatist organisation committed to the creation of an independent Catalonian state. This theoretical country of Catalonia would be based on Marxist theory and would encompass the Spanish provinces of Catalonia and Valencia.

Terra Lliure's terrorist activities were principally small-scale bombing attacks on property. TL frequently targeted foreign banks and corporations, but also attacked the diplomatic facilities of foreign countries such as the United States and Great Britain. During Spanish dictator General Franco's reign, Catalan culture and language were suppressed. Terra Lliure received some support from the Catalan people for its support of the Catalan culture. Even after General Franco's dictatorship ended in 1975, TL continued its terrorist attacks. The terrorist organisation never garnered broad support from the Catalan people and by July 1991, it was clear to even the militant members of Terra Lliure that their terrorist campaign would not be successful in creating a Catalonian state. The group's leaders published a statement that the group would cease its terrorist activities and would instead attempt to affect change through the political process. Terra Lliure is no longer an active terrorist organisation.

Also known as Free Land

The Extraditables

Continent: South America
Country: Columbia
Background:

The Extraditables were a group formed by drug traffickers of the Medellín Cartel in order to prevent their extradition to the United States. Colombia's Turbay administration had made an agreement with the United States government to extradite certain cartel leaders for trials in the US legal system. Certain members of both governments at the time preferred that leaders of the cocaine cartels be sent to the United States as opposed to the Colombian judicial system, which was rife with corruption.

Colombian policy was murky, and cartel leader's feared extradition even after the Colombian Supreme Court annulled the Colombia–United States extradition treaty in 1987. The Extraditables were formed in response to this ever-present threat, and focused their attacks on politicians and journalists suspected of supporting extradition. The most well-known figure involved with the group was Medellín Cartel leader Pablo Escobar. In addition to their higher-profile kidnappings, the Extraditables are thought to be responsible for dozens of further murders of government officials.

The Colombian government adopted a new constitution in July 1991 with specific prohibition on the extradition of Colombian citizens. Partially as a result of the probation, Pablo Escobar finally surrendered. He escaped from jail a year later and was shot by Colombian police in 1993. By the end of the early 1990s, the Medellín cartel had been effectively dismantled.

The Inevitables

Continent: South America
Country: Bolivia
Background:
A group calling itself "the Inevitables" detonated a bomb at the Bolivian offices of the Canadian Centre for International Studies and Cooperation (CCECI). CCECI is a firm that assists economic development throughout the world. The bomb was detonated at night and caused significant damage but no injuries. In a pamphlet, the Inevitables claimed to be fighting the forces of imperialism.

While lines such as "slayers, international players: Die before slaves live!" indicate that the group is radically leftist, there is reason to believe that the group was protesting America's Plan Bolivia, which aims at destroying coca fields through a combination of subsidised development of alternative crops as well as air sprayings of large coca fields. The attack occurred in Caranavi, a city which began cultivating coca in 1999, and the Inevitables warn that if groups such as CCECI insist on "destroying" Caranavi, they will be attacked. CCECI is involved in helping develop alternative crops to replace coca. This, combined with the insistence on driving American interests out of Bolivia and changing American policy, indicates that the Inevitables is driven more by economic considerations and reliance on coca production than by any particular ideology. The Inevitables has only been responsible for one attack and is not a serious threat in the future.

Tontons Macoutes

Continent: Central America
Country: Haiti
Background:
The Tontons Macoutes were a militia loyal to long-time Haitian dictator Francois 'Papa Doc' Duvalier, and later to his son, Jean Claude 'Baby Doc' Duvalier. The Tontons Macoutes, "boogeymen" in Haitian Creole, were created as a paramilitary force to be stronger than the Haitian Army, in order to guard the Duvalier regime against assassination attempts in the midst of Haiti's violent political climate. They eventually became a force for controlling public discontent and political adversaries of the Duvaliers, ensuring their continued reign in Haiti.

"Tonton Macoute" is a figure from Haitian folklore, usually represented as an old man who captures children and places them in a bag.

Political unrest has continued in Haiti well past the reign of the Duvaliers. Political-oriented armed gangs have become a major source of violence in the streets of Haiti, with frequent battles between supporters of ousted Haitian leader Jean-Bertrand Aristide and their opponents. Sources claim that anti-Aristide groups have in their ranks former members of the Tontons Macoutes, some of whom became integrated into the Haitian police and military services.

Also known as Boogeymen, National Security Volunteers

Tunisian Combat Group

Abbreviation: TCG
Continent: Asia
Country: Afghanistan
Background:
The Tunisian Combatant Group (TCG) is a terrorist entity dedicated to the creation of an Islamic state in Tunisia. The group is loosely organised and operates in small cells throughout Afghanistan and Western Europe. In addition to targeting Tunisian interests, TCG also attacks Western targets, including those of the United States.

TCG is nominally committed to a fairly specific objective, namely the creation of an Islamic state in Tunisia. However, TCG members have been linked to al-Qaeda and radical Islamist network in Western Europe that supports al-Qaeda and other terrorist operations. The Tunisian Combatant Group has assisted in recruiting, logistics, and the falsification of documents for the jihadist network in Europe. In addition to its ties to al-Qaeda, TCG members are also associated with the Salafist Group for Preaching and Combat (GSPC).

In December 2001, TCG's co-founder was arrested in Belgium for providing falsified documents to terrorists. In 2002, an Italian court sentenced several Tunisian Combatant Group members. These were the first convictions of al-Qaeda associates in Europe following the September 11, 2001 attacks.

Also known as Groupe Combattant Tunisien, Tunisian Combat Group, Tunisian Islamic Fighting Group

Tupac Amaru Revolutionary Movement

Abbreviation: MRTA
Continent: South America
Country: Peru
Background:
The Tupac Amaru Revolutionary Movement (MRTA) is based on Marxist-Leninist revolutionary theory. The group was founded with two primary goals. First, MRTA is dedicated to overthrowing the current Peruvian government and replacing it with a Marxist state. Second, the group aims to expel the U.S. commercial and diplomatic presence from Peru. The Tupac Amaru Revolutionary Movement takes great pride in the fact that it is an organisation of the people, and strives to connect with peasants, students, and members of trade unions.

The MRTA is the second-largest Marxist guerrilla movement in recent Peruvian history, following the Shining Path. While the Shining Path is characterised by an isolationist and elite terrorist leadership, MRTA has attempted to foster relationships with the Peruvian peasantry and other socialist groups. The MRTA's economic vision, enacted in a few small areas that were once controlled by the group, is that of a mixed economy based on communal planning.

The MRTA has not conducted a significant terrorist attack since the 1997 attack on the Japanese Embassy in Lima, Peru. Today, it appears that the MRTA is most concerned with achieving the release of imprisoned MRTA members, some of whom are being held in Bolivia.

Tupamaro Revolutionary Movement – January 23

Continent: South America
Country: Venezuela
Background:

The Tupamaro Revolutionary Movement is a terrorist organisation currently operating in Caracas, Venezuela. The group is based in a working-class Caracas neighbourhood, the 23 January District. The group first emerged in 1998 as a self-styled neighbourhood vigilante group. The Tupamaro Revolutionary Movement took it upon itself to exterminate alleged criminals in the 23 January neighbourhood.

Since its emergence, the Tupamaro Revolutionary Movement has demonstrated a penchant for extreme leftist beliefs, as well as support for current Venezuelan President Hugo Chavez. The terrorists have expressly criticised the Venezuelan Chambers of Commerce, owners of private schools, and "oligarchs." For their purposes, the Tupamaro Revolutionary Movement defines oligarchs as commercial bank officials, former Venezuelan foreign ministers, the Military Institutional Front, and the Construction Chamber. The terrorists have also criticised Venezuela's National Assembly. The Tupamaro Revolutionary Movement maintains public support for President Chavez.

In July 2003, representatives of the Tupamaro Revolutionary Movement claimed that they had ceased to cover their faces in public. The statement generally attempted to give credibility to the group. Moreover, by issuing this statement; the group distanced itself from reports of terrorism against oil companies. The group rejected reports that their members (wearing masks) were engaged in terrorist activities in Venezuela's oil fields. On the 10th October 2003, Tupamaro leader Jose Pinto expressed his solidarity of belief with the deceased leftist revolutionary Che Guevara.

Also known as Tupamaro Revolutionary Front, Tupamaros

Tupamaros

Abbreviation: MLN
Continent: South America
Country: Peru
Background:

Tupamaros, also known as the MLN (Movimiento de Liberación Nacional or National Liberation Movement), was an urban guerrilla organisation in Uruguay in the 1960s and 1970s. The MLN is inextricably linked to its most important leader, Raúl Sendic, and his brand of social politics.

The Tupamaro movement was named after the Inca revolutionary Túpac

Amaru II. Its origins lie in the union between the Movimiento de Apoyo al Campesino (Peasant Support Movement) and the members of trade unions funded by Sendic in poverty-stricken rural zones. It grew in proportion to the ascending powers of Uruguay's military, which culminated in a notoriously oppressive dictatorship between 1973 and 1984.

The movement began by staging the robbing of banks, gun clubs and other businesses in the early 1960s, then distributing stolen food and money among the poor in Montevideo. It took as slogan "Words divide us; action unite us".

At the beginning, it abstained from armed actions and violence; they have always made clear about not being a guerrilla group but a political movement; the eventual use of violent means would be made according to strategy and possibilities. In June 1968, President Jorge Pacheco, trying to suppress labour unrest, enforced a state of emergency and repealed all constitutional safeguards. The government imprisoned political dissidents, used torture during interrogations and brutally repressed demonstrations. The Tupamaro movement engaged then in political kidnappings, "armed propaganda" and assassinations. Of particular note are the kidnapping of powerful bank manager Pereyra Rebervel and of the British ambassador to Uruguay, as well as the assassination of Dan Mitrione, the FBI agent alleged to have taught techniques of torture to police forces in various Latin American countries. A very close friend to President Jorge Pacheco, the banker Pereyra Rebervel was highly unpopular, having "once killed a newsboy for selling a paper attacking him." He was released four days later, unharmed but a bit fatter. According to Langguth, the "poor in Montevideo were quoted as joking, 'Attention, Tupamaros! Kidnap me!'".

The peak of the Tupamaros was in 1970 and 1971. During this period they made liberal use of their Cárcel del Pueblo (or People's Prison) where they held those that they kidnapped and interrogated them, without using torture, before making the results of these interviews public. In 1971 over 100 imprisoned Tupamaros escaped the Punta Carretas prison. In the same year, in an uncleared episode, Pascasio Báez, a rural labourer that accidentally discovered one of their hideouts was killed.

Nonetheless, the movement was hampered by a series of events including important strategic gaffes and the betrayal of high-ranking Tupamaro Héctor Amodio Pérez, and the army's counteroffensive, which included the Escuadrón de la Muerte (Death squad), police officers who were granted repressive powers to deal with Tupamaros.

Along with police forces trained by the US Office of Public Safety (OPS), the Uruguayan military unleashed a bloody campaign of mass arrests and selected disappearances, dispersing those guerrillas who were not killed or arrested. Their usage of torture was particularly effective, and by 1972 the

MLN had been severely weakened. Its principal leaders were imprisoned under terrible conditions for the next 12 years.

Despite the diminished threat, the civilian government of Juan María Bordaberry ceded government authority to the military in July 1973 in a bloodless coup that led to further repression against the population and the suppression of all parties. The following month, the Tupamaros formed the Revolutionary Coordinating Junta with other leftwing groups pursuing urban guerrilla warfare in the Southern Cone. The following year, various South American regimes responded with the collaborative, international counterinsurgency campaign known as Operation Condor.

Also known as National Liberation Movement

Turkish Hezbollah

Continent: EurasiCountry: Turkey
Background:

Turkish Hezbollah was founded in south-eastern Turkey during the early 1980's. Its goal was the establishment of a Sunni Muslim theocracy in Turkey, which they attempted to achieve by overthrowing Turkey's secular regime. Despite the common name, Turkish Hezbollah is unrelated to the Iranian-sponsored Lebanese Hezbollah. It is suspected that Turkish Hezbollah has also received Iranian funding and support, as Iran sought to spread its revolutionary Islamic ideology into Turkey. Initially, Turkish Hezbollah members trained with members of the Kurdistan Workers Party (PKK), Turkey's main rebel Turkish group. A rivalry soon developed, and Turkish Hezbollah soon focused the bulk of its attacks on the PKK, which it accused of anti-Muslim activities. Turkish Hezbollah also focused on spreading its Islamic theology through Turkey through bookstores and publishing houses. Because the Turkish government's main counterterrorism efforts at this time were directed against the PKK, some accuse the government of supporting and funding Turkish Hezbollah as a proxy, a charge they deny. Regardless of official government complicity, their focus on combating PKK allowed Turkish Hezbollah to act without fear of government reprisal. Charges of connections to the Turkish government are furthered by the fact that from its founding until 2000, Turkish Hezbollah was not involved in any violent confrontation with Turkish police or security forces.

Turkish Hezbollah's situation greatly changed in the mid 1990's, as PKK's threat to Turkey waned, culminating in a 1999 truce. With the government's focus away from PKK, Turkish Hezbollah arose as a target for the Turkish government, who began to arrest its members. The lack of PKK as a serious adversary also caused Turkish Hezbollah to change its focus, and in the mid-1990's it began to target secular academics and journalists, feminists and religious Muslims who did not support its goal of establishing an Islamic state in Turkey. Full-scale operations against the group by the Turkish government began in 2000, resulting in the deaths of hundreds of militants throughout south-eastern Turkey. Turkish police, investigating the fraudulent use of a kidnapped businessman's credit card, were led to small house in the city of Beykoz, where a shootout ensued and the group's leader, Huseyin Velioglu, was killed. Also captured in the raid were chief lieutenants Edip Gumus and Cemal Tutar. This raid, which yielded a wealth of information on the group and led to the capture of other key members, is seen as the beginning of the end of Turkish Hezbollah. Many of its remaining members have escaped to Iran and Iraq. However, involvement of Turkish Hezbollah is suspected in the 2003 bombings of synagogues and British targets, although the links are unclear at this point.

Turkish Islamic Jihad

Continent: Eurasia
Country: Turkey
Background:
Like with Turkish Hezbollah, Turkish Islamic Jihad is believed to be financed by Iran yet not directly related to the Islamic Jihad group carrying out attacks in Israel and the Occupied Territories. The group has never publicly declared a specific ideology, but their name implies a fundamentalist Islamic orientation. In their only public statement, the group claimed to oppose the efforts of both the United States and Egypt at the 1991 Madrid Peace Conference, whom they accused of attempting to "divide up the Middle East."

Although they have not claimed an attack since 1996, the Turkish Islamic Jihad was mentioned in the Iranian press as late as 2000 as one of a number of groups continuing to "carry out clandestine political and military activities." The group is presumed to be inactive; however the Islamist movement continues to present a threat to Turkey.

Ugandan Democratic Christian Army

Abbreviation: UDCA
Continent: Africa
Country: Sudan, Uganda
Background:

The Uganda Democratic Christian Army (UDCA) was the main opposition force in Uganda in the early 1990s. The UDCA was the successor to Alice Auma's Holy Spirit Movement (HSM). Auma had claimed to be possessed by a spirit (called Lakwena) that would help her create a Christian nation in Uganda. However, HSM's reliance on magic and bullet-proof potions led to its destruction. Joseph Kony, inspired by Auma, consequently formed the UDCA in 1990. The UDCA was comprised mainly of former HSM members and other converted Acholi (a tribal group in Sudan). Even though he was driven by Auma's spiritual teachings, Kony engaged in brutal guerrilla tactics that proved highly effective in furthering the UDCA cause.

UDCA hoped to establish a government that ruled in accordance with an extremist interpretation of Christian scripture. Engaging in brutal tactics throughout northern Uganda, the UDCA maimed, killed, and enslaved non-Christian Acholi and attempted to overthrow the government of Yoweri Museveni. By 1994, military setbacks left the UDCA marginalised. Kony disbanded the group and reformed it as the Lord's Resistance Army (LRA) in an attempt to expand the group's support base. The UDCA is no longer active though it is essentially still operating as the LRA.

See the Lord's Resistance Army

Uighur Militants

Continent: Asia
Country: Turkistan
Background:

The Uighur (WEE-grr, also Uyghur) are an ethnically Turkic group of Muslims in the formerly independent Republic of East Turkistan, which the Chinese call Xinjiang Uighur Autonomous Region. The large region makes up one-sixteenth of China's territory and borders three former Soviet central Asian Republics. The latest Chinese census gives the present population of the Uighurs as slightly over 6 million. There are also 500,000 Uighurs in Western Turkestan, known as Uzbekistan, Kazakistan, Kirgizstan, Turkmenistan and Tajikistan. Almost 150,000 Uighurs have their homes in Pakistan, Afghanistan, Saudi Arabia, Turkey, Western Europe and the United States. In order to transform Eastern Turkestan into a Chinese province millions of Chinese have been settled there. Before 1949 there were only 300 thousand Chinese settlers in Eastern Turkestan. Now there are more than 6 million.

Uighur militants in Xinjiang have been struggling for decades to establish an independent East Turkestan. In 1933 and 1944, the Uighurs were successful in setting up an independent Islamic Eastern Turkestan republic. But these independent Islamic Republics were overthrown by the military intervention of the Soviet Union. In 1949 the Nationalist Chinese were defeated by the Chinese communists and Eastern Turkestan fell under Chinese communist rule.

The Committee for Eastern Turkestan, based in Alma-Ata, Kazakhstan, is probably the most radical national movement in Central Asia. The Committee has recently become more militant and has vowed to intensify their struggle in a bid to free Xinjiang from growing Chinese influence. It was originally formed by Uighur guerrillas who fought against the Chinese in the period of 1944-1949. In 1945 Muslim freedom-fighters took up arms and set up an independent Turkestan Republic in a mass-uprising supported by the Soviet Union. Their leader of the 1940s, Aysa Beg, fled to Turkey in 1949 after the Communists came to power.

The situation in Xinjiang for Muslims is extremely severe. Uighurs are being arbitrarily detained. Thousands of Uighur political prisoners are in jail and are being tortured. There have been very violent repressions of protest, mass closings of Koranic schools, a large number of death sentences for religious protesters.

In 1990, the Uighurs, Kirghiz and Kazakhs of Eastern Turkestan again rose up against Chinese rule. In April in the remote town of Akto, more than 1000 residents, furious at not being allowed to build a mosque, took to the streets. More than 60 people were killed in clashes with Chinese troops. In July 1990 the authorities in Xinjiang announced the arrest of 7,900 people in a crackdown on "criminal activities of ethnic splittists and other criminal offenders."

The "Strike Hard" anti-crime campaign launched in 1996 was announced as an initiative to answer citizens' legitimate concerns about rising crime through a high-intensity series of high-profile police actions. The "Strike Hard" campaign never officially came to an end, though it faded from the scene in most urban areas. In minority areas, however, it is a different story. Particularly in Xinjiang province, home to the Muslim

Uighur nationality, the "Strike Hard" work appears to be going full-tilt, clearly a tool being used to justify harsh measures against political activists, including many well publicised executions of accused pro-independence activists.

On the eve of Ramadan on 5th February 1997 in Ghulja, believers were offended by the arrests of 30 prestigious religious leaders by the Chinese Government. Six hundred young people took to the streets, walking toward city government, demanding release of those religious figures. On their way, they were stopped by police and the paramilitary forces. Police violently dispersed crowds using electrical clubs, water cannon, and tear gas in the freezing day. The second day, an even bigger demonstration was held after Uighurs all over town heard about the incident. Chinese police and paramilitary forces were ordered to shoot to the crowd, and killed 167 people, and succeeded in suppressing the rally. Afterwards, the Chinese policemen arrested over 5,000 demonstrators, including elder, young women and children in a single day on the charge of intending to split the motherland, conducting criminal activity, fundamental religious activity, and counter-revolutionary element.

The Chinese Government subsequently made the first open execution of seven Uighurs in order to 'kill the chicken to scare the monkeys.' Chinese military forces loaded them on to the open truck and drove slowly through the busy Uighur bazaar and neighbourhoods through a crowd. When the mourners got too close to the trucks, the Chinese soldiers opened fire and killed nine more people.

Anwar Yusuf, president of the Eastern Turkistan National Freedom Centre, was one of several independence leaders who gathered in Taiwan 25th to 28th February 1998, for public and private meetings and numerous press interviews. Invited by the World Federation of Taiwanese Association in the U.S., Yusuf was joined by prominent Eastern Turkistani activist Erkin Alptekin; Professor Thubtin Jigme Norbu, elder brother of His Holiness the Dalai Lama; Tashi Jamyangling, former Home Secretary of the Tibetan Government in Exile; and Johnar Bache, Vice Chairman of the Southern Mongolian People's Party. The independence leaders met with leading Taiwanese, in and out of government, including Liu Sung-pan, the president of Taiwan's Legislative Yuan; Shui-Bian Chen, Mayor of Taipei; and Frank C.T. Hsieh, Mayor of Kaosiung.

Following the death of the exile East Turkestan leader Isa Yusuf Alptekin, who advocated non-violence and was called the Turkic Dalai Lama, no-one has had the authority to prevent militant resistance against Chinese rule in Xinjiang. Branded as "Xinjiang's Hamas," the Home of East Turkestan Youth is a radical group committed to achieving the goal of independence through the use of armed force. It has some 2,000 members, some of whom have undergone training in using explosive device in Afghanistan and other Islamic countries.

Also known as Committee for Eastern Turkistan

Ulster Defence Association/Ulster Freedom Fighters

Abbreviation: UDA/UFF
Continent: Europe
Country: United Kingdom
Background:

The Ulster Defence Association is the largest loyalist paramilitary organisation in Northern Ireland, boasting a membership of 40,000 during its peak. As a loyalist organisation, the UDA is opposed to the unification of Northern Ireland and the Republic of Ireland and desires that the six counties of Northern Ireland remain part of the United Kingdom.

The UDA was formed in the early 1970s in response to the Irish Republican Army's (IRA) violent resurgence in Northern Ireland. Small, neighbourhood-based local groups, with the express intent of protecting Protestants from republican attacks, began to form. In 1971, the UDA was established as an umbrella organisation for many of these local groups. The group is closely connected to the Ulster Freedom Fighters (UFF), utilising the UFF as a covert terrorist organisation from the 1970s until the early 1990s. Through this deception, the UDA was able to maintain a legal status in Northern Ireland until 1991. However, the two groups have effectively merged into one organisation. The UDA's retention of its status as a legal organisation lead many republicans to cite it as an example of the collusion between loyalist organisations and British security forces and Northern Ireland police forces.

Although formed to protect Protestants from Republican terrorist attacks, the vast majority of attacks conducted by the UDA have been retaliatory killings targeting Catholic civilians or rival loyalists. The majority of the attacks committed by the UDA have been small-scale, individual murders as opposed to bombings or other large-scale tactics preferred by other terrorist groups in Northern Ireland. Operations are conducted by one of the organisation's six largely independent brigades.

Due in part to its cooperation with the Loyalist Volunteer Force (LVF), the UDA became embroiled in a feud with the LVF's founding group, the Ulster Volunteer Force (UVF), beginning in 2000. In addition, the UDA has been weakened by violent internal feuding, leading to reports of brigades breaking away from the organisation. However, the North Belfast brigade declared in August 2006 that it has since reunited with the UDA.

Beginning in October 1994, the UDA has declared numerous ceasefires, often as a result of similar declarations made by republican organisations, namely the IRA. However, members of the UDA remained active through the use of cover names such as the Red Hand Defenders (RHD) and Orange Volunteers (OV). Due to its continued feuding, both internally and with other loyalist organisations, and its utilisation of cover names, the British government stated in October 2001 that it no longer recognised a UDA ceasefire.

Plagued by internecine feuds and heavy involvement in organised crime and drug trafficking, the UDA announced in November 2005 that its leadership was reconsidering the group's future due to the standing down of the IRA and the LVF. Since its announcement, the UDA has engaged in internal cleansing, forcefully expelling controversial members and their supporters from the organisation and, often, Northern Ireland entirely. Despite these efforts, the Independent Monitoring Commission, established in 2004 to monitor paramilitary organisations in Northern Ireland, announced in April 2006 that the UDA continues to engage in paramilitary and criminal activities, especially drug trafficking and extortion.

See the Red Hand Defenders, Orange Volunteers

Ulster Volunteer Force

Abbreviation: UVF
Continent: Europe
Country: United Kingdom
Background:

The Ulster Volunteer Force (UVF) is a loyalist paramilitary organisation dedicated to maintaining Northern Ireland's ties with the United Kingdom. Loyalist organisations in Northern Ireland oppose the unification of the six counties of Northern Ireland with the 26 counties of the Republic of Ireland.

The UVF, as it exists today, was formed in 1966 to combat the threat of republican paramilitary organisations such as the Irish Republican Army (IRA). However, their inception was rooted in a unionist militia formed by Edward Carson during the early 1910s and 1920s whose name and symbols were appropriated in 1966. This original organisation sought to prevent the creation of an autonomous Ireland and therefore was dedicated to maintaining Ireland's ties with the United Kingdom. The original UVF was disbanded shortly after the creation of the Republic of Ireland.

Throughout its history, the UVF has conducted a multitude of operations, including: bombings, assassinations, kidnappings, and hijackings.

These attacks usually targeted Catholic civilians, republican paramilitaries, and rival loyalists, all of whom were located in Northern Ireland. However, beginning in the 1970s, the UVF expanded its terrorist bombing campaign to include Catholic civilian targets in the Republic of Ireland, often in retaliation for attacks by the IRA or other republican groups. A particularly violent group of UVF members, named the Shankill Butchers, is thought to be personally responsible for the kidnap, torture, and murder of over 30 Catholic civilians in Northern Ireland.

In October 1994, as part of the Combined Loyalist Military Command, the UVF declared a ceasefire in response to the IRA's ceasefire. However, numerous members were opposed to the ceasefire and participation in the peace process, which led to their separation from the UVF to form splinter groups such as the Loyalist Volunteer Force (LVF). It is also possible that former UVF members remained active through the use of cover names like the South Londonderry Volunteers.

The UVF has been consistently challenged by rival groups like the LVF and the Ulster Defence Association (UDA), where years of fighting has only recently tapered off. In addition to instability caused by fighting with these groups, the UVF has been weakened by internal feuding, the use of police informants within the group, and the arrests of leading members. The group has also become heavily involved in organised crime and drug trafficking, resulting in waning public support.

In September 2005, as a result of continued paramilitary activities and violent feuding with other loyalists, the British government announced that it no longer recognised the 1994 UVF ceasefire. Recently, the group's leadership has attempted to distance the UVF from criminal activities, although their success is debatable. The Independent Monitoring Commission, formed in 2004 to monitor paramilitary organisations in Northern Ireland, stated in its April 2006 report that the UVF remained an active and violent paramilitary organisation. In May 2007, the group declared that the "IRA's war is over" and as such, it would halt all terrorist activity. Whether or not this represents a step forward in resolving the conflict in Northern Ireland remains to be seen.

Underground Government of the Democratic People of Laos

Abbreviation: UGFDPL
Continent: Asia
Country: Laos

Background:

Little is known about the Underground Government of the Free Democratic People of Laos (UGFDPL), a group that has claimed responsibility for several small bombings in Laos in the past few years.

While the group has made few public statements giving insight into their aims and ideology, the lack of information surrounding the group is probably more a product of the secretive, hermetic nature of Laos and its communist government. For over 30 years, the Lao People's Revolutionary Party has ruled the country with an iron fist, crushing ethnic insurgencies (notably a low-level conflict waged by the Hmong minority group) and peaceful opposition alike.

While the Laotian government has been quick to blame any anti-government violence on "bandits" or ethnic "Hmong insurgents," the UGFDPL appears to be a pro-democracy group opposed to the authoritarian communist government. In a rare statement of claim leaked to the public, the group claimed responsibility for a November 2003 bombing at a national monument, saying, "All the bomb explosions...this time, as in the past, have been carried out by (Lao) people (our mission) is to dismantle the cruel and barbarian regime of the ruling Lao People's Revolutionary Party." The group also expressed an opposition to the presence of Vietnamese troops on Laotian territory.

Since 2000, the group has claimed responsibility for numerous attacks on markets, tourist venues, and transportation targets. Most prominently, the group claimed responsibility for a 2004 bombing at the Thai-Lao "Friendship Bridge," just days before a regional ASEAN summit was to take place in the Laotian capital. Due to the government's desire to downplay these incidents, very little information is known about the damage and casualties caused by the attacks. For the most part, UGFDPL seems more interested in publicising their cause rather than killing people.

Almost nothing is known about the size and structure of the UGFDPL. Some news reports speculate that the group is made up of disillusioned ex-military forces, but there is no concrete proof to support this claim.

The UGFDPL is an active organisation dedicated to bringing democratic rule to Laos. Authoritarianism is deeply entrenched in Laos, and until there is a significant change in governance within the country, the UGFDPL will most likely carry out bombing attacks on prominent targets in the near future.

Also known as Free Democratic People's Government of Laos, Free Democratic Government Committee of the Lao People

United Self Defence Forces of Columbia

Abbreviation: AUC
Continent: South America
Country: Columbia
Background:

The United Self-Defence Forces of Colombia (AUC) was formed to combat leftist terrorist organisations operating in Colombia, primarily the FARC and ELN. The AUC grew out of local paramilitary and self-defence groups formed in the 1980s. These groups were dedicated to protecting the economic interests of wealthy citizens and of the state from the Communist-inspired guerrilla movements that threatened them.

At first, the various paramilitary groups enjoyed the tacit approval of the Colombian military. The military even cooperated with the AUC in the fight against leftist guerrillas. Eventually, however, the close financial connections between the paramilitaries and local drug cartels forced the military to officially sever ties with the AUC in 1989. Despite this, the military and the AUC have been accused of continuing their collaboration unofficially, and the AUC recruits many former military personnel.

The AUC functions as an umbrella organisation comprised of independently-operated groups. One of these paramilitaries, the Peasant Self-Defence Group of Córdoba and Urabá (ACCU), is thought to have spearheaded the formation of the AUC. Furthermore, Carlos Castaño Gil, the co-founder and leader of the ACCU, is recognised as the on-again/off-again AUC leader.

The AUC serves the interests of Colombian economic elites, drug traffickers, and any local communities that do not support the leftist rebels. According to the AUC, its primary objective is to protect its supporters from leftist guerrillas. Clearly, however, the AUC is also keenly interested in controlling the drug trade, which is its primary source of earnings. AUC leader Carlos Castaño Gil claims that 70 percent of the AUC's operational costs are funded by drug-related sources.

The AUC began peace negotiations with the Colombian government in July 2004. The talks centred on the disarmament of AUC blocks and their reintegration into the Colombian Armed Forces in order to provide security in their local strongholds. Like in similar, previous negotiations (such as with Pablo Escobar's group), the AUC sought to negotiate surrender and disarmament for promises of non-extradition to the U.S. and reduced prison sentences for terrorist and narcotics crimes. Despite AUC pledges to work with the American and Colombian governments to take action against cocaine production in the areas in which they operate, the

American government has refused to drop their demands for extradition of AUC leaders.

Although the peace talks proceeded slowly at first (hurting the AUC's standing with the public), the disarmament process accelerated in 2005. By early 2006, more than 26,000 right-wing paramilitaries had reportedly disarmed in a series of weapons submission ceremonies. On the 12th April 2006, 1,700 fighters turned in their weapons in the town of Casibare. This action marked the final scheduled ceremony in the demobilisation effort. The disarmament process is now presumed to be over, having involved thousands more guerrillas than expected.

Now that disarmament is reputedly over, it remains to be seen what role former AUC troops will play in Colombian security and politics. Discouragingly, there have been reports from the north of the country indicating that a few small bands of officially demobilised AUC fighters are still involved in terrorist activities—including extortion, kidnapping, and even murder. The Colombian government has demanded serious efforts to control any outbreaks from senior commanders, particularly Salvatore Mancuso, though Mancuso has denied having any ability to control his former forces.

United Self Defence Forces of Venezuela

Abbreviation: AUV
Continent: South America
Country: Venezuela
Background:

The United Self-Defence Forces of Venezuela emerged in 2002 as the Venezuelan counterpart to the powerful Colombian paramilitary group, the United Self-Defence Forces of Colombia (AUC). The United Self-Defence Forces of Venezuela, known by its Spanish acronym AUV, echoes the ideological statements of the AUC, namely the criticism of leftist and Communist organisations. While the AUC principally targets members of Colombia's Communist terrorist organisations, the Venezuelan AUV directs its attacks principally at the acting Venezuelan government of Hugo Chavez, a leftist government with links to Libya and Cuba.

In addition to its attacks against acting government officials, the AUV condemns the Bolivarian circles, or citizens groups that support current Venezuelan president Hugo Chavez. Consistent with the views of their Colombian affiliate, the AUV also criticises the activities of leftist guerrillas.

Carlos Casta, the leader of the United Self-Defence Forces of Colombia (AUC), has admitted to training the United Self-Defence Forces of Venezuela. Casta claims that his interference in Venezuela's internal affairs is necessary due to its geographical location. According to Casta, the border area between Colombia and Venezuela is a legitimate battle ground.

It is likely that any continuing activities of the United Self-Defence Forces of Venezuela will take place in the border region of Venezuela, specifically in the western state of Tachira.

United Somali Congress

Abbreviation: USC
Continent: Africa
Country: Ethiopia
Background:

The United Somali Congress (USC) is one of the major political and para-military organisations of Somalia. Formed in 1989, it played a key role in the ouster of the government of Siad Barre, and became a major target of the so-called Operation Restore Hope campaign in 1993. It had devolved through numerous fragmentations throughout the years but by 2004 its members and alumni would be key participants on the Transitional Federal Government.

Based around Hawiye clan, its political wing was founded in Rome in January 1989. Its military wing was formed in 1989 in Ethiopia, and led by Mohamed Farrah Aidid until his death in 1996. He was succeeded by his son Hussein Mohamed Farrah, by which time the Aidid faction of the organisation was also known as the Somali National Alliance (SNA), often the USC/SNA.

The clan based militias were not patriotic to begin with. The only reason they existed was to gain power by any means necessary. Both SNM and SSDF hired tribesmen who operated in a manner of ruthless killings, rape and torture. Said Barre who most Somalis consider a patriot, commented in comparison, that Ethiopian rebels overseas and inside the country never done anything harmful to its countrymen while Somali opposition forces did anything and everything consequentially negative to the general life of the country. These people were mainly former government ministers and employees. One such example is now noble sounding ex-minister Ali Khalif Galaidh.

Military successes by the USC would be instrumental in bringing about the ouster of the Barre government on the 26th January 1991, but the USC failed to manage a political settlement with its rivals, the SNM, SPM and the SSDF, and also fragmented within its own leadership after Ali Mahdi Muhammad was declared interim President.

Upon the naming of Ali Mahdi Muhammed as President, the USC split into two. The USC/SNA emerged under Mohammed Aidid and the United Somali Congress/Somali Salvation Alliance (USC/SSA) of Ali Mahdi Muhammed. The USC/SNA came under the control of Mohamed Aidid's son, Hussein Mohamed Farah Aidid after the father's death in 1996. The USC/SSA eventually came under control of the Deputy Chairman, Musa Sudi Yalahow.

Both USC factions made peace with each other in August 1998, though this caused a violent split between Yalahow and Ali Mahdi Muhammed, and fighting continued in Mogadishu. Eventually both Hussein Aidid and Yalahow reconciled and joined the Somali Reconciliation and Restoration Council (SRRC) in 2002, in opposition to the Transitional National Government (TNG). This caused a rift between the USC/SSA supporters of Yalahow and Omar Muhamoud Finnish (also known as Mahmud Muhammad Finish), who continued to support the TNG. Fighting between the two caused many deaths in Mogadishu. Hussein Aidid, Yalahow and Finish all joined the Transitional Federal Government (TFG) in November 2004.

Uygur Holy War Organisation

Continent: Asia
Country: China
Background:

Almost nothing is known about the Uygur Holy War Organisation, but the struggle from which they emerged is well-documented. The Uygurs of Xinjiang province in South-western China have long had a complicated relationship with their rulers in Beijing. At various times throughout their history, the Uygurs, Muslims of Turkic background, have enjoyed freedom or religion and some degree of self-rule. But since the Chinese Communists came to power, Xinjiang has come much more directly under the control of the majority Han Chinese who rule the country. The Communist disdain for religion has provided much fodder for disagreement, for example, when local Party officials refused to allow a mosque to be constructed in the city of Kashgar. Violations of human rights by Communist forces have also been widely reported, especially concerning the violent suppression of Uygur protests. Beginning in the late 1980's, some Uygurs began to turn to terrorism in an effort to convince Beijing to grant them autonomy. Bombings and assassinations have plagued Xinjiang ever since, and the separatists even took the fight to the enemy, bombing the Chinese capital three times in the spring of 1997. Since September 11, 2001, Chinese officials have begun to crack down even more openly on the Uygurs, arguing that they are contributing to the "Global War on Terrorism."

The Uygur Holy War Organisation may have existed for only one day

– 21st November 2001. On that day, Uygur separatists claiming membership in the organisation raided a police station, killing the director, and the home of a judge, who was stabbed along with his wife. No further acts of terrorism have been claimed by, or attributed to, the Uygur Holy War Organisation, and none is expected in the future.

Waffen SS

Continent: Europe
Country: Latvia
Background:

There probably never was any organised terrorist group called the Waffen SS. More than likely, the group that attacked the World War II memorial in Dobele, Latvia, in May 1998, was made up of fanatical Latvian nationalists, who today lionise the older generation that served in Hitler's Waffen SS during World War II. Anti-Russian and anti-Semitic, this extreme form of Latvian nationalism has taken off since the fall of the Soviet Union. Former Waffen SS units hold parades in the streets of Latvia's major cities, and parliamentarians and military officials frequently attend; the President only stopped attending in the late nineties after much international protest. Spokesmen say that the celebration of Hitler's Latvian units is meant as anti-Communist, not pro-Nazi. But the bombings of Jewish cemeteries and the presence of swastika graffiti in parts of Latvia suggest that at least some of Hitler's ideas hold sway among segments of the population. Given the twisted view of history being taken by many Latvian nationalists today, it makes sense that the individuals responsible for the Dobele bombing would claim responsibility in the name of the Waffen SS.

Since 1998, no further acts of terrorism have been attributed to the Waffen SS, and this is not expected to change in the near future. However, since this group probably never existed as a firm organisation, it is certainly possible that some of its former "members" are still engaged in some of the violent nationalist activities that continue in Latvia today.

Wakefulness and Holy War

Continent: Middle East
Country: Iraq
Background:

Wakefulness and Holy War is an Arab Sunni Muslim group that operated in and around Fallujah. They videotaped one of their attacks on American forces and sent it to an Iranian television on the 7th July 2003. On the tape they said "Saddam and America are two sides of the same coin." They also stated they were carrying out more operations against American occupation in Fallujah and nearby cities.

West Side Boys

Continent: Africa
Country: Sierra Leone
Background:

The West Side Boys were an armed group in Sierra Leone, sometimes described as a splinter faction of the Armed Forces Revolutionary Council. It captured and held members of a mostly West African peacekeeping force (including members of the Royal Irish Rangers) in 2000, and was subsequently destroyed by units of the British Special Air Service, Special Boat Service and Parachute Regiment during September 2000 in Operation Barras, and follow-up operations by the Sierra Leone Army and Royal Irish Rangers. The group was influenced to some extent by American rap and gangsta rap music, especially Tupac Shakur, and the "gangsta" culture portrayed therein. The group was also known as the West Side Niggaz or West Side Junglers. Since the former would have been an unacceptable phrase to be regularly used on news programmes, the title was amended to render it innocuous.

Many members of the group were children abducted after their parents had been killed by the "recruiters". Some of these children were forced to participate in torturing their parents to death in order to brutalise and dehumanise them. The West Side Boys were heavy users of homemade palm wine, locally grown marijuana, and heroin bought with conflict diamonds. Conflict diamonds were also used to purchase many of their weapons, which ranged from SLR rifles, AK-47 rifles and RPG-7 grenade launchers to 81 mm mortars and ZPU-2 anti-aircraft guns. Most of their vehicles were hijacked from UN food convoys. One of the hostages rescued during Operation Barras has also claimed that the West Side Boys were supplied with ammunition by corrupt Jordanian United Nations Mission in Sierra Leone peacekeepers.

Also known as West Side Niggaz, West Side Junglers

White Arayan Resistance

Abbreviation: VAM
Continent: Europe
Country: Sweden
Background:

White Aryan Resistance (Swedish: Vitt Ariskt Motstånd), also known as

VAM, was a neo-nazi paramilitary group active in Sweden between 1991 and 1993. The name of the group was derived from the US White supremacist organisation WAR however the point of the acronym is lost in the translation. According to Stieg Larsson, a researcher of white supremacist organisations, the group was instead styled on the then already defunct US White supremacist group The Order, led by Robert Matthews. VAM was founded by Klas Lund; other leading members were Torulf Magnusson and Peter Melander, editor of the group's magazine Storm. The organisation's symbol was the "Wolfsangel". VAM has been implicated in many serious crimes in Sweden, including the infamous Police-murders in Malexander, car bombings of political journalists and murders of perceived opponents. Many former members of this violent organisation can today be found in present day neo-nazi organisations, according to a report prepared and jointly published by Sweden's four largest dailies; Aftonbladet, Expressen, Dagens Nyheter and Svenska Dagbladet, in November 1999.

After VAM, Klas Lund organised The Swedish Resistance Movement (Swedish: Svenska Motståndsrörelsen), another off-shoot to VAM is National Socialist Front (Swedish: Nationalsocialistisk Front) or NSF which were formed in 1994 by VAM-sympathisers in Karlskrona.

White Patriot Party

Abbreviation: WPP
Continent: North America
Country: United States of America
Background:

The White Patriot Party (WPP) was a paramilitary, Christian Identity faction of the Ku Klux Klan founded by Glenn Miller in 1980. WPP was extremely racist: they supported apartheid, and set up hotlines featuring telephone recordings of a black man being lynched. WPP won considerable support in North Carolina by blaming the bad economic climate for farmers on international Jewish bankers. Some estimates put the WPP's peak membership at 3000. Miller's goal was "southern independence. The creation of an all-white nation within the one million square miles of mother Dixie. We have no hope for Jew York City or San Fran-sissy-co and other areas that are dominated by Jews, perverts, and communists and non-white minorities and rectum-loving queers."

The Order gave some of the $3.6 million they stole to Miller and the WPP. Miller was subpoenaed to testify at The Order trial because Order member Bruce Pierce said that Miller received $300,000 from the Order. Miller testified that he had received $200,000.

The White Patriot Party was shut down by Morris Dees and the

Southern Poverty Law Centre (SPLC). Dees, an outspoken advocate for civil rights, became a target of the Klan after a 1981 confrontation with Louisiana grand dragon Louis Beam. Dees persuaded a court to issue an injunction protecting Vietnamese shrimpers who were being terrorised by the Louisiana Klan. Beam was so enraged that he challenged Dees to a duel. Dees was harassed by Beam and his associates, including Miller, for the next several years. Eventually the SPLC hacked into the WPP's computer network and discovered evidence that the group was planning to assassinate Dees. Based on this evidence, a judge issued an injunction forbidding Miller and the WPP from engaging in paramilitary activity. Miller violated this injunction and was convicted of threatening Dees. As part of a deal he struck with the government, Miller testified at the 1988 trial of 13 white supremacist leaders. He is now loathed as a traitor by much of the extreme right.

Y

Yarmuk Jamaat

Continent: Asia
Country: Russia
Background:

Yarmuk Jamaat is a militant Islamist organisation connected to numerous attacks against the local and federal security forces in Russian region of Kabardino-Balkaria in the North Caucasus. It became part of the Caucasian Front of the Second Chechen War.

In the late 1990s, intolerance of religious dissent by Valery Kokov, the administrator of the Kabardino-Balkaria region, forced many Muslim organisations to go underground.

The Jamaat of Kabardino-Balkaria became one of these organisations and many of its members fled to Chechnya for paramilitary training, reportedly under Ruslan Gelayev. After their training, these members returned and formed the current paramilitary off-shoot in 2002. The Jamestown Foundation reported that volunteers had indeed been operation in the North Caucasus, but that the Yarmuk Jamaat was officially established in August 2004 by Muslim Atayev.

The insurgency network in Kabardino-Balkaria was originally established by the Shagen brothers, who were Kabardins. In 2003, the brothers arranged for Chechen field commander Shamil Basaev to visit Kabardino-Balkaria. Both brothers were killed later that same year. Mussa Mukozhoyev was the self-proclaimed emir of the Jamaat and was widely known to be a moderate. He told "We are not fools. We don't want to bring the Chechen war into our homes," But even then, he explained, it was becoming harder and harder to hold back extremists intent on Jihad against the Russians they considered to be their oppressors. Those more radical members went on to form Yarmuk.

Yarmuk Jamaat issued a statement in January 2004 outlining their rationale for violent action and basing their turn toward violence on the Hanbali School of religious law, one of the four main schools within Sunni Islam. Its current leader, Anzor Astemirov took credit for the idea of establishing the Caucasus Emirate which was proclaimed in late 2007 by President of Ichkeria Doku Umarov.

Yemen Islamic Jihad

Continent: Middle East, Asia, Europe, Africa, North America
Country: Afghanistan, Libya, United Kingdom, United States of America, Yemen

Background:

Yemen Islamic Jihad is composed of Yemenis, Egyptians, Algerians, Saudis and other Afghan war veterans who followed Tariq al-Fasdli back to Yemen after the war to help President Ali Abdullah Saleh defeat the socialists of South Yemen in 1994. Al-Fasdli and several other leaders immediately joined the triumphant government, but the new government's failure to incorporate the hundreds of Islamic Jihad fighters into the Yemeni army left them to pursue their militant Islamist aims. Nevertheless, the group enjoys de facto support from political elites at many levels of Yemen's government, enforcing their own brand of Sharia in the South.

Yemen Islamic Jihad has also taken on foreign targets. In 1992, U.S. troops headed for Somalia were targeted in two hotel bombings during their stay over in Yemen and in 1993 Egyptian authorities blamed Yemen Islamic Jihad for an attempted assassination of the Egyptian Prime Minister. The government of Yemen continued to turn a blind eye until the attempted assassination of Egypt's president Hosni Mubarak in 1995 by Yemeni-based militants.

Tariq al-Fasdli met Osama bin Laden during his years in Afghanistan and Yemen Islamic Jihad is closely affiliated with, and substantially funded by, Al Qaeda. In 2000 the two groups, along with the Aden-Abyan Islamic Army, were implicated in the bombing of the USS Cole. The group is based in Yemen, but is believed to have militant wings in Palestine, Afghanistan, the US and the UK.

The goals of Yemen Islamic Jihad include the establishment of Sharia law in Yemen, the support of the Palestinian struggle against Israel, an end to western intervention in the Middle East (including the removal of foreign military, commercial, and civilian presences from Yemen, Saudi Arabia, and elsewhere in the Middle East), and combat against the 'enemies' of Islam, namely, Israel, the United States, and the West in general.

Also known as Islamic Jihad

Zapatista Army of National Liberation

Abbreviation: EZLN
Continent: Central America
Country: Mexico
Background:

The EZLN (Ejercíto Zapatista de Liberación Naciónal or Zapatista Army of National Liberation) is a political movement dedicated to pressing the Mexican government for more rights and better conditions for Mexican Indians in the country's impoverished southern provinces. Emiliano Zapata is a national hero in Mexico who fought during the Mexican Revolution and attempted to introduce agrarian reform to benefit the lower classes; the EZLN maintains that they are Zapata's ideological heirs. In January 1994, the EZLN launched a guerrilla war against the government, and has maintained a role on the fringes of Mexican politics ever since. The group is based in the state of Chiapas and has considerable support there. Dozens of villages have declared themselves under the control of the EZLN.

The EZLN was created on the 17th November 1983 by a shadowy figure called Subcomandante Marcos, who remains the group's leader to this day. Allegedly a former teacher, Marcos fled to the jungle with a couple of followers to begin an armed communist revolt. His movement struggled to gain adherents until he dropped orthodox Marxism sometime around 1990 and focused on the specific grievances of the rural peasants and indigenous peoples of Chiapas. Marcos' anti-government, anti-globalisation, and anti-American rhetoric took root amongst poor Chiapans. The group's membership expanded into the thousands with many sympathisers across the region.

The group launched its rebellion for democracy, equal rights, and better living conditions for Chiapans on the 1st January 1994. That date was chosen to coincide with the launch of the North American Free Trade Agreement (NAFTA). Approximately 150 people were killed in almost two weeks of clashes before a truce emerged. Since the uprising, the group has continued to agitate for native rights including negotiating with the government, publicly appealing to Mexican voters, organising marches and political rallies, and threatening further insurgent violence.

While the EZLN maintains many of the trappings of a terrorist group, such as appearing in public obscured by ski masks and retaining military capabilities, the group has kept a cold but persistent truce with the Mexican government since 1994. Subcomandante Marcos emerged after several years in hiding in 2005 to declare that the EZLN was entering mainstream politics. In addition to stumping around the country for indigenous rights, the EZLN also operates a radio station in Chiapas which broadcasts in Spanish and several local languages. The group is a favourite of anti-globalisation activists from around the globe and group members, including Subcomandante Marcos, are currently touring Mexico raising awareness and political and ideological support for their cause. Due to its political aspirations and the 1994 truce, the EZLN is not expected to engage in any major attacks in the near future.

Also known as EZLN (Zapatisas), Zapatista National Liberation Front

Zimbabwe African Nationalist Union

Continent: Africa
Country: Mozambique, Zimbabwe, (Rhodesia)
Background:

The Zimbabwe African Nationalist Union (ZANU) is Zimbabwe's most powerful nationalist organisation and now forms the basis for the ruling party in Harare, the ZANU-PF. It has been led since the 1960s by Robert Mugabe, Zimbabwe's current Executive President. The ZANU began as a group opposed to British colonial rule. As colonialism in Africa was ending in the 1960s, the UK refused to grand independence to Zimbabwe (then called Rhodesia) under the minority regime of Ian Smith. This prompted Smith to unilaterally declare independence in 1965.

After Smith's UDI, the nationalist struggle in Zimbabwe's main actors were Mugabe's ZANU and the Zimbabwe African People's Union (ZAPU) of Joshua Nkomo. The ZANU received economic and military aid from China and espoused some socialist principles, but their orientation was always primarily nationalist. The ZANU and ZAPU fought both each other and the Rhodesian government. In addition to conducting guerrilla warfare, the ZANU also targeted civilians and foreign missionaries. The group operated mainly out of guerrilla bases in FRELIMO-controlled areas of Mozambique.

The Civil War finally ended after British-mediated talks in 1980, leading to Mugabe's election as Prime Minister. Despite including Nkomo in his cabinet, Mugabe's ZANU and the ZAPU fought intermittently until 1987 when they merged their parties to form the ZANU-PF (Zimbabwe African National Union – Patriotic Front).

Mugabe, whose title is now Executive President after changing the constitution in 1987 remains Zimbabwe's ruler. The ZANU-PF has been accused of widespread electoral fraud, voter intimidation and lack of respect for civil rights, and Zimbabwe has increasingly been faced with international isolation. Particularly controversial was Mugabe's alleged support in 2000 of groups of squatters that violently took over white-owned farms.

The ZANU-PF received the majority of votes in March 2005 and 2008 parliamentary elections that were claimed to be rigged by Zimbabwe's main opposition group, the Movement for Democratic Change (MDC). Despite its lack of respect for democracy and human rights, however, the ZANU/ZANU-PF is no longer engaged in terrorist activity or guerrilla warfare.

Web Sites used to collate the information in this book and with grateful appreciation.

http://www.meta-religion.com/Extremism/extremism.htm
http://www.satp.org/satporgtp/countries/india/terroristoutfits/index.html
http://www.xs4all.nl/~afa/alert/engels/combat18.html
http://www.meta-religion.com/Extremism/White_extremism/Combat_18/combat_18.htm
http://www.tkb.org/Home.js
http://en.wikipedia.org/wiki/The_Return_(guerrilla_organisation)
http://www.freelebanon.org/articles/a167.htm
http://www.worldstatesmen.org/Terrorist.html#RIRA
http://www.blackpanther.org/
http://www.guardian.co.uk/alqaida/story/0,,1601506,00.html
http://www.alrashedeen.net/
http://warnewstoday.blogspot.com/index.html
http://www.cdi.org/terrorism/terrorist-groups.cfm
http://ftp.fas.org/irp/world/para/index.html
http://www.nps.edu/Library/Research/SubjectGuides/SpecialTopics/TerroristProfile/TerroristGroupProfiles.html
http://www.investigativeproject.org/
http://www.espionageinfo.com/index.html
http://www.milnet.com/state/2001/10254.htm
http://encyclopedia.thefreedictionary.com/Al-Jama'a+al-Islamiyyah+al-Muqatilah+bi-Libya
http://www.theinformationproject.org/orgindex.php?sort=a
http://www.atlapedia.com/online/countries/chad.htm
http://www.adl.org/terrorism/symbols/salafist.asp
http://www.country-data.com/cgi-bin/query/r-6553.html
http://cns.miis.edu/research/iraq/fedayin.htm

http://schema-root.org/region/middle_east/iraq/resistance/militias/falluja_squadron/

http://www.chinadaily.com.cn/english/doc/2004-06/19/content_340780.htm

http://www.mfa.gov.il/MFA/MFAArchive/2000_2009/2001/3/Force%2017%20Background%20Material%20-%20March%202001

http://www.jihadunspun.com/articles/18122003-Iraqi-Resistence/irailatir03.html

http://www.prophetofdoom.net/Islamic_Clubs_Lashkar-e-Tayyba.Islam

http://www.meforum.org/article/362

http://media.www.msuspokesman.com/media/storage/paper270/news/2002/11/22/WorldNews/Afrikaner.Extremists.Seek.To.Ignite.Race.War-330366.shtml

http://www.broadleft.org/ir.htm

http://onlinedictionary.datasegment.com/word/al-asifa

http://www.osac.gov/Groups/group.cfm?contentID=1301

http://www.globalsecurity.org/military/world/para/al-sunna.htm

http://www.encyclopedia.com/doc/1O48-ZapatistaNationlLbrtnFrnt.html

http://en.wikipedia.org/wiki/Wikipedia:Text_of_the_GNU_Free_Documentation_License

http://middleeastfacts.com/middle-east/fatah-fateh.php

www.newblackpanther.com

http://www.defenddemocracy.org/research_topics/research_topics_show.htm?doc_id=158407&attrib_id=7450

http://www.aph.gov.au/library/intguide/FAD/sea.htm

http://www.ribt.org/nuke/html/modules.php?op=modload&name=Organisations&file=organisation&id=36

http://www.homeoffice.gov.uk/security/terrorism-and-the-law/terrorism-act/proscribed-groups

http://www.state.gov/s/ct/rls/fs/37191.htm

http://www.broadleft.org/polmil.htm

http://www.baader-meinhof.com/

http://www.acs-onweb.de/hd/content/pres_c3_terrorist_or_revolutionary/terrorist.bib.htm

http://www.amlnetwork.net/tr-grps.html

http://countrystudies.us/lebanon/90.htm

http://www.sikhiwiki.org

http://www.answers.com

http://www.adl.org/extremism/moa/default.asp
http://www.worldnetdaily.com/news/article.asp?ARTICLE_ID=48868
http://www.eastarmy.nic.in/combating-militancy/klo-02.html
http://www.bookrags.com/wiki/Breton_Revolutionary_Army
http://www.acig.org/artman/publish/article_202.shtml
http://www.mundoandino.com/Colombia/
    Simon-Bolivar-Guerrilla-Coordinating-Board
http://www.allstates-flag.com/fotw/flags/co-polit.html
http://slate.msn.com/id/2104210/

Appendix A

Organisations Banned by the United Kingdom. List of proscribed terrorist groups (UK)

http://www.homeoffice.gov.uk/security/terrorism-and-the-law/terrorism-act/proscribed-groups

17 November Revolutionary Organisation (N17)
Abu Sayyaf Group (ASG)
Al-Gama'at al-Islamiya (GI)
Al Gurabaa
Al Ittihad Al Islamia (AIAI)
Al Qaida
Ansar Al Islam (AI)
Ansar Al Sunna (AS)
Armed Islamic Group (Groupe Islamique Armée) (GIA)
Asbat Al-Ansar ('League of Parisans' or 'Band of Helpers')
Babbar Khalsa (BK)
Basque Homeland and Liberty (Euskadi ta Askatasuna) (ETA)
Baluchistan Liberation Army (BLA)
Egyptian Islamic Jihad (EIJ)
Groupe Islamique Combattant Marocain (GICM)
Hamas Izz al-Din al-Qassem Brigades
Harakat-Ul-Jihad-Ul-Islami (HUJI)
Harakat-Ul-Jihad-Ul-Islami (Bangladesh) (Huji-B)
Harakat-Ul-Mujahideen/Alami (HuM/A) and Jundallah
Harakat Mujahideen (HM)
Hizballah External Security Organisation
Hezb-E Islami Gulbuddin (HIG)
International Sikh Youth Federation (ISYF)
Islamic Army of Aden (IAA)
Islamic Jihad Union (IJU)
Islamic Movement of Uzbekistan (IMU)
Jaish e Mohammed (JeM)

Jeemah Islamiyah (JI)

Khuddam Ul-Islam (KuI) and splinter group Jamaat Ul-Furquan (JuF)

Kongra Gele Kurdistan (PKK)

Lashkar e Tayyaba (LT)

Liberation Tigers of Tamil Eelam (LTTE)

Mujaheddin e Khalq (MeK)

Palestinian Islamic Jihad - Shaqaqi (PIJ)

Revolutionary Peoples' Liberation Party - Front (Devrimci Halk
    Kurtulus Partisi - Cephesi) (DHKP-C)

Teyre Azadiye Kurdistan (TAK)

Salafist Group for Call and Combat (Groupe Salafiste pour la
    Predication et le Combat) (GSPC)

Sipah-E Sahaba Pakistan (SSP) (Aka Millat-E Islami Pakistan (MIP) -
    SSP was renamed MIP in April 2003 but is still referred to as SSP)
    and splinter group Lashkar-E Jhangvi (LeJ)

Libyan Islamic Fighting Group (LIFG)

Jammat-ul Mujahideen Bangladesh (JMB)

Tehrik Nefaz-e Shari'at Muhammadi (TNSM)

Proscribed Irish groups:

Continuity Army Council

Cumann na mBan

Fianna na hEireann

Irish National Liberation Army

Irish People's Liberation Organisation

Irish Republican Army

Loyalist Volunteer Force

Orange Volunteers

Red Hand Commando

Red Hand Defenders

Saor Eire

Ulster Defence Association

Ulster Freedom Fighters

Ulster Volunteer Force

Appendix B

Organisations Banned by the United States of America. Current List of Designated Foreign Terrorist Organisations by the United States of America

http://www.state.gov/s/ct/rls/fs/37191.htm
  Abu Nidal Organisation (ANO)
  Abu Sayyaf Group
  Al-Aqsa Martyrs Brigade
  Ansar al-Islam
  Armed Islamic Group (GIA)
  Asbat al-Ansar
  Aum Shinrikyo
  Basque Fatherland and Liberty (ETA)
  Communist Party of the Philippines/New People's Army (CPP/NPA)
  Continuity Irish Republican Army
  Gama'a al-Islamiyya (Islamic Group)
  HAMAS (Islamic Resistance Movement)
  Harakat ul-Mujahidin (HUM)
  Hizballah (Party of God)
  Islamic Jihad Group
  Islamic Movement of Uzbekistan (IMU)
  Jaish-e-Mohammed (JEM) (Army of Mohammed)
  Jemaah Islamiya organisation (JI)
  al-Jihad (Egyptian Islamic Jihad)
  Kahane Chai (Kach)
  Kongra-Gel (KGK, formerly Kurdistan Workers' Party, PKK, KADEK)
  Lashkar-e Tayyiba (LT) (Army of the Righteous)
  Lashkar i Jhangvi
  Liberation Tigers of Tamil Eelam (LTTE)
  Libyan Islamic Fighting Group (LIFG)
  Moroccan Islamic Combatant Group (GICM)
  Mujahedin-e Khalq Organisation (MEK)
  National Liberation Army (ELN)
  Palestine Liberation Front (PLF)

Palestinian Islamic Jihad (PIJ)
Popular Front for the Liberation of Palestine (PFLF)
PFLP-General Command (PFLP-GC)
Tanzim Qa'idat al-Jihad fi Bilad al-Rafidayn (QJBR) (al-Qaida in Iraq)
    (formerly Jama'at al-Tawhid wa'al-Jihad, JTJ, al-Zarqawi Network)
al-Qa'ida
al-Qaida in the Islamic Maghreb (formerly GSPC)
Real IRA
Revolutionary Armed Forces of Colombia (FARC)
Revolutionary Nuclei (formerly ELA)
Revolutionary Organisation 17 November
Revolutionary People's Liberation Party/Front (DHKP/C)
Shining Path (Sendero Luminoso, SL)
United Self-Defence Forces of Colombia (AUC)

Index

Coming soon

This is the Concise Edition of Paul Ashley's *Complete Encyclopeadia of Terrorism*. 2012 however sees the publication of *The Comprehensive Encyclopeadia of Terrorism*, also by Paul Ashley. This will be a 1008 page hardback edition, ideal for reference for academics and the public alike.